THE THIRD WORLD WAR:
The Untold Story

Also by General Sir John Hackett and others:

THE THIRD WORLD WAR: AUGUST 1985

THE THIRD WORLD WAR:
The Untold Story

General Sir John Hackett

MACMILLAN PUBLISHING CO., INC.
New York

Macmillan Publishing Co., Inc.
866 Third Avenue, New York, N.Y. 10022

Originally published in Great Britain
by Sidgwick and Jackson Limited

Map on page vii by Jane Birdsell, all other maps by John Flower

Library of Congress Cataloging in Publication Data

Hackett, John Winthrop, Sir, 1910–
    The Third World War.

    Includes index.
    1. World War III.   2. Imaginary histories.
I. Title.
U313.H33   1982   355.4'8'09048   82-9879
ISBN 0-02-547110-4   AACR2

10 9 8 7 6 5 4 3 2 1

Printed in the United States of America

Contents

List of Maps

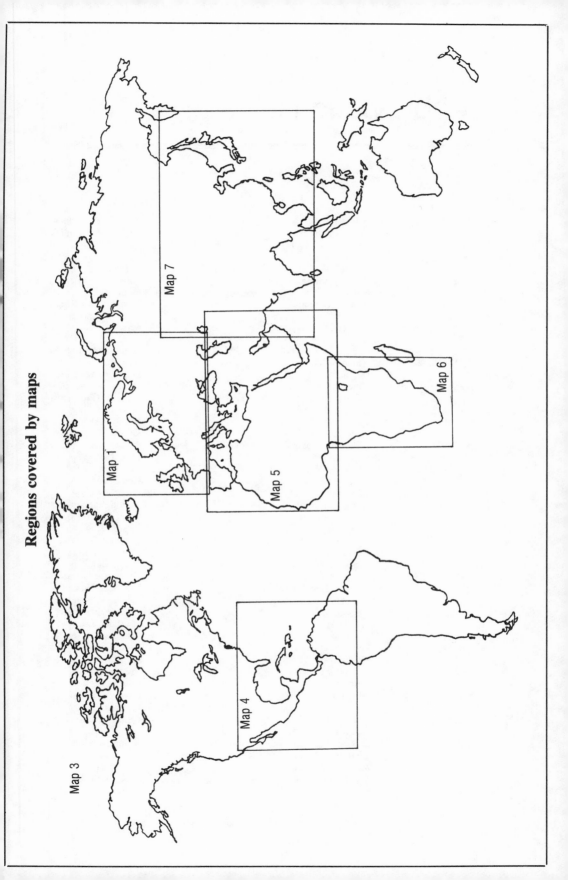

Regions covered by maps

Map 3

Map 4

Map 1

Map 5

Map 6

Map 7

Abbreviations

AAFCE	Allied Air Forces Central Europe	BATES	battlefield artillery target engagement system
AAM	air-to-air missile(s)		
ABM	anti-ballistic missile(s)	BMP	*bronevaya maschina piekhota* (Soviet armoured vehicle(s), infantry)
ACE	Allied Command Europe		
ACLANT	Allied Command Atlantic	BTR	*bronetransporter* (Soviet armoured personnel carrier(s))
AEW	airborne early warning		
AFCENT	Allied Forces Central Europe	CAFDA	Commandement Air de Forces de Défense Aériennes
AFNORTH	Allied Forces Northern Europe		
AFSOUTH	Allied Forces Southern Europe	CAP	combat air patrol(s)
		CCP	Chinese Communist Party
AFV	armoured fighting vehicle(s)	CENTAG	Central Army Group
AI	air-intercept		
AIRCENT	Allied Air Forces Central Europe	CEP	circular error probable
AIRSOUTH	Allied Air Forces Southern Europe	CINCEASTLANT	Commander-in-Chief Eastern Atlantic
ALCM	air-launched cruise missile(s)	CINCENT	Commander-in-Chief Central Region
ANC	African National Congress		
ANG	*Atlantique nouvelle generation* (French anti-submarine aircraft)	CINCHAN	Commander-in-Chief Channel
		CINCNORTH	Commander-in-Chief Allied Forces Northern Europe
APC	armoured personnel carrier(s)	CINCSOUTH	Commander-in-Chief Allied Forces Southern Europe
ARM	anti-radiation missile(s)		
ASEAN	Association of South-East Asian Nations	CINCUKAIR	Commander-in-Chief United Kingdom Air Forces
ASW	anti-submarine warfare	CINCUSNAVEUR	Commander-in-Chief US Navy Europe
ATAF	Allied Tactical Air Force(s)	CINCWESTLANT	Commander-in-Chief Western Atlantic
ATFS	automatic terrain-following system		
ATGW	anti-tank guided weapon(s)	CMP	counter-military potential
AWACS	airborne warning and control system	COB	co-located operational base(s)

COMAAFCE	Commander Allied Air Forces Central Europe	GNP	gross national product
COMBALTAP	Commander, Baltic Approaches	GRU	Glavnoye Razvedivatelnoe Upravlenie (the Soviet military intelligence service)
COMECON	Council for Mutual and Economic Aid		
CPA	Czechoslovak People's Army	GSFG	Group of Soviet Forces in Germany
CPSU	Communist Party of the Soviet Union	HARM	high-speed anti-radiation missile(s)
CW	chemical warfare	HAS	hardened aircraft shelter(s)
DIA	Defence Intelligence Agency	HAWK	homing-all-the-way killer (SAM)
DIVADS	divisional air defence system	HE	high-explosive
EASTLANT	Eastern Atlantic	HOT	high-subsonic optically teleguided (anti-tank missile)
ECM	electronic counter-measure(s)		
ECCM	electronic counter-counter-measure(s)	ICBM	inter-continental ballistic missile(s)
ELINT	electronic intelligence	I/D	interceptor/destroyer
EMP	electro-magnetic pulse	IFF	identification friend or foe
ENG	electronic newsgathering	IGB	inner German border
ESM	electronic support measure(s)	INLA	Irish National Liberation Army
EWO	electronic warfare officer(s)	IONA	Isles of the North Atlantic
FBS	forward-based system(s)	IR	infra-red
FEBA	forward edge of the battle area	JACWA	Joint Allied Command Western Approaches
FNLA	Front for the National Liberation of Angola (Frente Nacional de Libertação de Angola)	JTIDS	joint tactical information distribution system
FRELIMO	Front for the Liberation of Mozambique	KGB	Komitet Gosudarstrennoi Bezopasnosti (the Soviet committee of state security, or secret police)
FRG	Federal Republic of Germany	LAW	light-armour weapon
FROG	free-range over-ground (SSM)	LRMP	long-range maritime patrol(s)
FY	fiscal year(s)		
GAF	German Air Force	MAD	mutual and assured destruction
GDR (DDR)	German Democratic Republic (Deutsche Demokratische Republik)	MCM	mine counter-measure(s)
GLCM	ground-launched cruise missile(s)	MIDS	multi-functional information distribution system

MIRV	multiple individually-targeted re-entry vehicle(s)	SAC	Strategic Air Command
MLRS	multiple-launch rocket system	SACEUR	Supreme Allied Commander Europe
MNR	Mozambique National Resistance	SACLANT	Supreme Allied Commander Atlantic
MPLA	Movimento Popular para a Libertação de Angola (Popular Movement for the Liberation of Angola)	SADARM	seek and destroy armour (anti-tank munition)
		SAF	Soviet Air Force
		SALT	Strategic Arms Limitation Talks
MRCA	multi-role combat aircraft	SAM	surface-to-air missile(s)
MRUASTAS	medium-range un-manned aerial surveillance and target acquisition system	SHAPE	Supreme Head-quarters Allied Powers Europe
		SHQ	squadron headquarters
		SITREP	situation report
NAAFI	Navy, Army and Air Force Institutes	SLBM	submarine-launched ballistic missile(s)
NADGE	NATO air defence ground environment	SLCM	submarine-launched cruise missile(s)
NATO	North Atlantic Treaty Organization	SLEP	service life extension programme
NCO	non-commissioned officer	SNAF	Soviet Naval Air Force
NORTHAG	Northern Army Group	SOTAS	stand-off target acquisition system
NPA	National People's Army	SOUTHAG	Southern Army Group
OAS	Organization of American States	SP	self-propelled
		SRF	Strategic Rocket Forces (Soviet)
OAU	Organization for African Unity	SSBN	submarine(s) ballistic missile, nuclear powered
ODCA	Organizacion Democrata Cristiana de America	SSGN	submarine(s) guided missile, nuclear powered
PACAF	Pacific Air Force		
PLA	People's Liberation Army	SSM	surface-to-surface missile(s)
PLSS	precision location strike system	SSN	submarine(s) nuclear powered
RAAMS	remote anti-armour mine system	SS-N	surface-to-surface – naval (missile)
RDM	remotely-delivered mine(s)	START	Strategic Arms Reduction Talks
REMBASS	remotely-monitored battlefield sensor system	SURTASS	surface towed-array sensor system
		SWAPO	South-West Africa People's Organization
RPV	remotely-piloted vehicle(s)		
RWR	radar warning receiver(s)	TACEVAL	tactical evaluation

TACFIRE	tactical fire-direction	UNITA	União Nacional para a Independencia (National Union for the Total Independence of Angola)
TACTASS	tactical towed-array sonar system		
TAWDS	target acquisition and weapons delivery system	USAF	United States Air Force
TERCOM	terrain contour-matching (guidance system)	USAFE	United States Air Force Europe
TNF	theatre nuclear force(s)	USAREUR	United States Army in Europe
TOW	tube-launched optically-tracked wire-guided (anti-tank missile)	VELA	velocity and angle of attack
		V/STOL	vertical/short take-off and landing
UKAD	United Kingdom air defence	WESTLANT	Western Atlantic
UNIFIL	United Nations Force in Lebanon	ZANLA	Zimbabwe African National Liberation Army
UNIFISMATRECO	United Nations Fissile Materials Recovery Organization	ZIPRA	Zimbabwe People's Revolutionary Army

Foreword

Earlier this year, at Eastertide in 1987, we, a group of Britons deeply aware of how narrowly such freedoms as the Western world enjoys had been able to survive the onslaught upon them of the enemies of freedom in August 1985, completed a book about the causes, course and outcome of the Third World War. In the prologue to that book (a short piece of writing of which every word stands as firmly today, six months later, as it did then, and perhaps deserves re-reading) we wrote: 'Much will be said and written about these events in years to come, as further sources come to light and further thought is given to this momentous passage in the history of our world.'* A good deal more information has indeed become available since then.

The belligerent involvement of Sweden and Ireland, for example, was passed over in our first book, not through unawareness of its importance but through uncertainty about the political implications of some aspects of it which suggested an approach like that of Agag, who trod delicately. The same was true of the neutrality of Israel, under joint guarantees from the USSR and the USA. We could do little more than state this at that time as an end-product, since here too there were uncertainties in issues where precipitate judgment could have been prejudicial. We are now able to go more fully into the process which led to the establishment of an autonomous Palestinian state and the stabilization of Israeli frontiers under guarantee, though the reader will note that the great powers came very near to such conflict over this issue as could have caused the Third World War to break out at least a year before it did.

In Central America and the Caribbean there was also danger of a premature explosion. There has now been developing a Latin-American community (in which a non-communist Cuba plays a critically important role), with the interest and support of the United States but with no intent on its part of total dominance. These matters

---

* *The Third World War: August 1985* (Sidgwick and Jackson, London, and Macmillan, New York, 1978), p. 15.

were at a delicate stage when we last wrote. We can now report more freely on the development of this regional entity as it grows in robustness. It emerged in circumstances so dangerous that the USSR was almost able to secure the defeat of NATO before a shot was fired on the Central Front. We can now examine why.

In the Middle East, in north Africa (where the extinction of over-ambition in Libya was received with almost worldwide acclamation), in southern Africa, and in the Far East we are also now able to take the story further.

In the strictly military sphere, we have been able, with more information, to make some adjustment to the record. This is particularly important where the course of events is considered from the Soviet side. There is now quite an abundance of additional source material available – political, social and military – and we have made use of this as far as we could. The Scandinavian situation has already been mentioned. Operations in northern Europe have been looked at again in the light of it and operations at sea, much influenced by the participation of a belligerent Ireland. On the Central Front we have been able to give more attention to air operations. Those in the Krefeld salient in the critical battle of Venlo on 15 August, the relatively small but vitally important air attack on Polish rail communications to impede the advance just then of a tank army group from Belorussia in the western Soviet Union, the importance of equipment which, however costly, could not safely be foregone – these and other aspects of war in the air receive more attention.

As we said in the Prologue to the first book, 'The narrative now set out in only the broadest outline and, of our deliberate choice, in popular form, will be greatly amplified and here and there, no doubt, corrected.' To contribute to this process is our present purpose.

We are still very far from attempting any final comment on the war that shook the world but did not quite destroy it. The intention is largely to fill in some gaps and amplify various aspects of the tale. The lesson, which is a simple one, remains the same. It is worth restating.

We had to avoid the extinction of our open society and the subjugation of its members to the grim totalitarian system whose extension worldwide was the openly avowed intention of its creators. We had at the same time to avoid nuclear war if we possibly could. We could best do so by being fully prepared for a conventional one. We were not willing, in the seventies and early eighties, to meet the full cost of building up an adequate level of non-nuclear defence and cut it fine. In the event, we just got by. Some would say this was more by good luck than good management, that we did too little too late and hardly deserved to survive at all. Those who say this could well be right.

London, 5 November 1987

THE WORLD IN FLAMES

Chapter 1

Dies Irae

There could not have been many people in Western Europe or the United States who were greatly surprised when they learned from early TV and radio broadcasts on the morning of 4 August 1985 that the armed forces of the two great power blocs, the United States and her allies on the one hand and Soviet Russia and hers on the other, were at each other's throats in full and violent conflict. Preparation for war, including the mobilization of national armed forces, had already been proceeding for some two weeks in the West (and for certainly twice as long in the countries of the Warsaw Pact) before the final outbreak. Yet the magnitude of the assault when it was first felt in its full flood and fury was none the less astounding, particularly to those in the Western world (and these were the majority) who had paid little attention in the past to portents for the future. Bombs were bringing death and devastation on the ground, aircraft exploding into fiery fragments in the sky. Ships were being sunk at sea and the men in them hammered into pulp, electrocuted, burned to death, or drowned. Other men, and many of them, were dying dreadfully in the flaming clamour and confusion of the land battle. Yet another world war had burst upon mankind. While the course of life in the short three weeks of the Third World War had no time to be as radically affected as in the five or six years of each of the first two, the consequences of this war were likely to be more far reaching than any before it.

World war had really been inevitable since the Soviet incursion into Yugoslavia on 27 July, the event which had brought about the first-ever direct clash between Soviet and United States troops on a battlefield. Moscow had long sought a favourable opportunity to reintegrate post-Tito Yugoslavia into the Warsaw Pact, in the confidence that the frailty of the union when its creator had gone would in good time furnish a suitable opening for intervention. As the cracks in Yugoslavia began to widen, particularly between Slovenia and the Federal Government in Belgrade, the Soviet sponsored so-called Committee for the Defence of Yugoslavia had most injudiciously

staged an unsuccessful punitive raid into Slovenia. The Committee
called for Soviet help and the opportunity was seen to be at hand.
Within days Soviet units were in action against US forces from Italy.
Fearful of the consequences if this crisis should get out of control,
Washington had tried hard to cool it down and keep it quiet, but in
vain. ENG (electronic newsgathering) film smuggled out by an enterprising Italian cameraman, showing US guided weapons destroying
Soviet tanks in Slovenia, was flashed on TV screens across the world.
Few viewers in the West even knew where Slovenia was. Fewer still
doubted that the two superpowers were sliding with rising momentum towards world war.

There was no question where the focal point of any conflict between the armies of the two great power blocs would lie. It would be
in the Federal Republic of Germany, where the Group of Soviet
Forces in Germany (GSFG), largely stationed in what was known as
the German Democratic Republic (GDR), faced the considerably
weaker NATO forces of Allied Command Europe (ACE), in what
NATO called its Central Region. It was in the GDR that the Warsaw
Pact was even now staging manoeuvres of impressive size, so large as
to arouse at first strong suspicion in the West, and then to confirm,
that this was really mobilization in disguise. The manoeuvres had
been notified to other powers, in accordance with the Final Act of the
Helsinki Conference on Security and Co-operation in Europe. Some
smaller though still considerable manoeuvres of the Southern Group
of Soviet Forces in Hungary had not. It was from these that one
airborne and two motor rifle divisions had moved into Yugoslavia.

The move into Yugoslavia was very nicely calculated by the Soviet
Union. If the West did nothing to oppose it, a quick and easy gain
would result, not of critical importance but useful, if only as a rough
and timely warning to Warsaw Pact allies. If the West did oppose it
with force, this would constitute an attack on a peace-loving socialist
country that would justify the full-scale defensive action against
NATO, as the aggressive instrument of Western imperialism, for
which the Warsaw Pact was already in an advanced state of preparation. The fighting between Soviet and US forces in Yugoslavia
could very easily be presented as evidence of imperialist aggression.

The war, which some believed had begun already in Polish ship-
yards, mines and factories the previous November,* was now a certainty and could not be long delayed. The NATO allies tried strenu-
ously to complete their own mobilization, which had begun in the
Federal Republic on 20 July, in the United States on 21 July, in
Britain (where the co-operation of the trade unions – led by

---

* See General Sir John Hackett and others, op. cit., 'Unrest in Poland', p. 59.

England's leading Luddite – was not at first certain) on 23 July, with other allies following suit. In Britain in addition a strong and vigorous Territorial Army was constitutionally embodied and the lately formed but already highly effective volunteer Home Service Force, whose purpose was defence against both invasion by external forces and internal subversion, was activated.

The agreement of governments to evacuate from Germany the dependants of American and British service personnel and other civilian nationals was given, with inevitable reluctance, on 23 July, and they began to move out on 25 July. Reinforcements for the United States Army in Europe (USAREUR) began arriving by air from the United States on the same day, together with the first reservists for the formations in I and II British Corps, the latter, formed in Britain in 1983, having most fortunately been deployed in good (though not full) strength for exercises in Germany at the beginning of the month.

On the morning of 4 August 1985, there were many in European cities who had heard (with quite a few old enough to remember) how it had been when people were told in September 1939 in much the same way, if without TV, that we had again a world war on our hands. People in the United Kingdom, for example, had then slung on their mandatory gas masks and taken up their tin hats, if their duties required it, in the full belief that the end was very near. In 1985 those with access to a fall-out shelter tended to make for it, or at least to see that it was in order and well stocked, while those without wondered rather glumly whether it had been wholly wise to disregard advice about survival under nuclear attack. In the cities of Europe in both wars the worst was expected at once. In neither did it happen – not immediately anyway.

Some of the towns and cities in Western Europe had not long to wait for the thunderous, irregular, ear-splitting crash of Soviet bombardment from the air, and the agonizing uncertainty over who was still alive at home, or even where home was in the street now turned to rubble. The places first attacked were those of importance in the movement of NATO troop reinforcements to the European mainland. Channel ports in Britain, and in Belgium and the Netherlands, though not yet in France, received early and violent attention on the very first day from long-range missiles launched from Soviet aircraft. Coastal airfields, especially those handling military transports, and the air traffic control centre at West Drayton near London were among early targets struck. The United Kingdom Air Defence (UKAD) Command, with its complex of warning systems, interceptor aircraft squadrons and gun and missile defences, was fully extended practically from the start. It was almost overwhelmed at first by the volume of attack upon defences that had never yet been brought to the test in this new type of war, in which computer response and missiles had replaced the searchlight and visually-aimed guns of earlier days.

Operations in the north, up as far as the Arctic Circle, opened at once on account of their relevance to trans-Atlantic reinforcement. Attacks on Atlantic ports soon followed, swift moments of appalling noise, leaving, in a silence broken only by the crackling sound of gathering fire, the twisted steel of habour installations with little houses near the docks reduced to burning shells. As the Soviets gained airfields to the west, it was felt upon the French side too, with Brest and the Channel ports joining Glasgow, Bantry, Bristol and Cardiff on the list of towns hit.

It had taken the Soviets almost a full day to realize that, against their hopes and expectations, they had a belligerent opponent in the French Republic. Moscow had firmly believed that the French, pursuing as always the national self-interest with a single-mindedness unequalled anywhere, would find it more prudent to keep out. Yet for all the obstacles set in the way of Western defensive co-operation by de Gaulle's withdrawal from NATO, and for all the reliance the Soviet Union had placed upon some years of left-wing government in France, the French Republic abided most faithfully by its obligations under the Atlantic Treaty.

In spite of assurances broadcast worldwide from Moscow that France would remain immune from attack if it remained neutral, and that the punitive and prophylactic operation undertaken by the USSR against NATO would in that event go no further than the Rhine, II French Corps in Germany had already been quietly placed by the French Government under the full command of the Supreme Allied Commander Europe (SACEUR) on the night of 3/4 August. Three further divisions and an army headquarters soon followed, with the French Tactical Air Force also placed under command for the support of French ground forces. French ports, railways, military installations and, above all, airfields and airspace were put at the disposal of the Western allies. The bombing by Soviet aircraft of Boulogne, Calais, Dieppe and then Brest, and of other ports and a number of airfields followed very soon afterwards.

The great weight of the Soviet ground and air attack was to be concentrated on the Central Region of Allied Command Europe (ACE), within which SACEUR, an American, was responsible for operations from the northern tip of Norway to the southeast corner of Turkey, and from the Caucasus in the East to the Pillars of Hercules at the gates of the Mediterranean in the West. The Central Region, under its German Commander-in-Chief (CINCENT), stretched from the southern edge of Schleswig-Holstein down to Switzerland, with Allied Forces Northern Europe (AFNORTH) on its left flank under a British general, and Allied Forces Southern Europe (AFSOUTH) under an American admiral on its right. Behind ACE lay the area of responsibility of the Supreme Allied Commander Atlantic (SAC-LANT), an American admiral operating from Norfolk in Virginia, while in between there was the newly-created Joint Allied Command Western Approaches (JACWA).

Götterdämmerung was to be staged in Germany. But wars are made by people; it is a truism hardly worth repeating that without people there would be no wars. What is more, it is people who fight and die in them, who injure and destroy other people in them, who suffer from them, and yet who seem to be so far unable to prevent their occurrence as to provoke quite intelligent men and women to the infantile conclusion that if only you could take away all the weapons no fighting would be possible. Because reflection upon people, and above all upon the people who get themselves caught up in wars, must lie at the heart and centre of all reflection upon war and peace, we turn now from contemplation of the scene upon which this stupendous tragedy was about to be played to make the acquaintance of one minor actor in it, someone whose whole life up to its very end had become totally dominated by it, whose conscious being was to be completely absorbed in it, whose capabilities and energy were to be applied exclusively to the discharge of his own part in it, and who was to have no influence whatsoever on its outcome.

Chapter 2

Andrei Nekrassov

Andrei Nekrassov was born on 13 August 1961 in Rostov on Don into a military family. His father had been an officer in the Red Army but ill health had compelled his retirement from military service and he now lived, a widower, quietly at home in Rostov. Andrei's mother had died in his youth and his father had never married again. From childhood both Andrei and his elder brother had dreamed of becoming officers too. In 1976 the elder brother entered the Ryazan Air Force Academy and four years later became a paratroop officer in 105 Guards Airborne Division, quite soon to find himself in Afghanistan.

When in 1978 Andrei left school, where he had shown some promise in mathematics but an even greater inclination to literary and philosophic studies, he too entered a military academy, the Armed Forces Command Academy in Omsk.

He was not by nature a convivial or even a gregarious young man. He was in fact a little shy and did not make friends easily. Happily, he found a contemporary in his own intake to the Academy who was of much the same disposition as himself, and between this young man, Dimitri Vassilievitch Makarov, the only child of a history lecturer in the Lomonossov University in Moscow, and Andrei Nekrassov there developed, in its quiet way, a deep and enduring friendship.

It was just before he left the Academy in Omsk, after four years, that Andrei learned of the death of his brother in Afghanistan, in an action, of which he had no details, against the Mujaheddin. He grieved for the loss of his brother but he was particularly sad for his father, whom he now so rarely saw. In a family with no mother, the three of them, the father and two sons, had been very close. His father would feel still lonelier now.

On graduating from the Academy in 1982 Andrei was promoted to the rank of officer and posted by the Ministry of Defence to the Southern Group of Forces in Hungary, where he was given command of a platoon in the motor rifle regiment of 5 Tank Division. Soviet forces abroad were normally in Category One, at operational

7

strength, including the officers. Young officers beginning their service abroad did so at the lowest level. Most of Andrei's fellow cadets who had received postings within the Soviet Union were given command, not of platoons but of companies, immediately after graduating from the Academy. By sheer good luck Dimitri too had been sent to 5 Tank Division and was commanding a platoon in another company of the same motor rifle regiment.

In 1984 Nekrassov was transferred to the Belorussian Military District, where he took over a motor rifle company in 197 Motor Rifle Division of 28 Army. All divisions in 28 Army belonged to the Group of Soviet Forces in Germany, although in peacetime they were largely stationed in Belorussia. Together with its normal combat training, 28 Army was in constant practice for a swift move into East Germany, where, even in peacetime, its mobilization stores and much of its heavy equipment were located.

In Hungary Andrei Nekrassov had had a platoon of thirty-two men. In Belorussia he was given command of a company comprising three platoons, but with no more than thirty men in all. Like most other such companies, his was thinly manned, with only a cadre of indispensable specialists: junior commanders, drivers of BMP infantry combat vehicles, and heavy weapons operators. The 'cannon fodder' – submachine gunners, machine-gunners, grenade throwers and the like – joined the company only on mobilization. The standard of training of these reservist soldiers was abysmally low but no one seemed to mind. After all, there was an almost inexhaustible supply of them.

In June 1985 extensive training exercises began in Belorussia. Under the guise of these, as became clear later, the Red Army was partially mobilized and divisions were reinforced to their regular strength. The reservists came from Moslem republics – Uzbeks, Tajiks, Kirghiz. After two months of refresher weapon training (the men had by now almost forgotten how to handle weapons), sub-units had been formed. Even when this training programme had long been completed, no order to release the reservists came through. On the contrary, the instructions were to continue with the training.

No. R341266 Senior Lieutenant Nekrassov, 001, was beginning to get worried. As one of the regiment's best officers he had been put forward as a candidate for the Frunze Military Academy. For junior officers the Military Academy meant escape from the stifling monotony of service in the lower ranks to more interesting and creative military work on the staff. Nekrassov had already passed the preliminary medical board and had been recommended by superior reporting officers, including his divisional commander. He had received a summons to sit the Academy entrance examinations and was required to be in Moscow on 10 August. But the training of reservists dragged on. Nekrassov feared that, if he missed these entrance examinations, perhaps next year some other officers in the regiment might have better luck and he would be left out, or next year something might go wrong in the company and once again he would have another year to wait. If this went on, he might never get into the Academy at all. It was important for him to know. Nekrassov, who was approaching his twenty-fourth birthday, wanted to get on with it. There were only two weeks left before the examinations but he had still not received confirmation of permission to attend, and there was no sign of an end to the exercises. The only consolation was that in the division there were many other officers who had applied for military academies, and they too remained in uncertainty.

One of these, it so happened, was none other than his old friend Dimitri Vassilievitch Makarov, who had just turned up in another motor rifle regiment of the same division.

On 26 July intensive training had begun on the loading and unloading of heavy equipment for movement by rail. Next day the divisional headquarters and the headquarters of the regiments were reported, as the two friends heard, to be working out the problems of concealed advances over long distances. Soon afterwards 197 Division did a night march of 200 kilometres and by morning had taken cover in a large area of thick forest. The officers knew that their division was already in Polish territory. The troops did not. Soldiers were not allowed to carry maps, nor were they shown how to read them. Herein lay, Nekrassov had been taught, an advantage of the system: Soviet forces had to be prepared to fight anywhere without argument and did not need to know where they were. In the clearings in the dense forest, camouflaged shelters for thousands of vehicles had already been prepared in advance. This, if surprising, was convenient.

The following night, in good summer weather, the division made another move westwards and by morning had again taken cover in the woods, in positions that had again clearly been occupied by some other division before them.

Nekrassov had already become aware that many other divisions in addition to his own were involved in what was clearly a very large troop movement. Exercises? Of course. But one thing was unusual. There was a completely unprecedented intensity of ideological work. Political commissars of every rank were conducting hundreds of individual and group discussions about the bestial face of capitalism and its blood-sucking nature, about unemployment, inflation and aggressive capitalist intentions. This went on, of course, during any training exercise, but not with such high intensity. There was something even more unusual. During training, the tanks, artillery, mortars, BMP, and other fighting equipment normally had only drill rounds and blanks. The division was now issued with live ammunition.

On the evening of 1 August, once the ammunition had been stowed and all vehicles had been replenished and checked, officers of the General Staff carried out an inspection. Shortcomings were pointed out which had to be put right within the next few days, but on the whole the inspecting officers were satisfied.

At 2300 hours on the night of 3/4 August the division was put on full alert. It was again a warm summer night. Battalions and companies stood-to in the forest clearings. Something important was clearly afoot. A message was then read out from the Government of the Soviet Union. NATO forces, it said, had treacherously attacked forces of socialist countries with no prior warning. All ranks, the message ended, soldiers, sergeants, warrant officers, officers and generals must now do their duty to the end, to crush this imperialist aggression by destroying the wild beast in its den. Only thus could the peoples of the world be kept free from capitalist enslavement. The soldiers enthusiastically shouted 'Hurrah!' as was expected of them. Nekrassov looked at the greyish-green crowds of men and wondered how long this rush of enthusiasm could last. There were deficiencies in the training of Soviet forces which would come to light in the very first battle. The poor co-operation between the various arms of the forces, for example, would become obvious. The majority of the infantry, in spite of all the training they had been doing, were still little more than a herd. The level of training of young officers was also clearly inadequate.

Nekrassov did find some comfort in reflecting on the wisdom, intuition and foresight of the Soviet High Command. Our enemies have only just begun the war, he thought, but already our troops have been mobilized and we are in position. We have received our reservists and drawn our ammunition and have moved forward to our forming-up points. How did our leaders manage to calculate and anticipate the enemy's perfidious intentions so exactly as to be able to deploy our own forces on the very day before the enemy attack? There was food for thought here.

———

It was still dark when Nekrassov pushed his way out of the lean-to roughly fashioned from the branches of young fir trees in which he had spent the last few hours of the night. The summer weather had broken and turned cold. Wrapped in his greatcoat he had not felt it, and was grateful that there had been no rain, but he had slept little.

There was much to think about. The 197 Motor Rifle Division was now dispersed north-west of Kassel and would move forward this morning into the battle. That thought lay like a grey leaden weight in the back of his mind and he tried to keep it there. Though baptized already in battle under bombardment from the air, he had never been in action against an enemy on the ground before but he was confident that he would know how to handle his company. What concerned him now was to get it on the move in the best possible shape. There would be no other chance today to put things right before it would find itself engaged against enemy he had been told would be British. As he moved round with the Sergeant Major, a portly Ukrainian called Astap Beda, who had just come up to report, Nekrassov looked with more than usual care at what was being done.

The motor rifle company commanded by Nekrassov was, when complete, 105 men strong, mounted in the ten infantry combat vehicles (BMP) in which they would ride into action. He could just distinguish the outlines of the vehicles, now dispersed 30 metres apart round the edges of a woodland clearing, as the first light of an August day crept out of a clouded sky. There was activity all about him, for they would soon be moving off. Men tried not to hear the mutter of gunfire from the west as they checked the stowage of equipment on their vehicles, grateful that at least they had not yet been ordered into their grossly inconvenient chemical warfare clothing.

Each BMP carried four *Malyutka* M anti-tank rockets, an automatic 73 mm gun, two PKTM machine-guns of 7·62 mm calibre, a *Strela* 2-M anti-aircraft rocket launcher (similar to the American *Redeye*), an RPG-16 anti-tank grenade launcher, ten *Mukha* single-shot disposable grenade launchers, which you shot off and then threw away, a sniper's rifle, and five *Kalashnikov* automatic rifles. It was a complicated little army that Senior Lieutenant Nekrassov had to handle, but he had fired every weapon in it and done his best to practise the men – no easy task since they spoke half a dozen different languages, of all of which he was ignorant, and almost none spoke Russian.

Key personnel were usually Russian, or if not were at least proficient in the language. The driver of Nekrassov's own BMP, a silent, watchful man by the name of Boris Ivanienko, came from Poltava. You could never know, of course, who was an informer and who was not and Nekrassov would hardly have confided in his driver in any case, but the Senior Lieutenant had come to have some confidence in this quiet and competent man, who so often seemed to know what was wanted of him even before he was told. It would be good to have someone like that close at hand in the battle.

Another member of the company whom Nekrassov had got to

know quite well was a funny little rifleman, from Kazan on the Volga, called Yuri Youssupof, who was also carried in the company commander's BMP. Nekrassov had said a kind word to this man soon after his arrival as a reservist, something which so startled a simple and lonely youth very far from home, completely baffled by what went on around him, that he attached himself to Nekrassov from then on in an almost dog-like devotion. Junior officers in the Red Army had no personal servants but it was customary for one of the rank and file to be made available for small services to an officer, to enable him to get on with his job without minor distraction. In No. 3 Company Yuri thus became the Senior Lieutenant's personal orderly, trying to see that he got something to eat and somewhere to sleep, longing in his simple way to be able to do more for one of the very few people, since he was torn from his family and friends, who had treated him as a human being.

At this time Nekrassov's company, to which six new men had come yesterday, was still eight under its authorized personnel strength. Three such companies, together with a battery of 82 mm automatic mortars with a maximum rate of fire of 120 rounds per minute,* at either low or high trajectories, made up the motor rifle battalion. Three of these battalions, plus a battalion of tanks, an artillery battalion, and six other separate companies – reconnaissance, air defence, multiple rocket launcher, communications, engineers, and transport – formed the regiment. The other two of the three infantry regiments in 197 Motor Rifle Division were organized on the same lines but, instead of BMP, which were fighting vehicles, were equipped with armoured transporters (BTR), thus making up in the whole division one heavy and two light regiments of motorized infantry. In addition, the division contained one tank regiment, one self-propelled artillery regiment (now incorporating a battalion of BM-27 multi-barrelled rocket launchers), an anti-aircraft rocket regiment and several other battalion commands, a reconnaissance unit, a communications unit, a rocket (FROG 7) unit, an anti-tank unit (IT-5), engineers, chemical defence, transport, repair and medical. There would also be two or three KGB battalions attached to the division.

The 197 Motor Rifle Division was due on the morning of 7 August

---

* This formidable new weapon was carried in a BMP, whose back door let down to form the mortar base plate. The bomb weighed 4 kg and was carried in packs of five, ninety rounds travelling with the mortar, with further ammunition in a back-up armoured load carrier. It could not, of course, be kept in sustained action at maximum rate of fire, any more than the *Kalashnikov* automatic rifle, which could fire in one minute all the ammunition the rifleman carried. A pack of five rounds fired off in ten seconds would represent an average engagement for the 82 mm automatic mortar.

to relieve 13 Guards Motor Rifle Division, which now for three days had been making slow progress against I British Corps.

Even before it had crossed the boundary between the two Germanies to move up into the battle in the Federal Republic, 197 Motor Rifle Division, whilst still 50 kilometres to the rear in the second echelon, had come under heavy NATO air attack, with quite considerable losses. Personnel casualties were, as usual, recorded with neither promptness nor exactitude. The breakfast ration brought up for No. 3 Company, Senior Lieutenant Nekrassov's, which had lost more men than most from air attack, was therefore issued as for a company up to strength.

The Sergeant Major poured out double the prescribed summer ration of 100 grams of vodka for Nekrassov and gave him two biscuits instead of the regulation one.

'A little more vodka, perhaps, Comrade Senior Lieutenant?' A solicitous fellow, the Sergeant Major.

'No, to hell with that. We'll drink it this evening if we're alive.'

'Exactly,' agreed the Sergeant Major, tipping his own double ration down a well-trained throat. He would have liked more, but did not care to take it without the officer's permission.

'How are the men?'

'Hungry, Comrade Senior Lieutenant. And pretty savage about it.'

'Savage is no bad thing. Everything ready?' Nekrassov adjusted his throat microphone.

'Yes, Sir!'

'Then let's go.' He gave the order.

At once No. 3 Company came to life in a stutter of starting engines and in its ten BMP moved off into a misty dawn and an uncertain future which no one in the company found particularly attractive.

THE BALANCE OF POWER

Chapter 3

The State of the Alliance

The resolve and the military capability of the West had since 1918 been sapped by an uncritical hankering for peace. It was hardly surprising that after the war of 1914–18, in which the full potential of highly developed industrial nations was for the first time totally applied to the destruction of national enemies, a deep and wide-spread revulsion against war set in. The tide of pacifism in the 1930s, particularly in war-scarred Europe, was running strongly, fed by a genuine emotional concern which often blinded quite sensible people to what should have been obvious. Some strange aberrations resulted. At a time when Hitler's long march in Europe had already begun, for example, the annual Labour Party Conference in Great Britain voted not for the reduction of the Royal Air Force but for its total abolition.

On the other side, the nature and the purposes of peace were seen rather differently. 'Peace,' said Lenin, 'as an ultimate objective simply means communist world control.' The policy of the USSR, both internally and externally, from the end of the First World War to the outbreak of the Third, was not only wholly consistent with this principle. It was consistent with no other. The Third World War was its inevitable consequence.

There were, of course, plenty of Marxists around, in the West as well as the East, to whom Lenin's dictum would be no more than an axiom. There were also Western artists, writers and other intellectuals in the 1930s who enthusiastically embraced communism, since it seemed to offer to suffering humanity real hope for a better world. Some of them claimed later that they had been misled as to the true nature of communism and its methods. This was a claim received on the whole with scepticism.

There were also many honest folk who were simply sickened by the very thought of war, with its savage and appalling slaughter and its apparently mindless cruelty. Among them those whom Lenin described as 'useful fools', and found so helpful for the purposes

16

he had in mind, occurred in some numbers. In free and generous societies they flourish in abundance.

After the Second World War, which was in some ways little more than a continuance of the First, a new and dreadful danger appeared in the weapons of mass destruction which men had been clever enough to invent, and to manufacture, but which mankind was neither wise enough nor good enough to be trusted with.

It was Soviet policy to move in and exploit, to the advantage of the USSR, fears found everywhere of nuclear annihilation. The so-called 'peace movements' of the Western world were one result, unobtrusively orchestrated and largely paid for by the USSR, with maximum utilization of Lenin's 'useful fools', who were often men of impeccable respectability and even occasionally of some distinction. Peace movements flourished in the fifties. This was the time of the Stockholm Appeal and the World Peace Council and other manifestations that were discreetly directed from Moscow and generously financed through the so-called Peace Fund. The principal target of all such peace offensives was the United States of America.

It is hard nowadays, when so much is known of the manoeuvres of the deeply dishonest regime under which the Soviet Union suffered for more than half a century, to believe that people in other lands not under its imperial dominion could be so foolish. The Soviet Union had, since the end of the Second World War, annexed and enslaved three free nations on the Baltic coast (Latvia, Lithuania and Estonia); bound two other nations (Belorussia and the Ukraine) in unwilling servitude; continued to massacre its own people to maintain the supremacy of the Communist Party of the Soviet Union (CPSU); imposed harsh and unwelcome regimes by force in Eastern Europe; financed and organized subversion in democratic countries which, though ripe for the plucking, were too far from its frontiers to invade; built a wall across part of Europe, with mines and guns and dogs, not to keep miscreants out but unwilling citizens in; invaded Afghanistan; behaved towards the inhabitants of the Soviet Union with a savagery which passes description; lied and tricked and cheated wherever it found advantage in dishonesty . . . and yet, so great were Western fears of nuclear war that, adroitly handled, these fears could be turned to suspicion and dislike of a nation whose leaders were the elected choice of the people, with no history of the massacre of millions behind them, still less of the enslavement of nations – the United States. It would be foolish to claim that there are no weaknesses in Western democracy. Ugly faults abound on every side, sometimes so monstrous as nearly to drive sensitive and intelligent observers to despair. But it was the height of absurdity to suggest that, whatever the weaknesses of the parliamentary democracies of the

West, the grim, implacable, repressive incompetence of a Marxist tyranny would be preferable, that the policies of the Soviet Union were the only real source of world peace and that the only real threat to it lay in those of the United States. Yet this was the message put across by Soviet propaganda and spread by its agents, whether they knew what they were doing or not.

The 1980s opened to a swift crescendo in the orchestration of anti-nuclear protest. Mass rallies were organized in Germany, France, the Netherlands, Belgium, Britain, and the United States, in every one of which it was America that was cast as the villain of the piece. 'Reduce the arsenal of the warmongering West,' was the cry, 'and give the peace-loving Soviet Union and its devoted associates the opportunity and the example to reduce their own.' There were, it can be confidently asserted, no such demonstrations at all in the cities of the USSR.

The adroitness with which Lenin's useful fools were exploited, and the degree to which the genuine fears of honest people were turned, in the Soviet interest, to the obstruction of their own governments was almost unbelievable. Eventually, common sense began to win back ground abandoned to hysteria. The hollowness of the unilateral nuclear disarmers' arguments showed up ever more clearly and the gross travesty of truth which laid the blame for increasing armaments, particularly in the nuclear field, solely upon the United States was less uncritically accepted. By the summer of 1983 the scene was calmer, and though much damage had been done this was not irreparable. The Soviet Union's peace offensive did not, in the end, cripple Western defensive efforts as completely as those who mounted it had hoped.

It must also be said that the public disquiet aroused by the growth of nuclear arsenals at the disposal of both superpowers did something, on the Western side at least, to alert governments to the necessity to explain fully to their own publics what was being done and why, instead of simply assuming that they could pursue these dramatic defence policies without any questions being asked. In the Soviet Union, of course, the problem never arose.

In addition to the general malaise which it created, nuclear policy was one of the causes of disunity between the Western allies, but by no means the only one. Another was something as vague as the difference in style between the actions of government on the two sides of the Atlantic. The uncertainty and soft centre of the Democratic presidency gave way in a single election to the hard-line and defiantly stated policies of a Republican era, even though there was still a marked lack of consistency between the policies announced from one day to the next. Neither style was attractive to the European leaders, with the partial exception of Britain's Prime Minister. They preferred on the whole a more patient and consistent approach to policy-making, weighing one thing with another and often having to agree on more balanced and less adventurous policies than some of them would have liked, as the price for reaching agreement within the European Community. The latter as an instrument of policy in the world had never recovered the ground lost in the failure of the European Defence Community and the European Political Community in 1954. Much time had subsequently been wasted in trying to re-create institutions which would have replaced these brave efforts at the formation of a United States of Europe. The nationalist obsession of General de Gaulle, followed by the less blatant but equally damaging half-heartedness of Britain with regard to any positive move towards a new structure for Europe, had led to the spending of more time in the Community on what can literally be described as bread and butter issues than on the discussion of how Europe could wield a degree of influence in the world commensurate with its economic strength and the importance of its worldwide interests.

It was not until 1981 that the Genscher-Colombo proposal, supported behind the scenes by the Action Committees for the Union of Europe, showed the way to a new mechanism and a new act of political will. By adopting this proposal in 1983 the members of the Community, soon to be increased by the adherence of Spain and Portugal, equipped themselves with a capability for making decisions and an embryonic apparatus for putting them into effect. The great merit of this proposal lay in accepting things more or less as they stood, namely that the European Council, consisting of the heads of government of the member states of the Community, had set itself up as the top decision-making body both for matters within the normal operations of the Community and, more important for our present purpose, for the making of decisions in matters of foreign policy jointly between the governments of the member states. And now it had finally succeeded in adding to its tasks the search for identity of view in defence policy and co-operation between the armed forces of the Community's members.

This was achieved through two kinds of measures, both of which seemed quite simple when they had been done but to get them done had required a leap of the imagination over the institutional hurdles which the theorists of the Community had placed in the way of any such pragmatic development. The European Council made an Act of Union declaring that it constituted a unified authority for whatever purposes it might choose then or later. It also decided to set up new secretariats for the preparation and execution of decisions in the fields of foreign policy and defence. Foreign policy had previously been co-ordinated, and so far as possible harmonized, by means of an impermanent bureaucracy consisting of the officials of the state which was furnishing the presidency of the Community at the time. As this changed every six months, continuity was difficult to ensure and efficiency suffered.

It was clear as soon as the decision to include defence matters in the activities of the Union had been taken that such an arrangement was totally inadequate. Defence decisions have either to be taken a long time in advance, owing to the time needed for the working out of operational doctrine upon which requirements for military equipment are based and then the long lead-times in its production, or alternatively have to be taken under heavy pressures in a very short time in some emergency or crisis requiring common action. A basic minimum of staff is required both to monitor the long-term processes and to prepare the data and intelligence material (for example, information on force dispositions) necessary for the taking of emergency decisions within the Alliance and for crisis management. The logic of this argument was in the end enough to overcome French hesitations, while Britain finally accepted that in order to maintain the levels of defence which the Conservative Government judged necessary, without offending its monetarist principles, some radical means of obtaining greater cost-effectiveness must be sought. The only available route to this objective lay through co-operation with the other states of Western Europe both in the production of armaments in common, with a far higher degree of standardization, and by the acceptance of a certain degree of specialization in the roles of the armed forces of member states. No dramatically swift results could be expected from this new institutional arrangement but at least it provided a framework in which improved and better shared planning could take place, once the essential decision had been taken to improve the conventional strength of the European forces in the Alliance in the circumstances which will be described below.

In addition to the disunity within the European Community, there had been a continuing rumble of disagreement between Europe and the United States over the roles that they should respectively or together play in protecting their interests throughout the world. These differences had been expressed with particular sharpness over the subjects of nuclear policy and the Middle East. The nuclear argument was frustrating to the Americans since they had believed that in the production and deployment in Western Europe of modernized long-range theatre nuclear forces (TNF) they were acceding to the wishes of the Europeans, who felt themselves threatened by the installation in the territory of the Soviet Union of improved systems obviously targeted on Western Europe. The resolution of this particular and vital difference of opinion was at least partially achieved by the opening of serious negotiations with the Soviet Union in late 1981 followed by the Strategic Arms Reduction Talks (START) which are described in the next chapter; partly also by a reassessment of the proper role of the European defence effort within the Atlantic Alliance, which is more immediately germane to what follows. While it was perfectly right and proper that the Europeans should wish to have on their territory nuclear missiles equivalent to those facing them from the other side, or to try to negotiate for the abolition or reduction of such weapons on both sides, the acceptance of this did not begin to deal with one of the cruellest dilemmas with which Western statesmen might find themselves faced: namely the choice whether to be the first to use nuclear weapons if they were unable to hold off attack by conventional Soviet forces in Europe.

The new TNF were logically required as part of the general scheme of deterrence which had worked so well ever since the acquisition of a nuclear capability by the Soviet Union, on the general principle that like can only be deterred by like. The popular agitation against the stationing of these weapons in the territories of Western European states was therefore misconceived, as was apparently perceived by the great majority in those countries who did not accept that the example of unilateral disarmament given by the West would be followed by the East. The raising of this issue in the public debate led at last, however, to the focusing of attention on the much more real and difficult problem inherent in the doctrine of flexible response. This included the proposition that in certain circumstances, that is to say in the event of a Soviet attack by conventional forces in Europe which could not be successfully stopped by the conventional forces of the West, the choice would have to be made whether to allow the attack to succeed and vast areas of Western Europe to remain in Soviet occupation, or whether limited and selective use of nuclear weapons should be authorized by the West in order to impose a halt on the military operations. This would afford a pause in which an attempt might be made to end the dispute, at the same time advertising the readiness of the West to escalate to whatever degree might be necessary in order to prevent a Soviet victory.

The reason why Western leaders might be faced by this agonizing choice was briefly and bluntly that their conventional forces were not enough by themselves to be able in all circumstances to bring to a halt an attack by the more massive Soviet conventional military machine. This situation represented an unfortunate legacy of the decision of the 1950s, at a time when the United States still had nuclear superiority, that it was sufficient to threaten to use this superiority to deter – and if necessary to bring to an end – aggression of any kind in

Europe. What was attractive to politicians in this formulation was not simply the overwhelming advantage of force on the Western side which was present at the time, but also the economy of means which it allowed them to enjoy in the provision of conventional forces in Europe. Long after the Western nuclear advantage disappeared and nuclear parity was accepted, with even some advantage on the Soviet side, the financial benefits of the reliance on nuclear weapons by the West persisted in the minds of short-sighted politicians, who finally persuaded themselves that the West could not afford to provide the necessary conventional level of forces and to maintain the level of social expenditure which seemed necessary in order to prevent the further dissolution of Western society.

Some unsung genius in the new Genscher-type defence secretariat managed to launch the idea and have it accepted by his European masters that the popular opposition to nuclear weapons could be fruitfully diverted into this other argument, namely that one of the most debatable not to say reprehensible possible uses of nuclear weapons by the West could be avoided if the level of conventional forces on the Western side were increased. If there was a reasonable chance that these forces could hold up or at least delay significantly a Soviet conventional attack then the choice whether to be the first to use nuclear weapons in Europe would be landed on the Soviet side and TNF would be required on the Western side in their original and proper purpose of deterring such first use by the Soviets and not in the much more unacceptable mode of possible first use by the West.

The creation of adequate Western conventional forces for this purpose clearly lay outside the scope of the possibilities of increased expenditure by individual European nations and could only be achieved both by the greater efficiency of co-operative defence efforts and by a manifestly equitable sharing of the load, such as could only be obtained through the operation of a united European defence.

This would have the further advantage that it helped greatly to bridge one of the main differences which divided Western Europe from America. The United States had for long felt it was paying more than its fair share in the defence of Western interests. For example, the concept of the rapid deployment force for use, say, in the Indian Ocean included the belief that it might involve the earmarking for operations there of forces which would otherwise have been available as reinforcements from the United States to Europe. It therefore seemed in many American eyes an obviously fair consequence of this proposal that if the United States had to use its forces in an area where the West Europeans were unable to operate militarily but where their interests were no less in need of defence than those of the

Americans, the Europeans should 'take up the slack'. That is to say that they should put themselves in a position to make good in Europe any deficiencies which might result from the fact that the US was obliged to operate in the general Western interest elsewhere. There was some West European objection to this train of thought not only because of the extra expense which would be required if European forces had to be increased in order to make good American deficiencies in Europe, but also because it seemed to give an automatic support by Western Europe to American policies in the rest of the world which might not have been adequately discussed or on which it might not have been possible to reach agreement. This caveat was reinforced by the manifest disagreement which was felt to exist between some aspects of American policy in the Middle East and that pursued by the European Community. The Americans seemed in many European eyes to be so much subject to the influence of the Jewish vote in the United States that they were unable to impose moderation on the policy of Israel, even though the latter depended on them for financial support and the supply of war material; and in particular because the United States would not accept, or could not prevail on Israel to accept, the necessity for including in a solution of the Middle East question due consideration of the rights of the Palestinians and the creation of a separate Palestinian state.

With this degree of divergence over the area in which it was most likely that the United States might have to take military action or, at least, use military force in a deterrent role, it was particularly difficult to expect that the West Europeans would, so to speak, endorse a blank cheque for American policy by agreeing in advance to take up the slack in Europe.

It was clear throughout the industrialized Western world, as well as in Japan, that if Arab oil dried up, industry would slow down – or even, here and there, come to a virtual stop. The unwillingness of successive administrations in the United States, under pressure from powerful political groups (particularly in New York) to accept the simple fact that to secure the oil flow would involve more sympathetic consideration of Arab interest in finding a solution to the Palestinian problem, was a major obstacle to progress. It also introduced further friction into US relations with Europe, where governments were able to take a rather less constrained view of the international scene in the Middle East than was easy for an American administration. To secure the oil flow and to solve the Palestinian problem, while not arousing dangerous political hostility at home, was for the United States a major problem. The attitude of European states, both to their responsibility in NATO and the possibility of joint action outside the NATO area, in defence of common interests, was to play an important part in encouraging Washington to find a way out of this involved and delicate problem.

The search for a way through this maze was greatly (and unexpectedly) assisted by no less than the Prime Minister of Israel with his virtual annexation of the Golan Heights in late 1981 and his subsequent cancellation of the strategic agreement with the United States which had provoked such outspoken European criticism. These actions and the consequent sharpening of relations between the United States and Israel at last made it possible for the former to adopt a policy with regard to the Middle East which was more in line with a reasonable interpretation of the position of the Arab countries and, at the same time, more in line with the views of Western Europe. This development removed the main obstacle to tacit acceptance by Western Europe of the doctrine of taking up the slack and thus provided yet another argument for the improvement of Western European conventional forces.

There were two other important consequences. The countries of Western Europe had been the better able to harmonize their policies towards the outside world the more these differed from those of the United States. They seemed to feel that West European positions were only to be announced as such when it could be shown that in so doing Europe was flexing its independent muscles and showing to the world that it did not necessarily have to behave as a satellite of the United States. This too had largely had its origin in the sharp opposition of the respective Middle East policies, and when that particular difficulty was on the way to being overcome it became easier for Europe to think in terms of a joint effort with the US to promote the interests of the whole Western world. But once it was decided to make the effort, the means of co-ordinating the defence of these Western interests were found to be greatly lacking. They were occasionally discussed at the so-called Western summits such as that which took place in Guadeloupe in 1978, but these meetings did not include all those who felt they should be included and moreover had no continuing machinery to see that such decisions as were made were carried out effectively. The usual answer to such criticism was that consultation within the Atlantic Alliance could take place over the whole world. This was formally true to the extent that consultation sufficed. Action, however, was another matter since the area of responsibility and operations of the Atlantic Alliance was specifically limited by its treaty to Europe and the Mediterranean and the North Atlantic area, thus excluding many of the countries and regions in which the more acute threat to Western interests was now being perceived. Here, too, new machinery was required and the need for it was partly met just in time before the onset of the Third World War.

The Western summit of 1982 not only attempted to formulate the policies to be followed by the Western world generally with regard to the safeguarding of essential supplies and the use of its economic predominance as a means of influencing world events and deterring further Soviet adventurism, but also took the first tentative step to set up a framework to which action on the lines of these decisions could be reported and further consequential decisions prepared. The mere extension of NATO's areas, which might have seemed a simpler course, was not possible because not all its members were prepared to agree to it. So the alternative solution had to be adopted of a decision by those willing to participate in action outside the area to equip themselves with the necessary means of doing so. The Western Policy Staff was the rather cryptically-named organ to which at their summit meeting heads of government entrusted these new tasks and which in the event had just two years to begin to get into its stride before its utility was conclusively demonstrated.

The final cause of trans-Atlantic disunity – the difference in style and tempo – was more difficult to resolve. Over much of the period of the Atlantic Alliance there had been talk of completing it by an 'Atlantic Community', but this had never really amounted to more than conference rhetoric. The concept had been invoked when the Alliance was in trouble as, for example, after the Suez operation when relations between the United States and Britain and France were particularly strained. Resolutions were passed in favour of its creation but, in practice, nothing happened except two additions to the functions of the Alliance which were important in potential but never achieved their full impact. One of these was that the Alliance should concern itself with economic policy. This, however, was being handled in so many other international bodies that the NATO contribution to it never achieved significance. The other was more fruitful. The allies agreed that they would improve the consultation which took place within the Alliance about matters of common concern and this was extended from the original NATO area to all other areas of the world, with the severe handicap already mentioned that while it was possible to talk about out-of-area dangers it was still not possible within the Alliance, as part of the operations of the Alliance, to take concerted action with regard to them.

In later years the Atlantic Community concept had been relegated more clearly to the limbo of unrealized theories because of the growth and development of the European Community, to which the majority of the European members of the Alliance were prepared to devote much more effort than to the shadowy Atlantic concept. This dichotomy was specifically recognized by the advocacy in the middle 1960s of the 'twin pillars' by which it was understood that the Alliance should be composed of the United States and Canada on the one hand and a united Europe on the other hand. This, too, had not been fully realized. The proposition did little more, in fact, than serve as yet another obstacle to the realization of anything which could properly be described as a community embracing both sides of the Atlantic.

The clearest reason for the difficulty of giving reality to the 'Atlantic Community' was, of course, the disparity in size and power between the United States and the countries of Western Europe. The United States since the Second World War was the only country on the Western side that aspired to or had thrust upon it a world role, whereas the ex-imperial countries of Western Europe, while conscious of the loss of the world position that they had once enjoyed, had not always been able to reconcile themselves to the position of middle-ranking regional powers.

There was the further difficulty that the method of American policy-making was not geared to participation in an integrated community. It was difficult for allies to introduce their views into the agonizing process of public discussion and decision-making which was the method favoured by the United States, with its rigid separation of powers, and once a decision was taken it was difficult to expect that the Americans would be prepared to go through it all again in order to accommodate views coming from outside their own borders. The Alliance continued, therefore, with hard-headed appraisal on both sides of the outstanding value to all participants of a 'Trans-Atlantic Bargain', which was the phrase used by one distinguished American representative at NATO as the title of an illuminating book on the relationship. The essence of the bargain was the American guarantee that it would consider an attack on Western Europe as if it were an attack on the United States and the European assurance that Western Europe would provide an equitable share of the effort needed for its common defence. The bargain was only in danger when the Europeans seemed to be reluctant to make the same assessment as the Americans of what was equitable; or when the United States through force of circumstances felt it necessary to divert its attention and its effort in varying degrees away from Europe and particularly, as in the case of Vietnam, when this diversion was generally disapproved of by the Europeans and turned out, moreover, unsuccessfully.

The abrasive style of the Republican Administration in the early years of the 1980s and the growing United States preoccupation with the Middle East, South-West Asia and Central America coincided with the increasing volume of noise coming from Europe about nuclear disarmament. It also coincided with the kind of negative auction carried out between the smaller political parties in the Netherlands and Belgium which resulted in the reduction of their conventional defence effort and, at the same time, an expressed reluctance to allow the stationing of the new TNF on their territories. It was noted too in Europe that at a time when economic sanctions were much discussed and much advocated to show displeasure in Soviet action in Afghanistan and on the military seizure of power in Poland, the United States appeared unable to use for more than a very short period the one sanction which would seem to the man in the street to have the most possibility of success, namely to stop grain exports to the Soviet Union; and this not from any doubt as to its efficacy, but because American middle-western farmers, whose votes were so important to the US Administration, were unwilling to forgo the vast sales to the Soviet Union on which their farm economy was largely dependent.

It was fortunate for the West that the war broke out when it did and not later. The United States and Europe were to some extent on divergent tracks.

Chapter 4

Nuclear Arsenals

The early 1970s had seen the achievement by the Soviet Union of strategic nuclear parity with the United States. The Strategic Arms Limitation Talks (SALT) produced in May 1972 an agreement which set ceilings upon numbers of strategic ballistic missile launchers and a treaty which imposed limitations on anti-ballistic missile defence systems. Together these appeared to suggest that both superpowers had accepted the principle of mutual and assured destruction (MAD). In fact, neither had. To the USSR, deterrence lay in a demonstrable ability to fight, win and survive a nuclear war. The USA relied on a continuing technological superiority to check any Soviet confidence that this was possible. On both sides the 1970s witnessed a sharp growth in the numbers of deliverable warheads, largely owing to the introduction of multiple individually-targeted re-entry vehicles (MIRV), and a marked increase in the efficiency of guidance systems and thus in accuracy of delivery. The United States had doubled the numbers of its strategic warheads from around 5,000 in 1970 to over 11,000 in 1980; in the USSR the increase was from about 2,500 in 1970 to about 5,000 at the end of 1980, though this figure was due to rise to some 7,500 in the next few years. Meanwhile, accuracy in strategic weapons had improved on both sides, from circular error probable (CEP – the radius from a target within which 50 per cent of warheads directed at it would probably fall) of two and even three thousand feet down to (for missiles launched from the ground but not, as yet, from submarines) six or seven hundred.

The technological advantage, in terms of strategic weapons, of the USA over the USSR in 1980 was much less than it had been ten years before. Moreover, the total lethality of the American strategic armoury (its counter-military potential, in the jargon, or CMP), which was almost three times that of the USSR at the end of the 1970s, was overtaken and surpassed by the Soviet Union in the early eighties. The USA had some advantages in both bombers and submarines (of the thirty or so US ballistic missile submarines constantly held in readiness, up to twenty were at sea at any one time, as against no more than ten for the Soviet Union) and in anti-submarine warfare (ASW) techniques Western navies were definitely in front. In inter-continental ballistic missiles (ICBM), however, the USSR would remain a good way ahead until the US *Trident* II submarine-launched ballistic missile (SLBM) – a very accurate missile – and the MX ICBM would become operational in the second half of the eighties.

When the Soviet Union's much more advanced arrangements for the protection of government and industry and for civil defence were taken into account, it was clear that the first half of the eighties would indeed open what the analysts tended to call, after Henry Kissinger, a 'window of opportunity' for the USSR. In spite of the enormous technical difficulty of launching a fully co-ordinated strategic nuclear first strike against US land-based ICBM and the certainty that even with optimum results this would leave a considerable strategic nuclear force in the United States as well as an intact US submarine force still able to reply, the opportunity open to the USSR to use its strategic nuclear lead in the first half of the 1980s to apply political pressures in international affairs was clear. If these failed to achieve decisive results there was always the possibility of open warfare in the field against NATO in Europe. In any case, the so-called 'window of opportunity' would not remain open for more than a few years.

Wherever the arguments led in the field of inter-continental nuclear strategy (that is to say, in what was unkindly described by some military men as 'military metaphysics'), it was in connection with shorter-range theatre nuclear forces (TNF) that critical divisions and uncertainties developed in the Western Alliance. At the begin-ning of the eighties, the USSR was able, in the prevailing state of uneasiness in the West over the nuclear threat, to exploit these most effectively, through a massive propaganda campaign and with the aid of the 'useful fools'.

For all the Soviet Union's often displayed maladroitness, there is no doubt that its handling of Western concern over nuclear weapons was most skilful.

When the American strategic nuclear superiority in the 1960s gave way to the state of rough parity between the two superpowers, their vulnerability to each other's inter-continental weapons was perhaps of less importance in the Alliance than the vulnerability to nuclear attack of the European allies. Whatever marginal advantage might accrue to either superpower from improved accuracy, the hardening or concealment of launchers, their increased mobility and so on, the simple fact remained that neither could be so hard hit by the other in a first strike as to be incapable of a devastating response. The critical question that began to emerge in the seventies was how far the US would be induced by the difficulties of the European allies in wartime to initiate a central attack on the Soviet Union. If the willingness of any American president to invite the appalling reprisals this would produce would be questionable (as it could hardly fail to be), what could be done to find an acceptable alternative? Thus was born, out of European uncertainty whether the USA could be relied upon to accept truly appalling damage at home on behalf of allies abroad, the debate on TNF and their modernization, a debate which did much to throw the Alliance into disarray and to offer the Soviet Union opportunities it did not fail to exploit.

The introduction into service by the USSR of the SS-20 ballistic missile and the *Backfire* bomber (to use the NATO term) in the late 1970s gave the Warsaw Pact new options for an attack on Western Europe, although Soviet military thinking saw this as only a continuance of an established line of policy. It was now possible, given the SS-20's range of 3–4,000 miles (as against 1–2,500 for the SS-4 and 5 it was replacing), for the USSR to attack almost any major target in Western Europe from inside its own territory. None of NATO's land-based missiles in Europe could reach beyond Eastern Europe into the USSR itself and the few nuclear-capable aircraft possessed by the Alliance, even if of just sufficient range, could not confidently count on penetration. There were, it is true, 400-odd *Poseidon* SLBM warheads assigned to the Supreme Allied Commander Europe (SACEUR), but the use of any of these would be likely to invite Soviet attack on the continental United States itself, while attack by ICBM from the US, of course, would be certain to do so.

European concern over the imbalance in theatre nuclear capabilities led to NATO's decision in December 1979 to install on the territory of European allies, through the next decade, 572 American missiles of greater range and accuracy than those at that time available. Thus 108 *Pershing* II intermediate-range ballistic missiles would replace the *Pershing* I-A stationed in Germany, giving about 1,000 miles more range and, with their terminal radar guidance system, far greater accuracy. At the same time, 464 ground-launched cruise missiles (GLCM) would be installed, with a range of some 1,500 miles and a highly accurate terrain contour-matching guidance system known as TERCOM. Of these, 160 would be located in the UK, 96 in the Federal Republic of Germany, 48 each in Belgium and the Netherlands, and 112 in Italy. This decision, unanimously arrived at in the NATO Council, was accompanied by a proposal to negotiate with the USSR for the reduction of theatre nuclear systems. The deployment decision and the arms control proposal were seen as one package.

To the West the installation of these modernized weapons would do no more than correct a critical imbalance. To the Soviet Union, however, as Brezhnev had already warned, in an unsuccessful effort in October 1979 to avert the impending NATO decision, it was clearly seen as an attempt to change the strategic balance in Europe and give the West a decisive superiority. This would lie in affording the USA an option not hitherto available of attack upon the Soviet homeland (always an interest of paramount importance for the USSR) without using central strategic forces and so inviting attack on the American continent.

An immediate offer to halt the deployment of SS-20s would have cut the ground from under NATO's feet. They were already being installed and would reach a total of some 250 by mid-1981, with a final total of 300 in 1982. Since in Soviet eyes this did no more than improve the effectiveness of an already established policy, no need was seen to depart from it and the offer was not made. The SS-20, the argument ran, was only replacing less efficient SS-4 and 5, with a greater range which would, as a bonus, enable all China to be targeted from inside the Soviet Union as well. The NATO move, however, was seen by the Soviet Union as a new and threatening departure, even though none of the modernized missiles would be ready before 1983 at the earliest.

The TNF decision also began to generate a heightened public uneasiness in Europe. The greater range, flexibility and accuracy conferred by the introduction of *Pershing* II and GLCM was seen as raising the possibility of actually fighting a nuclear war in Europe which could leave the USA unscathed. There was concern that US military thinking might be moving towards the concept of a containable or limited nuclear war, which would clearly, of course, be a war contained in Europe.

The proposal made by NATO that negotiations should begin upon limitation of TNF was followed up by preliminary discussions between the USA and the USSR in Geneva in the autumn of 1980, which had to be abandoned when the US Administration changed. Little was achieved other than a slightly clearer definition of positions, though it was at least agreed that the talks should remain bilateral and include continental systems based in Europe, though the Soviets were still hoping to bring in the so-called forward-based systems (FBS) as well, including SLBM and nuclear-capable aircraft on aircraft carriers in European waters.

The new US Administration made no attempt to restart the negotiations and the prospects for them were not greatly helped by Brezhnev's offer at the 26th Party Congress in February 1981 of a moratorium on new medium-range missiles as soon as effective talks began. The SS-20 deployment programme was at that time nearing completion, with one missile coming into service every five days. The NATO deployment was still two to three years off.

Though many in the West saw in Brezhnev's offer no more than blatant cynicism, it did reflect a genuine distinction made by the Soviets between what they were doing, which was much the same as before, and what NATO proposed, which to the Soviet way of thinking introduced an entirely new principle. It was also symptomatic of the unsettled state of public opinion in Western Europe at the time, that the Brezhnev proposal was welcomed by some (including the opposition Labour Party leadership in Britain) as a helpful concession.

The circumstances which more than anything else had led to President de Gaulle taking France out of NATO in 1966 looked now like being reversed. One of his chief objections was that in the Atlantic Alliance Europe was too closely linked with the United States. The Alliance, in fact, looked like becoming no more than a structure for the projection of American interests in Europe. Now, at the beginning of the eighties, there was a tendency to uncouple the defence interests of the United States from those of Europe and set up a situation which might have been rather more to de Gaulle's liking. There is little doubt, however, that this tendency was seen by many thoughtful people in the West as presenting a serious threat to the Alliance and to world peace.

To prevent this diversion of interest from growing dangerously great it was imperative that the modernization of theatre nuclear weapons should be very closely associated with negotiations between the USSR and the USA for their reduction.

It was made abundantly clear to the US Administration (perhaps this had not been taken as seriously in Washington before now as it should have been) that uneasiness among the European allies and the highly vocal expression of popular discontent in which it was being manifested must be allayed, and this could only be done by what was seen to be a genuine move on the part of the United States to enter into serious negotiations with the Soviet Union on arms control.

In September 1981 the new US Secretary of State and the Soviet Foreign Minister met in New York to discuss a resumption of TNF talks which could start at the end of November in that year. There were still considerable reservations in Europe as to whether the United States was wholly serious in its stated intention to reach an agreement. It was only through strenuous efforts on the part of the US Administration that public opinion in Europe was eventually persuaded, at least in part, that real progress was being made. The process that was eventually to result in what came to be known as the START Treaty of 1984 was none the less truly under way. Its culmination in the summit meeting in January of that year might, it was thought, have had as much to do with the coming presidential campaign as with the conclusion of the business of negotiations.

An arms control treaty is an advantage to a conservative in an election year though an encumbrance to a liberal. This point was underlined by the fact that the ratification process in the US Senate was complete by the summer. The negotiations had been difficult but (though the outcome failed in differing ways, but to about the same degree, to satisfy both sides) not as difficult or as protracted as was expected, and the work that had gone into the abandoned SALT II Treaty of June 1979 saved much time in the formulation of definitions and of types of limitation.

The new treaty justified its descriptive acronym of START, Strategic Arms *Reduction* Talks. The term, proposed by the Americans at the outset of the new negotiations, was only accepted with misgivings by the Soviets, not so much because they rejected the explicit aspiration to reduce armaments, but because they wished to preserve continuity with the established SALT process. The substitution of 'reduction', however, for 'limitation' had such wide popular appeal, in Warsaw Pact countries scarcely less than in Western and even (to the limited extent that this was possible) in the USSR itself, that its acceptance was inevitable.

Unlike the SALT II agreement, which would only have lasted for five years, the START Treaty was to be of indefinite duration. In addition to this and the actual achievement of cuts, the key feature of START was that it also incorporated an interim agreement of the previous year to limit TNF in Europe.

Although much work had to be done on the rest of the Treaty, the US had pressed hard for an early deal on TNF to accompany the actual deployment of the first new *Tomahawk* GLCM in Britain and Italy in late 1983, with more to follow in West Germany and Belgium, but with none in the Netherlands, which had opted out. From December 1979, when the decision had first been taken by NATO to modernize the TNF, there had been a curious and ambivalent relationship between the implementation of the decision and arms control. Unless there was some chance of a serious diplomatic effort through arms control measures to remove the military requirement (or at least to reduce the number of weapons), it was not certain that any of the European nations would be willing to take these missiles in and very likely that some would refuse. At the same time, unless there was some chance of the programme being implemented, NATO would have no bargaining position, and without it would be unlikely to secure any cuts at all in the 250 Soviet SS-20 or the 350 older SS-4 and SS-5 missiles which also remained in service.

In their early stages the discussions on TNF arms control were not easy. This was in part a consequence of the mutual suspicions in the tense international climate following the Soviet invasion of Afghanistan, crisis in Poland, and the election of a US Administration bent on major rearmament. But the difficulties were even more a result of the sheer intractability of the issues: the USA wished to focus primarily on land-based missiles in the USSR that could hit Western Europe, which included many SS-20s based east of the Urals; the USSR wished to exclude weapons based outside Europe but include the American FBS, notably aircraft such as the F-111 and F-4 and even some aircraft carriers whose A-6 *Intruder* and A-7 *Corsair* aircraft could only attack Soviet territory with difficulty but which constituted a significant danger none the less. Lastly, because the Soviet SS-20 missiles were fitted with MIRV with three warheads (while the *Pershing* II and GLCM had only one warhead each) the US wished to use warheads as the basis for comparison while the USSR wished to count only the launchers. There was also the tricky question of the British and French nuclear forces which the Soviet Union wished to take into account, while Britain and France wanted them left out.

Not one of these issues was close to resolution by the time the talks (not yet in their new guise of START) began in mid-1982. This new beginning provided an opportunity to break the deadlock. The basic conceptual breakthrough was to try to identify a class of weapons which, though deployed in theatres, were essentially strategic in nature in their yield and in the targets they were likely to engage, and so ought to be linked with the other strategic weapons that had been considered appropriate for SALT.

Any demarcation line with nuclear weapons is inevitably arbitrary, but this approach made it possible to accept that the only United States TNF that deserved to be called strategic were the *Tomahawk* GLCM and *Pershing* II due for deployment, and the F-111 aircraft already based in Europe. On the Soviet side, account would have to be taken of the SS-20, SS-4 and SS-5 missiles, and the *Backfire*, *Badger* and *Blinder* aircraft under the command of the Soviet Long-Range Air Force. This allowed for all shorter-range systems to be excluded, perhaps for another negotiating forum, and got round the problem of how to justify the inclusion of Soviet systems facing China and some medium-range US aircraft based in the United Kingdom that would otherwise have been left out. The formula still could not accommodate the British and French strategic nuclear forces, but it was agreed to put off this issue, once again, for the next stage in the talks.

This broader definition of strategic weapons having been agreed, the issue then switched to how they should all be counted. In the past, the basic unit of account had been missile launchers or aircraft, with special categories for missiles with multiple warheads or bombers with air-launched cruise missiles (ALCM). The Americans attempted to introduce new counting rules whereby full notice would be taken of the properties of the various weapons, such as yield, accuracy and number of warheads. These proved complicated to formulate, however, and raised verification difficulties, and were anyway strongly resisted by the Soviet side. Eventually the Americans gave up on these new rules but pressed instead for stricter restrictions on MIRV missiles and greater co-operation on verification procedures. The main concession that the US made was to accept that major deployment of submarine-launched cruise missiles (SLCM), then being contemplated by Washington, would undermine any agreement. This concession led to the resignation of the US Navy Secretary.

The eventual agreement reached was to place a limit of 2,000 on the strategic forces (bombers, ICBM and SLBM) on each side (compared with a figure of 2,250 that had been part of the 1979 SALT II agreement). However, the new ceiling also had to accommodate the weapons based in Europe. Ceilings were placed on missiles with MIRV (including the SS-20) and aircraft carrying ALCM (1,000) and on ICBM with MIRV (650). The Soviets made a token cut of fifty in their giant 'heavy' ICBM (to 250) and accepted that the USA could build weapons of a similar size should they desire (which was unlikely). Each side would be free to mix its weapon types and their geographical distribution within these limits but at least 200 could be based in Europe. NATO decided that this figure would be sufficient for its needs in Europe. Since this meant a cut to a quarter of the planned complement of missiles and aircraft it was readily accepted as a significant arms control achievement – achieved multilaterally.

Such was the situation reached in the mid-eighties as mankind moved on towards an uncertain and forbidding future. Both sides stood like brooding giants, each guarding a store of weapons more than enough to destroy the entire population of the planet. Both deeply hoped that none of these deadly engines would ever need to be employed but their hopes were based on different thinking. On the Soviet side the aim was to offer to Western democracies a choice between a war of nuclear annihilation on the one hand, or acceptance on the other of piecemeal absorption into a communist world. If, in the event, the use of force had to be initiated it would, in the Soviet concept, be in the first instance with conventional weapons but sufficiently powerful to make the use of nuclear means unnecessary. On the Western side the most widely favoured aim was to possess sufficient non-nuclear war-fighting strength to halt an initial thrust by conventional means alone. This would leave the Soviets to choose between calling a halt, or invoking a nuclear exchange which would mean appalling and unpredictable disaster on both sides with little possible advantage in the outcome to anyone.

Western hopes lay, therefore, in the creation of an adequate non-nuclear armoury, in which the early years of the 1980s had shown disquieting deficiencies. What had been done to correct these, how far it was effective and how far it fell short we shall now enquire.

Chapter 5

Weapons

New tools for the battlefield, that is to say, weapon systems based on advances in technology, often remain without being tried out upon the battlefield itself for many years. The Israelis, for example, had used equipment produced in the United States in the 1973 war and the Americans themselves had had their last opportunity to try out major new systems in the war in Vietnam. Some of the newer equipment on the Soviet side was seen to work successfully in the hands of Egyptian clients in 1973 and the Soviet Union was itself able to employ newer versions of it, as well as the older and better known, behind the screens set up round Afghanistan from 1980 onwards. In helicopters, for example, in which the USSR had made very considerable advances, variants of the MI-24 type known as *Hind* D and E, were particularly useful for the location and destruction of pockets of Mujaheddin tribesmen. In Afghanistan, also, the Soviets used scattered mines which, although produced and issued in considerable numbers elsewhere had hitherto had little use. They also used some chemical agents.

Such situations as these, however, differed widely from that of the central conflict towards which the great powers were heading in the summer of 1985. In north-western Europe much of the equipment of both sides and their war-fighting techniques – which in some respects had developed radical differences – had never yet been tested in battle.

It was generally agreed that the tank, though there had been over the past score or more years occasional attacks upon its supreme position, was still the key factor on the land battlefield. Both on the Western and on the Soviet side there had been very considerable improvements in the tanks now in service, mainly in better protection, higher mobility, greater lethality in the main armament and in more effective fire control.

In the United States tank fleet the well-tried M-60A3 (which had been replacing the M-60A1) was now itself being replaced by the new M-1, the *Abrams*. Some of the earlier types were still in service in the US Army at the beginning of the eighties but by 1985 the *Abrams* was widely deployed. It had an advanced 1500 hp gas turbine engine and when it first came into service had used the 105 mm rifled gun as its main armament. The *Abrams* was now being furnished with the same type of 120 mm smooth-bore gun as was to be found in the German *Leopard* II. It had been the intention that all tank battalions in the United States Army in Europe (USAREUR) should be armed with the *Abrams* by the summer of 1985, but owing to delays in budgetary procedure little more than half the US main battle tank units in Europe were equipped with the *Abrams* carrying the new gun.

There is still argument between those who favoured the rifled gun and those who favoured the smooth bore as the more effective tank destroyer. This will no doubt continue, since results from the use of both these two guns on the Allied side in the war we are studying have not yet offered conclusive evidence one way or the other.

The British *Chieftain* was still as effective a fighting machine as any on the battlefield. It had a powerful and reliable engine, a highly effective 120 mm gun, a new laser range-finding system together with night-vision sighting, as well as well-proven stabilization equipment, impressive armour and useful speed. *Challenger*, with its superbly protective so-called Chobham armour (named after the establishment where it was developed) and its 120 mm rifled gun was also coming into regimental service. It was a magnificent tank but its introduction to British regiments in 1984 had so far only resulted in the addition of 100 or so of these outstanding fighting machines to Allied Command Europe at the time war broke out.

For the German *Bundeswehr*, the *Leopard* II was a marked improvement on *Leopard* I. In addition to its powerful new gun, *Leopard* II had a fully integrated fire control and stabilization system, a shorter response time, laser sighting, a higher first-round hit probability and, with the new sub-calibre ammunition, more effective penetration. Two thousand of these tanks had been scheduled in 1981 for procurement by 1987, but no more than half of these were in service with Federal German troops in 1985.

On the Soviet side, too, there had been improvements. Their newest tank, the T-80, was beginning to come into use shortly before the outbreak of war, but the main battle tank of the Warsaw Pact forces was the T-72, which had succeeded the T-64. The latter was still widely deployed, however, particularly among non-Soviet members of the Warsaw Pact. Produced in Kharkov, in the Ukraine, the T-64 had a powerful 125 mm smooth-bore gun with mechanical loading, allowing a rate of fire of up to eight rounds per minute at ranges out to 2,000 metres, with a three-man crew, improved armour, a newly

designed 780 hp engine, better suspension, advanced infra-red sighting and (like the *Chieftain*) laser range-finding. This tank, however,
was not popular with its users. They found it unreliable. It shed its
tracks. It had, in fact, been brought out in haste as the answer to the
projected NATO main battle tank known as MBT-70, which was
never produced. Its successor, the T-72, was built in the Urals. It still
at first had the same 125 mm gun as the T-64 but this was shortly
succeeded by a newer and much more effective type of gun of the
same calibre. The next tank model, the T-80, was manufactured in
Leningrad and showed still further improvements in armoured protection, with a new engine and a new suspension. Comparatively
few T-80 tanks were to be found in 1985 in service with the Red Army.

Soviet tanks were generally simpler and of rougher design than
those of the Western allies. They were less complex to maintain but
on the whole lacking in engine power and liable to break down. The
much lower level of sophistication in Soviet armoured equipment was
very noticeable, the result of a requirement to produce tanks which
could be readily manned by crews with a relatively low level of
intelligence and education.

All of the three types of Soviet main battle tank which would
chiefly be encountered in the war weighed round about 40 tons.
Higher weights were to be found among those of the Western allies.
As for ranges, NATO tank armaments were capable of engaging
targets out to 4,000 metres. There had long been argument as to
whether this long range was really an advantage and whether it would
not have been better to sacrifice some of it to secure other advantages. Certainly the ranges of Soviet tank guns were nothing like as
great. The theory behind Western tank design was that Warsaw Pact
opponents could be expected to concentrate tanks in high numerical
superiority, given choice in time and place of attack and given also the
greater number of tanks they had in the theatre. This meant that the
attrition of the armoured enemy had to begin as soon as possible to
diminish the probability of being overwhelmed by numbers when the
enemy got closer in, and it therefore had to begin at the furthest
range. It is true that the fullest exploitation of such long ranges, out to
3,000 and 4,000 metres, depended much on visibility and also on the
openness of terrain. In poor weather, mist or smoke, or in close
country, it was never easy and often impossible to acquire targets at
anything like these ranges. The tactical handling of tanks with the
longest ranges, like the *Chieftain*, came more and more to be dominated by the search for suitable firing positions giving the furthest
range of vision. Allied fire control systems, with laser range-finding
and sighting equipment, ensured a high probability of first-round hits.
Thermal imaging sights, such as those used in the US *Abrams*, and

other sighting equipment for use in very poor visibility did much to extend the usefulness of the main armaments of Allied tanks.

In the need for the earliest possible attrition of the enemy's tank numbers, surveillance of the battlefield was of the highest importance. There were still regrettable gaps in NATO in the availability of adequate equipment for this purpose. The British, for example, had had a project, known as *Supervisor*, or under the ungainly title of the medium-range unmanned aerial surveillance and target acquisition system (shortened into the mouth-cracking acronym MRUASTAS), which had been cancelled in 1980. A new system, *Phoenix*, which would fill this gap in the British capability for effective indirect fire, was just coming into service, however. New munitions were being developed to kill tanks at ranges of up to 30 kilometres but the means of acquiring targets for them had fallen behind. *Drones*, or what were more precisely described as remotely-piloted vehicles (RPV) (such as the Franco-Canadian-German *Drone* CL-289) were, within their limitations, of considerable use in the acquisition of hard targets in depth. The most consistently reliable means available up to the outbreak of war was still that of observation by men on the ground with sensors which were simple and robust but not, of course, as flexible or controllable as other systems would have been. They also made heavy demands on the men carrying out the observation.

What was known as sideways-looking airborne radar also had a useful role to play. It could indicate from an aircraft the location of tank concentrations which could then be plotted and attacked with area weapons. The acquisition of hard targets in depth, however, still had a long way to go.

There was an interesting and promising heliborne system in the United States forces known as SOTAS (stand-off target acquisition system) with a moving-target indicator radar. This had just begun to come into service by mid-1985. The few aircraft that had this capability when war broke out were to prove of high value in tracking the movement of enemy vehicles and providing divisional commanders with adequate information to permit them to attack second echelon forces with mass fire power as the prelude to planned counter-attacks. Attack upon the second echelon, or follow-up forces, had long been seen to be one of the most important ways of diminishing the forward momentum of the Soviet attack. Anything that could contribute here was valuable. Another sensor system, the remotely-monitored battlefield sonar system (or REMBASS, in the uncouth language of technical acronyms which military equipment seems to spawn so freely) was expected to come into NATO service in 1983 or 1984, but this was another of those battlefield aids of the highest importance that had been held up in the pipeline.

It was ironic that by August 1985 the means of attacking hard targets in depth was still well ahead of means of finding targets to attack. The new ammunition available to 155 mm guns in NATO from the US armoury included *Copperhead*, the cannon-launched guided projectile. *Copperhead* required a laser beam to be reflected from its target by a source known as a designator. The projectile then homed in on this. The problem was to keep the laser directed at the target tank during the critical time. Stay-behind parties of stout-hearted men had been trained in this and had the necessary communications to synchronize their target designations with the firing of missiles from up to 15 kilometres behind them. Following targets moving at 30 kph across country is no easy matter, however. Moreover, laser designators were still in 1985 bulky items of equipment, not easy to conceal and almost impossible to move around by stealth.

The remote anti-armour mine system (RAAMS), which could also be delivered by guns, proved to be an important and lethal partner to *Copperhead*. It was highly effective in attacking the bellies of tanks where the plate was not more than 20 mm thick. Several salvoes from a 155 mm artillery battery produced small minefields scattered around tank concentrations which restricted movement and gave better opportunities for *Copperhead*.

A novel and useful munition came into service in USAREUR in 1984 called seek and destroy armour, shortened into the not infelicitous little acronym SADARM. An artillery projectile exploding in an airburst releases sub-munitions, which then descend by parachute, swinging and scanning for hard targets. Their sensors emit millimetric wave signals and where there is a response (which would hardly come from anything but a tank or self-propelled gun) the sub-munition fires a charge through the top of it. Although a virgin weapon in 1985, these looked like being winners and V and VII US Corps took in the relatively small numbers available most gladly. The very high importance of early reduction in the numerical superiority of Soviet tanks fully justified the accelerated funding of this project in the early 1980s.

Artillery guns (as opposed to rocket equipments) were of course of the highest importance. Happily the Western allies had long agreed on a common calibre of 155 mm. A towed version of a British-German-Italian gun in this calibre (the FH-70) had already been operational for some years. What was needed was the self-propelled version of the same gun, the SP-70. Such of these as were in service in 1985 were expected to survive well on the battlefield and prove themselves to be agile and effective, the improved ammunition and range of up to 29 kilometres being most welcome. In far greater numbers, however, the familiar American-built SP M-109s and M-110s would still provide the main means of artillery fire-delivery in depth.

Dangerous though the numerical superiority of Warsaw Pact armour would be, its attrition was not the only task of the artillery. The traditional role of counter-battery fire, to reduce the effectiveness of the enemy's artillery, would still have a high priority. It was to be expected that on both sides, after every engagement, guns would have to move to another site to avoid the enemy's counter-bombardment. Location of gun position was with modern techniques too efficient to permit of sitting around. The calls for fire support that could be expected on FH-70, SP-70 and M-109 and M-110 guns, were bound to be heavy and might in the event far outweigh their ability to respond, demonstrating all too clearly NATO's relative shortage of artillery.

The Soviet Union disposed of a heavy 122 mm mortar called the BM-21, which was capable of firing forty rockets either singly, or in groups, or in what is daintily described as 'ripples' in which one huge deafening and destructive impact is closely followed by another, and another. The 240 mm successor to this equipment was also in service by the summer of 1985. The huge quantity of fire that multiple rocket launchers can put down has enormous shock effect. The NATO response to the introduction of these Soviet multiple rocket systems was to develop a new American-German-British multiple-launch rocket system (MLRS), which fired two packs of six rockets, also singly or in ripples, out to a range of 40 kilometres. It was just as well that the first batteries of NATO's multiple rocket launchers had been introduced in all Allied armies by 1984, giving troops some idea of the scale of bombardment to be expected. To experience this on the receiving end in complete surprise for the first time would be totally stunning.

Rivers and canals in the Federal Republic were developed, in the short time available, into the best possible obstacles. Bridge demolition chambers had been built into new bridges in the Federal Republic until the mid-seventies, but since then their design had incorporated no easy system for destruction. The engineer effort involved in preparing the demolition of all sizeable river crossings was enormous. Much more could have been done if even modest funds had previously been devoted to the development of more rapid demolition systems. As it was, many major bridges had to be left intact.

Soviet tanks were at one time required to have a swimming capability but this turned out to be a total failure and the USSR had no amphibious tanks in service in 1985. All types of Soviet main battle tank could, however, be waterproofed and fitted with a snorkel for air intake. Their self-propelled (SP) guns and armoured personnel carriers were expected to swim.

Where recent Soviet experience would be likely to stand them in good stead would be in the use of helicopters. Their MI-24 *Hind* types, the *Hind* D and *Hind* E particularly, which had been developed as gunships, that is to say as flying weapons platforms, had given them in the occupation of Afghanistan the most valuable possible experience and now provided formidable weapon systems. A variety of weapon fittings had evolved (*Hind* D now carried a turreted gun) in addition to heavier protection, while in the development of their tactics the Soviets had made great strides. These two really powerful gunships would certainly prove to be more battleworthy and far less vulnerable than the MI-24 *Hind* A, which was still in service, from which they had been developed. Their pilots had been trained to operate without friendly ground support. Their casualties would be numerous, that was certain, but the effectiveness of this new highly-developed instrument of war was likely to be reaffirmed at every major obstacle and whenever the pace of the armoured battle began to flag. The pattern to be expected was that *Hind* attacks would probably be followed up with landings, in at least company strength, from *Hip* troop-carrying helicopters, of which MI-8 – *Hip* E – was a late assault development. The deep penetration of sorties such as this would naturally cause commanders to worry about disruption in the rear but the real successes that these helicopter operations would seek to achieve would lie in the maintenance or renewal of forward momentum in the mainly armoured attack.

Would the helicopter now be taking over from the tank, as the tank's most lethal enemy? This was by no means certain. What had to be ensured, if war came, was that the *Hind* should not be allowed to become the undisputed owner of low-level airspace. The helicopter did look, however, like laying a claim to be the tank's heir presumptive.

Other helicopters whose performance reinforced this claim, in addition to *Hind*, were the now well-established US UH-1 *Cobras* but even more the new AH-64 *Apache* with its *Hellfire*, fire-and-forget laser-guided anti-tank missile. Outright dogfights between opposing helicopter forces on any scale would probably be avoided, since neither adversary had a truly effective helicopter air-to-air weapon, though both sides were proceeding hastily in the early 1980s with promising developments. With equipment in service the best results would come where imagination was most actively applied. It was very likely that those Western allies who possessed relatively few helicopters would tend to hold their precious fleets in hand for special situations while those with more extensive assets could use them from the outset more boldly in the forward areas. The British Army *Lynx*, introduced in the early 1980s and fitted with the TOW (tube-launched optically-tracked wire-guided) missile for anti-armour use, would tend, for example, to be kept out of contact until the Soviet attacking forces had closed right up. The *Lynxes*, which might be said to be more vulnerable than the gunship helicopters, could play a highly important part in dealing with a well-defined enemy breakthrough. By hovering low and using the full 4,000-metre range of the TOW missile, *Lynx* would be able to keep out of range of enemy air defence and out of sight of ground-to-ground weapons, while still delivering an effective attack. The high mobility of these aerial vehicles and the lethality of TOW would make them a natural counter-attack force. The use of scatterable mines (or RDM – remotely-delivered mines) to delay and distract the attention of Soviet armour could improve the kill rate of *Lynx* and other anti-armour helicopters considerably. The United States' helicopter force would work in much the same way as this, but with deeper forays beyond the forward line of troops, in conjunction with fixed-wing strike aircraft such as the A-10 *Thunderbolt*. Attack upon the second echelon would be of high importance.

The Franco-German HOT (high-subsonic optically teleguided) anti-tank missile system, used in the helicopters of both France and the FRG, with a range from 75 to 4,000 metres and sufficiently massive penetration to defeat any known tank in service in the mid-eighties, could not fail to make a valuable addition to the NATO anti-tank armoury.

The part likely to be played by rotary-wing aircraft has been stressed here because of its intimate association with the land battle. A truer air war could also be expected to range widely and deeply, with 2 and 4 ATAF (Allied Tactical Air Forces) initially intent on winning the air battle in the face of greater numbers of aircraft and of really formidable Warsaw Pact air defence. The opening high explosive and chemical attack on NATO airfields could expect success to the extent that, delivered with surprise, it would leave the Western allies with somewhat reduced resources and less flexibility. Defence against chemical warfare would severely reduce the efficiency of personnel and increase turn-round time on airfields. Shelters had been hardened, however, and alert procedures improved to ensure the survival of as many as possible of the aircraft attacked on the ground.

Interdiction, wherever possible, and attrition of enemy forces in depth would form the major offensive role of the Allied air forces, with the ground forces getting relatively little close support in the early stages except in cases of extreme urgency. The devastating tank-busting capability of the US A-10 *Thunderbolt*, though its full exploitation invited uncomfortably high losses, would be especially effective in these emergency situations, as well as when working with anti-tank helicopters in seeking out and destroying the Soviet armour, as is described in the next chapter.

In its ground forces the United States had by the summer of 1985 replaced many of its M-113 APC with the new *Bradley* M-2 infantry fighting vehicle. The *Bradley* M-2, which was not just a new 'battle taxi' but a true fighting machine, could make a world of difference since it gave each squad its own TOW missile, to be fired from under the shield of armour, and for close-in protection a 25 mm electrically-fired *Bushmaster* gun capable of destroying light armour and firing a high-explosive anti-personnel round as well. The squad also had the *Dragon* medium-range ATGW (anti-tank guided weapon). The infantry could not yet be said to be a match for armour but it could certainly now give a better account of itself under armoured attack than before.

If there was one area of almost desperate deficiency in Allied Command Europe (ACE) in the middle 1980s it was in air defence. Overall air defence planning in NATO only began to take real shape at the beginning of the eighties with the formulation of the Air Defence Planning Group's programme. This was to take in all air command and control (both offensive and defensive), NATO airborne early warning, NATO IFF (identification friend or foe), the multi-functional information distribution system (MIDS) and air defence weapons. In a programme initiated in 1980, intended to be implemented over fifteen years, it was sad, if inevitable, that little progress had been made in the five years before the war. NATO looked like going to war with air defences of very uneven capability which cried out, as with so much else in NATO, for standardization.

Medium- and high-level missile air defence in ACE was still provided by HAWK (homing-all-the-way killer) and *Nike*. *Patriot*, a far superior system to either, could probably have replaced both, operating (as the sales talk put it) 'from treetop level to very high altitude'. It had proved expensive to develop and was not available in time to be generally deployed in Europe before the outbreak of war, though it was just coming into service in early 1985. Its absence would be felt. At lower levels, protection was afforded by *Rapier*. The new type of tracked *Rapier* system introduced in the early eighties enormously enhanced air defence in both Northern and Central army groups in the Central Region. The very low-level cover provided by the American man-portable *Redeye* (in British and Canadian formations by *Blowpipe*), all too sparsely spread, would leave vulnerable points too often totally exposed. *Stinger*, a US shoulder-fired anti-aircraft weapon, began to supersede *Redeye* in 1981 and was generally in service in USAREUR in 1985. It used passive infra-red (IR) homing, the missile operating independently after initial arming and launch by the operator. This was a great step forward in low-level air defence. Among NATO allies the Federal Republic of Germany was the first to adopt *Stinger* but others followed. It was in wide (but unhappily not general) use in the Central Region in 1985. The US, German and Dutch formations had air defence weapons not greatly dissimilar from the Soviet ZSU-23-4 radar-controlled anti-aircraft gun. The US divisional air defence system (DIVADS) offered promise and the German SP armoured anti-aircraft system *Gepard* (*Cheetah*), with its twin 35 mm guns, was costly but might prove its value against air attack, even at $4 million per copy. One advantage to NATO was that Soviet pilots had neither the equipment nor the training to fly quite as low as those of 2 and 4 ATAF. They would therefore be more exposed to earlier radar detection and subsequent attack.

In the whole vital problem of controlling battlefield airspace, NATO IFF was one case of particularly badly needed rationalization and improvement. It is worth enlarging upon this as an example.

It is essential to know very quickly whether an approaching aircraft is hostile. IFF interrogates it by sending out a group of pulses to which another group of pulses is sent back in reply by what is known as a transponder. If this answer is correct – that is, as expected – the aircraft is friendly. If not, it is hostile.

The system, long in use, had been adequate when warfare was less complex, electronics less advanced, and airspace, especially lower airspace, less crowded. It was scarcely adequate in the 1980s. It could be jammed, either accidentally or deliberately. It could be 'spoofed' by an imitation of the right answer. The emission, whether of interrogation or answer, could be tracked to source and serve as a beacon to bring in guided- or homing-attack. It had blind spots. It had reliability problems. What was good for the 1960s was hardly good enough for the higher pressures of the 1980s. A soldier in a trench with a *Stinger* would have an advanced IFF with him but if he got it wrong, and pressed the trigger when he should not, he could destroy a $20 million aircraft and a pilot. It is said that in the early days of the 1973 Arab-Israeli war the Egyptians shot down eighty-one Israeli aircraft and sixty-nine of their own.

As the 1980s opened, the urgent need for a new identification system for NATO was realized and a development programme launched. Its cost was estimated to be at least $250 million, and the resultant replacement of the current IFF, in which some $2,000 million had already been invested, could hardly be complete by the end of the century. NATO would have to go to war with the IFF it had, depending more and more upon procedural method in the management of airspace.

Soviet air defence systems in the probable battle zone ranged from SA-2 up to SA-14, with the new generation starting at SA-8. The mobile medium- to low-level SA-6 and the hand-held low-level SA-7 had proved themselves, without any question, many years before in Sinai, and the successor equipments were even more effective, lethal and mobile. The ZSU-23-4 radar controlled anti-aircraft gun was still in service in 1985 in spite of its age and no equivalent equipment in NATO came anywhere near to matching it in terms of numbers. It was probably the most feared item of the Warsaw Pact battlefield air defence armoury.

In the US artillery the automated tactical fire-direction system (TACFIRE), so long awaited, began to come into service in USAREUR in 1981 and was well established in 1985, giving much increased responsiveness and control. The British battlefield artillery target engagement system (BATES) was another example of the application of microprocessor technology to the central control of artillery, transmitting accurate fire orders from observer to gun in milliseconds and producing the swift response necessary for the engagement of fleeting targets. The use of this system, though it had faults, marked a quantum jump in British methods of artillery control and was expected to do much to compensate for the shortage of guns in the two British corps in NORTHAG. In both cases, in TACFIRE and BATES, the failure of government, in the US no less than in the UK, to ensure adequate and timely funding resulted in dangerous delays in bringing systems of incalculable value into service.

It was fortunate for NATO in 1985 that the *Assault Breaker* concept, already in 1978 under research and development in the United States but threatened by budgetary hazards thereafter, had been at least partially rescued in time. This was an attempt to provide non-nuclear response to armoured superiority, with improved effectiveness against first-echelon forces but with the emphasis on second and third echelons up to 160 kilometres in depth. It had been from the first a joint US Army/Air Force project, involving an airborne target acquisition and weapons delivery system (TAWDS) and a ground-based army element. The full exploitation of the potential of *Assault Breaker* depended on the development of systems such as the helicopter-borne SOTAS mentioned earlier. The *Patriot* missile (originally intended as a surface-to-air missile, or SAM, but now also to be used as a surface-to-surface missile, or SSM) could be guided both from a ground-based command and control centre or from an airborne command post if the ground centre were out of action. An essential element in *Assault Breaker* was to be the use of terminally-guided sub-munitions. Each bomblet (or *Smartlet*, as these developments of 'smart' munitions came to be called) was furnished with a terminal seeker and a limited degree of manoeuvrability. The seeker would send out a millimetric wave signal to which there would be from the unwitting target an involuntary response. The weapon would then lock on to the response and find its path to the target. It was unfortunate that funding in the US for the development of *Assault Breaker* was so far reduced in the early 1980s that the whole system was only partially in troop service by 1984.

In the field of chemical warfare (cw) the offensive capability available to Warsaw Pact armies in the field was well known, as well as the use to which in Soviet military practice it could be put. Specialist cw personnel, perhaps numbering in the aggregate 150,000, were deployed in the Red Army down to battalions. Some 15 per cent of all Soviet artillery ammunition carried chemical fillings, with up to 50 per cent of theatre and strategic missiles armed in the same way. The availability of aircraft fitted with spray tanks was high.

The practice would be to employ non-persistent non-lethal or incapacitating agents in the advance in bombardment preparatory to attack, for example, on positions it was intended to overrun or occupy. Such agents would disperse in a matter of minutes. Tear gas, or the cs used in civil disturbance, are good examples of such agents. What are known in the West as DM and DC, with secondary effects such as nausea, giddiness and reduction of the will to fight, are military versions. Non-persistent agents include chlorine and phosgene, lethal when sufficient is inhaled, but by the early 1980s thought to be of little use on account of unreliability.

More persistent agents, including blister gases – for example mustard and nerve agents such as the highly lethal Tabun (GA) and Soman (DC) – would be used to seal flanks and deny areas not intended for occupation, as well as to attack airfields, often in conjunction with delayed-action bombs.

The purpose of all cw attack would be twofold: to inflict casualties, and by causing opponents to take full protective action to impede performance.

It is difficult for anyone without experience of exacting work done under full cw protection to realize how far it saps efficiency. Protective clothing is burdensome and hot, and physical work in it is very exhausting. Staff work, though not so demanding physically, is difficult in respirators and thick gloves. The maintenance of effective seals over apertures such as windows, doors and hatches is time-consuming and involves severe self-discipline. Decontamination demands not only appropriate equipment and a plentiful water supply, but also minute care, which diverts attention and resource from other essential tasks. Men get accustomed to some degree to the discomforts and distractions of cw precautions but they are rarely more than 50 per cent efficient under them and tire quickly.

It was known that Warsaw Pact defensive capabilities in the field were inferior to those of the West, where British protective clothing and equipment were of outstanding quality, and alarm and other precautionary procedures were well practised. Other NATO members followed in varying degrees of effectiveness. The great disadvantage on the Western side was the general lack of a retaliatory capability everywhere but in USAREUR. Stocks of offensive toxic agents in the US had once been high but had deteriorated, or been dispersed, or destroyed so far that by 1980 they could be said (and were, by the Chairman of the Joint Chiefs of Staff) to be virtually non-existent. One SACEUR after another from the late 1970s onwards had emphasized that only the availability of an adequate retaliatory capability could be considered an effective defence against Soviet cw.

Interest lay chiefly in what is known as the binary round, a projectile in which two substances of a non-toxic nature are combined in flight and become a toxic substance before impact. Though there were technical difficulties (a short flight, for example, put obstacles in the way of effective combination of ingredients), the great merit of the binary round lay in safety of handling and storage, and a possible reduction in the sensitivity of Allied countries about hosting it in peacetime. The production of the binary round was recommended in the US in the early 1980s but it had not proved possible to store any in European countries by the summer of 1985. A useful step forward, however, had been the bilateral agreements between the United States on the one hand and Federal Germany and the UK on the other for the manufacture of quantities of such munitions for 155 mm artillery. They were to be stored for the time being in the US and brought forward when required.

Thus the armed forces on the Soviet side were in 1985 well prepared for offensive cw action but not over-well equipped to withstand attack, and on the other side quite well (in the case of the British, very well) prepared in defence but with a retaliatory capability confined entirely to the Americans. It was unlikely that, if a Warsaw Pact attack involved early and widespread use of cw in the field, the Western allies would fail to make use of the US capability to respond. This, however, would involve delay on the Western side and give the Soviets some initial advantage. This was almost certainly what was intended.

The Soviets would without doubt employ cw from the start of any offensive and the Western allies were well and truly warned to expect it. It was also highly probable that the two US corps would not be attacked in this way since it was a fair guess that the Supreme Allied Commander Europe (SACEUR) would find some way of employing the American retaliatory capability on his own authority in support of US troops, using munitions flown in for the purpose. This would be well known on the other side, as would also be the inability of other Western allies to retaliate in kind, at least for the time being, on their own behalf. Allied casualties, if war broke out, could be confidently expected but if precautions were taken and discipline prevailed they need not be high.

In aircraft the Alliance was compelled on the whole, in the years leading up to the war, to make do with what it had, or at any rate to improve it as best it might by stretching existing capabilities a little further, rather than to try to introduce far-reaching innovations. Given the financial constraints, Allied air forces, with an immense concentration of effort, did not do too badly.

The EF-111, for example, was an improved jammer built into an F-111 airframe, capable of Mach 2-plus speeds at height and a supersonic performance at sea level. Being also highly manoeuvrable it was a good survivor. The EF-111 carried ten high-powered jammer transmitters and a terminal-threat warning system which detected weapons-associated radar emissions and would provide flight crews with warning of impending attack from SAM anti-aircraft artillery or interceptors. These aircraft, beginning to enter service in 1983, were expected to prove very effective as deep-penetration escorts. In the Second World War the protection of deep penetration by an air force was provided by fighter escort or, when beyond its range, by the capacity of the bomber to fight its own way through the enemy's interceptors, as in the US 8th Air Force. In the 1980s the penetrating aircraft had to be protected primarily from the result of electro-magnetic emissions, whether its own or the enemy's, which would serve to guide gun, missile or interceptor attack towards it. The EF-111 development typified modern trends.

So did the TR-1, a retooled version of the old U-2 (what the press called the 'spy plane'), a high-altitude (over 70,000 feet), long-range (over 3,000 miles) reconnaissance and surveillance platform providing battlefield information to tactical commanders. This aircraft, too, was a definite plus. It had advanced electronic counter-measures (ECM), synthetic aperture radar systems, and capability to direct precision strikes against enemy radar emitters (PLSS – precision location strike system) and to collect ELINT (electronic intelligence) data. It began coming into NATO service in the early 1980s.

The story was the same with the F-4G, a modified F-4E *Phantom*, containing advanced electronic warfare equipment and armed with anti-radiation missiles, of which the latest, AGM-88 – HARM (high-speed anti-radiation missile) – was just coming into service when war broke out.

The F-15 *Eagle* was still in service, with a newer version, the *Strike Eagle*, carrying improved systems and possessing a better all-weather capability. The F-16 *Fighting Falcon*, which began to come into squadron service in 1981, represented a real advance. Its equipment included a multi-mode radar with a clutter-free look-down capability, head-up displays, internal 'chaff' (strips of foil which act as decoy to enemy homing missiles) and flare dispensers, a 500-round 20 mm internal gun and ECM, all in an aircraft with speed around Mach 2, a ceiling of more than 50,000 feet and a ferry range greater than 2,000 miles. This was a great improvement on any fighter the Western allies had hitherto seen. The F-18 *Hornet*, a one-man multiple-mission fighter bomber of even more advanced type, attractive to both navies and air forces, had suffered many delays in development and was not yet in service when war broke out.

A further development of high significance was the E-3A *Sentry* airborne warning and control system (AWACS). Into a Boeing 707 airframe had been fitted equipment which made up a mobile, flexible, jamming-resistant, surveillance and command, control and communications system, capable of all-weather, long-range, high or low surveillance of all air vehicles, manned or unmanned, above all types of terrain. Its look-down radar gave it a unique capability hitherto absent. *Sentry* could operate for six hours, on station 1,000 miles from home base, with a maximum speed of 530 mph and a ceiling of 29,000 feet. Details of how it worked are given in the next chapter. Its entry into service in 1980 and into NATO in 1982 marked a great step forward.

The improved *Harrier* came into service with the US Marines as the AV-8B in 1983 and with the RAF as the GR-5 a year later. More than one attempt was made by the US Administration in the late 1970s to kill the AV-8B. Happily Congress remained firm and the very valuable inter-Allied (US/UK) development of an advanced vertical/short take-off and landing (V/STOL) aircraft was saved.

Three major developments in the late 1970s and early 1980s emphasized the joint sea/air character of modern naval operations. First, the advent of ocean-ranging, high-performance bombers, such as the Soviet *Backfire*, armed with stand-off anti-ship missiles; secondly, the increased anti-submarine potency of long-range maritime patrol aircraft (LRMP), such as the *Nimrod*; and thirdly the much extended range of shore-based fighter protection of shipping and naval forces made possible by in-flight refuelling. The air capability of these forces was much improved also, at little extra cost, by the invention in Britain of the ski-jump flight deck, first fitted in HMS

Invincible, often publicly described as an aircraft carrier but more correctly designated a cruiser. Its use considerably enhanced the combat performance of V/STOL *Harrier* aircraft and led to the adaptation of the hulls of container-type merchant ships to be escort carriers. Unfortunately only one of these, the *British Traveller*, was operational by mid-1985.

Anti-submarine warfare (ASW), always difficult, costly and complex, was made even more so by the introduction of an effective anti-sonar coating for submarines. This reduced the detection-range of active sonar dramatically, although its use for the precise location of submarines, in order to bring weapons to bear, remained virtually indispensable. Fortunately passive sonar, which is not affected by coatings on the submarines, had made great strides by 1985. It took three main forms. For very long-range detection, surveillance arrays, called SURTASS (surface towed-array sensor system), towed by ocean-going tugs, were used; destroyer/frigate types, and submarines on anti-submarine patrol, towed tactical arrays, called TACTASS (tactical towed-array sonar system); and LRMP aircraft were equipped with much improved passive sonobuoys. All these measures would impose considerable restrictions upon the mobility of hostile nuclear-powered attacking submarines.

Increasingly the systematic deployment of both active and passive sonars in ships, submarines and aircraft, and where possible on the seabed, had come to be seen as the basis of an effective counter to the submarine. Without the energetic application of information technology this could not have been achieved. By this means data obtained from any submarine contact, however fleeting, in any theatre of war, could rapidly be collated, after processing, with other submarine contact data and intelligence to be analysed, compared, and stored for further use. A continuously updated master submarine plot could thus be maintained, which would be accessible electronically to any NATO commander engaged in anti-submarine warfare, at any level, at sea or on shore. In addition, the exercise of command and control over the forces engaged in fast-moving and extensive air-sea combat would be much facilitated by the development and adoption of narrow-band, secure, voice communication equipment for tactical use.

Amongst the more important new weapons in the sea/air battle would be *Stingray*, the air-dropped or surface-ship-launched, high-performance homing anti-submarine torpedo; and the *Captor*, a mobile, homing, anti-submarine mine. *Lynx*, an ASW helicopter coming into service in the Royal Navy in the early 1980s, was a particularly useful guided weapons platform. The underwater-to-surface anti-ship missile *Harpoon* was another effective new weapon, in use in NATO submarines. Without these weapon systems the exiguous naval, naval air, and maritime air forces of NATO would have been at a severe disadvantage in trying to protect merchant shipping and seaborne military forces against all-out attack by the Soviet Navy and Soviet naval aviation.

The fighting power of the US Navy, and hence of NATO, had by mid-1985 been augmented by the first fruits of two remarkable procurement programmes, namely the building of the *Ticonderoga*-class cruisers, *Aegis*-equipped (*Aegis* is an integrated computer-controlled air defence system), and the conversion of the Second World War *Iowa*-class battleships into what, as a cross between battleships and carriers, were nicknamed 'battliers'. The former were the first major surface warships to have been conceived since the microchip came in to join the missile, and could engage air, surface and underwater targets simultaneously at all ranges out to hundreds of miles; the latter, with an assorted armament of 16-inch guns and guided missiles, both surface-to-surface and surface-to-air, coupled with the survival capability conferred by vast size and heavy armour protection, provided the US Marines with devastating and reliable naval gunfire support, as well as air cover offered by v/STOL aircraft.

Finally, in a far from exhaustive survey, we come to *Tornado*, the multi-role combat aircraft (MRCA) combining the activities of a new strike/attack and reconnaissance aircraft, and in another variant an advanced interceptor, which though a joint Allied (UK/FRG/Italy) development of the first importance, more than once nearly came to grief in Allied budgeting. Happily *Tornado* too survived, even if its production rate was slower than it should have been. Its role is covered in more detail in the next chapter, which deals specifically with air warfare.

Military operations in Europe in August 1985 were to last for only three weeks. They would demand, none the less, optimum performance against opponents who were for the most part resolute and almost always well equipped. Penalties for inefficiency or irresolution on NATO's part would be high. The war was not in the event long enough to extract the fullest value from developing techniques, nor even to draw the best dividends from material already in use and now becoming familiar. It was quite long enough to show where weaknesses lay. It was also long enough to demonstrate very clearly not only that non-nuclear defence is expensive (if it is to be effective), which was something that had been realized for a long time, but also that nuclear war can hardly be avoided unless the high cost of the alternative is met. The margin of NATO success would have been safer if the improved techniques and equipment, of which a few have been looked at here, had been available sooner, or in greater quantity, or if some which never came into service had not been strangled at birth. What the West had, and the way it was used, was just enough to prevent the catastrophic use of battlefield nuclear weapons with all its dreadful consequences. It might easily have been otherwise.

There is an old Roman saying: '*Si vis pacem, para bellum*': if you want peace prepare for war.

It could be reworked, on lines more appropriate to the late twentieth century, to read: 'If you want nuclear peace prepare for nonnuclear war: but be ready to pay the price.'

Chapter 6

The Air Dimension

The flexibility of air power is so far undisputed that people have tended rather to tire of the phrase. There is no escaping the fact, however, that it takes years for air forces to adapt to new fundamental concepts of operation. It takes at least ten years to develop a major air weapons system and air crew need four to five years after recruitment to become operationally effective in the more demanding roles. So it was not surprising that in the late 1970s, little more than a decade after the switch from a NATO strategy of massive retaliation to one of flexible response, the Allied air forces were still heavily involved with the technical and training tasks of developing a tactical capability to match possible battle scenarios of a war in central Europe under new politico-strategic terms of reference. Nor was it surprising that the reorganisation of the Soviet Air Force (SAF) on more flexible lines (described later in this chapter) was only beginning to come to fruition in the early 1980s.

In the United States Air Force (USAF) and the British Royal Air Force (RAF) the lion's share of the air appropriations had throughout the 1970s been going to tactical forces. For the USAF this meant emphasis on contemporary fighters – the F-15 *Eagle* and *Strike Eagle* and F-16 *Fighting Falcon* – and A-10 *Thunderbolt* tank-busters. For the RAF it meant, among other things, Anglo-French *Jaguars*, the astonishingly versatile vertical/short take-off and landing (V/STOL) *Harriers*, F-4 *Phantom* fighters bought from the United States in the late 1960s and *Buccaneers* of a type that was a capable variant of an earlier naval aircraft. Most of these aircraft had been around for some years. By 1985 the RAF had had nearly fifteen years of experience in operating the V/STOL *Harriers*, for example, from dispersed sites around their base at Gütersloh well forward on the north German plain.

That dispersal was to serve them well when Gütersloh was attacked by Soviet *Fencers* on the morning of 5 August and not a single *Harrier* was on the airfield – although some RAF *Puma* helicopters and a charter aircraft evacuating civilian baggage were

caught with heavy casualties. The *Harrier* pilots knew the area back-
wards and their association with I British Corps in the Northern
Army Group (NORTHAG) was especially close. It was out of that
association, and years of exercise together, that the British doctrine
of counter-armour operations from the air had grown. The principle
was to exploit the speed of the fixed wing aircraft to turn the flank of
the enemy's armoured echelons and then fly up or down to attack
them some 10 to 20 kilometres in the rear, at the critical point where
the armour would be fanning out from its line of march on to the
battlefield. These tactics, which depended, like so much else, on air
reconnaissance and rapid response, were to be vindicated in the war,
and the air losses, though high, were sustainable for at least a while.
This did not, in the event, take the immediate pressure off the troops
at the forward edge of the battle area (the FEBA) when they were being
forced back by the momentum and fire power of the enemy's tanks.
The effect would be felt later. In slowing momentum at the FEBA the
army was to rely primarily on the long-range fire power of well-sited
tanks and anti-tank guided weapons (ATGW), as well as ATGW helicopters hovering in ambush over dead ground or concealed in woodland.
The *Harriers* and *Jaguars* would of course intervene directly at the
FEBA when the clamour for help became especially loud and insistent.
When they did so their losses would usually be high and the trade-off
between tanks and aircraft could only be justified at times of the
direst need.

The Anglo/German/Italian multi-role combat aircraft (MRCA)
brought into service as the *Tornado* in its specialized long-range
interceptor role in the UK, and its interdiction and counter-air role
for the European continent, was a very recent and promising arrival.
The German Air Force (GAF) was tied by political and geographical
logic to the defence of its own air space, direct support of the land
forces of CENTAG (Central Army Group) and NORTHAG, and
interdiction and counter-air operations over enemy territory. By
1984 the GAF had received most of its *Tornados* and its air defence
force was made up of F-4 *Phantoms* and a residue of F-104 *Star-
fighters* left over from the 1960s.

Each of the Allied air forces was backed up in some degree by air
transport and helicopters. The helicopter was an unknown factor in
operations on the scale and at the intensity that were to be experienced in the Third World War. In the event it played a versatile and
often indispensable part in many roles, and notably so with the Warsaw Pact forces. But as had always been expected, losses were high
and it remains an open question as to how long the helicopters could
have remained on the battlefield in a longer war. The United States
Army and Air Force, with Vietnam experience behind them, were to

use large numbers in the gunship and logistic roles, with great skill and often with decisive local effect. In the first days of the war German and British helicopters were virtually to save the re-supply situation in NORTHAG's rear area. The threat to soft-skinned vehicles from SAF armed reconnaissance aircraft had been seriously underestimated and the roads were blocked with wrecked trucks as well as civilian refugees. To compound the chaos and confusion the FEBA was falling steadily back to the west and it was chiefly through a non-stop shuttle of medium-lift helicopters that the ammunition and fuel would reach the front.

In a more offensive mode RAF *Puma* helicopters were to be used to move army anti-tank teams and their *Milan* weapons across the axes of the enemy's advance to new positions as his thrust lines swung. When they achieved surprise and found good firing positions this proved an excellent way of keeping the anti-tank weapons in action against the enemy. The British Army's *Lynxes* were effectively used in a similar way. But the British had always been hesitant about helicopters, partly because of their vulnerability, and partly because of their cost. By 1985 the British Army and the RAF had still to agree upon whether the helicopter should be regarded as an air or ground system. In consequence the capabilities of this remarkable, but admittedly vulnerable, machine were not always fully exploited in the battle in the north.

This was not true of the Soviet forces, which had always loved helicopters and built models for every kind of task and weapon. They were to use them as self-propelled guns flying above and ahead of their leading armour, as anti-tank platforms and as electronic counter-measure (ECM) stations. They even armed some with air-to-air weapons. Not surprisingly they fell easily and in large numbers to the US *Patriot* missiles (which were coming into service but were not yet plentiful) and the British *Rapier* and French *Rolands* and *Sicas* deployed by the NATO armies. Nevertheless, Allied ground force commanders at all levels would have cause to reflect that the need to strengthen their defences against marauding helicopters had not been fully appreciated.

Bringing offensive air support to bear on the enemy's vulnerable articulation points in a fast-moving battle places a high premium on tactical air reconnaissance, with its rapid reporting and subsequent response. This was done in the main by interdictor or fighter aircraft operating with specialized crews and equipment. Over the sea, maritime aircraft patrolled against submarines and surface ships, with land-based helicopters working closer inshore. The whole Western European theatre was enclosed by the NATO air defence ground environment (NADGE), a radar warning system within which, in addition to the air fighters, there were arrays of ground-based surface-to-air missiles (SAM) for point and area defence. In the event the demand for air reconnaissance far exceeded the limited numbers of aircraft and crews available to carry it out. Whether there should have been more tactical reconnaissance squadrons must remain a moot point. More here would have meant less somewhere else. To give an idea of scale, it is worth noting that the USAF possessed approximately five times the number of aircraft of the whole of the RAF and GAF together.

On the broader front of intelligence – and that was very broad indeed – it had always been feared by the sceptics that in a major war the Allied intelligence system with its computerized 'fusion centres' would get clogged up – and it did. The input from satellites, airborne radars, electronic sensors, photography, and a host of other sources was vast and although the computers swallowed it all at great speed and spat it out again obligingly enough, they did so in an uncomprehending way. When war broke out intelligence centres had to be diluted with inexperienced or out-of-practice staffs and this was to hinder the speed at which the significance of bald data could be appreciated – as for example after the Gdansk incident, described at the end of this chapter, when the crucial information about the Soviet Air Force *Cooker* frequencies took forty-eight hours to reach the operating units that so desperately needed it. But the learning curve is steep in war and processing and evaluating times were to be greatly reduced in the first few days. Nevertheless, the human burden in handling the nearly overwhelming volume of data that the sensors, computers and communications could collect, store and deliver was tremendous and was to remain so throughout the war.

The British and German air force commanders had long seen that they would need an agile air-superiority fighter to replace their *Phantoms* in the 1980s, in order to counter the growing tactical air power that the Warsaw Pact would be able to bring to bear over a land battle in the Central Region. For political reasons this had to be tackled as a multi-national collaborative project and joint studies were started by the UK and the FRG with the French, who had a similar need. This well-intentioned collaboration got nowhere and the project was dropped. Differences in specifications and timescales could not be reconciled and the costs of the *Tornado*, which were getting badly out of control, squeezed out what little room was left in the forward defence budgets of the Federal Republic and the UK. The French kept their thoughts and their plans to themselves as the British and German staffs accepted that they would have to make do with their *Phantoms* for the rest of the decade. This was unfortunate but for the British there was at least the consolation that there was now room for a handsome increase of some eighty aircraft in the *Harrier* force. This would be welcome in the land battle but one result would be that Britain and Germany, if forced into a war in the 1980s, would be using fighter aircraft that were more than twenty years old in concept and design – the *Tornado* excepted – and that they would have no contemporary air-superiority fighter for the air battle.

The smaller northern NATO countries had managed their admittedly simpler resource problems rather better by plumping for the US F-16 *Fighting Falcon* tactical fighter in the mid-seventies. Although 'buying American' when there was so much drive behind the idea of developing the European aerospace industry had been a controversial decision, the war was to show that the Norwegian, Belgian, Dutch, and Danish air forces had made a sound and timely choice. Although the separate national air force orders were not large, the aggregate of more than 200 F-16 *Fighting Falcon* fighters, some with an enhanced night and bad-weather capability, together with the new *Mirage* 2000 of the French Air Force, did much to redress the RAF and GAF deficiencies in this area.

The French Air Force could not of course be included in the NATO order of battle – nor in any formal NATO plans or calculations. But its air defence was tied in with NADGE and military liaison with NATO was close. Although France had an interest in a new tactical fighter its need was not as pressing as that of Germany and Britain. The French Air Force had a satisfactory and well-assured programme for the early 1980s of replacing its earlier *Mirage* interceptors with the *Mirage* 2000 in both the tactical and interceptor roles. The interdiction and tactical attack roles were covered by the Anglo-French *Jaguar*. The French Air Force, with ample opportunities for dispersal and the advantage of operating on internal lines of communication, looked, and turned out to be, an effective, well balanced and modern force.

The British and German dilemma was critical. The turn of the decade saw a conservative government in Britain (as in the USA) committed to defence improvement. The United Kingdom soon ran into budgetary difficulties, while in Germany economic stringency and the soaring costs of the *Tornado* had already produced a virtual freeze on all air force procurement plans.

It was here that the Spinney Report made a quiet but telling entry. Franklin C. Spinney, an analyst, headed a research team in the USA tasked by the Pentagon with analysing the day-to-day availability of tactical aircraft. He unearthed some disquieting facts, not least that the reliability and serviceability factors for USAF front-line aircraft were far below what would be needed for intensive operations in war. Spinney concluded his astringent report in 1980 with the painful conclusion that 'Our strategy of pursuing ever-increasing technical complexity and sophistication has made high technology solutions and combat readiness mutually exclusive.'

This conclusion, although unlikely to be universally true, chimed sufficiently well with the experience of the air forces of the larger powers to make the report very uncomfortable reading. Although obviously unwelcome, the report was taken seriously and had a significant impact on later events. Understandably, it was played down publicly and those few commentators in the media who latched on to what sounded like bad news missed the point that Spinney had been inveighing against complexity rather than high technology. There could be no question of air power turning its back on science and technology, for to do so would be to turn its back upon itself. In different ways, however, and sometimes for different immediate reasons, the Allied air forces started taking account of what Spinney had said.

While the big increases in the US defence appropriations for fiscal years (FY) 1980 and 1981, and their five-year projections, swung resources for the USAF back to the strategic elements (for well recognized politico-strategic reasons) they still left substantial room for improvements in the tactical forces. These took the form of further purchases of F-15 *Eagle* and F-16 *Fighting Falcon* fighters, more A-10 *Thunderbolts* and eight more KC-10 air refuelling tankers, which were to be so important for the trans-Atlantic reinforcement of Europe by fleets of tactical bombers and fighters. In FY 1983, perhaps with an eye to Spinney, no less than $3.6 billion was included for increased spare-part holdings and reliability improvements.

By the start of the war some of the USAF's A-10 *Thunderbolts* had been given a bad-weather and night capability, but so had the Soviet SAM, so that any advantage to the A-10s was to some extent offset. When surprise was achieved, or the enemy defences were degraded, the *Thunderbolts* with their massive firepower could wreak havoc on the enemy's armour, but in less favourable circumstances their losses would be almost too heavy to sustain. It was with some misgivings about the likely loss rate that the staffs of 4 Allied Tactical Air Force (ATAF) and CENTAG had approved, a year or so before the war, a programme of tactical trials to modify their existing co-ordination between the US Army anti-tank helicopters and the USAF *Thunderbolts*. The approved doctrine hitherto was for the helicopters, hovering in ambush, to open fire on the armour with their guided weapons for thirty seconds before the *Thunderbolts* came in, and then to pop up again to give the surviving tanks another thirty seconds' worth when the *Thunderbolts* had finished. The idea came from the US Army *Cobra* helicopter pilots that their own effort might be better directed at the easily recognizable Soviet ZSU radar-controlled anti-aircraft guns and SAM vehicles which would be providing the tanks with anti-air protection. If they did that, it was argued, the *Thunderbolts* would have, if not an unrestricted, at least a much less fiercely opposed run at their targets. Ground force commanders were sceptical. The threat was from the tanks and there would never be enough anti-tank weapons in the right place at the right time. What there was should be directed at the main threat. The *Thunderbolts* might not arrive anyway.

The trials were promising, but without real action no one could be sure what would be best. In the event, adoption of the new tactics was at first cautiously limited to the new Hughes AAH-64 helicopters of 8 Aviation Combat Division of the US Army Air Corps at Finthen, Germany, working with USAF *Thunderbolts* deployed forward to Germany from their English base in East Anglia. The wooded knolls around Fulda, for example, were to give excellent cover to the ambushing helicopters with their *Hellfire* missiles, and the enemy's defence vehicles were, as predicted, clearly visible against the squat Soviet T-72 tanks and BMP around them. With the ground defences at least temporarily stunned and degraded, the *Thunderbolts*, in relatively slow runs, could concentrate their fire with deadly effect against the tanks. Happily it had just been possible in the two years before the war to extend these tactics widely. Helicopter attack on tanks, sometimes in conjunction with A-10 *Thunderbolts*, on the lines worked out between the US Army Air Corps and the USAF were to be a frequent and powerful element everywhere along the Central Front.

The five-year projection in FY 1983 also provided for substantial increases in USAF flying hours, which had been cut back, just as they had been in European airforces, to dangerously low levels under budgetary pressures in the late 1970s. While this USAF programme was one to excite the envy of airmen across the Atlantic, much of its emphasis was nevertheless consistent with what Europe was having to do – namely, enhance and develop what already existed rather than insist in vain on new types.

The RAF was the only air force in the alliance to operate all the roles of air power (in the USA the maritime role was discharged by the US Navy Air Force). It is therefore instructive to look back at some of its problems in the five years before the war.

Although the British Government endorsed and generally adhered to the 3 per cent annual growth of defence spending in real terms agreed by the NATO Council in 1977, each year saw greater difficulty in containing the programme costs within the increased defence budget. Something always had to be dropped or deferred. A formidable 'bow wave' of unfulfilled operational requirements was being pushed ahead of the defence programme. As economic pressures increased, existing capabilities had then to be trimmed back because of rising running costs – a process that came to be termed rather bitterly in British defence circles 'salami-slicing'. As matters got worse in the years of economic recession, flying hours and ground transport fuel were cut and (almost incredibly) officers and men were sent on leave to save money. The shoe, and more especially the flying boot, was pinching hard.

As in the USAF, the RAF had suffered a drain of experienced air crew in the second half of the seventies because pay and prospects compared badly with those to be found in civilian life in times of some economic buoyancy. Experience levels in the front-line squadrons began to cause anxiety, and subsequent cuts in flying and training, although effective enough in saving money on current account, were to cast a long and dangerous shadow over the force in the immediately following years. It fell to the British Defence Secretary to take a serious look at this declining situation in the summer of 1981 after yet another of a long series of what the British called 'Defence Reviews' – a well understood euphemism for further cuts in the defence programme. This time the review cost Britain 20 per cent of its naval surface fleet. As the Royal Navy was the major contributor to NATO's Eastern Atlantic (EASTLANT) and Channel forces this in turn meant a cut of some 15 per cent in available surface escorts in the EASTLANT area.

The other two British services did not go unscathed but the RAF was at least authorized to keep in service two squadrons of *Phantom* fighters that would otherwise have been phased out. These were to augment the air defence of the United Kingdom and spoke for a proper recognition of the crucial importance of the British Isles in war as a forward base for United States land and air reinforcements and a rearward base for the air forces of the Supreme Allied Commander Europe (SACEUR) should things go badly on the ground in Germany.

Explicitly the review laid stress on increasing weapon and logistic stocks. Implicitly it was an acknowledgement that if war should come to Europe it was likely to go on rather longer at the conventional level than previous planning and provisioning had been prepared to admit. If ever there should be good reasons for 'going nuclear', running out of ammunition and other war stocks after a few days should not be allowed to be among them.

The shock of the naval cuts was sharp but as the pain wore off it came to be seen that there was an inevitability about what had happened. At last realities were being faced, including the central one that the cost-growth of technology was going through the roof while most of the world was running out of money. Those who took any interest in current affairs knew that the strategic and theatre nuclear balance was unfavourable to the Alliance at the end of the 1970s. Until that imbalance was redressed by reductions on the Soviet side or new deployments on the Allied, the next six or seven years would indeed offer, in the now currently accepted phrase, a window of opportunity for the Soviet Union. The dangerous years were now upon the Alliance and its air forces had to take a long, cool look at the situation.

Using once more the British model, things would have been a lot worse but for the sound foundations laid in the seventies. Aircraft such as the *Tornado*, the *Nimrod* in its maritime and airborne early warning (AEW) roles, and the latest *Blindfire* all-weather version of the *Rapier* air defence missile, were among the leaders in the world league. Apart from having to keep the older aircraft in service much beyond what was originally planned, some other weaknesses lay in the increasing vulnerability to the developing Soviet Air Force of airfields in the UK and the shortage of alternative bases for dispersal – especially with the need to accept large reinforcements from the United States in war and the possibility of rearward redeployments of aircraft from the continent of Europe. Average experience levels in the front-line squadrons in some roles were uncomfortably low and the big gap for the rest of the decade was going to be the lack of a current-generation tactical fighter for operations over the forward area in Germany. It must also be said that ECM equipment, while all right as far as it went, was well behind the general state of this important art. Precious little extra resources would be forthcoming – that much was clear – and remedies would have to be sought by making better use of what there was or what was in near prospect.

Inevitably some good came from this enforced period of austerity. Some of the changes it imposed were radical. The opening of all ground branches not involved in direct combat duties to women, for example, tapped a reservoir of valuable recruits. Similarly, wider uses were found for auxiliaries and reservists of both sexes to considerable advantage. The USAF went further, in allowing women to be employed on flying duties. It was not long before this was extended to combat duties. In fact, it was a 29-year-old woman who was to lead the first offensive action from the United States in the Third World War. This deserves closer attention.

For some years the Soviet Navy had been using Conakry in Guinea, West Africa, as a turn-round base for their long-range *Bear* maritime reconnaissance aircraft and , occasionally also, *Backfire* bombers and supporting air tankers. In this way their aircraft could sweep down the length of the North Atlantic one day and up again the next. All of this was well observed by the US and British surveillance systems and it was naive if the Soviet Navy expected aircraft at Conakry to be unmolested in war. Nevertheless, on the evening of 4 August 1985 there were four *Bears*, two *Backfires* and a tanker on the airfield and the USAF responded promptly.

At midnight a mission of four B-52D bombers from the California Wing at March Air Force base took off from their war deployment base in Florida for a direct attack with 120 tons of high-explosive bombs under the command of Major Ed Lodge in the lead aircraft. They started their bomb runs to the target nine hours later from a clear blue sky. There was no fighter opposition and the Soviet SAM, which only started coming up as the bombing neared its end, were easily confused by the B-52s' ECM. Runways, control facilities, hangars and fuel installations were taken as precision targets and systematically destroyed as the B-52s ploughed their furrows 10,000 metres up in the sky. Their success was total and the airfield was put out of use to such a degree that the Soviet Navy made no attempt to use it again.

Some of the wiser leaders in Africa saw the moral. Client states or surrogates would do well to ensure that their patron countries had the power and the reach to protect them from the dangers to which politics and geography might expose them. Guinea had painfully failed to foresee these risks.

Back at their base in Florida, as the citations for medals for the bomber crews were read out, the media were electrified to discover that the mission commander's full name was Edwina Tinkle Lodge. She was among the first of a small group of young women who graduated from the US Air Force Academy and was accepted for training in the Military Airlift Command in the 1970s, where she had excelled as a pilot and aircraft capain. With a little help from her congressman, who was out for the women's vote, she had been transferred to the B-52 Bomber Wing at March Air Force base which trained for a wide range of conventional bombing tasks. The Conakry raid was just one of them.

The example of the USAF was not generally followed in other Allied air forces even though there was an all-round shortage of experienced pilots stemming from the lean recruiting years of the 1970s. The critical difficulty lay in the restrictions placed on flying hours by governments for economic reasons. In due course corrective action had to be taken and in the RAF, for example, measures to keep experienced pilots longer on front-line duties helped to offset the dilution of experience which was exacerbated in the early 1980s by the need to cream off the best of the 'fast jet-set' to man the

Tornado as it came into service. An important step in tackling that problem was when the British Government and its Treasury advisers were at last shaken out of the wrong-headed notion that there was an easy money-saving Midas touch in cutting back on flying and training. But it took a costly accident rate to persuade them of the folly of keeping an air force out of the air. A sustained drive was mounted to improve reliability of all equipment and to streamline the flow of logistics to the flight lines in the forward areas – wherever the fortunes of war might decide that they would be. This campaign paid off handsomely when the war came. Spinney's report turned out to have had a very long tail.

What was done in the RAF was characteristic of the sort of effort and improvement programmes mounted by all the Allied air forces. The benefit of such measures came through steadily to the front line and evidence of this showed up in the rigorous evaluations under simulated war conditions imposed by independent multi-national NATO inspection teams. But certain innovations in the use of civil resources in Britain were of a rather special nature and deserve mention because they played a positive part in preserving and exploiting the strategic importance of the UK base within the Alliance.

In this connection it is worth recalling that in 1979 the United States Strategic Air Command (SAC) first publicly announced the intention to designate eighty B-52Ds in support of NATO forces. The bomb bay of the B-52Ds had been enlarged in 1967 to carry up to 70,000 lb of conventional free-fall bombs and in 1977 the aircraft were given further structural and avionic improvements to extend their operational life and to enchance their conventional bombing capability. In September 1978, B-52s from 7 Bomber Wing at Carswell, Texas, participated for the first time in the NATO exercise 'Cold Fire'. Thereafter, they trained more and more frequently in European conditions.

On some occasions in their training they flew directly across the Atlantic, simulated attacks on 'hostile' forces in Western Europe and returned to their bases in Texas and California with the assistance of air-to-air refuelling. By 1981, regular deployments were being made to forward operating bases such as Brize Norton or Marham in England. Tactical response was thus being quickened without the political implications of permanent basing. But this exacerbated the nagging problem that air bases in the United Kingdom were becoming heavily overcrowded, and therefore increasingly attractive as targets to an enemy. While regular SAC deployments to Lajes in the Azores, which began in 1983, eased the overcrowding to some extent, the problem remained.

Although there had been hundreds of airfields in Britain by the end of the Second World War, by 1982 there were less than fifty in the hands of the RAF and the USAF – the latter having long maintained both strategic and tactical wings in the UK. Recovering the old wartime airfields was out of the question and for some years the RAF had been eyeing the civil airports with their modern runways and ground facilities. But nothwithstanding goodwill from national and municipal authorities, commercial, constitutional and communications problems had always stood in the way of their military use. By 1984, however, twenty-three airports had been earmarked and were exercised as satellites of main RAF and USAF bases. The rationalization of military and civil communications had been the main hurdle to clear; once that was done, and with a wider public appreciation of the threat to the country, the other difficulties fell away. The plan was to use these civil airports as dispersed sites for flights of up to eight aircraft and thereby distribute the precious air eggs in that many more ground baskets.

The difficulty lay in knowing how to sustain operations without technical facilities and logistic stocks. To ease the problem the airmen's eyes had been resting on the civilian helicopter fleet which had grown to more than a hundred aircraft around the North Sea oil industry. The operating companies were very willing to play their part in national plans and readily agreed to a scheme, in emergency, of attaching up to four of their aircraft to each of the main RAF and USAF bases so as to form a logistic chain to the newly earmarked satellite airfields. The plan was exercised a few times before the war and when the real need came the civilian helicopter crews performed herculean tasks in ferrying technicians, weapon reloads, test equipment and spare parts. They did this by day and by night without regard to weather, often plying between airfields under missile attack. Hardened air crew that they were, some were heard to comment, with a nice taste for understatement, that it was quite relaxing after the rigours of flying to the North Sea rigs in winter.

A signal success came to these helicopters in the first days just before and after the outbreak of war as the 'air bridge' was swung across the Atlantic and US Boeing 747s and Lockheed C-5s were landing up to 300 troops in central England every four minutes. The commercial helicopters ferried thousands of troops and hundreds of tons of their supplies from the airfields to the railheads and east coast ports. This eased what threatened to become an unmanageable congestion on the roads and railways and cut vital hours off the reinforcement time from the United States to the continent of Europe.

None the less, what the Commander Allied Air Forces Central Europe (COMAAFCE) had described in 1982 as 'the Achilles heel' of his Command, the insufficient availability of stocks of fuel, ordnance, spares and other requirements on dispersal airfields, continued to give concern. Co-located operational bases (COB), from which both USAF and RAF aircraft could operate, alleviated the difficulty. It was never quite to disappear. The danger that reinforcement aircraft, together with those withdrawn from further forward, would arrive in such numbers as to swamp support facilities remained.

First priority in the British dispersal plan went to the large air tankers, the AEW aircraft, and the *Nimrod* anti-submarine patrol aircraft, all of which had key roles but existed only in small numbers. They were anyway far too big to be protected in the hardened shelters which had been built with NATO common funds at most of the operational airfields; but the smaller RAF aircraft like the *Tornados*, *Buccaneers* and *Jaguars*, as well as the *Hawk* jet-trainers in their secondary air-defence role, were also thinned out and sent to the dispersed sites when it looked as if the main bases might become too hot to hold them.

By 1984 British Airways Boeing 757s had been modified to carry out refuelling which was to be invaluable when the almost insatiable demand for air tanking started in the first hours of the war. Sadly a proposal by British Airways in the late 1970s that their new jumbo-jet cargo carriers should be built with floors strengthened for military loads got bogged down in a bureaucratic argument about who would pay for the airline's payload penalty in peacetime. The Western allies were in consequence denied a very badly needed addition to their airlift for military vehicles.

And so it was that in these sorts of ways, and with a very free exchange of ideas within NATO, the Allied air forces made the best of the seven lean years before the war. But while their attention was turned to improving current effectiveness, rather than to bidding for solutions in the future, technology and its opportunities were of course not standing still.

The airborne warning and control system (AWACS) was arguably the biggest 'force multiplier' of any recent developments and its impact on the war exceeded the expectations of even the most ardent proponents of its introduction to USAF service in 1977. The E-3A *Sentry* aircraft, based on Boeing 707 airframes, were readily distinguished from other 707s by the 30-foot diameter radome enclosing the radar and other antennae by which the aircraft was able to exercise much of the capability which put it so far ahead. An illustration of how it worked is worth giving.

In July 1985 the eighteenth and last of the E-3A *Sentries* assigned to NATO arrived at the German Air Force base at Geilenkirchen, near the Dutch border, to join the newly-formed European NATO squadron. The last of the thirty-four aircraft retained in the USA had joined 552 Airborne Warning and Control Wing at Tinker Air Force Base near the city of Oklahoma earlier in the year. Crews on this Wing had amassed considerable experience on regular deployments to Keflavik in Iceland, Ramstein in Germany, Cairo West, Dhahran in Saudi Arabia, and in South Korea and Japan. The crews of the NATO squadron, drawn from eleven Allied countries, had not travelled so far afield but had become very familiar with the airspace of central Europe, Norway, Italy and Turkey.

By the beginning of 1985 a regular surveillance pattern had been established in the Central Region of Europe. One *Sentry* from the NATO squadron was always aloft near Venlo on the German-Dutch border; a second from the USAF flew over Ramstein; and a third, also from the NATO squadron, patrolled to the west of Munich in Bavaria. Stand-by aircraft were held on fifteen minutes' readiness. Their racetrack patterns were flown at over 25,000 feet. The serviceability of *Sentry*, based on a well-tried type of aircraft, had always been better than that experienced by new generations of aircraft and by 1985 COMAAFCE could confidently expect a daily 80 per cent serviceability rate from both the USAF and the NATO units. Moreover, with a four-man flight crew, additional to the thirteen men manning the equipment, extensive crew space, in-flight cooking and in-flight refuelling, each *Sentry* could extend its normal six-hour patrol time by several hours if necessary, which afforded great advantages.

From 1983 onwards, *Sentries* in both NATO and USAF squadrons had been built with almost identical equipment. The original computer speed had been increased threefold and the storage capacity fivefold. The *Sentry* computer could now process an incredible $1 \cdot 25$ million operations per second and, if necessary, could communicate with up to 98,000 air and ground users by the joint tactical information distribution system (JTIDS), a digital communications system resistant to ECM. Not surprisingly, in the early years of deployment the technical capacity of the aircraft had tended to outrun the imagination of those responsible for its operation, while there were many who considered its introduction into service premature and its technology potential excessive. In 1981, however, a separate subordinate NATO AWACS Command had been established at Maisières near Brussels and an Allied staff had worked steadily both to exploit its functions more fully and to integrate *Sentry* operations with those of the British AEW *Nimrod*.

Sentry's first and most obvious role was to look out for intruders into NATO airspace. Hitherto, low flying *Floggers* or *Fencers* could be detected only at some 30 miles' distance by the scattered mobile forward radars close to the inner German border (IGB). Now that aircraft at any height could be clearly identified at least 200 miles away, and if flying at 5,000 feet or above, 300 miles away or more, the practical implications for NATO's air defences were startling. Warsaw Pact aircraft could be observed taking off from bases anywhere in Eastern Germany, for example, or from others half way across Czechoslovakia, or as they were flying close above the Baltic waves beyond Bornholm. Aircraft climbing to a high-transit flight level could be detected in eastern Poland and all the way across Eastern Europe as far as the Soviet border. Instead of three or four minutes' warning of a surprise attack, *Sentry* could give an air defence sector headquarters, like that at Brockzeitel not far west of Düsseldorf, up to thirty minutes' warning.

That was not all. Additional wiring had been asked for in the eighteen NATO aircraft to incorporate electronic support equipment, the peacetime euphemism for what was required to gather electronic intelligence. In 1983, after extensive debate in the Western Alliance, funding had been provided for this equipment to be installed. Thereafter, for the next two years, data on Warsaw Pact command and control procedures, surveillance radars, SAM guidance wavelengths and even individual Warsaw Pact aircraft call signs and pilot voices had been assiduously collected and fed into the system's data banks. Indeed, the problem was not the accumulation of data, but the constant pressure on over-stretched NATO ground staff to ensure that it was all categorized, processed and fed into the seemingly limitless capacity of the new generation of computers. Perhaps, as some thought, there was too much of it all.

The Warsaw Pact, of course, was well aware of *Sentry*'s potential, publicized proudly as it was in the regular editions of Western military aviation journals. And, indeed, they had in 1982 deployed their own IL-76C *Cooker* to perform much the same function.

Under *Sentry*'s long shadow, the Warsaw Pact air forces had tightened signals discipline considerably, sought to decrease their air crews' dependence on ground control and accelerated the introduction of their own digital secure communications links. Increasingly, Warsaw Pact squadrons were deployed back to central USSR for periods of intensive operational training unobserved, but there was now no way to maintain squadron effectiveness in Eastern Europe, or exercise their surface-to-air defences, without adding to *Sentry*'s data bank. There had been, not surprisingly, a determined attempt by the Soviet Union to mobilize public opinon in the FRG against the modification of the Geilenkirchen base to accommodate these aircraft. This had failed in 1982 in the face of patient and well-reasoned explanations by the Federal German Government of *Sentry*'s enormous contribution to deterrence. One thing was sure. Quick and violent counter-measures against the system could certainly be counted on if war came.

In the spring of 1985 the *Sentries* began to detect small but significant changes in Warsaw Pact air activity. SU-24 *Fencers* had been stationed in eastern Poland for four years, steadily replacing both MiG-21 *Fishbeds* and, latterly, early marks of SU-17 *Fitters*. The bulk of the *Fencer* squadrons, however, had remained at bases in the eastern Ukraine, in the Kiev Military District, or the Baltic Military District. In January 1985 regular rotations of the USSR-based squadrons began first to eastern and then to western Polish airfields. *Sentry* quickly detected the changing voices and call signs of the new crews, who were obviously very experienced. In May and June reconnaissance sorties by *Foxbat* G, equipped with sideways-looking and synthetic-aperture radars, and digital information instantaneous downlinks, were greatly increased along the IGB and were duly noted by the *Sentries*.

Throughout the spring the weapons range at Peenemünde in the GDR was used round the clock by *Flogger* Gs and Js during the day and by *Fencers* at night. *Sentry* could track both medium-level approaches to the range and the actual ground-attack procedures. This information was added to all the other indicators available to the Western allies which suggested steadily increasing Warsaw Pact military activity.

In mid-July the major Warsaw Pact exercise began which was to be used as cover for mobilization.

By 2359 hours on 3 August, the *Sentries* had watched five regiments of *Hind* E gunships deploy, as part of the 'exercise', to forward bases 30 miles from the IGB. Two regiments of SU-25 *Flatfoot* ground-attack aircraft had returned to their major bases north of Leipzig, which placed them in range of both the area around Fulda and the north German plain. More significantly, the intensity of the jamming now rapidly increased. Only spasmodic attempts had ever been made to jam the *Sentries'* surveillance radar before. Triangulation from the three *Sentries* constantly on station quickly pinpointed the sources of the jamming as eight AN-12 *Cubs* operating in their ECM mode, cruising some 100 kilometres beyond the IGB. However, because of the narrow beam width of the Westinghouse AN/APY-1 radar installed in the E-3A *Sentries* and its low side-lobe characteristics, the effect on the AWACS' radar screens was negligible and their effectiveness remained high.

The *Sentries* were not the only targets for the jammers: below and in front of them were the inviting targets of the NATO ground radars – static, still in process of modernization, and highly vulnerable both to direct jamming and to side-lobe penetration. One after another these reported to their sector commanders that their medium- and high-level surveillance was becoming impaired, despite rapid switching through the frequencies available to them. The effectiveness of Soviet *Click* jammers, long suspected, was now being confirmed.

It was at 0315 hours on 4 August, 25,000 feet over Ramstein in the Federal Republic, that the radar operators of the *Sentry* aircraft E-3A 504826 of 965 Squadron, detached from Tinker to USAFE (United States Air Force Europe), first saw twelve blips appear on their screens, crossing eastern Poland at 35,000 feet, apparently from the central Ukraine on a westerly heading, at a speed of just under Mach 2. Within seconds they were also spotted by the *Sentries* over Venlo and west of Munich and identified as *Backfires*. All data were flashed immediately down to COMAAFCE's battle staff. The Ramstein, Wildenrath (RAF) and Neuburg (FRG) battle flights were immediately scrambled and climbed away to their intercept positions, still well west of the IGB. The *Backfires* crossed the Polish frontier into the GDR but then broke formation and in six pairs fanned out on headings in an arc towards Hamburg in the north and Bavaria in the south. All twelve were maintaining radio silence.

Then, while still 50 miles inside Warsaw Pact territory, they banked steeply and within a few seconds one after another inexplicably turned back towards Poland. The senior controller in 504826 began to express his surprise, speaking in a somewhat relaxed tone on his secure encoded downlink to his colleagues in the bunker 30,000 feet below. As they listened his voice suddenly stopped, and at the same moment the steady, friendly IFF (identification friend or foe) signal from 504826 which was being received by the two other *Sentries* abruptly disappeared. As subsequent events showed, even if the USAF crew had heard the warning shouted by the Dutch ECM operator in the Venlo *Sentry* there was little they could have done .

It should be recalled that one important modification to the original E-3A *Sentry* had been the fitting of hard points under the wings and fuselage which could carry chaff dispensers and air-to-air defensive weapons. Chaff comprised strips of metal foil exactly cut to simulate and amplify a given wavelength. A cloud of these would give the same response as an emitter on the same wavelength, and thus act as a decoy to attract a homing missile. At the same time as the electronic support measure (ESM) refit in 1983, and in a rare example of refusal to spoil a ship for a ha'p'orth of tar, NATO had also funded provision of these chaff dispensers. The USAF had taken a little longer to be convinced that the E-3A might not always see its attacker and be able to avoid him. Consequently, not all their AWACS carried this kind of protection. It was the misfortune of the crew from 965 Squadron that their aircraft that night had not yet been modified.

Lieutenant De Groot in the Venlo *Sentry* saw on his screen the *Backfires* suddenly turn for home. He guessed at once why. They would use their stand-off anti-radiation missiles, which had a range of 150 miles, and these would home on the radars of the *Sentries* and destroy them. Without waiting for any order from his commander he hit the chaff dispenser key and simultaneously shouted his warning. The well-drilled Italian ECM operator in the Bavarian *Sentry* heard the warning and immediately reacted in the same way. A few seconds later each of these two *Sentry* aircraft was rocked violently as Soviet anti-radiation missiles exploded harmlessly several hundred feet behind and below them in the cloud of drifting metal foil. The third *Sentry*, unprovided with chaff, was less fortunate. The missile struck. The seventeen USAF crewmen of the E-3A *Sentry* of 965 Squadron, far from their Oklahoma home base, became the first airman casualties of the Third World War. The wreckage of the aircraft fell over a wide area in the woods of the upper Mosel valley. The missile had ripped off the radome from the stricken *Sentry*'s mainframe and the aircraft had disintegrated.

The *Backfires*, however, had attacked not just the three *Sentries*. Each *Backfire* probably carried at least two anti-radiation missiles. They also destroyed six ground surveillance radars and damaged two others between Hanover and Mannheim. Yet, because of the rigid rules of engagement imposed by NATO on its air forces, they were able to return unscathed to their Ukrainian bases. The war had begun, but NATO airspace had not yet 'officially' been violated.

The crews in the two remaining *Sentries* had no time either to applaud the initiative of the Dutch officer or to grieve for their lost colleagues. On the encoded voice-link the clipped tones of the British duty commander, the air vice-marshal acting as deputy in COM-AAFCE's bunker, instructed both aircraft to adjust their patrol racetracks to cover the gap left by the Ramstein E-3A until the relief aircraft could come on station. The Venlo *Sentry* turned south, the Bavarian north; surveillance across the IGB was uninterrupted. At Geilenkirchen, the NATO *Sentry* on fifteen minutes' stand-by was scrambled; at 0329 hours it climbed away, turning south to replace 504826.

The wisdom of placing all such high-value assets under the direct command of COMAAFCE was thus clear from the outset of the war. There was now much to survey. As the *Backfires* turned for home, swarms of blips began to appear on the *Sentries*' radar screens, as, in accordance with well-publicized doctrine, the longer-range offensive Warsaw Pact aircraft prepared to punch through NATO's air defences in the area already partially blinded by the *Backfire* attack. Five years before, NATO forces would have had no way of identifying the main axes of the air threat until it struck across the IGB. Now, the *Sentry* controllers could watch the formations massing in much the same way as forty-five years previously hazy RAF radars had watched the *Luftflotten* assemble over the Pas-de-Calais. But in 1985 the controllers were assisted by the micro-processor. Warsaw Pact jamming was largely filtered and almost entirely limited to two or more azimuth bearings on the narrow sweeping beam. The keyboards rippled and details of aircraft type, height, speed, heading and numbers were flashed by the computers to the fighter controllers below. The information was there in abundance.

———————

Throughout the 1970s Soviet air power had steadily increased in strength as a new generation of *Flogger, Fitter, Fencer* and *Foxbat* fighters and *Backfire* bombers, supplemented by the *Hip* and *Hind* helicopters and the *Cock, Candid* and *Camber* transports entered service. In the early 1980s the Soviet Union had flexed these new muscles in several parts of the world. Military strength had been unequivocally used to prepare a more favourable political situation in Angola, Mozambique, Ethiopia, South Yemen, Syria, Libya and Afghanistan. All these efforts had not been uniformly successful but the long reach and hitting power of Soviet aircraft had everywhere become more and more apparent.

Western military concern at what was clearly an attempt to close the gap in quality between Warsaw Pact and NATO aircraft was tempered by reassuring knowledge of several serious and apparently endemic weaknesses in the Soviet Air Force itself. Effective air power demands far more than improved aircraft. It must have highly-trained and dedicated people, a professional and complex maintenance system, flexible and resilient command and control organization, and above all the inspiration of imagination and initiative in both practice and theory. The SAF, on the other hand, appeared to be handicapped by the quality of its largely conscript ground crews, by low morale and corruption (as described in such detail in the published accounts of evidence from the defecting Soviet airman Lieutenant Belenko who landed his MiG-25 *Foxbat* B in Japan in September 1976), by a rigid command structure which hampered the flexible use of air power and by a social and political system in which the encouragement of initiative and imagination was hardly prominent.

Beginning in late 1982, however, shreds of evidence began to reach the Defence Intelligence Agency (DIA) in the Pentagon and West European intelligence centres which seemed to suggest that the Soviet Union was making determined efforts to eradicate some of these weaknesses and that, despite the deadening effect of the Party bureaucracy on all levels of the SAF, it was having some success. During 1983 clearer evidence began to emerge which ultimately was to compel the NATO air forces to revise their overall estimate of the potential effectiveness of their Warsaw Pact opponents.

As early as 1979 the SAF had attempted to improve the quality of maintenance by introducing new warrant officer ranks and by offering improved pay and promotion incentives to encourage conscript ground crew to extend beyond their mandatory two year's service. By 1983, as the Soviet colleges of science and technology continued to produce more graduates each year, there was in the conscripted manpower of the SAF an increased proportion of highly-skilled young men. Moreover, as the Soviet Union came to lay greater emphasis on conventional war-fighting methods, previously very much in second place to nuclear doctrines, the pay of SAF ground crew was raised to match that in the nuclear-armed Soviet Strategic Rocket Force (SRF), hitherto the pre-eminent branch of the Soviet armed services. Living and messing conditions were improved and though still far below levels demanded in the West were nevertheless much higher than those of the majority of conscripts in their civilian life. The retention rate of ground crew began to rise, their status began to improve, and during 1985 the serviceability rate of SAF front-line squadrons in Eastern Europe began to show a steady but marked improvement.

The second cause for unease concerned changes in SAF operational procedures. Throughout the 1970s, although the SAF re-equipped with aircraft able to carry three times the payload over twice the range of their predecessors, its squadrons tended to fly the same rigidly controlled, highly predictable patterns of attack and defence which had been evident for thirty years. From 1979 onwards, however, articles began to appear in *Red Star* and some air force journals, purporting to be written by senior officers, which openly commended pilots who had shown initiative in departing from pre-arranged plans and procedures which, in exercises, they had found to be inadequate. No such noises were heard from the Red Army, which was carrying on in the old familiar straitjacket.

The causes of these changes in the SAF can now be seen more clearly. To operate the *Fencer* under conditions of inflexible command and control would undermine its long-range potential. Moreover, the considerable investment which the Soviet Union had made in computer-assisted command and control procedures was beginning to pay dividends in easing the enormous airspace management problems created by the large-scale SAM deployment in Eastern Europe. Hitherto, rigid control had not only been politically desirable but it had been adequate for short-range offensive operations and air defence, and had enhanced flight safety in airspace shared at many heights with SAM and guns. There was another factor. Soviet air power doctrine assumed the application of large numbers over very large areas. In the Red Army, with a similar basic philosophy, initiative was expected not so much from a lieutenant as from the commanders at not less than divisional level. In the SAF the operational concept required control and command to be exercised at a level appropriate to the reach and hitting power of the aircraft concerned. Moreover, in pre-planned offensive operations of a kind envisaged by the Warsaw Pact, conformity on the part of individual air crew to the plan had seemed more important than an ability to exercise initiative in adversity. This was the exact opposite of what was to be found in the numerically inferior NATO air forces.

By 1985, however, it was apparent that far-reaching reorganization of command and control in the SAF had been completed. The general staff now controlled the heavy bombers, *Bears* and *Bisons*, and the medium bombers, *Badgers* and *Backfires*, as two virtually independent air armies. They could, therefore, be directed not only against targets in Europe but in the Mediterranean, the Middle East and, if necessary, the Far East. The shorter-range *Floggers* and *Fencers* were controlled at the lower theatre headquarters level, while the fixed-wing aircraft with the shortest range, the SU-17 *Fitter* Js and SU-25s and remaining MiG-21 *Fishbeds*, stayed under control of frontal aviation headquarters. Below them, the close air support *Hip* and *Hind* helicopters were controlled by the armies. The net result of this reorganization had been to match the level of command with the combat radius of the aircraft, thereby ensuring greater flexibility and concentration of force in relation to the demands of tactical control and rapid response. As has been indicated, however (and we shall be seeing some lively evidence of this in chapter 11), there was room for difference of opinion on what was really meant by flexibility.

At the same time as the command infrastructure had been revised, Soviet operational training also began to approach more closely the potential of the new aircraft. The MiG-23 *Flogger* G, hitherto flown only as an interceptor, was fitted with underwing rails to take air-to-surface rockets. *Flogger* squadrons in Eastern Europe began to assume multi-role commitments. Periodically they would deploy to armament camps in central USSR to develop new ground-attack techniques away from the prying eyes of *Sentry*. On their return, each would demonstrate a marked improvement in weapon delivery. More ominously, exercises involving the co-ordination of three or more air regiments increased in frequency. In the 1970s it had not been uncommon for a squadron of ground-attack *Fitters*, for example, to be given top cover by a squadron of MiG-21 *Fishbeds*. By 1984, *Flogger* Gs or Js could be escorted by entire regiments of other *Flogger* Gs. Some Western military analysts had expected to see such escort provided by the most recent addition to the MiG-25 family: the two-seat *Foxbat* F with its improved pulse-doppler radar and long-range air-to-air missiles (AAM). But its basic airframe still made it quite unsuitable for the low-level air-superiority role and its additional weight had actually restricted its combat radius still further. It therefore remained on traditional *PVO Strany* (Air Defence Force) combat patrols working with IL-76C *Cooker*, the SAF's new AEW aircraft developed from the *Candid* transport.

The advent of *Cooker* had long been forecast in the West, but even when it began to enter service in 1982 very little was known about its operational capabilities. Its trials and development flying had been carried out in Central Asia out of range of most Western electronic intelligence (ELINT) agencies. It was well known that Soviet radar engineering was in many respects as good as that in the West and that the *Candid* airframe could provide ample space for bulky Soviet equipment which had not yet fully benefited from the microprocessor revolution. It was possible, therefore, that *Cooker's* radar range was similar to that of NATO's AWACS. If that were so, and if it had similar powers to identify low-flying aircraft and communicate instantaneously with ground and air defences, the task of NATO aircraft attacking deep behind Warsaw Pact lines would become much more difficult.

By January 1985 twenty-four *Cookers* had come into service. Ten were based in south-eastern Poland out of range of most NATO aircraft, strategically located to fly standing patrols either up towards the Baltic or south-east across Czechoslovakia, Hungary and Bulgaria. Others patrolled former report lines across the northern USSR. A third detachment operated in the Black Sea, Caucasus and Caspian areas, while three were regularly deployed to the Chinese border regions. The Soviet crews were apparently well trained and well disciplined. Within a very short time NATO specialists were convinced that *Cookers* were not using anything like all their frequency range or transmitting power while on routine patrols over Eastern Europe. These suspicions were heightened by regular deployments of individual aircraft back to central USSR with two or more regiments of *Foxbats* and *Flogger* Gs. Satellite information was sketchy but was sufficient to indicate that the SAF was holding regular exercises similar to the NATO *Red Flag* series in Nevada run by the USAF in which Soviet air opposition was realistically simulated. In these, *Cooker* appeared to be locating several low-flying aircraft and either vectoring interceptors directly on to them or relaying target information to ground control units. But unless the full extent of *Cooker's* frequencies could be identified, and its operating ranges established, comprehensive ECM could not be prepared by NATO. Not for the first time, however, at least one of NATO's problems was to be dramatically reduced as a result of endemic weaknesses within the Soviet system, which in this case culminated in what became known as the Gdansk incident. The account of it given below appeared in the December 1986 number of the *RUSI Journal* published by the Royal United Services Institute for Defence Studies, London.

❢ On 27 July 1985 an IL-76C *Cooker* of the AEW 16 Guards Regiment of the SAF climbed away on a routine evening patrol from its main operating base south-east of Krakow. The aircraft captain, Major Anatoly Makhov, was not in the best of moods. Just before the take-off his second pilot had been replaced by the regimental political commissar, Lieutenant Colonel Yuri Gregorian. In 1980 the Political Directorate had ordered their regimental officers to show greater affinity with the operational crews. Gregorian, who had earned his pilot's wings several years before but was now known to hate flying, took care to ensure that he had at least one signature each month in his log book to lend authenticity to figures which could easily be falsified. The power and influence of a regimental commissar were far more attractive to him than the dull routine of *Cooker* patrols and he did as few of those as he could.

This particular *Cooker* patrol began uneventfully. It was observed by the Venlo *Sentry* to reach its routine patrol track north of Bydgoszcz, cruising at slightly more than 350 knots at 30,000 feet. Then abruptly it was observed to lose height and, heading north towards Gdansk, it disappeared below *Sentry's* long-range surveillance reach. It was several days before NATO air intelligence was able to reconstruct the events of the next few hours but, happily, there were good secondary sources.

Major Makhov was determined to be as courteous as possible to the Colonel who, after all, could make life very miserable for him. But as the *Cooker* levelled off on its patrol circuit, Gregorian was clearly losing interest. He took out from his brand-new flying suit a well-thumbed paperback novel which, Makhov was interested to note, was a lurid example of highly illegal Estonian pornography from Tallin. Relieved, the Major relaxed and concentrated on the undemanding job of flying the *Cooker* on a predetermined track, height and speed while his navigator busily cross-checked their position with the senior fighter controller in the cabin behind them.

Then, for no apparent reason, the red fire-warning light from No. 2 port inner engine began to flash on the main instrument panel in front of Makhov at the same moment as the warning hooter blasted in his headset. Makhov was no beginner, with 2,500 hours on IL-76 aircraft behind him. He swiftly reached down, closed the No. 2 throttle and watched the flashing red light. It stayed on. So he reached across and flicked the No. 2 fire extinguisher switch, at the same time closing the No. 2 stopcock. The flashing light disappeared and the hooter stopped.

Major Makhov noticed, with amusement, that an ashen-faced Colonel Gregorian in the right-hand seat was staring with stupefaction at the panel. But Makhov had no time to enjoy the commissar's discomfiture. Even as he began to call to his flight engineer to check the port wing visually, No. 1 port outer light flashed and the hooter blared a second time. This time he could sense the tension on the flight deck as he swiftly killed this engine too and released the No. 1 extinguisher.

"No visual signs of fire," reported the flight engineer.

Makhov had no doubts about his ability to handle *Cooker* on the two starboard engines only and he strongly suspected that the problem was simply an electrical fault. But the *Cooker* carried fourteen men without parachutes who were depending on him; his professional competence was on the line.

"Where is our nearest field?" he asked the navigator.

"Gdansk Civil," came the nervous reply, "Forty kilometres on heading 355."

Gregorian picked this up on intercom and began to shout objections to the use, without authority, of a Polish civil airfield. Makhov ignored him and switched to the international distress frequency. In quiet but good English he began to describe his emergency and his intention to make a straight-in two-engined approach to Gdansk Civil Airport. He then switched back to his own operational channel and informed his base of the situation.

In fact, the next few minutes, though tense, were comparatively uneventful. Major Makhov again demonstrated his professional skill by putting the heavy *Cooker* down without mishap. As he taxied towards the main apron in front of the terminal building he called the tower to arrange a guard on the plane while the port wing and engines were examined. He knew from long experience that even if it had only been an electrical fault, his Soloviev turbo-fans would need flushing from the effects of the fire extinguishers and the *Cooker* could be on the ground for several hours. But this was a civil airport; there were no Soviet soldiers or airmen stationed there. Since the troubles began in 1980, all Soviet military personnel in Poland had kept as far as possible a low profile, restricted to military airfields or barracks. To the conscript crewmen of the *Cooker* the bright lights of the civilian terminal looked very inviting. Colonel Gregorian had recovered his composure sufficiently to begin thinking about the possibilities of the duty-free shop.

The *Cooker* was marshalled to a halt some 30 yards beyond the last Polish civil airline TU-134 at the end of the dispersal area. As the white-overalled ground crew of the Polish state airline LOT pushed the trolley ladder up against the forward door, a dozen armed Polish soldiers fanned out around the aircraft and the Gdansk Aeroflot agent hurried across the tarmac towards it. The conversations that followed were overheard by both Lot ground crew and the guards, but by what means they were so quickly relayed to London has not yet been made known.

Colonel Gregorian described to the agent and the senior Polish NCO the emergency they had come through and how single-handed he had overcome the panic of the rest of the crew and brought this valuable aircraft safely to earth. Major Makhov went pale and was clearly very angry. He said nothing until one of the Polish guards, in quite good Russian, asked him what had really taken place on the flight deck, and was told.

What exactly happened in the next hour is not public knowledge. What is known is that just before the outbreak of war, details of *Cooker*'s IFF codes, operating frequencies, transmitters and receivers, all of absolutely critical importance, reached the Radar and Signals Research Establishment at Malvern in England for analysis by British scientists. According to press reports at the time, the crew of a Polish LOT TU-134 made a scheduled run from Gdansk to Copenhagen late on the evening of 27 July and the crew then asked for political asylum in Denmark. Passengers on that flight described how Soviet airmen led by a portly, noisy Colonel were allowed into the duty-free shop of the Gdansk terminal and also said that as they were taking off they saw Soviet troops replacing Polish guards and Soviet uniformed ground crew taking over from the Polish engineers in their overalls who had been examining the port wing of a Soviet military aircraft near the front of the terminal. Whether there were disaffected men among the Polish guards, or among the ground crew, or whether Major Makhov allowed his anger at the bragging behaviour of the Colonel to distract his attention from his aircraft for a few minutes we do not know. But an elderly Polish cloakroom attendant, born in the Ukraine, alleged that while he was on duty one night just before war broke out an SAF Colonel was in the lavatory in the terminal building when a highly excited Soviet airman rushed in.

"The operating and maintenance manuals have gone from the aircraft!" he is alleged to have said.

His excitement was understandable. These were classified documents of high importance. Their loss was a serious matter. He was shortly followed into the lavatory by a grim-faced Major. Unaware that the attendant could understand Russian, the three men argued furiously for several minutes about whether and how the manuals could have disappeared and who was responsible.

Then the Colonel said: "Understand one thing: *NO* documents have been removed from my aircraft. If it is necessary to replace certain damaged manuals on our return to base, you will do so; but if one word of this reaches the ears of the regimental commander I will personally ensure that every member of this crew sees nothing but a Gulag for the rest of his life." **,**

History, therefore, had almost repeated itself. In 1939 the Poles had given *Enigma* to the West; in 1985 they seemed to have passed over the secrets of *Cooker*. Because of a political commissar's fear of his superiors, and the airmen's fear of the commissar, it looks as if the loss was never reported. By 3 August NATO commanders began to receive complete operational and technical data on *Cooker*. This did not get down to squadrons for another forty-eight hours, which was only just in time.

Chapter 7

The Warsaw Pact

Soviet hopes and aspirations for a world position of compelling power had by the beginning of the 1980s passed through two phases and entered a third. In the early days of the revolution it was confidently hoped that Marxist-Leninist ideology would prove an irresistible magnet to the peoples of the world and the Soviet Union would sit supreme above all nations as its unique source and sole interpreter. In the background, of course, would be the additional solid support of powerful armed forces. Hopes of ideological supremacy were never realized. There has never been a mad rush on the part of other nations to follow the example of Soviet Russia and set up Marxist-Leninist states. These hopes were before long replaced by the equally confident expectation that the Soviet Union would become an economic superpower. It would easily overtake the United States and exercise thereafter unchallenged authority as the world's richest and most productive nation. There would, of course, still be the support of powerful armed forces. These hopes too were disappointed. The gross national product (GNP) of the Soviet Union by 1984 had not yet reached $3,000 per head of population, which put it in nineteenth place among European nations. By the early 1980s the Soviet Union had indeed become a world power of truly formidable might and influence, not through the attractions of its revolutionary ideology, nor yet through its economic performance. The Soviet Union's power, which was very great, was almost exclusively military.

Its development, and above all the desperate efforts to achieve military parity with the United States, had been costly. The economic growth of the USSR was at this time slowing down. None the less, its defence expenditure continued to rise at rather more than 5 per cent per annum and was probably taking up more than the whole increase in gross national product. One-third of all mechanical products in their final form were for military stocks, which was a serious handicap in an economy gravely short of equipment and machines. Most of the available research and development effort went to defence, as well as one-fifth of all metal production, together with one-sixth of the chemical output and about the same proportion of all energy consumed. Though the figures were made to look smaller by the Soviet Union's internal pricing system it seems likely that by 1983 defence expenditure was absorbing something between 15 and 20 per cent of total GNP.

The Soviet Union's ageing leadership, the character and outlook of which had been formed in the great patriotic war, had always relied heavily upon, and been very close to, the military. On grounds of age alone changes at the top were inevitable before long. Brezhnev had never made the mistake (from which, when it was made by others, his own career had so signally benefited) of indicating an heir apparent in the leadership, but change in the mid-1980s there would certainly be and with the introduction of younger men into the Politburo and the military high command, men who had not been conditioned in the same way as their predecessors, a shift in outlook and priorities could be expected.

Newcomers would hardly be likely to adopt more liberal policies. They would be hard-line realists, to whom the absolute supremacy of the Communist Party of the Soviet Union (CPSU), and the safeguarding of their own positions in it, would override all other considerations whatsoever. Nevertheless, changes in structure, organization and style would certainly take place, if only to demonstrate that the leadership had changed. For the old guard, therefore, time was running out. They had until about the mid-eighties and probably no longer to extract full benefit in their own way from the Soviet Union's military strength and its recently developed capability for projecting that strength at a distance, and to consolidate the world position this created. Beyond that time the distortion demanded of the economy for maintaining that position could not be indefinitely sustained, even with a populace long accustomed to its drearier consequences. Moreover, the growth in Soviet military strength had quickened defence expenditure in other countries and this in turn had reacted on the Soviet Union which, even if it had been inclined to recast priorities and spend less on defence, found itself, as the direct result of its own policies, constrained to spend more.

There also loomed the spectre of an extensive and costly military re-equipment programme to replace material, much of which had been developed more than twenty years before to embody a rather different war-fighting philosophy. This would not happen all at once but could not, without encouraging growing weaknesses in the whole defence structure, be long deferred.

There were other tendencies which also pointed to an approaching climacteric. The population of the Soviet Union increased in the years between 1974 and 1984 by some twenty-five million, but only about a quarter of this was Russian. Most of the rest was Asiatic, in which the increase was at about four times the rates found among Muscovites. The greatest increase was in Central Asia. By the early years of the 1980s the population of the USSR included some seventy million Moslems. Impermeability to external influences continued, as always, to be a prime factor in the maintenance of the supreme objective – the total dominance of the CSPU. The complete exclusion of such influences, however, could not be guaranteed, even in the Soviet Union itself.

Hunger for Western-style consumables was found everywhere. Listening to Western broadcasting was common. Probably as many as fifty million people in the Soviet Union in 1981, according to Vladimir Bukovsky, were already receiving the BBC, the Voice of America, *Deutsche Welle* and other Western radio stations. Very often listeners tuned in for the music and then stayed with the news.

The other Warsaw Pact states were even more open than the USSR to outside influences, especially in view of the inability of COMECON to satisfy their consumer needs and resultant closer contacts with, as well as indebtedness to, Western economies. In the event, therefore, that the USSR should seek a direct military confrontation with the USA it would clearly be unwise to defer this beyond, say, 1985. In the more likely contingency of consideration in the Soviet Union of how far it could proceed with high-risk policies, in which the danger of a military confrontation would be considerable, it would clearly be more prudent to pursue such policies in the early 1980s than later on. The window of opportunity would not remain indefinitely open.

The Soviets in their international relations after the Second World War and before the collapse of Soviet imperialism in the Third, though they were thought by so many to be masters of a shrewd and far-sighted strategy, often demonstrated a quite surprising degree of maladroitness. This was often so striking as to arouse comment at the time. Their extraordinary mismanagement of affairs in Austria in 1946 was a very early example, when their conviction that Austrian gratitude for liberation by the Red Army made it safe to allow free elections, in the confidence that a communist majority would be returned, resulted in the election of an Assembly without a single communist member. There was also their mishandling of affairs in Yugoslavia, in Hungary, in Czechoslovakia, in the Middle East, in the Indian sub-continent and with China, and their dramatic expulsion, lock stock and barrel, in 1972 from what looked like a deeply entrenched position in Egypt. Rarely, however, has the history of international relations shown a more outstanding example of maladroitness than the bringing about of the NATO Alliance and West German rearmament. The Reich lay prostrate before its four principal enemies – the USA, Britain, the Soviet Union and France – totally defeated. Within four years of that time, Soviet policy had so antagonized its former allies that, with their patience exhausted, the other three saw no alternative but to form a defensive alliance and then bring in the defeated enemy re-armed. Pro-Soviet fantasists in the West sought in vain to disguise the simple truth. NATO, a purely defensive structure, was brought into being by the USSR and by the USSR alone. The Soviet Union was itself the only begetter of what was to become its greatest bane.

Citizens of the Soviet Union, as the 1970s moved on into the 1980s, may well by now have come to accept their lot with resignation, without any confidence, or even any hope, that it would ever change for the better. It would be wrong to suppose, as many did in the West, that they were also wholly lacking in awareness of what went on in the other world, outside the closed system which constituted their own. In addition to what came in through radio broadcasts from outside, the circulation of information within the Soviet Union itself was a good deal freer than was commonly realized in the West. It was certainly much freer than the Communist Party liked. A country in which a huge black market flourishes, however, is not one in which information does not circulate, especially when the black market is not only permitted by the authorities but even, as compensation for their own extraordinary ineptitude, actively encouraged, though the circulation of information, of course, is not. Though the concept of public opinion as a political force in a communist state is hardly valid, it was inevitable that in the Soviet Union, in the four or five years before the war, there was not only widespread awareness of what was going on in the outside world but strong currents of political opinion flowing from it. The boycott of the Olympic games made a far greater impression than was commonly realized abroad and the attempts by the Party to play down its effects and claim an outstanding public relations success produced in Moscow a veritable flood of the sick jokes whose volume and venom had long been the only reliable index of public reaction to events. The invasion of Afghanistan aroused wide interest and deep unpopularity and, as it dragged on with no satisfactory end even remotely in sight, it was more clearly recognized as a blunder of the first magnitude. The disposal of the dead in the Afghan campaign threw a particularly interesting light on popular attitudes. At first they were flown home for burial, but as the flow continued and the numbers grew this was seen to be unwise. Public concern in the Asiatic republics, from which most of the first troops engaged in Afghanistan came, was so marked (particularly in

Kazakhstan) that from mid-1981 the practice ceased. The dead were now buried in the country where they died.

It will long be argued, with the benefit of hindsight, whether the West should have made greater efforts in the early 1980s to take advantage of the Soviet Union's difficulties, for example in Afghanistan and Poland. In the former, massive supply of arms to the 'rebels', or the active suborning of Soviet troops, would have required a greater degree of collusion by Pakistan than it was wise for that country to give. Moreover, Afghan disunity was almost as powerful a source of weakness as lack of heavy weapons. The Polish case too was a genuine puzzle. Could the West have saved Solidarity? After the imposition of military government, how far was it in the Western interest to do economic damage to the country in the hope that the Government and not the people would suffer, and so be led to allow the progress towards democracy to be resumed?

Ineffective though pre-war efforts in the West had been to exploit Soviet difficulties, they had some interesting by-products. Very little was done in peacetime by Western governments, however tempting the opportunities, to prepare for intervention in the internal affairs of Warsaw Pact countries if war should break out. It was too risky for the CIA or other such agencies to make any large-scale preparations and their governments in general warned them not to try. The period of hostilities when war did break out was too short to organize much more than the support of subversion by the massive injection by air of supplies. What governments had failed to do, however, was in large part made up for by the efforts of those active individuals who had pressed hard for better exploitation of opportunities to harm the Soviet system in peace. Governments in the West found ready to their hand organizations, personnel, training arrangements and even stocks of equipment brought together by activist expatriates of the Baltic States and the Ukraine, and other constituent republics of the Soviet Union, let alone of Warsaw Pact countries. Those in the West whose national origins and interests lay in these countries flooded in, when war threatened, to offer their services. There were many more than could be used during the actual period of hostilities, but good use was made of some, particularly in Poland, the Baltic States and the Ukraine. More useful still were some of those exiles, driven out by communism, who on the collapse of the Soviet Union were more than willing to return to their own countries and contribute to their recovery. Since these often included many of the ablest men and women in their own nations, some with very high capabilities as administrators, their availability in the establishment of successor regimes was invaluable.

The plan which was finally accepted in the Kremlin for the invasion of Western Europe by forces of the Warsaw Pact envisaged a swift occupation of the Federal Republic of Germany, to be completed within ten days, followed by consolidation of a front along the Rhine and the negotiation of a ceasefire with the United States from a position of strength.

There were several very important reasons why the USSR should seek to secure the Rhine stopline with the least possible delay. The first was the need to achieve a decisive military success and a strong and clearly defined political base for negotiation before trans-Atlantic reinforcement could develop a truly dangerous momentum. The second was to give the West as little time as possible to resolve doubts and hesitations over the initial release of nuclear weapons – for it was naturally assumed that the West would need them first, to offset the conventional superiority deployed against them by the Warsaw Pact. A third and scarcely less important reason lay in the necessity to reduce to a minimum the strain of prolonged operations upon the coherence of the Warsaw Pact, particularly where those countries were concerned which, up to the war, had been described as the Pact's Northern Tier – the German Democratic Republic, Poland and Czechoslovakia. The first two of these reasons are explored in the next chapter. The third merits attention here.

The armed forces of each of these three countries, though all had been set up (ab initio in the GDR, in reconstituted form in Poland and Czechoslovakia) under close Soviet control, differed radically. All armed forces, even when they are raised within an externally imposed straitjacket, reflect the ethos and outlook of parent nations. The part to be played in the Third World War by the armies of the Northern Tier can hardly be said, in retrospect, to have been surprising.

A role was planned for these armies, and initial tasks assigned, in a swift and violent invasion of Western Europe which was to be speedily successful. The plan was only one of many contingency operational plans kept constantly updated in the Kremlin, but it was of the highest importance. It was inevitably the plan which to the three countries concerned was of more importance than any other.

Each of their armies had been organized, equipped, trained and oriented in the basically offensive mode of the Soviet armed forces and integrated into them as closely as differing circumstances allowed. The impatience of certain older and more doctrinaire officers of the Soviet High Command at the apparent unattainability of total integration was understood in the Defence Committee of the Politburo, its most important element, but had to be restrained. The armed forces of these three countries remained, as events proved, very different, each retaining marked characteristics derived from different parentage and upbringing.

The army of the GDR (the National People's Army or NPA) emerged as a totally new creation in the 1960s. It was always the smallest of the three, at little more than 120,000 strong at the outbreak of war, of which half were eighteen-month conscripts. It had no military tradition of its own (the re-emergence in the 1970s of historic distinctions between Saxon and Prussian units was of no great significance) and was entirely subservient to a Party regime whose interests were closely consonant with those of the Soviet Union. Fear of a threat from West Germany, carefully cultivated by the USSR, was helpful during the formative period, but *Ostpolitik* and detente reduced the value of this threat as a bonding material, and defection from the NPA to the West in the 1970s was considerable. This was rarely found, it must be said, among officers above the rank of lieutenant colonel, which was evidence of the degree of reward and encouragement offered to the military by the Party. While the two tank and four motor-rifle divisions of the NPA were to be assigned a fully forward role in the offensive of the Group of Soviet Forces in Germany (GSFG) in August 1985, the reliability of the NPA (not so much in the officer cadre, particularly at higher levels, as in the rank and file) was always to the Soviet High Command a cause for uneasiness. When the lightning successes of Warsaw Pact forces over NATO, upon which the loyalty of the East German NPA within the Pact depended, even more than it did with others, failed to materialize and there was civil commotion, starting with sabotage and violence first of all in Dresden on 11 August, it was not thought prudent to use the NPA, at least in the first instance, to suppress it. The *Bereitschaftspolizei* of the Ministry of the Interior were called in first and then, when the rioting spread on 14 August to Leipzig, a *Wachregiment* under the orders of the Ministry of State Security moved in. When disorder spread further, Soviet permission was, with the utmost reluctance, sought by the GDR to withdraw NPA regular troops to suppress it, and permission was as reluctantly given. The three NPA motor rifle regiments brought back for the purpose on 17/18 August proved unmanageable. Orders were disobeyed, desertion was rife, officers were shot. The Party was still supreme in the GDR but from now on it was progressively less able to govern.

How different was the case of Poland. The Polish armed forces, having refused in 1970 to intervene against the near-rebellious civil population, felt obliged to take complete control of the country in 1981. It is still not clear whether General Jaruzelski imposed martial law because in his view as a Polish patriot it was the only alternative to an outright imposition of Soviet administration, or because, as a communist, he genuinely believed that Solidarity's power was incompatible with the orderly government of the state. Whatever the answer to this riddle, the assumption of power had two effects on the Polish Army. Its manpower was deeply committed to the maintenance of internal security, and so could make less contribution to an external military operation. On the other hand, fighting West Germans might be more attractive to many Polish soldiers than repressing Solidarity. In fact they were soon to have the worst of both worlds, when it became clear that one of the Polish Army's main roles in the war would be to prevent Polish partisans from cutting the Soviet supply lines across Polish territory into Federal Germany.

The threat to Polish national independence posed by the FRG, heavily emphasized by the Soviets, had become increasingly less credible during the 1970s. There was little else to bind Polish military interests to the USSR in its obsession with a blind hostility to NATO. The unwillingness of the Soviet military to treat their Polish colleagues as professionals of the same standing (which, at equivalent levels, they undoubtedly were) and the reluctance of Moscow to furnish the Polish Army with modern equipment did little to bridge the inevitable gap between nations that had been more often enemies than friends. On the Soviet side, moreover, the tendency of the Polish military to allow professionalism to take precedence over ideology was in the late seventies arousing increasing uneasiness.

Poland could never, therefore, have been regarded by the Soviets at that time as a wholly reliable military ally. One condition alone did more than anything else to keep Poland lined up with the Warsaw Pact plans for a swift invasion of Western Germany. This was the certainty that if Poland came out of the arrangement, a Warsaw Pact-NATO battle would be fought not on German territory but on Polish. A swift, decisive invasion of Western Germany was infinitely preferable. In the event, the invasion though swift was not decisive and Soviet fears about the military reliability of Polish troops were soon realized. When the Soviet lines of communication through Poland became increasingly disrupted from partisan activity, plentifully and ably supplied (though with very considerable losses) by NATO air forces, the move of Polish formations back from Germany to look after the security of communications inside Poland was a total failure. The mutiny in Poznan on 17 August in one of Poland's eight mechanized divisions, the first formation to be sent home for internal security duties, was the signal for a general showdown with the Soviet High Command.

In Czechoslovakia, the events of August 1968 not only put an end to all hopes of steady progress towards the eventual total identification of Czechoslovak and Soviet interests. They also virtually destroyed the Czechoslovak People's Army (CPA).

Early hopes of a fusion between Czech and Soviet interests were never, in fact, wholly justified. It is true that the USSR could regard Czechoslovakia, in the early years of the inter-war period, as the most pro-Soviet of all its new client states. The Czechoslovak elections of 1947 were not conducted, as many have alleged, under duress from the Red Army, which was at that time quite thin on the ground in Czechoslovakia. The setting up of a communist government was in the first instance the result of a more or less respectable democratic process, if somewhat tarnished by the coup in 1948, and was, ironically enough, almost as decisive as the massive rejection of communism by the Austrians in the free elections which the Soviets had so unwisely permitted the year before. In the following years the steady re-emergence of Czech national sentiments, of anti-Soviet opinion and of restlessness with external repression of free institutions, resulted, in Dubcek's time, in a level of dissatisfaction with Soviet hegemony too dangerous in itself and too likely to spread infection outside Czech frontiers to be disregarded.

Within the CPA there had been for at least a decade before 1968 a growing disenchantment with Soviet insistence on the total subordination of Czech interests to those of the Soviet Union, which was particularly galling to an officer corps deeply concerned for national security. Almost equally galling to military professionals was the growing intrusion of political considerations into military affairs. This was especially resented among highly qualified younger officers who often found their careers suffering from their own strong disinclination to accept Soviet doctrine, structures and interests as of unique and paramount importance in the sphere of Czechoslovak defence.

The invasion of August 1968, ordered and led by the Soviet Union but with a token inclusion of forces from other client states, tore the CPA apart. It also put an end to hitherto quite marked pro-Soviet tendencies in the country as a whole. The army never recovered, in size and professionalism, its previous standing. Up to the outbreak of war in 1985, in spite (and partly because) of persistent Soviet efforts to reimpose total Soviet control over the Czechoslovak military apparatus, the CPA could never be counted on as a wholly reliable Soviet instrument. It remained firmly tasked, none the less, to offensive action in a quick war against the West. Even before the advance slowed down, however, as a result of NATO defensive action in the Federal Republic of Germany, the mutiny which broke out in the CPA 4 Motor Rifle Division at Cheb on 17 and 18 August was predictable.

All in all the Soviet planners could not count very much on the military contribution of their Warsaw Pact allies. The purpose of the Pact was not, as in NATO, that a group of nations should pool their war efforts in a common cause. It was much simpler and more brutal.

What the Soviets wanted from the Pact was a security apparatus under their control to prevent the territory of the other members being used as a springboard or corridor for an attack on the Soviet Union. They needed a glacis, not an alliance. Both the definitions of 'glacis' given in the *Oxford English Dictionary* are apposite: 'A place made slippery by wet lately fallen and frozen on', or 'The parapet of the covered way extended in a long slope to meet the natural surface of the ground, so that every part of it shall be swept by the fire of the ramparts'. It is not a place on which to expose friendly forces.

Chapter 8

Plans for War: Politburo Debates

Major General Igor Borodin, a member of the Central Committee and of the Secretariat of the so-called Administrative Department, in effect the controlling element of the Red Army and the KGB, escaped the carnage of the last days of August 1985 in Moscow and found his way to the headquarters of VII US Corps. His debriefing at Supreme Headquarters Allied Powers Europe produced the following document (SH-003-47B-5320) dated 17 September 1985, declassified 5 June 1986.

Except in a time of crisis the Politburo would only meet once a week, on Thursdays at 3 pm, when members and candidate members assembled in the old Senate building of the Kremlin.

The Politburo was the embodiment of the Party's absolute power over all aspects of life and society. This was somewhat disguised by cosmetic devices such as the post of President, who had no power whatsoever, and the Parliament, or Supreme Soviet, which ratified every Politburo decision unanimously and whose members were appointed from amongst the most devoted Party officials and could be replaced without any difficulty. There was no doubt at all where real power lay.

The agenda for a normal Politburo session were drafted several months in advance by the Secretariat of the Party Central Committee and then approved by the Politburo members. The Secretariat of the Central Committee prepared and distributed all necessary material in good time, besides summoning people required to furnish information, such as ministers, marshals and generals, diplomats and intelligence officers, the editors of leading newspapers, writers, scientists and judges, the leaders of Gosplan (the state planning organization), of the penal system, of the ideological propaganda front, of agriculture and so on.

For some of these the summons by the Central Committee Secretariat was a catastrophe. For others it marked the beginning of an
upward turn in their careers. In crucial cases some, after the summons
to the Secretariat, would then have to give evidence before the
Politburo itself.

The Politburo was interested in everything and had its own resolute
opinion on all matters. It could decide that a given opera conformed
to the interests of socialism, but that a particular ballet did not and
must not be performed.

On 6 December 1984, the Politburo discussed the situation in
Europe. It was accustomed to use several sources of information.
Two reports had been prepared for this meeting, one by the political
intelligence service (the First Main Directorate of the KGB), the
other by the military intelligence service (the Second Main Directorate of the Soviet Army General Staff – the GRU). The two reports
relied on different methods of analysis. They both reached the same
conclusion: Western Europe was dying of decay.

The KGB was able to take some credit in suggesting that the
unbridled power of the trade unions was at the heart of the West's
economic and political decline. With memories of Solidarity in
Poland still fresh in Soviet minds, this struck a sympathetic note. The
communist political parties in the West had largely turned out to be
unsatisfactory instruments of Soviet infiltration, either because they
were notably unsuccessful in the political arena, as in the United
Kingdom, or politically unreliable, as in Italy. But they had achieved
real success in industrial organization, in penetrating or influencing
the trade union structure both locally and nationally. The bourgeois
governments of Western Europe had not been able or willing to apply
the Polish remedy of martial law in order to control the self-
destructive strikes and go-slows which contributed so satisfactorily to
the decay of Western capitalism. Their efforts to improve matters by
'social contracts' and similar devices had been laughably ineffective,
and Western society was, in accordance with Marxist doctrine, riven
by economic contradictions. Governments were prepared to tolerate
massive unemployment as an alternative to inflation. The workers
were prepared to destroy large parts of industry in order to maintain
their historic working practices. The time was ripe for the Soviet
Union to act, before the accumulated frustrations of the bourgeoisie
led Western governments at last to take adequate measures to control
industrial anarchy.

The GRU believed that the reason for Europe's decay lay in the
unprecedented spread of neutralist and pacifist attitudes. Europe did
not want to defend itself. It seemed to believe that its best defence lay
in helplessness. The more determination the Soviet Union showed in

the international arena, the weaker Europe would become. Soviet military intervention in Afghanistan had not been followed by a strengthening but by a noticeable weakening in NATO and Western Europe. The same was true of the troubles in Poland. These neutralist and pacifist attitudes might not persist.

During discussion the most important question was whether the fruit was ripe enough. Was this the right moment to shake the tree?

Opinions differed. The GRU advised that the moment had come. Thanks to a policy of detente the Soviet Union had been able to deploy a whole new generation of nuclear weapons for the European theatre, as well as improved conventional armaments, which the West, for political and financial reasons, had been unable to match. Europe might in the future change its mind and give more support to the tougher attitude recently apparent in the United States.

The KGB believed that an even more favourable situation would develop in a couple of years' time. The suggestion that the Western Alliance would become more coherent in the future could, of course, be dismissed. Europe would become still further detached from the USA and within itself more divided. Further sharp increases in the price of oil, economic recession, widespread strikes and increasingly violent demonstrations would lead to deep uncertainty and general discontent. This would culminate in the collapse of several Western European governments, soonest of all in those countries which, having nationalized heavy industries, had proved wholly unable to run them effectively.

Both intelligence services agreed that the best opportunity for military action would follow mass riots in Western European cities, organized by trades unionists, advocates of peace, students, the unemployed, racists and conservationists. National communist parties, largely working through the trade unions, would be particularly helpful here. Western European governments would be so destabilized and paralysed by these riots that it would not be hard for the Soviet Union to find an occasion to intervene.

The question was asked whether the Soviet intelligence services were confident that disturbances could be organized on a large enough scale. The representatives of both services gave a positive reply.

The Defence Council then examined the Operational Plan. The Defence Council was the most powerful part of the Politburo, made up of only those members directly involved in the most important military matters. These were the General Secretary of the Central Committee of the Party, the Supreme Party Ideologist, the head of the Organizational Department of the Central Committee (that is, the head of the Party machine), the Minister of Defence, and the Chairman of the KGB.

The Operational Plan was the war plan drawn up among the 100 generals and 620 colonels who made up the First Main Directorate of the General Staff. It was based on an analysis of known intentions and probabilities, and of Soviet forces and those of likely enemies, the latter supplied by the GRU.

The Operational Plan was worked out at the end of each year for the following year and then approved by the Defence Council. In practice, the Operational Plan for the current year was usually last year's plan, adjusted in respect of changes in the international situation and the correlation of forces.

On the basis of the General Staff Operational Plan, the General Staffs of the Strategic Rocket Force (SRF) and of the national Air Defence Forces (*PVO Strany*), and also the Staffs of Strategic Theatres, made their own operational plans. In their turn the headquarters of military districts, naval fleets and army groups worked out plans for their own areas of responsibility. The headquarters of Operational Directorates based their planning both on information from the General Staff intelligence service and on reports from their own intelligence directorates. These formed part of each main headquarters, disposing of their own networks of agents, guerrilla subunits, and electronic, airborne and other means of surveillance.

The Eastern European states did not make their own operational plans. Instead, the Warsaw Pact headquarters informed the Eastern European commands only of what was of particular concern to them in their allotted tasks.

The Operational Plan for the year 1985 embraced every possible theatre.

The fifty Soviet divisions in the Far Eastern and Trans-Baykal districts (of which only eight were in Category One – that is, at operational strength) were sufficient to watch this frontier for the time being. China would without doubt develop into a major threat at some time in the future. A world crisis might give it earlier opportunities. For the moment that theatre was stable.

In South-West Asia there were always possibilities of conflict with the United States, with or without some of its satellites.

In the Middle East the USSR had already in this very year come quite close to a war with the USA. This had arisen largely from local mischief-making, with Syria and Israel, from opposite sides, as chief mischief-makers. Strenuous efforts had made it possible to avoid open conflict and the neutralization of Israel under guarantee, with the creation of an autonomous Palestinian state, had established some sort of stability in the area. This, without prejudice to longer-term political aims, afforded some tactical advantage in the shorter term. It was desirable to keep Israel neutral.

Policies designed to destabilize the Caribbean and Central America, and distract the attention of the United States and particularly that of the American public, from Europe, had had only moderate success. These should be pursued further.

The Operational Plan set out detailed contingency planning for military operations in any likely circumstances – in the Far East and the Pacific, in South-West Asia, in Africa and in Central and South America. Top priority was given to possible operations in Europe.

Document OP-85E-SSOV (Operational Plan for the year 1985, Europe, Top Secret and of Special Importance) consisted of that part of the Operational Plan which related to possible operations against NATO in Europe. No copy of this has come to light. Major General Borodin, however, gave what he maintained was a clear recollection of its contents.

'The first part of the document was an analysis of the probable enemy's forces. The second part concerned the strength of Soviet and Warsaw Pact forces in Europe. The third part dealt with the plan for the utilization of these forces.

'Of the plan put forward in the third part, there were three versions.

'**Variant A** was divided into five phases, set out as follows:

'*Phase One* (duration 24 minutes): a sudden mass nuclear attack throughout the entire European theatre, including Spain and Portugal, in total depth. The following forces would take part in this first strike: 1 Missile Army of the Strategic Rocket Force; the missile brigades of the thirteen Front Tank Armies and Tank Army Groups (in all twenty-six missile brigades); the missile brigades of the Combined Armies and Tank Armies (in all twenty-eight missile brigades); the missile battalions of all motor rifle and tank divisions within range; the missile submarines of the North, Baltic and Black Sea Fleets and those of 5 Nautical Squadron. Their salvoes would be fired simultaneously by all missile units from their permanent deployment points or their positions at the time. Of the divisional missile battalions (equipped with missiles of up to 150 kilometres' range), only those would take part in the attack that were located in the immediate vicinity of the frontiers. The first strike was intended to neutralize all enemy forces down to divisions, brigades and regiments, with particular attention to headquarters, together with missile bases, airfields, the principal communications and administrative centres and the air defence systems.

'*Phase Two* (duration 96 minutes) follows immediately after Phase One. Eight Air Armies, the aircraft of three fleets, two corps of long-distance strategic aircraft, sub-units of the civil aviation

Aeroflot and all military transport aircraft will take part. During this phase a maximum effort will be made to determine the results of the first nuclear attack. At the same time, a heavy air attack will be made on any targets seen to have survived the first attack. These would largely be mobile targets, such as field command posts and mobile missile units.

'Nuclear and chemical weapons will be used. At the same time, the military transport aircraft and Aeroflot transport will drop guerrilla sub-units of *Spetsnaz* (Special Assignment Force) in areas not under nuclear or chemical attack. As soon as the Phase Two attack begins, all the missile launchers which took part in the first attack will when possible be reloaded and tactical missiles not used in the first strike because of their limited range, but which can now be brought to bear, will be moved swiftly forward into the main attack. Missile sub-units will receive target information directly from reconnaissance aircraft.

'*Phase Three* (duration 30 minutes): all missile sub-units again deliver a massive nuclear attack, as soon as the aircraft are clear. This attack is intended to destroy newly revealed targets and targets insufficiently damaged in the first attacks. Chemical warheads will predominate, although the density of nuclear warheads will remain high.

'*Phase Four* (duration 7 days): the success of this phase of the operation depends on surprise. Most Soviet and Warsaw Pact forces are not put in a state of readiness at the preliminary alert. The stand-to signal for these divisions is given only as the first nuclear attack takes place. The two and a half hours required for the first three phases of the operation is sufficient time to prepare their echelons and to move them forward from their stations. Detailed plans of action for each division, each army and each front, are worked out in advance and kept sealed. All that remains for commanding officers to do is to unseal the appropriate package and carry out the orders prescribed in it. All others will be destroyed. Even if the assault echelon divisions have not had time fully to prepare themselves in two and a half hours, they must nevertheless be moved forward into action. In these circumstances the enemy divisions will be at a disadvantage. The assault by the first echelon divisions will take place simultaneously along the entire front, to drive in wedges as quickly and as deeply as possible wherever enemy defences permit. On the second or third day of this action the Front Tank Armies will be put in where success has been greatest. On the fourth day of the operation, in any zone where enemy resistance has been effectively suppressed, the Belorussian Group of Tank Armies will be put in to strike across Europe towards the Atlantic coast. During the fourth phase, aircraft and missile sub-units will take supporting action as required by ground and naval forces. On each of the first three days there will be a parachute drop of one airborne division. If the availability of military transport and Aeroflot aircraft permitted, all divisions would have been dropped simultaneously on the first day of the operation. This is not possible.

'*Phase Five* would be carried out only in the event of Soviet and East European forces being brought to a halt in West Germany and becoming involved in sustained operations. This could lead to the development of a static front with a linear deployment of NATO forces from north to south. In this case the Ukrainian Group of Tank Armies will move at maximum speed from Hungary through Austria (neutrality notwithstanding) on the axis Linz-Frankfurt-Dunkirk. The purpose of this phase is to disrupt the Allied lines of communication and cut their line of retreat and then press on to the sea.

'**Variant B** was almost identical with Variant A, although nuclear weapons are not employed. Instead, all missile formations and units deliver a concentrated chemical and high-explosive attack whilst at the same time maintaining a state of constant readiness for the use of nuclear weapons. Variant B envisages a period of tension in Europe before military operations begin, lasting for anything from several days to several months or even one year. The troops on both sides will be in a state of readiness for all this time, carrying out exercises close to the enemy's lines. The longer this period of tension lasts the better it will be for the Soviet Union. Weariness, boredom and false alarms will combine to reduce alertness. Soviet and Warsaw Pact formations can then be swiftly put on the alert and moved into the attack forthwith. To this the response of NATO forces is likely to be sluggish. Variant B also provides for a possible lightning attack from peacetime locations without chemical weapons. This can best be done when the West is most vulnerable: for example, in August during the holiday period.

'**Variant C** was divided into a preliminary and a main stage.

'*Preliminary Stage* (duration 10 days): during this period several dozen civilian special service groups formed in Western and Asiatic non-communist countries will head for Western Europe. Each group acts independently and will not know that its mission is part of a general plan. At the same time, *Spetsnaz* sabotage units numbering some 5,000 men will cross into Western Europe as tourists. Simultaneously, Soviet merchant ships, with sub-units of marines and sabotage troops hidden on board, will sail towards Europe's main ports.

'*Main Stage:* at an appointed time the *Spetsnaz* groups will destroy key electric power stations with explosives. If sixty of these can be put out of action, the whole of industry and all communication systems in

Western Europe will be paralysed and rail transport will come to a standstill. All other means of transport including aircraft will be severely handicapped by lack of communications. In these circumstances it can be expected that water supplies will be cut off, radio and television broadcasting will cease, refrigeration will be impossible and produce will perish in warehouses. In buildings, lifts will stop, lights will go out, and telephones and alarm systems will be cut off. In large cities traffic chaos will result. Petrol and oil fuel supplies will give out. The underground railways will come to a halt. The work of government establishments, military headquarters and police forces will be disrupted. Crime will increase enormously and panic will set in. Pro-Soviet saboteurs in civilian clothes should now be able with little difficulty to destroy the principal communications systems of the main NATO headquarters and put out of action the command posts of the air defence systems. At the same time, Soviet military transport and Aeroflot aircraft will carry out a mass drop of paratroop divisions. These landings will be safeguarded by Soviet *REP Osnaz* (Special Electronic Counter-Measures Force) sub-units which will 'blind' NATO's radar stations. The mission of the airborne divisions is to seize government establishments, military headquarters and command posts, and to disrupt all state and military administration systems. Once this has been accomplished and before it has been possible in the West to evaluate what has happened, the Soviet Government will urgently appeal to the US Government to refrain from a nuclear response and will give guarantees that the Soviet Union will not use nuclear weapons.'

Several points of outstanding importance were raised when Document OP-85E-SSOV was discussed in the Kremlin. The first was whether the attack should be nuclear from the outset, as in Variant A. Arguments for this were strong. The USSR had a lead over the USA in land-based missile weapons of inter-continental range, though not in those delivered by aircraft or from submarines.

The bomber aircraft mattered less than the submarines. It was noted that Britain and France had obstinately maintained, and even modernized, independent submarine-launched ballistic missile (SLBM) capabilities which, though modest, could do critical damage in the Soviet Union. The USSR was well ahead of the West in military and civil defence provision and in the hardening of launching sites, communications and administrative accommodation. Its size and the dispersal of its population conferred significant advantage. In theatre nuclear forces (TNF) the START Treaty had reduced the Soviet Union's lead but this was still considerable. It had not been possible, unfortunately, to prevent the beginning of the installation of the new TNF, the *Pershing* II and cruise missile weapons, though the refusal of the Netherlands to host any had been helpful. The great strides made in generating anti-American and anti-nuclear tendencies in the Alliance reflected considerable credit on those responsible. The billion dollars' worth of hard currency this had cost the Soviet Union was money well spent. It was difficult to believe but nevertheless true that the conviction was widely held in Britain that if there were no nuclear weapons in the British Isles they would be immune from nuclear attack. This conviction was particularly creditable to Soviet disinformation services and those responsible were to be congratulated. Since the British Isles were of paramount importance to the NATO war effort in Europe they would, of course, without any question be attacked and neutralized, whatever the circumstances.

Although in TNF in general the USSR was superior, it could not be absolutely guaranteed that the United States would refrain from the use against the Soviet Union of nuclear weapons of inter-continental range, if a nuclear attack were mounted on Western Europe, though the probability that the USA would use strategic nuclear weapons if its European allies were facing early defeat by non-nuclear means was low. Nor could it be guaranteed that a first strike on the United States would destroy so much of its ICBM capability as to rule out the possibility of a highly destructive response. It almost went without saying that what was known in the muddled jargon of the West as 'escalation' would certainly take place. That meant that a decision to use any nuclear weapon was in effect a decision to go the whole way into the full strategic exchange.

Would this, for the USSR, be worthwhile? Even if the USA were devastated, would the Soviet Union in the aftermath be in a position to retain full control over its own people, let alone those of restless client states? This was doubtful. Heavy damage and high casualties in Warsaw Pact states would loosen ties in the socialist world rather than strengthen them, while the progress of the USSR itself would be set back so far as to open dangerous opportunities to China. Opinion in the Politburo appeared to be hardening against the option of a nuclear opening.

None the less there was a deep and manifest difference of opinion here which could not be overcome. One group, resolutely led by the Chairman of the KGB, Army General Sergei Athanasievich Aristanov, ably supported by the Minister of Defence, Marshal Alexei Alexandrovich Nastin (each a member of the Defence Council of the Politburo), maintained that the Soviet approach to war demanded the swift and violent use of the most powerful weapons available. This suggested, logically enough, a nuclear opening, in total depth, including, it went without saying, ICBM attack on the continental United States. In the strategic exchange between the central systems of the two great powers the Soviet Union would suffer grave damage which would put its progress back significantly. But it would survive and in time recover. The United States, on the other hand, would be destroyed, leaving the Soviet Union to establish progressive socialist societies in its own good time throughout the present capitalist West.

The arguments for a conventional opening were well known. There would clearly be advantage in a non-nuclear victory and this, with good timing and the correct handling of field operations, was not impossible. If, however, the advance into Western Europe were so far delayed that the Rhine could not be secured within ten days there must be no question but that the *whole* of the Soviet Union's nuclear capability must be applied and quickly used. There must be no withholding of the more powerful weapons in the hope that the enemy would do the same with his, and no concession at all to the fallacious Western concept of escalation, which is not only fundamentally incorrect but wholly out of keeping with the now well-established, and even traditional, Soviet method of making war. If there were any uncertainty over the achievement of very early success by non-nuclear means, however, the whole operation should without any doubt be nuclear from the start.

The Supreme Party Ideologist, Constantin Andrievich Malinsky, who was a member of the Politburo Defence Council, supported by the leader of the Organization of the Party and State Control, Otto Yanovich Berzinsh, and Taras Kyrillovich Nalivaiko, responsible for relations with socialist countries (both being members of the Politburo but not of the Defence Council) demurred. It must be the aim of the Soviet Union to realize Lenin's grand design of a world under communist rule. A world of which much would be charred rubble or irradiated desert would hardly be worth ruling. What was wanted was supremacy in a living world, not over a charnel house it would be death to enter. Nuclear weapons were to frighten rather than to fight with. Their use would set up a contradiction in socialist practice which should be avoided except in the very last resort and only after the deepest thought.

For the time being, at least, the majority were in favour of a non-nuclear opening and the meeting passed to consider other matters.

The position of European neutrals was discussed. Sweden, in spite of signs of restlessness in recent years, could almost certainly be cowed into maintaining its traditional stance. France was an unknown quantity. It was a member of the Atlantic Alliance but not of its military organization, NATO. France's record of self-interest suggested that it might, and probably would, abstain from belligerence if the advantage offered were sufficient. Ireland would probably follow France's lead, though recently improved Anglo-Irish relations raised doubts here and it would be as well to target key installations in Ireland for conventional destruction in order to deny their use to the Western allies. The chance would have to be taken that Irish facilities would become available to the enemy, which could raise problems for the Soviet Navy in the Eastern Atlantic.

To occupy France would impose a serious burden on Soviet resources and involve a significant addition to occupied territories which would certainly raise security problems of their own.

What would help France to stay out would be a guarantee of total immunity. This suggested that, though offensive action should be planned to cover the whole of Western Europe, the immediate aim should be to occupy and dismantle Federal Germany, stopping, for the time being at least, at the Rhine, while the Federal Republic was being dealt with and negotiations were in progress with the USA. The intention to stop at the Rhine would be widely publicized with maximum pressure on France to accept the Soviet guarantee of immunity and abstain from belligerence, which it almost certainly would. The destruction of Federal Germany would then inevitably cause the collapse of the Atlantic Alliance.

This policy received approval.

The question of distracting the attention of the United States from Europe was again discussed. If the USA could be involved in active warfare in Central America and the Caribbean, American public opinion would be unlikely to favour massive support for NATO in Europe. The Warsaw Pact should then have an easy victory. Energetic action to this end should still be pursued, with particular attention to Cuba.

A suggestion to mount an amphibious and airborne threat to the western seaboard of North America, as a further distraction from war in Europe, was dismissed as implausible. The support of even a small amphibious force across the Bering Sea was impracticable in the face of United States maritime and land-based air strength, while the inability of the Soviet Air Force (SAF) to lift and then maintain all of its seven airborne divisions at once was well known.

The question was then raised of action in Asia to distract the attention of the United States from the focal point in Europe. Would the setting up of crises either in East Asia, as for example in the area of Indochina, or in South-West Asia, perhaps in the oil-producing areas, be useful? The conclusion was that they would not be productive either in the right way or at the right time, with the possible exception of the Korean peninsula. It would be a mistake to alarm China before Federal Germany was destroyed. Operations in

South-West Asia would draw off Soviet and US forces in about equal strengths, which would show a net advantage to the Soviet Union in global terms. There were, however, too many unpredictable factors in that region. What would Pakistan do? What of the Arab world? What of the Moslem population of the Soviet Union? It was thought best to take one thing at a time. The speedy liquidation of the Federal Republic of Germany was the primary objective and nothing must distract attention from this. Where disinformation and action in support of progressive policies was showing promise among native populations, as in southern Africa, these activities should continue. Major initiatives outside Europe, however, should not now be undertaken until the primary objective had been realized and the Alliance destroyed.

Offensive action in space was also discussed. Obviously the highly developed Soviet capability for interference with US space operations would be fully exploited. Would nuclear weapons be used? The 1963 agreement not to employ weapons in space could, of course, be disregarded. The chief question that arose was whether nuclear weapons could be used in space or at sea without initiating the central exchange. It was thought that they should not be used at all unless it was accepted that the inter-continental exchange would inevitably follow. The question of electro-magnetic pulse (EMP), however, was of particular interest. To the less technically inclined members of the Politburo it was explained that a fusion weapon exploded outside the atmosphere, say 200 kilometres up, would cause no thermal, blast or radiation damage on the earth but would generate a pulse of immense power which could damage or destroy electric or electronic equipment over a wide area, disrupt electricity distribution and communications and severely disorient instrumentation, with what could be catastrophic operational results. The West was far more vulnerable to EMP than the USSR. Should the electro-magnetic pulse be exploited?

There was considerable support for this discriminate use of a nuclear weapon but in the end it was agreed that it would probably be taken as a clear indication of intention to wage all-out thermonuclear war, with all that that implied. It should not, therefore, be done unless all-out nuclear war were intended.

In discussion of the operational alternatives, Politburo members drew attention to shortcomings in the planning. They instructed that a revised Plan be submitted in two weeks for final approval.

On 20 December 1984 that part of the revised Plan of the First Main Directorate of the General Staff which concerned operations against NATO was once again submitted to the Defence Council. A map-room exercise was held, with the head of the First Main Directorate of the General Staff acting as leader of the 'Eastern' forces and the head of the GRU leading the 'Western' troops. The task of the head of the GRU was to stop the 'Eastern' forces. He would consider every possible manoeuvre and weapon available to the enemy in battle. The head of the First Main Directorate had also to take appropriate measures to overcome 'Western' opposition. It stood to reason, of course, that if in the real battle the enemy were to use unexpected techniques, equipment or tactics which would halt the Soviet breakthrough, of which the Soviet military intelligence service had given no warning, the GRU chief would be court-martialled.

The Chief of the General Staff supervised this duel between his two subordinates and acted as umpire. The Politburo members observed the battle closely. For the moment, at least, it was only being fought on maps. The conclusion was that a favourable outcome was likely.

When the map exercise was over, the Chief of the General Staff, the heads of the Main Directorates and their deputies were all subjected to rigorous questioning by Politburo members, not on the particular operational matters under discussion but generally on the state of Soviet and NATO forces. It is a curious and interesting fact that in committees the world over, however powerful and important, there is a tendency to explore matters, often in some detail, which are not of the highest importance in themselves but which attract the interest of some of the members – the lay members particularly. This is sometimes exploited by other members as a device to avoid discussion of points which might prove embarrassing. The Politburo was no exception.

Once again there arose the old question of what happens to NATO's obsolescent armaments. The members of the Politburo refused to believe that all the tanks, artillery and armoured personnel carriers which NATO had taken out of service would actually have been disposed of. Knowing in advance that this question was bound to crop up yet again, the chief of military intelligence had brought with him secret reports about the destruction of obsolete weapons in the West, with a film showing the destruction of such weapons. This did not succeed in dispelling doubts. Again and again it was asked if all these documents might not simply be the product of Western disinformation services which, though less widespread and effective than those of the Soviet Union, were known to be far from idle. The GRU chief explained that it was completely true, that he had detailed accounts of the destruction of old equipment. There then arose the question of why NATO did this. The Soviet intelligence service found that hard to answer.

The West's policy in relation to obsolete armaments thus remained a mystery. The Soviet Union did not destroy its old military equipment. It preserved it. A thoroughly obsolete tank can be buried in the ground up to its very turret. The turret may then be additionally fortified with armour plates. The tank does not have to move at all. Its engine and caterpillar tracks are already of no use, but its armour is as strong as it used to be. Its main armament and machine-guns may be fired as before. Its optical instruments and signals equipment remain. According to the Soviet view, two or three old tank crew members with one obsolete tank buried in the ground might, suitably sited, effectively defend a wide frontage, perhaps replacing a whole company or even a first-rate infantry battalion. The buried tank is invaluable in both nuclear and chemical warfare and its crew live in warmth and comfort. If the turret is reinforced with additional armour and well camouflaged, one obsolete tank can stop several of the enemy's advancing tanks. The Politburo simply could not understand why NATO had withdrawn from service literally tens of thousands of tanks, including those real armoured fortresses the *Conqueror* and the M-103, with their powerful guns, when in actual fact any sort of tank buried in the ground was a far better alternative to two or three infantrymen with rifles in a dirty, disintegrating trench. If NATO had secretly kept all its old tanks, then during the period of a threat of war, or even once war had begun, an impregnable steel defence could have been created.

Some of the members of the Politburo, of course, had had experience of tank warfare in the Great Patriotic War, some forty years before. None had served in airborne forces and few had any idea of the capability of helicopter assault in vertical envelopment.

On the following day, 21 December, an extraordinary meeting of the Politburo took place, for discussion of the situation in Eastern Europe and the possible behaviour of the USSR's allies in the event of war. The report was given by the Commander-in-Chief of the Combined Armed Forces of the Warsaw Pact, Marshal of the Soviet Union V. G. Kulikov. In the Soviet hierarchy this post, it must be said, commanded little respect. For a Soviet marshal, appointment to it meant honourable retirement from the real centre of power. A principal reason for its invention was to hide the simple fact that all decisions for the Warsaw Pact were actually made within the Soviet General Staff. The Supreme Commander was the titular military head of the Warsaw Pact armies. He was officially no more than one of the deputies to the Soviet Minister of Defence. The Soviet Minister of Defence gave orders to the Commander-in-Chief of the Warsaw Pact as his deputy. The latter then delivered the orders to the 'allies' and saw to it that they were carried out as correctly as possible. He reported back on the execution of the orders to the Soviet

Minister of Defence, who in turn reported back to his colleagues in the Politburo.

Kulikov's report to the Politburo referred to above brought little satisfaction to its members. From a military point of view Eastern Europe was well armed, but there was some lack of confidence in the willingness of Eastern European countries to fight. For example, Poland had been able, at the expense of reducing the living standards of its people and thanks to astronomical Western credits, to create armed forces with four times as many tanks as the British Army. Poland had a marine infantry division. Only two or three countries, notably the USA, allowed themselves such a luxury; the Soviet Union was not prepared to maintain such a division. However, the situation in Poland was radically changing. Polish workers had thrust a wedge into the Party structure. The movement had been incompletely suppressed. Polish anti-socialist forces might be able, in the worst case, to hamper their country's war effort very seriously. This would not only reduce the value to the Soviet Union of its most powerful military ally, but would also do much to disrupt the maintenance of Soviet forces operating in West Germany.

For the moment, East Germany continued to remain faithful, but how would its troops react to closer contact with Western influences and better opportunities to defect? The defection rate in the GDR was already quite high.

Czechoslovakia had remained in a state of ambivalence, almost of torpor, since 1968. At that time its army did not want to fight against the Red Army. Would the Czechoslovak People's Army now fight against anyone else?

In Hungary the situation was quite the opposite. The events of 1956 had been followed by economic developments which had unfortunately led to some erosion of socialism and a lessening of Party authority. What would the Hungarian Army do if war broke out? How far would it be disposed to fight for socialism?

Bulgaria had been deeply corrupted by Western influence. Every year there was in Bulgaria one Western tourist for every three inhabitants. The country was thriving on tourism and on little else. If Western Europe went socialist, there would be no more Western tourists and the hard currency they brought would cease to come in. Where would the advantage lie for Bulgarians in a change in the existing situation?

That left Romania. In some ways it appeared to be unfriendly but the Soviet Union could not afford to lose Ceausescu. He certainly had no desire to see the USSR collapse and he might well be a constant ally. It was a pity that Romania's army was so very weak and its economic situation scarcely less than catastrophic.

When the report was finished the Supreme Party Ideologist stood up and gave the Commander-in-Chief of the Combined Forces of the Warsaw Pact the following order:

'At the forthcoming meeting of the Warsaw Pact Political Advisory Council three fundamental points must be very diplomatically, but clearly and candidly, put forward:

a. It is not only wrong to betray friends, especially at war, it can also be suicidal.
b. The Soviet Union will always have a powerful nuclear capability in reserve for the punishment of traitors.
c. Western Europe will undoubtedly be destroyed, leaving those who have deserted socialism with no refuge. It is much safer to remain on the winning side.'

Chapter 9

Nekrassov's View

Andrei Nekrassov, Party member though he was (as he had to be), did not wholly trust Soviet propaganda. He could not disclose this publicly, of course. As pressures built up inside him, however, he felt an urgent need to share the load he was bearing with someone else. It was a great boon to him that the one person outside his family whom he wholly trusted, someone with a great, if different, awareness of the sort of things over which he was himself puzzled, was at hand. Nekrassov was able, in private and personal conversations held always well away from the possibility of eavesdropping, at least to say some of what was on his mind to Dimitri Vassilievitch Makarov. The bond between these two was stronger now than ever. Makarov's widowed father, the lecturer in history in the Lomonossov University, whom Dimitri, his only child, had not seen for over a year, had had a sudden heart attack and died. The two young men, reserved in their attitude to other people, began to see themselves more and more almost as brothers.

Andrei Nekrassov naturally did what was expected of a Soviet officer. He nodded his head, as was proper, and recited all the propagandist statements required of him in front of his men. But some of what was disseminated he, as a professional soldier, simply could not believe. Soviet propaganda claimed, for instance, that American soldiers were pampered. It was said that each American company had its own cook and that each American soldier had his own sleeping bag, just like a tourist. However, Nekrassov was perfectly well aware (and probably all other Soviet army officers were too) that this could not possibly be true. A company is a military sub-unit meant solely for fighting battles. A company cannot have a cook, for everyone in a company must fight. A regiment needs to have a cook, but only one for 2,000 men. Every night a few infantry soldiers are detailed as fatigues to help him. At least, that is what happens in peacetime; during war, there is absolutely no need for a cook at all.

He did not believe the propaganda and tried to sort out the position for himself. But it seemed, when he compared figures, that the Soviet propaganda might be right after all. A Soviet tank company had thirteen tanks and forty-three men – thirty-nine in the tank crews and four maintenance men, who were responsible for technical upkeep, supplies, discipline, provisions, morale, medical treatment, uniforms, ammunition, and so on. In an American tank company there were seventeen tanks but ninety-two men. What work, Nekrassov wondered, could all these people do? Perhaps they were penal infantry, expendable troops deployed to defend the tanks from light anti-tank weapons. But why keep penal soldiers in tank companies during peacetime? They should be made to do hard labour in prisons during peacetime, and only when war broke out should they be sent out to penal battalions, as wholly expendable manpower.

The figures just did not seem to work out at battalion level. A Soviet tank battalion had forty tanks and 193 men. An American tank battalion had fifty-four tanks but more than 500 men. The staff of a Soviet battalion numbered a total of three, two officers and a sergeant, with a signals platoon of thirteen men. For twenty-four hours a day over a period of many months the battalion's staff had to cope with directing combat operations and seeing to all the necessary documentation. However, within an American battalion, for some reason or other, they had devised a staff company, which had the same number of men as a whole Soviet battalion. It was completely impossible to understand what all these people could be doing. Moreover, hundreds of vehicles would be needed to transport them all, whereas only thirteen assorted vehicles were used to support a Soviet battalion with forty tanks.

In the Soviet infantry, problems of maintenance were resolved even more simply than in tank sub-units. In a Soviet motor rifle company everyone takes part directly in battle. Its officers are armed with the same weapons as their soldiers. The company sergeant major is responsible for discipline, order and the cleanliness of weapons, and also for supplying the company with everything it needs including fuel, provisions, ammunition, spare parts, uniforms and weapons. But even he, the only man involved in administration, has to take part in the fighting. As soon as the company goes in to fight on foot, the sergeant major either controls the movement of the BTR or directs BMP fire or both. In a Soviet motor rifle battalion there are only thirty men to deal with communications, repairs, medical and technical support, and the supply of stores, provisions and virtually everything else. They also have to deal with all the administration, while the remaining 413 men participate directly in the action. One result of this sensible use of manpower is that a Soviet battalion has a mortar battery, whilst an American battalion twice its size does not. Instead it seemed to have an incredibly long tail of unprotected vehicles full of administrators.

A Soviet motor rifle division of 13,800 men has 272 tanks and 108 self-propelled howitzers. A similar American division has 18,500 men but only 216 tanks and seventy-two self-propelled howitzers. A Soviet division is completely independent, with its own reconnaissance battalion and a company of anti-aircraft missiles (besides the anti-aircraft weapons of the regiments, battalions and companies), whilst an American division has to rely on outside support, in particular on the battalions of HAWK air defence missiles.

Andrei Nekrassov simply could not fathom, as he explained to his patient friend, why they did not transfer all their clerks, cooks and supply people to make up new tank battalions, or mortar batteries, or air defence regiments.

In Europe there were altogether 200,000 American soldiers. That would have been sufficient to form fifteen full-bodied Soviet tank or motor rifle divisions and all the auxiliary units and services needed to support and maintain them. If one had to use this manpower to form weaker divisions without, for example, reconnaissance battalions or heavy anti-aircraft missiles, but with 216 tanks per division, this number of men would be sufficient for twenty-five such divisions.

The US Army in Europe, with all that manpower, had only five incomplete divisions. However hard he tried, Nekrassov simply could not understand what work all these other people could be doing. Surely they were not *all* in penal battalions? His friend Dimitri was equally puzzled.

There were other things that neither Senior Lieutenant could understand. Within the US Army there were sub-units of military police. Why? Could it be that a battalion or regimental commander was unable to establish strict order without outside help? Surely a commander has enough authority to keep his own sub-unit under control?

As far as women were concerned the whole thing was quite incomprehensible. Where can a woman be used in an army? In a hospital or in a signals sub-unit, perhaps, but even then only in places where these were stationary: in rear communications centres and rear hospitals. Where else? In administrative posts? Only two typists were needed in a field army or tank army headquarters. There were five Soviet armies in the German Democratic Republic. That made ten typists in all. No more were needed. Why were there tens of thousands of women in the US Army? What did they do? Was it possible to find some kind of army job which involved only light physical work? What if these women worked in divisions, where, if they were not fighting, divisional personnel had to do extremely heavy work for a minimum of ten hours a day? Could the US Army really have different standards? In a twenty-four-hour period a Soviet soldier had twenty-five minutes of free time. Could this be sufficient for a woman? A soldier must be ready to sleep in the snow with only his greatcoat to cover himself, he may have to wash himself with snow and go for months without hot food. These American women are poor wretches, thought Nekrassov, driven by accursed unemployment into the monstrous hardships of a soldier's life. This procedure would really have to be changed! But perhaps in the US Army even the men each had a whole *hour* of free time per day? Perhaps it was true that they all, male and female, had sleeping bags, just like tourists? Perhaps they really did have one cook for every 200 soldiers, and that they took cooks along with them on exercises, and perhaps even to war as well? Perhaps even all the men in the army were allowed a standard of comfort appropriate to their female colleagues?

Naturally, as both young officers well knew, when there were not enough men the Soviet Union used women as well as men in the armed forces. A large part of the fixed air defence sub-units were staffed by women, but these were completely female. Women were also used for other light work. For example, 46 Guards Air Regiment had an entirely female staff. There was a woman commander of the fighter aircraft regiment, a female chief of staff, women pilots, engineers and technicians. But flying and air battles, from a physical point of view, are only light work. No one ever dreamed of sending women to join the Soviet land forces, for the work load there was exceptionally heavy and it was simply impossible to devise some sort of light work. In the Red Army's land forces there was no work that could be called 'light', thought Nekrassov, none at all.

Soviet experts also took a very critical view of the level of combat training of the American forces. The volunteer system had had, it was true, its darker sides. In the days of the draft everyone was called up for military service, but in a zero-draft army many of the volunteer recruits had been society's failures, unable to make a success of anything else. The system of voluntary service inevitably led to a weakening and a loss of efficiency within the forces. Of course, most Soviet forces were also poorly trained or even sometimes completely untrained, but they had an unquestionable advantage: the barrage battalions of the KGB, which would not allow a Soviet soldier to retreat or to surrender to the enemy. A Soviet soldier had no choice. He must kill his enemies with determination – and quickly – to save his own life. This is an incentive which counter-balances many deficiencies in combat training.

Both Andrei and Dimitri knew, of course, that voluntary service had been abandoned in the United States and had heard that this was for two main reasons. The pay had long been too low to attract any but poor quality volunteers, including men who could not read or write – like so many in the Red Army of course – and many others so dull as to be virtually untrainable. With the highly complex equipment used in the West – far more difficult to handle than the simpler, more rugged things Nekrassov was used to – this mattered much more than it did, for example, in No. 3 Company. The second and more compelling reason for going back to conscript service in the United States had been, it seemed (for reasons they had never fully had explained to them), that under the voluntary system essential reserves of military manpower had simply melted away. If a volunteer system could not produce the very large number of reservists needed in wartime it had to be replaced by conscription. It was as simple as that.

They had been taught that the American soldier was a poor fighter, physically and mentally soft and very apt either to surrender or to run away. Much of this would without any doubt be due to extraordinary weaknesses in American notions of organization and tactical method.

According to Soviet ideas, as both young officers well knew, American tactical method was a compound of criminal negligence, ignorance and incomprehension of the art of war. The US Army, they had been taught, dispersed whatever resources it had more or less evenly along the entire front, with approximately the same proportion of support weapons at each commander's disposal. However, victory had always been won by concentration, at the right moment, of all resources at a critical point.

All Soviet commanders, from battalions upwards, had a powerful striking tool in their hands. A battalion commander had under command a mortar battery; a regimental commander had a tank battalion, a battalion of self-propelled artillery, an anti-tank company and a battery of multi-barrelled mortars; a divisional commander had a missile battalion, a tank regiment, a self-propelled artillery regiment, a battalion of multi-barrelled rockets and an anti-tank battalion. The higher the level of command the more extensive the resources under the commander's own hand. The Supreme Commander had enormous powers at his disposal in the units or formations called 'Reserve of the Supreme High Command'. These were linked to the air corps, breakthrough artillery divisions, special-capacity artillery brigades, anti-tank brigades and sometimes to the tank armies. No commander from the rank of battalion commander upwards dispersed his reserves or distributed his men in equal groups. No subordinate commander had the right to ask for, let alone insist upon, reinforcement or further support.

Every superior commander used his offensive capability as a whole and then only in the critical sector of the battle. A battalion's mortar battery is not split up among rifle companies, but is used at full strength to support only one company: the most successful one. The anti-tank weapons at the disposal of the commander of a battalion, regiment, division, army or front were never split into groups but always held concentrated. Only at the most crucial moment were they put in, at full strength, at the enemy's weakest point. The same applied to tanks, artillery and aircraft.

If an army attacked sluggishly, its commander could expect no air support. On the other hand, if an army attacked with determination and energy, it received the support of the entire front air army, including an airborne assault brigade or division, and in addition possibly even further support from an air corps of the Supreme Commander's Reserve. This policy was not limited only to weapons such as those with nuclear warheads or to air defence missiles. All resources were concentrated in the hands of senior commanders and what was required was filtered down from top to bottom. A divisional commander, for example, had a medical, an engineer and a mainten- ance battalion plus other support battalions. He did not divide these resources among his regiments, but instead used them all to support the most successful of his regiments. The divisional motor transport battalion would deliver three times the normal ammunition supply to the regiment registering a success, and perhaps none to any other.

Everyone must work to exploit success, at any level. If one army in a front of three had broken through whilst the other two were held up, the front motor transport brigade would bring this army three times as much ammunition as usual, at the expense of the other armies. The front pipeline brigade would lay its pipes right up to the breakthrough zone, ignoring the rest, and all the fuel for the whole front would be given to the most successful army. The front commander would rush all his bridge-building and road-building regiments and brigades to the area of success. If the front commander received, for example, a re-supply of 100 anti-aircraft missiles, all of them would be given to the most successful army.

This sort of concentration of effort on a narrow sector was not impossible, even in a nuclear war. Each Soviet commander had to search out and destroy the enemy's nuclear weapons with whatever resources he could muster – from missiles and aircraft to saboteurs and secret agents. But first of all any of the enemy's weapons that might threaten the successful joining together of his various forma- tions would be sought out by the commander and destroyed. An army commander would seek first to destroy any threat that endangered his best division. A front commander concentrated all his forces to search for and destroy those of the enemy's weapons that might endanger the front's best army.

All forces were directed along one principal axis. The advance must be swift and in separate groups on the principle: 'move separately, fight together'. The enormous power of the cutting wedge would be mustered suddenly, right at the critical point of the enemy's defensive positions. The advancing wedge would manoeuvre past the enemy's pockets of resistance, leaving them hostage. It was very difficult to deliver a nuclear strike on a tank army that had broken through. Its units were agile as quicksilver, manoeuvring between massed groups of enemy forces, bearing down upon large cities but swiftly by-passing them. Assault on NATO forces in Western European cities would always be too risky.

The two young officers knew all this. They had been well taught. They were also well aware of the penalties awaiting those who disregarded what they had been taught.

Any failure within the Red Army to stick to the principle of sudden concentration of forces in one principal direction meant dismissal, and in wartime could mean brief trial followed by execution. They both knew that. In 1941 the Commander of the Western Front Army, General D. G. Pavlov, had been given only eight minutes in which to explain why he had dispersed his forces. His explanations were deemed insufficient and he was shot there and then. His Chief of Staff, General V. E. Klimovsky, had even less time to speak in his own defence and was also immediately shot. Soviet generals knew that the practice of executing failures was still followed. Not four stars on his shoulder straps, not even the diamond insignia of the rank of marshal, could save a failure from paying the final penalty.

In the US Army everything seemed to be quite the opposite. Commanders did not have a strike force at their disposal. The commander of an American battalion did not have a mortar battery, but only a mortar platoon. A brigade commander had absolutely no heavy-fire weapons of his own, and relied on divisional artillery. It was this organizational factor that appeared to compel a divisional commander to divide his artillery amongst his brigades. But shortage of guns was not in itself particularly terrible. What was indefensible was the deliberate policy of dispersing resources. A US divisional commander tried to share out his artillery equally, giving to each brigade as much as to every other. The brigade commander in his turn divided the artillery evenly amongst his battalions. These in turn distributed it to the companies. As a result, the blow to the enemy was never delivered like a punch from a fist, but as though from single poking fingers. American superior commanders also spread their resources in roughly even proportions amongst their divisions. As a result of this, no single commander was able to influence the battle by his own action. He simply did not possess enough of the proper tools himself and could not count, if he had an early success, on their provision.

American experts had attempted to justify this policy as the best defence against the threat of nuclear weapons on massed groups of forces. This came from a purely theoretical understanding of warfare, for it was quite unnecessary to assemble all the artillery in one area for concentrated fire on the major target. The artillery of a whole army could easily be kept under unified control and fire from different points, but its fire must always be concentrated in support of the one division or brigade on which, at that moment, would depend the fate of all other divisions, and perhaps also the fate of the whole operation.

It was always expected of the US Army by Soviet officers that its equipment would be technically very good, if complex, that its air support would be plentiful, and that its ammunition and warlike stores would be abundant. It was also expected that its tactical handling would be inexpert and that its morale would be low.

Those in the Soviet forces who, like the two Senior Lieutenants, expected low morale in the US Army were in for something of a surprise. There had been some quite marked changes in the past few years. The American soldier was far from being the alienated, drug-sodden, pampered pushover that these two and their Soviet brother officers had been led by their own propaganda to expect. Rumours that had reached them, however, suggested that, for whatever reason, the propaganda line about United States troops could be very far from the mark.

Chapter 10

Ireland

Beneath all the sound and fury of the IRA and Mr Paisley in the early 1980s, two or three constructive trends were in fact beginning to appear in Irish affairs. Unification of the whole island had always been the aim and the stated commitment of politicians in the Republic. In this they agreed with the IRA, but they dissociated themselves with varying degrees of emphasis and sincerity from the IRA's determination to bring this about by force. None of them, however, before Dr Garret FitzGerald in 1981, drew the obvious conclusion that if force was to be ruled out to coerce Northern Ireland into union, persuasion would have to be used instead. He at least pointed his finger clearly and unequivocally at two of the outstanding barriers to union: the claim in the Republic's constitution that its territory rightly extended over the whole island, and the subordination of the state to the moral and social dictates of the Roman Catholic Church, and hence, among many less contentious consequences, the prohibition of divorce, abortion and birth control. These two clauses encapsulated the objections of northern Protestants to the idea of closer relations with the Republic – the fears of domination by Dublin and the Vatican. Their removal, after much anguish on the part of backwoodsmen of the Republic, made possible at last a less inhibited dialogue on a future in which material interests, and the realities of the world political and strategic scene, could play a greater part than tribal animosity.

The effervescence of 'loyalist' feeling from the end of the 1970s onwards had an effect on British opinion which led indirectly in the same direction. The IRA had failed in their attempt to drive the British out of Ulster by terrorism. But the verbal attacks of Ulstermen against the British Government, for not being prepared to make even greater sacrifices on their behalf, finally succeeded where the IRA had failed, in bringing about a mood of general disillusion on the mainland. Why, it was asked, should British lives be lost to preserve the exclusivity of an ungrateful Protestant community as bigoted as their Catholic opponents, and an international frontier which, by its very nature impossible to control, only made it more difficult to overcome terrorism?

This popular mood gave the British Government greater room for manoeuvre in pressing forward with talks and studies jointly carried out with the Government of the Republic. These had begun cautiously but by 1982–3, greatly helped by sympathetic support from the US presidency, swept on with gathering momentum to the solution of trans-frontier problems of trade and energy, and to the grant of real powers to an Anglo-Irish Council, together with the introduction of parliamentary members as participants in this body. Such terms as federalism between north and south continued to be avoided, but the essence of what was in mind was not very different, and the ultimate goal of a confederation of the Isles of the North Atlantic (for which the happy acronym IONA had already been coined), began to glimmer less faintly on the horizon. This would involve a recognition that once the bitterness of the Ulster confrontation was removed or diminished, the present common interests of Ireland and Britain could at last predominate over the hostility of the past, and a sub-system within the European Community could begin to take shape. The Netherlands and Belgium had had their moments of bitterness, and perhaps more competitive economic interests than Britain and Ireland, but this had not prevented them from seeing national interest in the formation of Benelux.

Britain and Ireland started with some advantages: they had had a common monetary unit before the pound and the punt were so unwisely allowed to diverge in 1978. Citizens of the two countries had the unique privilege of voting in each other's elections (not quite reciprocally until 1983) and they had long anticipated the EEC's enforcement of free movement of peoples by being able to travel between the two countries without passports. The main requirement for breaking the psychological barrier to confederation was that politicians on all sides should stop peppering their speeches with emotive references to the Norman Conquest, the Battle of the Boyne, 1916 and so on. The upsurge of civil disorder following on the Protestants taking to the streets in 1983 did much in the end to discredit these tired old slogans on either side. The practical needs of security on both sides of the border encouraged both governments, by mutual agreement, increasingly to disregard its existence, and when relative calm returned, the mass of the people were surprised but by no means dismayed to find that some kind of confederal union had *de facto* come to birth.

There were two incidental clues in this story to foreshadow what came next. It was Isles of the *North Atlantic* which were moving towards a Benelux type of agreement. This was not an empty geographical expression. The term North Atlantic carried unmistakable echoes of the fact that thirty-four years earlier a group of countries had come together under that very name to express in the treaty that gave birth to NATO their common interest in resisting external threat. The group extended beyond the islands of the North Atlantic ocean to include countries on its continental coasts – Belgium, Federal Germany, the Netherlands, Norway, Portugal, France (which remained bound to the Alliance even when in 1966 it left the Organization), Spain (which joined later), some countries (Greece, Italy, Turkey) which had no Atlantic coastline but shared the defensive interests of those who had, and above all, the lynchpin of the Alliance, the United States.

The need to restore internal security had now become a further powerful motive to express in concrete form the common interests, within the Atlantic Community, of IONA. It did not require a great leap of the imagination to see that external threat could easily feed on internal disorder; indeed there was good reason to think that Irish terrorists had received aid from various potentially hostile sources in addition to what they were given by misguided Irish-Americans.

An unconnected circumstance pushed coincidentally in the same direction. When the European Community at last agreed on a fisheries policy it became necessary for this to be enforced throughout the maritime economic zone surrounding Community countries and extending to 200 miles from their coasts. The prospective admission into the Community of Spain and Portugal with their activity and expertise in distant deep-sea fishing reinforced the requirement. A glance at the map is enough to show that a very large area of this common maritime zone in the Atlantic is defined by reference to the coast of Ireland and can most easily be supervised by vessels and aircraft operating from its territory. It was equally clear that Irish military resources were inadequte to meet this requirement, and, with some nationalistic misgiving, it became necessary to accept that the ships and aircraft of other Community countries should help to police the operational area, and should in some cases be stationed on Irish territory. All this helped to break down the historical Irish reservation about becoming involved in a common effort for defence. The extension of political co-operation in the European Community from foreign policy to security policy, begun under the British presidency in 1981, had accustomed Irish representatives to taking part in discussion of matters relating closely to the Atlantic Alliance, and enabled them to learn what the others knew about the Soviet military build-up, and the increasingly dangerous situation arising from Soviet opportunism round the world and from the deepening concern of Soviet leaders facing rebellious subjects in Eastern Europe.

All these strands seemed to lead almost insensibly towards the goal so long desired by Western strategic planners: Ireland's recognition that it is of, and not only in, the West, and that some practical consequences could now be drawn from this recognition. To begin with there was no need even for formal alliance. It was enough to agree that the forces of friendly countries participating in the policing of the maritime zone should be authorized to take such steps as were necessary to protect themselves and their shore installations against any possible threat. Then, as the international situation deteriorated and the risk of hostilities grew more acute, the fishery protection ships could be replaced by anti-submarine naval vessels and maritime reconnaissance aircraft augmented by such further air support as was necessary.

For an account, from a rather different angle and from an Irish pen, of how events moved in the last few years before the war we are privileged to reprint here an article entitled 'The Irish Dimension' from the all too short-lived literary and historical periodical *The Wexford Pirate* (its first and last edition, in fact) published in June 1986.

_____

It has been said that in Ireland what is self-evident has quite often in the past been stubbornly denied if politics, prejudice or the faith found it inconvenient. Irish insistence on neutrality furnished a case in point. Its futility had long been clear. It was only the problem of the north which, under all three of these counts, had prevented general acknowledgement in the Republic of something so obvious to the world outside.

After the establishment of the Anglo-Irish Inter-Governmental Council in 1981, and a series of firm but friendly interventions by the US Administration, the regular semi-private meetings between the Irish Taoiseach and the British Prime Minister became more important, even if they also sometimes became less bland.

One such meeting in 1983 was billed in the press as having touched on two subjects almost always avoided, the so-called 'British army of occupation', and 'the possibilities of eventual confederation'.

The two leaders did not find themselves all that far apart. The *Times-Guardian* reported on the first subject:

The Taoiseach said that British soldiers in Ulster, though carrying out a well-nigh impossible job with great courage and such tact as they could muster, were regarded as an army of occupation even by moderate Catholics who ought to know better. That is to say, youngsters threw stones at British soldiers in the belief that they were thereby 'demonstrating for Ireland', whatever was meant by that, and unfortunately even middle-class Catholic fathers did not disabuse them.

The troops' presence was preventing a Catholic massacre. Their task' would be easier, however, if they were not operating under the flag of Britain, a country against which old Catholic animosities continued to smoulder and were all too easily fanned into flame.

According to the report, the British Prime Minister said that she warmly agreed. Although the task could hardly be handed to United Nations peacekeeping forces (the parading of Indian or Nigerian troops down the Falls Road might cause more problems than it solved), it would be most welcome if this dangerous, thankless and costly job could eventually pass to NATO or EEC forces, including, after an interval, even some Irish troops. But this would be easier if Ireland had some association with NATO, and if NATO could come to regard 'this fight of all free Irishmen, against Soviet-armed and communist-financed murderers', as, if not actually something of a NATO obligation, at least as a matter of pressing interest to NATO.

The Taoiseach was reported to have said that he took at least the first of these points, and intended to do something about it.

Shortly afterwards an arrangement was arrived at which neatly sidestepped public repugnance in Eire at official alliance with Britain, by the use of Ireland's ancient connection with another traditional enemy of England – France. A bilateral defence agreement was made between the Irish and French republics, under the benevolent gaze of NATO, which provided for the stationing of Irish troops overseas, in the joint defensive interests of both, under French command. Poets heard the beating of the wings of wild geese in the night. The ghost of Maréchal McMahon smiled, and many another. An Irish Brigade would serve with the French again, as others had served three centuries ago.

The Federal Republic positively welcomed the location of an Irish contingent in southern Germany, provided someone else accepted the stationing costs. Eire itself could not – that was obvious. In the event, as might have been expected, the United States picked up the tab, and in the spring of 1984 an Irish brigade group moved into hastily erected but good barrack accommodation, under command of II French Corps, in the neighbourhood of Trier.

It consisted of a brigade group headquarters and three mobile battalions, a field artillery regiment, an anti-aircraft artillery regiment and reconnaissance squadron, with engineer, ordnance and supply companies, all in a highly satisfactory state of training. Its commander was a promising young one-star general with considerable experience in UN peacekeeping, supported by a hand-picked staff, many of whom (like the commander) had the advantage of professional training in British defence establishments. For, of course, however far apart the Irish Government felt obliged to keep from Britain, out of deference to the deeply rooted animosities of earlier generations and to Irish-American opinion, in which long out-dated attitudes still thrived, Irish defence leant quite heavily on British support, freely given with an unostentatious friendliness which made it doubly welcome. There also now duly appeared in Supreme Headquarters Allied Powers Europe a modest Irish increment to the considerable liaison staff maintained there under a major-general by the French, non-membership of NATO notwithstanding. The whole arrangement was one which suited everybody who faced the facts of life in Eire's relations with the outer world as they really were, and not as they were imagined to be.

Irish neutrality in a major East-West conflict, however loudly trumpeted by successive Taoiseachs, had never in fact been a starter. Eamonn de Valera had once roundly declared that the defence of the British Isles was one. It was abundantly clear at the turn of the 1970s that the only way to avoid the direct involvement of Ireland in a world war, given that island's geographical position, would be to tow it away and anchor it somewhere else.

Even before the London *New Statesman* disclosed in early 1981 that critical installations and other facilities in the Republic had almost certainly been targeted for attack by both sides it was perfectly clear that they would play a very important part in a war between the Atlantic Alliance and the Warsaw Pact.

The use of Shannon and west coast sites was vital for maritime operations in the Atlantic; availability of the Irish airfields and ports was essential for the successful operation of the Atlantic 'air bridge' reinforcement operations into France and Britain for the European front; and the deployment of mobile radar and other surveillance systems would give much needed depth to NATO's air defence against Soviet attack, by sea or air, from the West.

To be quite blunt about it, if these facilities were not used by consent they would be seized. Otherwise they would be destroyed, if not by one side then by the other, to deny their use to the enemy. Sir John Junor, one of the most honest and outspoken commentators in the journalism of these offshore islands, made no bones about it. 'In an East-West war,' he wrote in London's *Sunday Express* in June 1983, 'a declaration of Irish neutrality would afford about as much protection as a fig leaf in Antarctica.'

On the second subject, the future association of component parts of the British Isles, the *Times-Guardian* reported:

The two prime ministers agreed that the ideal eventual solution would be a confederation or federation of Ireland, maybe indeed eventually leading to some confederation of all territories in the British Isles.

The Taoiseach said he had taken great political risks to make this more readily attainable. Ireland's constitution had been changed so that it was now a secular instead of a Catholic state. Divorce, contraception, abortion, secular education and dual citizenship in provinces that became in any way integrated into an Irish confederation or federation were all now accepted.

Could not the British Prime Minister for her part now take some political risks also? He recognised that she could not formally break her promise that there would be no change in Northern Ireland's status until a majority in the north agreed. But could she not take the line that those who stirred up hatred against the Catholics in the north were breaking the law under British race-discrimination legislation? And could not British political parties start indicating their support for moderate candidates in Ulster parliamentary elections?

If there could be one breakthrough whereby any constituency in the north elected a reasonable person ready to consider confederation, instead of always electing either Protestant bigots or rabid Republicans, people who longed for peace could start to hope.

The British Prime Minister agreed with the Taoiseach's views on general lines, but said direct intervention by herself would only be counter-productive. If she indicated support for a moderate candidate in any election, both sects of the Northern Irish would swing all the more violently to their usual support of the most extreme candidate available.

Some day special circumstances might arise in some election, and she would seize the chance to try to get other politicians in other British parties to act responsibly with her on the moderates' side. She had already turned her back on any coalition with the extreme Ulster Unionists in the British parliament, although Callaghan when in office, and Foot in opposition, had behaved badly about this. She would look for an opportunity to do more.

The opportunity arose because of the Christmas shopping bombs in 1983, and because of the emergence of that most unexpected of all Irish folk heroes, the 24-year-old Patrick McBride.

In early December of 1983, a bomb exploded amid shopping crowds in London's Oxford Street, killing eighty-three people, including a store Santa Claus and seventeen handicapped children who were queuing to get free presents from him. The so-called Irish National Liberation Army (INLA), claiming 'responsibility' for these hideous crimes, declared that this was a justified attack upon a double military objective. The stores group had as a non-executive part-time member of its board a former General Officer Commanding in Northern Ireland and the INLA had understood (wrongly, as had to be admitted later) that the Santa Claus was a retired regimental sergeant major from the Irish Guards. Two days later bombs exploded in a shopping centre in Dublin, killing thirty-two. A Protestant para-military group called the 'Battlers of the Boyne' said that loyalist Ulster was striking back in the heartland of popery. Several more bombs went off in both Protestant and Catholic pubs in Northern Ireland, and, with appalling results, five in separate sectarian schools.

The British Special Branch took a keen interest in certain unusual features of the Oxford Street and Dublin bombs, although the Belfast ones were of the usual home-grown sort made in local factories, against which London and Dublin had by now rather sophisticated detection devices. The usual leakiness of Irish terrorist sources in London enabled the Special Branch to catch those who planted the Oxford Street bomb fairly early, and some interesting developments followed. Police in Eire and the Province carried out dawn raids on the headquarters of several extreme Catholic and Unionist groups. Communiqués that evening explained why.

The materials for the Oxford Street bomb had been picked up by those who had planted it from a rendezvous in London, where they had been cached by a group of German students now known to be members of the reconstituted Baader-Meinhof gang. The materials for the Dublin bombs were similar, but had apparently been brought in from Italy by a party from the still very active Red Brigades. Raids on the extremist Catholic and Protestant political groups had produced clear evidence that people in each of those headquarters knew what was happening, and had in fact drawn a good deal of personal money as well as weapons and explosives from sources known to enjoy Soviet support. 'Although most people in each group thought they were fighting each other,' ran the joint communiqué from the British and Irish heads of government, 'these outrages have been financed and organized by agencies very close to the Soviet Union, clearly with interests other than those of Ireland in mind.'

Nobody could with certainty define which Catholic and Protestant extremists had been paid traitors to the West, and which had been merely megalomaniac nationalists, but fairly strong fingers of suspicion were pointed at two people who happened to be in the news at this time. A parliamentary by-election was pending in the marginal (for Northern Ireland) constituency of mid-Ulster, and a lady Catholic extremist and a gaunt, outrageous Protestant demagogue were already the main candidates in the field. Up to now it had been assumed that these two malign people would share 90 per cent of mid-Ulster's votes. The central parties (the Moderate Catholic, Non-Sectarian Alliance and so on) by now usually put up a joint candidate, but he or she rarely polled more than 10 per cent. After the killing of those seventeen handicapped children, the centrist parties hoped they might get more than 10 per cent of the vote in mid-Ulster, provided the right candidate for them could somehow be found.

He emerged in the most dramatic way at 4 pm the next Saturday afternoon, with bloodstained headband and three broken ribs, pounding down through the middle of the Twickenham Rugby Union football ground, with every Irish televiewer north or south cheering him along at every step.

Diminishing shamateurism and increasing sponsorship had brought it about that this winter saw the first Rugby Union World Cup, with teams from all four home countries of the British Isles and all the old dominions, plus France, Argentina, the United States, Romania and the Netherlands. From the top half of the draw the runaway entrants to the final were the powerful All Blacks of New Zealand; from the bottom half a green surprise packet from Ireland, made up, as always, of players from any part of the island, north and south.

With injury time already started in the final half, New Zealand led 28–23, and their ferocious forwards pressed once more on the Irish line. Ireland's gentle giant redhead Pat McBride, lock forward and captain and fiftyfold hero already that day, fell yet again upon the ball. He emerged from the scrummage with forehead bleeding, kicking for touch. A brief bandaging. 'Feet Ireland' from the line out. A loose maul. A heel and a Garry Owen forward punt. The New Zealand full-back fielded it just inside his 22-metre line, sidestepped the onrushing Irish forwards to his left, and went to kick to the right as Pat McBride, and he alone, had anticipated. The New Zealander's boot, the ball, and the front of Pat McBride's ample torso occupied the same space at the same instant, with a sickeningly audible cracking of McBride's ribs. But the ball was clutched to that green jersey regardless. McBride was past the full-back now, loping with dragging right foot the last 20 metres to the line like a wounded hare. Before two million television sets from Cork to Belfast all Ireland rose to its feet as he dived (no, actually flew)* the last eight metres to land between the posts. The conversion was a formality and Ireland had won the World Cup 29–28.

At the many TV interviews afterwards McBride developed a fine strain of Irish blarney, which was just what his country needed at this moment of shopping-centre tragedy and showplace triumph. As the winning team had been half from his north and half from the south, and 'one-third Catholic, one-third Protestant, one-third heathen, all in old Ireland's green', McBride said that he himself felt Northern Irish nationalism for one day a year only, which was when he rallied

---

* A small group in the County Donegal who averred that they had actually seen McBride in flight, and sought an opinion from the parish priest as to whether this miraculous occurrence did not merit consideration for canonization, were quite properly sent up Croagh Patrick, on their knees, for their pains.

his club side in Ballymena for the annual match against Sean O'Driscoll's Cork. After that match, when it was in Belfast, he preferred to drink in Sean's brother's pub in Andersonstown rather than bomb it. As for those who blew up schools in the name of the Christian religion, in any of its forms, 'or those who for one instant give any votes or sympathy or shelter or offer weasel words of partial excuse for any of these child murderers, whether from UDA or IRA or anyone else, my whole team would like to have each one of them for two, or better three, minutes under an All Black scrum' (here the team burst into applause behind him) 'and for that scrum I would nominate . . .' (here he named the toughest eggs from the tournament, including three from Australia, a Welshman and an Afrikaner who had been sent off during it). 'Ireland means this,' declared Mc-Bride, holding aloft the World Cup, 'it does not mean the bombers.'

There were some nasty funerals after that month's bombings, including one where the IRA declared a military burial for a thirteen-year-old who had belonged to one of their brigades. The boy's parents declared that they wanted no such thing, and wished the 'antagonisms between our neighbouring communities to be buried with our poor Michael'. As the saintly local priest invited some notables from the Protestant community to come to the funeral, there was likely to be a trial of strength. The TV cameras gathered like jackals.

The cameras showed that Pat McBride, still hobbling on a stick, was one of the party with the parents; so were some other members from the victorious national team, for the father was connected with a local rugby club. At the graveyard six masked IRA men appeared as if from nowhere, and raised rifles to fire a salute. Pat McBride hobbled over to the nearest gunman, struck his hand with his stick and caused him to drop the rifle, which later proved to be loaded only with blanks. The other rugby players disarmed and unmasked the other five gunmen. The unmasked gunman wriggling in McBride's huge hand was held before the TV cameras. He was a frightened teenage boy. McBride gently kicked his backside and said 'now take your beastly mania away'. In TV interviews afterwards McBride launched his main attack not on 'these posturing but actually unarmed children'. He said the most disgusting news of the day was a speech against all Catholics by the Protestant extremist at the mid-Ulster by-election.

The next day McBride was asked to stand as the centrist candidate at mid-Ulster. He accepted, and said he would call himself a candidate for 'confederacy'. During his campaign he was supported by the British Prime Minister and the leader of the other three mainland British parties, and also by the three main parties in the Republic of

Ireland. Unprecedentedly, he received a telegram of support from the Moderator of the Church of Scotland, and then on the last day another from the Pope.

It would be splendid to be able to report that McBride therefore won the seat. Because this was Northern Ireland he came merely second, 2 per cent behind the Protestant extremist and 8 per cent in front of the Catholic lady, who made a rather good speech in defeat. 'If there were a proportional, transferable or alternative voting system,' she said, 'all my supporters would have switched on second ballot to Pat McBride, who is a Protestant we respect. We should then have had an MP here who was liked by most of the people, instead of this Paisleyite who is detested by 63 per cent of them.'

This was significant. Way back in 1973 the Ulster Assembly that led to the brief Sunningdale agreement on power-sharing was elected under a system of transferable voting. It has been agreed that the new and long delayed constitutional assembly in Northern Ireland will also be elected under this system.

In 1987 public opinion polls suggest that in Northern Ireland the centrist parties (including the Confederate Party) hold a sufficient block of votes in the majority of constituencies to force the counting of the second votes. If that happens, nearly all the second votes will go to the centrist parties, and there is now a real prospect that the elected majority in Northern Ireland will vote in 1988 to get Britain off the hook of its 1973 declaration that there can be no change in Northern Ireland's constitutional status unless a majority of its inhabitants concur. A majority of its elected representatives will probably vote for a confederate Ireland.

This is a far more peaceful outcome in Ulster than appeared conceivable even as late as 1982. It is not uncharacteristic that as the world seemed threatened by incineration through thermonuclear war Ireland was moving at last towards internal peace.

———

We must now leave the thoughtful and lively prose of the sadly defunct *Pirate* and pass on to consideration of the impact of Irish belligerence, deepening in successive stages of association with other allies, including the United Kingdom, upon the war in the air and at sea which erupted in August 1985.

It had to be acknowledged that the happy outcome of Ireland's afflictions had not, by the spring of 1985, been perceived in Whitehall as so certain as to justify rejoicing; but it was decided, in a spirit of optimism, to develop plans for utilizing to the best advantage the air bases and harbours which might in consequence become available.

Even so, there were those who believed, as a letter to the *Times-Guardian* of 28 December 1984 pointed out, that 'simply redrawing the existing border so as to make the Irish Republic conterminous with the island of Ireland will just exchange a situation in which up to half a million people feel that they are in the wrong country for one in which at least double that number feel so'.

Ever since the formation of the Atlantic Alliance it had been possible to count upon the use of naval and air bases in Northern Ireland, and the readiness of the people there to support the British war effort, despite the existence of Republican sentiment in some parts of the Catholic community. These bases were of vital importance. First of all, without them it would be much more difficult to safeguard the approaches to the Clyde submarine base. It was in these waters that Soviet electronic surveillance vessels, taking advantage of Britain's retention of a three-mile limit of territorial waters, had persistently maintained watch over the comings and goings of both the British and the American ballistic missile and fleet submarines. From time to time, also, intrusive submarines, known not to be Allied, had been detected in the Clyde approaches. In times of international tension, or if war should break out, intensive operations using Northern Irish bases would be required. Secondly, the already daunting task of safeguarding shipping in the North Atlantic would be rendered even more so by the loss of these bases, especially the airfields. Hence the Defence Staff insisted that any all-Ireland constitutional agreement must include the retention of NATO's use of the Northern Ireland bases as required.

As to Eire, it was ideally placed to command the Western Approaches to the Channel, and to strengthen the defence of shipping in the Eastern Atlantic. But its naval and air forces consisted of six patrol vessels, only two of which had helicopters, and a dozen or so light aircraft; there was no military infrastructure capable of handling even the most elementary naval/air operations; and there were no coastal surveillance radars, let alone gun or missile defences. Nor was there any reserve of trained people to man operations rooms, communications networks, or even look-out stations. Fortunately advantage could be taken of the universality of air traffic control procedures, and the wide range of facilities at an international airport, to make operational use of Shannon immediately war broke out. Plans were made, also, to include the whole of Ireland and its territorial waters in the 'extended air-sea defence zone' under the newly-established Joint Allied Command Western Approaches (JACWA). Its Commander-in-Chief was British, equal in status with the Supreme Allied Commanders Europe and Atlantic (both American), and his area of responsibility incorporated Channel Command, and that part of the Eastern Atlantic which fell within the UK air defence zone and included all waters over the Continental Shelf.

Following the Franco-Irish special entente in 1983 the Ministry of Defence in Paris sought Dublin's agreement to the occasional deployment of one or two maritime patrol aircraft of the *Aeronavale* (French Naval Air Arm) to Shannon to facilitate their operation in peacetime out in the Atlantic. The twin-engined *Atlantique* was a very capable and well-tried aircraft and the latest version (*Atlantique Nouvelle Generation*, or ANG) with which the *Flotilles* at Lann-Bihouie in Brittany were now equipped was an excellent anti-submarine aircraft which also had a limited anti-ship capability. But compared with its four-engined counterparts (the US Navy's *Orion* and the RAF *Nimrod*) it was just a little short on range and endurance. The lengthening of its sea-legs by working from the west of Ireland would enhance its use in many of its peacetime tasks and, although this was not the basis of the French request, it would be a real 'force multiplier' in war.

Irish agreement was gracefully forthcoming provided that advance notice was given (save of course in emergency) and an agreed quota of visits per year was not exceeded. To these stipulations France readily agreed and a system of liaison officers and communications teams was established with Ireland as it had been for several years with the United Kingdom.

The Soviet naval staff were keenly aware of the strategic importance of Eire in any future battle in the Atlantic. Soviet policy was directed urgently to the denial to NATO of the use of air and naval bases there, and of the use of Irish ports and tanker terminals for trans-shipment. It was too much to hope, perhaps, that Irish bases could be made available to Soviet forces, but as a long-term aim it was borne in mind.

It was not the Naval Correspondent of *The Times*, but merely 'Our Correspondent in Dublin', who reported on 12 December 1981 'an application from the Russian airline Aeroflot to operate regular passenger services into Shannon . . . Last year the airport authority built a special fuel depot to enable Russian and other Eastern European airlines to refuel there. Russian tankers deliver the oil directly to Shannon . . . The inauguration of an Aeroflot service would be welcomed by the IRA which has won consistent moral support from the Russians for their terrorist campaign in Northern Ireland.' It was therefore with considerable chagrin that the Soviet naval planners learned of the sequence of events by which the Republic of Ireland gradually became committed to a degree of support for the NATO cause. But, as the strength of the Soviet Navy and its Air Force increased, and the prospect of breaking down the Atlantic 'air bridge' improved accordingly, the neutralization of Ireland by military means became part of Soviet war plans.

These plans had not, however, fully matured when the Soviet aircraft carrier *Kiev*, escorted by two *Krivak*-class frigates, arrived in Cork on 27 July 1985. The group was said to be on a training cruise which would take it to West Africa and Cuba. It had, of course, been tracked by NATO surveillance forces since leaving its home waters in Murmansk and in the normal course of events it would have remained under routine surveillance as it resumed its way south-west on 2 August. For various reasons, however, contact with the *Kiev* group was lost during the night of 3 August.

Early on 5 August, JACWA received a garbled and delayed report of a very large oil tanker damaged and on fire in Bantry Bay. She had struck a mine. Later that day reports came in of an Irish patrol vessel sunk off Cork, the Fishguard to Rosslare ferry sunk near Wexford, and a Dutch coaster sunk in the approaches to Dublin.

Not until after the war was it learned that while the Soviet aircraft carrier and her escorts had been visiting Cork a comprehensive mine-laying operation was being carried out by six Soviet *Foxtrot*-class (conventional) submarines. They laid delayed-action mines off Lough Swilly, Bantry Bay, Cork, Wexford, Dublin and Milford Haven, which sank five ships. Only Milford Haven was cleared of mines before a casualty occurred. The shortage of mine counter-measure vessels at JACWA's disposal resulted in the majority of Britain's western ports being closed to shipping for several days at a most critical time. Only one of the Soviet *Foxtrots* was sunk, No. 132, which attempted to withdraw through the North Channel after laying mines off Dublin. Her snort mast was detected by a surveillance radar very recently mounted on the Mull of Kintyre, and *Sea King* helicopters from Prestwick were actually in sonar contact with the *Foxtrot* when they received orders, early on 4 August, to commence hostilities against the Soviet Union. It was particularly heartening to the helicopter squadron that the first attack with the new *Stingray* torpedoes was successful.

Given the excellent liaison already established at Shannon between the French naval airmen and the Irish airport authorities, the arrival there on 4 August, within hours of the outbreak of war in Europe, of four ANG caused little stir. Nor did the landing, shortly afterwards, of a US Navy *Orion*. This aircraft had been following up a submarine contact some 100 miles south of Cape Farewell, which had been obtained by a Canadian frigate using a towed array passive sonar. Unfortunately the scent had gone cold, and the aircraft was ordered into Shannon, to operate under the Commander, Maritime Air, Eastern Atlantic.

On the morning of 5 August the *Orion* and two ANG were allotted tasks that took them far out into the Atlantic. Amidst the excitement of that day's news this did not attract much attention. But what did cause a loud buzz of rumour and speculation in the Shannon communications centre and control tower was when, at 1722 hours, a distinctly French voice came over the loudspeakers monitoring the international distress frequency: 'MAYDAY MAYDAY MAYDAY' it called, 'THIS IS SIERRA QUEBEC BRAVO CHARLIE WE ARE BEING ATTACKED BY FIGHTERS LATITUDE 52.12 NORTH LONGITUDE . . .'

Here, as in many places all over Europe, the outbreak of war was signified not by any dramatic public announcement like Chamberlain's address to the British people forty-six years earlier, but by a series of swift and violent encounters.

In this instance, the response was immediate and well orchestrated for the Mayday signal could mean only one thing: a *Kiev*-class carrier was out to the west and it must be found and sunk before it did any more damage. The two remaining ANG at Shannon and two *Nimrods* from an RAF base in Cornwall were launched on a search within half an hour. As the ANG climbed out on their search tracks the crews could see smoke rising from the refinery and the main hangars at Shannon and guessed correctly that a salvo of air-launched missiles, probably from a *Backfire*, had found their mark.

The search area was very large because of the missing and all-important longitude figure, but a fast westbound merchant ship broke wireless silence to report sighting a *Forger* aircraft on the horizon and this clue shrank the area of probability dramatically. With a new datum to work from, dawn was breaking when a *Nimrod* picked up the *Kiev* and its escorts on its radar.

At JACWA headquarters the operations staff were looking disconsolately at their meagre forces for attacking the enemy group. The specialized anti-shipping *Buccaneers* that had survived a raid on Murmansk the day before were being held at Bodö, Norway, to guard against Soviet naval incursions along that coast and they could muster only two or three aircraft from the UK. These would need in-flight fuelling and a fighter escort against the carrier. It could hardly be called a balanced force. But help came unexpectedly in the shape of fourteen *Marineflieger* (Federal German Naval Air Force) *Tornados* which arrived at Kinloss air base in Scotland as the planners were puzzling over the problem. This force, thanks to the decisiveness of its commander, Captain Manfred Steinhof, had got away from Nordholz in Schleswig-Holstein under the very noses of the advancing Soviets.

By 0900 hours, and after the French Ministry of Defence had got Irish agreement for the *Marineflieger* aircraft to refuel at Shannon despite the previous day's damage, eight of the *Tornados* landed and refuelled. They were in the air again in half an hour to join their fighter escort of RAF *Tornados* backed up by a VC-10 tanker. A United States Navy *Orion* had by then taken over the shadowing of the *Kiev* force on its radar and it homed the *Tornados* in for the attack. The carrier was holed with her steering disabled and one of her escorts badly damaged as the force withdrew and the submarine *Splendid* arrived on the scene to despatch the stricken ships. Three *Tornados* were lost, one to a *Forger* and the others to missiles from the escorts. Manfred Steinhof's aircraft ran out of fuel short of the Irish coast but he and his navigator were picked up by a fishing boat.

The Third World War had broken out thirty-seven hours earlier, and this was just one action in the great tide of war that was engulfing Europe.

WAR

Chapter 11

The Central Front

The contingency plan formulated by the Defence Council of the Politburo for the defence of the Soviet Union and its socialist allies against the aggressive designs of Western capitalism had two supreme aims: to cause the collapse of the Atlantic Alliance and to bring about the neutralization of neo-Nazi Germany. The second would lead to the first. The dismantling of the Federal Republic must, therefore, receive primary and very close attention.

To the Chief of the Soviet General Staff, Marshal P. K. Ogurtsov, an old cavalry soldier brought up in his profession in the 1930s to the use, incredible though it sounds today, of the sword as a weapon from the back of a horse (as, incidentally, was the main author of this book), the analogy was simple. Federal Germany was the point of the sword presented at the enemy; the outstretched right arm ('at cavalry, engage – point!') was Allied Command Europe; the hilt, which would come up against the victim's body with extreme violence once the point was through, was NATO; the rider on the horse's back, swinging forward with the thrusting, outstretched sword, planning, placing and timing the thrust, was the United States; the galloping horse giving the chief strength and impetus to the hilt, which, directed by the rider's swinging body and extended arm, would hammer the pierced enemy out of his saddle, was Western capitalism. Reflecting by the stove in his dacha, the vodka bottle handy, the Marshal always admired the aptness of his analogy, only regretting that no one understood it any more. What had once been cavalry, riding horses and wielding *l'arme blanche*, had been suffocating in stinking tanks for nearly half a century.

The destruction of Federal Germany would mean the collapse of the Atlantic Alliance, the total demoralization of Europe, the withdrawal of the USA across the sea and swiftly widening opportunities for the spread of socialism throughout the world. The importance of the FRG was such, however, that an attack upon it would be no less than a total attack on NATO and would be resisted as such. It would have to be planned accordingly.

The initial assault had to be massive. To carry out the intentions of the Defence Council, ten fronts would be activated, two in the GDR, one each in Czechoslovakia, Hungary, Romania, Bulgaria and the far north, all in the front line, with follow-up fronts in the Leningrad Military District, in Poland and in the Ukraine, while in Belorussia and the Ukraine there would be also two groups of tank armies comprising three tank armies each, making six tank armies to exploit success in the centre, or to be used otherwise as circumstances dictated. The initial assault at dawn on 4 August, following action in space to restrict surveillance, undercover operations to frustrate command and support, deep air bombardment in Europe to interdict forward movement of war material and reserves, and action at sea to begin the interruption of maritime reinforcement, would open with the utmost violence along the whole Warsaw Pact-NATO interface, from Norway to Turkey.

Since the Central Region of Allied Command Europe (ACE), against which three fronts threatened, with a fourth standing by in Poland, was to be the focal point of this immense operation, it is upon the Central Front that we now concentrate. In our earlier book, *The Third World War: August 1985*, published in the spring of 1987, we described at length and in some detail the course of the main operation in this theatre and other accounts have appeared in other places. We do not intend here to recapitulate all that has been written. It is upon more personal aspects of these events that we shall focus instead, sometimes at very close range.

———

No plans for a major land offensive in modern war can ever be followed for very long after the offensive opens. The plans are made as part of a long-term concept. They embrace the object of the operations as a whole; the dispositions and movements of the enemy as they are known at the time; the probable reactions of the enemy's commanders; and, perhaps most important of all, the estimate of what will be necessary for logistic support. Preparations for this demand forethought and imagination. They must be made far in advance and have to cover a period much longer than that during which the original operational plan of attack can continue to be followed. The operational plan may at any time have to be radically altered in a matter of days, or even hours, as commanders respond to the requirements of a developing situation. Logistic support, involving the movement and positioning of huge tonnages of material of all kinds, from bridging equipment to missile and gun ammunition, from fuel and food to medical supplies, cannot be as

NORTH SEA
NETHERLANDS
Amsterdam
Rhine
Waal
Nijmegen
Maas
Venlo
Krefeld
Brüggen
Geilenkirchen
Wildenrath
Brussels
Maastricht
BELGIUM
Aachen
Jülich
Maisières
Meuse
Bremen
FEDERAL
NIEDERSACHSEN
TEUTOBURGER WALD
Weser
Minden
Hanover
Münster
REPUBLIC
HARZ MOUNTAINS
Gütersloh
Wesel
Lippe
Duisberg
Dortmund
Düsseldorf
Neuss
OF
Kassel
Fulda
Cologne
Bonn
Nörvenich
GERMANY
Rhine
Mosel
Finthen
Würzburg
Trier
LUXEMBOURG
Mannheim
Ramstein
FRANCE
Metz
Karlsruhe
Stuttgart
0 Miles 100
0 Kilometres 100
ARCTIC OCEA
Andöya
Tromsö
Bardufoss
TROMS
Evenes
Narvik
Mörsvik
NORWEGIAN SEA
Bodö
NORD-TRÖNDELAG
SWEDEN
Umeaa
Vaernes
Kristiansund
Örland
Trondheim
The Faeroes
Bothnia
Sundsvall
NORWAY
Bergen
Flesland
ATLANTIC OCEAN
Shetland
Oslo
Kolsass
Uppsala
Västeraas
Aaland
Rygge
Stockholm
Orkney
Kragerö
Stavanger
Sola
Hiiumaa
NORTH SEA
Saaremaa
Lista
Hebrides
Skagerrak
Kattegat
Göteborg
Kinloss
Lossiemouth
JUTLAND
Frederikshavn
Aalborg
Gotland
Kalmar
Öland
MULL OF KINTYRE
Karup
Aarhus
Kallinge
BALTIC
Firth of Clyde
Edinburgh
DENMARK
Karlskrona
Lough Swilly
North Channel
Copenhagen
SEA
Ballykelly
Prestwick
FYN
ZEALAND
Bornholm
LITHU
Belfast
UNITED KINGDOM
LOLLAND
FALSTER
Kiel Canal
Kiel
Gdynia
Clare Island
Clew Bay
Irish Sea
SCHLESWIG-HOLSTEIN
Rostok
Peenemünde
Gdansk
Dublin
Elbe
Hamburg
Wista
EIRE
Liverpool
GERMAN
Shannon
Upper Heyford
NETHERLANDS
FED.
Warta
Bydgoszcz
Wexford
Birmingham
Marham
Amsterdam
Berlin
POLAND
Rosslare
Oder
Frankfurt-an-der-Oder
Cork
Fishguard
Malvern
Cottesmore
Magdeburg
Warsaw
Bantry Bay
Milford Haven
Cardiff
Northwood
REP. OF
Poznan
Brize Norton
DEM. REP.
Bristol
London
Rhine
Leipzig
Southampton
Calais
Brussels
THÜRINGER WALD
Dresden
Wroclaw
Boulogne
BELGIUM
Bonn
English Channel
Cassel
Bamberg
Cheb
Prague
Dieppe
Krakow
Nuremberg
Channel Islands
See inset map for this area
Paris
GERMANY
CZECHOSLOVAKIA
Brest
Augsberg
Neuburg
Vienna
Munich
Linz
Danube
Budapest
Lann-Bihouie
Bern
AUSTRIA
HUNGARY
FRANCE
SWITZERLAND
ITALY
Bay of Biscay
0 Miles 200
0 Kilometres 300
Belgrade
ADRIATIC SEA
YUGOSLAVIA

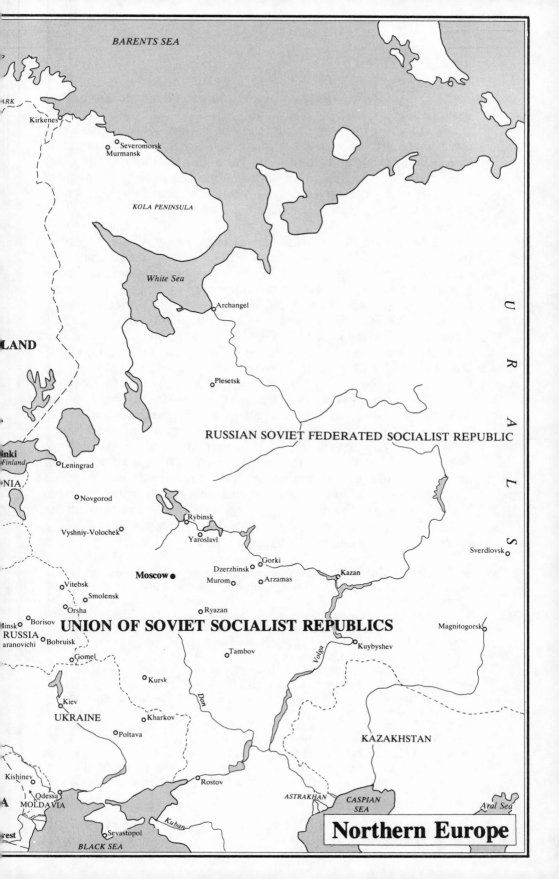

BARENTS SEA

Kirkenes

Severomorsk
Murmansk

KOLA PENINSULA

White Sea

Archangel

LAND

Plesetsk

U
R
A
L
S

RUSSIAN SOVIET FEDERATED SOCIALIST REPUBLIC

inki
Finland
NIA

Leningrad

Novgorod

Vyshniy-Volochek

Rybinsk

Yaroslavl

Sverdlovsk

Moscow

Gorki

Dzerzhinsk

Kazan

Murom

Arzamas

Vitebsk

Smolensk

Orsha

Ryazan

Magnitogorsk

insk

Borisov

UNION OF SOVIET SOCIALIST REPUBLICS

RUSSIA

aranovichi

Bobruisk

Volga

Kuybyshev

Gomel

Tambov

Kursk

Don

Kiev

UKRAINE

Kharkov

Poltava

KAZAKHSTAN

Kishinev

Rostov

A

Odessa
MOLDAVIA

ASTRAKHAN

CASPIAN
SEA

Aral Sea

rest

Sevastopol

Kuban

BLACK SEA

Northern Europe

easily adjusted as the fighting formations can be moved around the battlefields.

Soviet logistic planning was on the whole sound. It recognized that some unforeseen movement of divisions, or even armies, would be forced upon the High Command as the action developed, and made preparations accordingly. Notwithstanding the rigidity of much of Soviet planning, the movement of formations, as the flow of the battle dictated it, was carried out on the whole successfully in spite of Allied air interdiction, and the logistics proved generally adequate.

One formation directly affected by regrouping, as the pattern of the battle changed, was 197 Motor Rifle Division. It had come into the forward area as part of 28 Army, whose headquarters had been located in Belorussia in peacetime but whose main fighting strength and equipment was always held in the Group of Soviet Forces in Germany (GSFG). The outbreak of hostilities on 4 August found 28 Army to the south-east of 1 Guards Tank Army which had just moved forward westwards from near Dresden. On 5 August, 197 Division was transferred from 28 Army to come under command of 8 Guards Army, operating west of Leipzig, involving a move for the division in a north-westerly direction of about 100 kilometres. This was almost completed on the night of 5/6 August, relatively little hindered by the movement westwards of rear echelons of 1 Guards Tank Army, now heavily engaged further forward. To keep routes open for 197 required some radical measures on the part of KGB troops none the less. It was fortunate that the traffic blocks which sometimes took an hour or more to clear received no attention from NATO air forces. The movement of 197 was completed early on the night 6/7 August, the division being due to move forward into the battle on the morning of the following day, 7 August.

❛The 197 Motor Rifle Division was warming up to go into action. There was the continuous roar of a thousand motors, as tanks, armoured personnel carriers (BTR), infantry combat vehicles (BMP) and self-propelled weapons lumbered in long columns out of woodlands in the early mist of an August morning on to German country roads, where the upland hills of the Harz softened down into the plains. The division was pushing towards the forward edge of the battle area, 25 kilometres away.

The 13 Guards Motor Rifle Division had been pressing against British formations there for three days, but with few gains. It was exhausted. Now, at last, in the dim light of dawn, there seemed to be the chance that a fresh division would be brought up into their sector. The battle-worn soldiers of 13 Guards Division might soon be taken back to the rear, fed there and allowed to get some sleep. The fire power of hundreds of guns and scores of multiple rocket launchers firing salvoes of heavy rockets would cover the approach of the fresh division. Both 13 Guards Division and the new division's own artillery, manoeuvred into firing positions during the night, would take part in the artillery programme. In addition, the commander of 8 Guards Army had allotted his own army artillery brigade as further support for the deployment of the new division, bringing in an extra ninety 130 mm self-propelled (SP) guns.

A sudden salvo at 0700 hours from the two BM-27 battalions and the eight regimental batteries of multiple rockets started off the artillery programme. Over 1,000 shells, many of them chemical, suddenly burst on the British division. This deafening chorus was at once enormously increased by 340 guns and howitzers and 120 automatic 82 mm heavy mortars. At first the sound of distant gunfire and the thunder of nearby explosions could be distinguished by men in the advancing division one from another. Very soon the high and growing rate of fire set up a continuous roar.

The fresh 197 Motor Rifle Division pushed on fast towards first contact with the enemy. The 13 Guards Motor Rifle Division had prepared and marked out the lines of advance and covered them with smoke. The rate of artillery fire increased. As the column advanced, Nekrassov in something of a dreamy state watched formations of silvery planes flying over the battlefield like birds, almost touching the treetops.

The 13 Guards Division bade farewell to the enemy. Tanks in contact fired off all the ammunition they had, directly into enemy locations. The heavy multiple rocket launcher batteries coughed fire. The division was, in fact, shooting off all its remaining ammunition – perhaps to save hauling it back to the rear. It was faced with only one problem. This was to keep the enemy's head down in that vulnerable time when the fresh division was just on the point of engagement.

The columns of the fresh division as it came up had been met by dirty and mutilated machines of 13 Guards Division moving back. Spirits sank in Senior Lieutenant Nekrassov's company. Grey-faced men of the retiring Guards, hardly able to keep their red eyes open, their cheeks hollow and unshaven, were not an encouraging sight.

"How goes it?" went up a cry from the men in the fresh division.

The answer came.

"Wait till you meet a *Chieftain*, or better still a *Challenger*, then you'll know . . ."

There was laughter from the fresh column. "We've got instructions about what to do with a *Chieftain*!"

"You try fighting it with instructions!" The laughter, this time grim and sardonic, came from the other column.

Senior Lieutenant Nekrassov smiled cheerlessly. He was going into battle for the first time. Perhaps it was for the last time. He'd had a double ration of vodka that morning, thinking it would make things easier, but it hadn't. There was this voice in his head – "What's it all for, why am I *here*, why is *anyone* here?" His BMP was for the moment stationary. Its soldier driver, Boris Ivanienko, was watching his officer, whom he loved, with care.

"There they are!" The word went round among anxious men at the sharp end in 13 Guards Division. "Here's that other lot – and high time too!"

The two incoming light motor rifle regiments of the fresh division deployed swiftly into action. Two tank battalions led, with six motor rifle battalions behind them. Barely a kilometre ahead, enemy tanks could be seen in action. Breaking down the bushes, filling the air with the stench of exhaust fumes, eighty tanks and 200 other armoured vehicles thundered creaking and clanking through the smoke in horrifying menace over the last few hundred metres. Multi-barrelled rockets from the Soviet side brought down enormous concentrations of fire to cover the moment when the infantry left their vehicles. The positions of the British enemy were still obscured by the continuous smoke of exploding shells, rockets and mortar bombs, as the BTR slackened speed and the troops spilled out of them. The grey-green mass of grimly silent infantry spread across the ground and, forming some sort of lines, followed closely behind the tanks.

Suddenly the artillery fire ceased and the air was filled with a savage, if somewhat forced, "Hu-r-r-ah". Even the terrifying whiplash of automatic rifle fire could not drown that blood-chilling howl. As if reluctant to give voice again, the artillery was silent a moment and then lifted to more distant targets.

The two light motor rifle regiments, now for the most part attacking on foot, had the job of searching out the enemy's weak places. The whole of his anti-tank front could not, for sure, be uniformly strong. The moment a weak point was discovered the division's tank regiment and its heavy motor rifle regiment would be deployed there. These two regiments were even now lumbering slowly towards the forward areas, where it would soon be their turn.

Now, as the artillery and air preparation seemed to have passed its climax, and dismounted infantry from the two light motor rifle regiments were probing in on foot, all saw the signal of three green rockets for the general attack. The divisional tank regiment and its heavy motor rifle regiment slowly moved ahead. Clumps of mud flew up from the caterpillar tracks, accelerating motors roared. Gunfire broke out again – it was the tank regiment, now deployed into battle order, engaging the British battle groups. Spread out behind the tank regiment came the heavy motor rifle regiment. First the tank battalion of the regiment, then the first of its three motor rifle battalions. The second came up on the left, the third on the right. Each battalion was formed into identical columns of companies: the first company moved straight ahead; the second, at great speed, off to the left; the third to the right. The rumble and clash of iron filled the smoke-laden air. The armoured fighting vehicles spread out from their columns into battle formation as the tank guns hammered out their deafening drumbeat. This dreadful clanging noise, this terror and confusion, this necessity to do what you had to do when everything happening around was driving you away from it, was a battle.

Nekrassov scanned around him from the command BMP through his periscope, swinging it from side to side. Smoke drifted everywhere. Explosions ploughed up the open ground close by. Red flames leaped and licked over the armour of a T-72 tank not twenty metres distant. Beyond was another with its tracks broken, perhaps by one of the anti-tank mines the enemy dropped by air. Where the hell *were* those *Chieftains*? The Soviet tanks and BMP filled the landscape like an avalanche. The enemy was somewhere at hand but not to be seen. The British tanks were there all right, firing not directly from the front but from the flank or from far back, in well-chosen positions behind low crests in undulating ground.

Now the enemy's anti-tank helicopter gunships were coming in, with their deadly guided weapons. These would zoom down, attacking the ZSU-23 air defence guns and missile launchers, and then withdraw to open a way into the defence for the fixed-wing American A-10 *Thunderbolts*, storming in with tremendous weapon power, their swift and thunderous onslaught on tanks and BTR followed up again by the helicopter anti-tank gunships. Armoured vehicles in some numbers, whether tanks or BTR, fell victim to these attacks but attacking aircraft suffered too. No sortie withdrew without explosion in the air and flaming wreckage left on the ground. Nekrassov had not expected this. He had been told that the American tank destroying aircraft would be operating further south. They were wrong!

The BMP was fast and clung close to the ground. It was a difficult target for a tank gun, or a ground-based anti-tank guided weapon (ATGW), but as Nekrassov watched, one of them took a direct hit from a powerful shell. All that was left of the BMP seemed to be pieces of armour flying through a cloud of rubbish like rags in the wind. Almost certainly that was a *Challenger* gun. Mercifully there were said to be relatively few in the British Army. Nekrassov would have welcomed some of these on his own side, stronger though it was.

By mid-afternoon on 7 August, 197 Motor Rifle Division had pushed 6 kilometres into the enemy defences. But that was all. The division had ground to a halt. In Nekrassov's company only six of the original ten BMP remained. His own was still on the road, with Boris Ivanienko as its careful, steady driver. When the tanks had gone as far as they could, the infantry threw themselves forward under cover of tank fire, followed up by their BMP. One difficulty emerged quite early: the reserve riflemen had not been well enough trained to conserve their ammunition. As they moved they were firing off their automatic weapons without restraint. The 120 rounds each carried could not last very long. Without ammunition they took cover where they could. The enemy's anti-tank defences were still intact. Soviet tanks were halted.

Nekrassov lay in the grass, gnawing his fist. If there were a counter-attack now, the entire regiment, without ammunition for its riflemen, would probably be wiped out. But there was no sign of a counter-attack. The enemy had clearly had a hard time too.

Two East German and two Soviet motor rifle divisions had now been taking turns pounding at one British division for several days. There would have been severe losses on the enemy's side, but not as many as we have had, thought Nekrassov as he looked around at his own company. Only twenty-three dismounted men were left, plus six remaining BMP with their crews. But what was happening? The troops on the ground had gradually begun to drift away, slowly crawling to the rear.

"Back! Back!" shouted Senior Lieutenant Nekrassov. It was no use. They did not understand him. These were all Uzbeks or Kirghiz, with scarcely a word of Russian between them. Nekrassov had taught them what he could. They had all learnt the command "Advance". Not "Withdraw", naturally; there was no such order. They might misunderstand what he was saying now, and go on making for the rear instead of back to the battle. Those heavy multiple rocket launchers on the other side were enormously destructive and very frightening, that was sure. But this had to be stopped.

"Back to where you came from," shouted Nekrassov, "not to the rear. The KGB will shoot you!"

The soldiers who were creeping back stopped and looked towards their commander. Still keeping close to the ground, he pointed to where No. 2 Company, also drifting back, was coming under the machine-gun fire of the KGB barrage battalion, whose function at the rear was to ensure, by any means, that the forward momentum of their own troops was maintained. The Uzbeks understood and took cover. They turned and grinned at Nekrassov. Their expression clearly said: "Thanks, Sir! You told us just in time!" But only their eyes said this. They had never been taught enough to be able to say it in Russian.

It was late evening before the ammunition arrived. In some ways its arrival was welcome, in some ways not. It is impossible to manage without ammunition in a war, that's certain, but now they'd be sent in to attack again. Who would survive this time?

Along with the ammunition came meagre rations for lunch and supper rolled into one as well as the next morning's breakfast. There was vodka for 105 men, very little bread and only ten jars of meat paste. Nekrassov cursed the supply services in a rage.

"Comrade Senior Lieutenant," explained the stout Sergeant Major, Astap Beda, doing his best to calm things down, "the regimental doctor says it's dangerous to eat a lot during a battle. What if you are wounded, and have to be operated on with a full stomach?"

"That man's a lickspittle liar!" burst out Nekrassov. "They've no bread, they can't feed the troops, so with the help of the medics they dream up bogus scientific theories." Then he stopped himself. ❡

―――――

The Warsaw Pact offensive opened with considerable advantage to the attack. The ratio of forces gave them a general superiority over their opponents of rather better than three to one in ground troops, with an even more marked numerical advantage in tanks and tube artillery, though with no great advantage in quality. Indeed the latest generation of NATO tanks, the US M-1 *Abrams*, the German *Leopard* II and the British *Challenger*, which represented an improvement even on the formidable *Chieftain* (though this still formed the core of the British tank fleet) were every bit as good as the T-72s which constituted the main Soviet tank armament, and even had the edge on the T-80s, of which some but not very many were already in service with Soviet troops in 1985. Allied ATGW were fully as efficient as those of their opponents, though their air defence weaponry was less so.

In their tactical air forces, as in target acquisition and battlefield control techniques, the Western allies had had to accept disappointment in the pre-war years, when budgetary restrictions deprived them of much needed innovations. They had largely had to make do with what there was, but with a deliberate attempt to do so more effectively, exploiting to the full such improvements as tight budgets permitted.

The Warsaw Pact side also enjoyed the advantage on 4 August 1985 of having had, roughly speaking, about two weeks' more time in which to mobilize than NATO.

A further advantage to the offensive lay in the initiative over nuclear and chemical weapons. It was clear that biological weapons would not be used, but operations on the Western side had to be conducted in initial uncertainty over the other two. This meant accepting the penalty of operating under nuclear and chemical precautions with a degradation of efficiency which in some situations could be something like 50 per cent.

The greatest advantage of all to the offensive, however, lay in the choice of time and place for attack, which put in the attackers' hands the power to concentrate a high superiority of force almost where they wished.

In fact, topography exercised so compulsive an influence on choice of thrust line that Soviet hands were not as free as in theory they should have been, while Allied formations were fighting on ground they now knew very well indeed, which the enemy did not. None the less the speedy identification of main thrusts, so that defences and counter-offensive means could be moved to meet mounting threats in good time, formed one of the main preoccupations of Allied corps and divisional commanders.

A message that came out from Supreme Headquarters Allied Powers Europe (SHAPE) to the world at large on 4 August 1985 read as follows:

'Warsaw Pact attacks Allied Command Europe. First light undercover and parachute operations followed by massive armoured assault along entire front. Heavy fighting in Central Region. Allies under severe pressure. Soviets claim action "purely defensive". Situation confused. MFL.'

There was, indeed, scarcely any part of the forward positions of NATO in the Central Region which in the early hours of that August day of 1985 did not come under violent air and artillery attack, with chemical weapons freely in use.

The position in NATO over chemical warfare (cw) was far from satisfactory. Up to the very moment of the outbreak European allies had not been able to reach general agreement on the acceptance of chemical munitions to be located in their own countries in peacetime. The US, as we have seen earlier in Chapter 5 on weapons, had been manufacturing binary rounds since the early 1980s and under bilateral agreements with the UK and the FRG producing stocks also for them, to be held on their account in the United States until needed. The UK took in some of the stock held on their behalf in air shipments from the United States starting on 1 August and were ready to retaliate on 6 August. The FRG followed suit two days later. Typically, there was on 4 August still no decision in the NATO Council. The Supreme Allied Commander, as Commander-in-Chief of all US troops in Europe, would not wait. In that capacity, with the approval of the Joint Chiefs of Staff in Washington, he ordered immediate retaliation by US troops on 4 August. The I British Corps opened retaliatory action on 6 August, the three German corps on 8 August.

Other allies had no such capability. There was no great difficulty in furnishing them fairly soon, however, with compatible binary round artillery munitions and in lending 2 Allied Tactical Air Force (ATAF) a squadron of F-4s fitted with spray tanks, with which to reply. Warsaw Pact protective equipment was less effective than that on the Western side and chemical casualties were proportionately higher for the same weight of attack. After 8 August chemical attack on ground troops dwindled everywhere, though it continued on air-fields where, with the additional use of delayed-action bombs, there was sometimes a serious lengthening in turn-round times of aircraft as a result.

On 11 August 1985 Mr and Mrs George Illingworth of Bradford, Yorkshire, received a letter from their eldest son Brian, a senior aircraftsman instrument mechanic serving with the RAF at Bruggen in West Germany when war broke out. It ran as follows.

❛Dear Mum and Dad,

I will tell you straightaway that I am all right except for a broken leg and cuts and bruises. That's because you will see that this was written from the RAF Hospital at Wroughton. The Doc says I can write and tell you how I got it and I suppose he knows all about secrets and all that stuff.

Me and the lads were on early shift down the HAS [hardened aircraft shelter] with the Squadron. You remember I moved over to 17 a month ago. I say early shift but that's not really right because we had all been called up on the base the previous day. There was a lot of talk about the war starting and we had listened in to Forces Broadcasting but we thought it might be just a gimmick by the TACEVAL blokes (you remember Mum, those exercises when we had to wear our noddy suits for hours and play at soldiers), because they were always clever at kidding on that the exercises were for real. Anyway we got a talk from the CO – he's a bit strict but he's not bad – and then we got another one from the Squadron Commander who didn't seem to know whether he wanted a DFC or to go home to Mum. And we were told that this time it was for real and that the Tornado Wing at Bruggen would be a No. 1 target for old Ivan.

We'd practised a lot for the real thing. We knew that Ivan might attack with ordinary bombs, gas or even nukes, so at midnight when the siren sounded it didn't take long for all of us to get kitted up in the noddy suits. I couldn't understand why we simply sat back and waited if we knew Ivan was going to hit us. I'll bet the Israelis wouldn't have. It was something to do with the "* * * ing politicians", according to our Sergeant (sorry, Mum, but he does f and blind it a bit). Anyway, sure enough at half past six the tannoy hollered "RED – RED – RED" which meant that we were about to get attacked. Most of the big iron doors on the HAS were already shut and those that weren't quickly were, all except ours. You wouldn't believe how many times we'd practised and never once had it jammed. You can close them by hand but it takes more time than we thought we'd got. So there we were, with a four-foot gap right in front of our two Tornados.

Luckily, as it turned out, our HAS faced south. Because about seven minutes after the warning there was a thundering roar and at least sixteen, or so some of the other lads said, Soviet bombers came over the airfield. I could only see two or three through the gap in the door as they flashed past over the runway. We thought they might attack with gas but, this time at least, they didn't. It all seemed to have been ordinary bombs. There was an enormous bang on the roof of our HAS and a shower of paint and muck came down but the concrete didn't even crack. Just as quickly as they'd appeared they'd gone again and Corp and me and the other lads rushed out to see what had happened. We were a bit daft really, and Sarg didn't half tell us so too, because of course Ivan could have come round for a second go. But in fact he didn't and for a minute or two we just stood and stared at the mess he'd left.

Over to our right the central servicing hangars were on fire – a right old mess, with smoke everywhere. The air traffic control block was badly damaged and so were several of the barrack blocks and SHQ. Some of the fuel bowsers were in flames and a bulldozer belonging to the runway repair engineers was on its side and very bent. Black smoke began to pour across the airfield from one of the other Squadron dispersals and I heard here in hospital that one of the Squadron areas had really been hammered – all the bowsers and one shelter had been hit. Most of us though, to begin with at least, had been lucky, because we'd been in the HAS with the aircraft and I don't think any of them were damaged. Some of the rockapes (that's what we call the RAF Regiment lads) and some of the cooks on guard duty got caught out in the open nearer the perimeter wire and one of them's in the next bed. He says that he lost a lot of mates even though most were in slit trenches.

The fire tenders were quick off the mark and I saw one tearing down to the near maintenance hangar when it suddenly blew up. Just a flash and a bang and it had gone. That was a bit frightening. That's when we realized that Ivan had put delayed action fuses on some of his bombs, turning them into mines. That was really nasty because you never knew when there would be another one waiting to go off in a crater or a pile of rubble. The only way you could check was by looking at every square yard of concrete. I could see large bits of the runway untouched and several Tornados were able to get airborne quite quickly, but it must have been dodgy when they had to taxi past craters or rubble. And all movement was slowed down – aircraft, bowsers, fire tenders, ambulances and even the NAAFI wagon. Would you believe the old NAAFI wagon still kept going!

But you can guess what happened can't you? I had to walk out across our dispersal to check that 17 Squadron's area was clear for taxiing. We knew that the Tornados only needed a short bit of runway and if they could get to it they could counter-attack, which was obviously a very popular move. As I was passing a pile of rubble about 30 yards away it suddenly went up. I was very lucky. The blast knocked me sideways up against the wall of the pan and I broke my leg. The bits of flying rubble cut me up a bit but I'm luckier than a lot of my mates who are still (it's now 48 hours since) being brought in as a result of delayed-action bombs. But we're all well looked after and I'll soon be home. Give brother Willie a kick for me.

Love,
Brian ❢

Artillery and air preparation all along the front of the Central Region was soon, on the morning of 4 August, followed by very heavy concentrations in four areas which preceded four powerful armoured attacks, each on a divisional frontage, on thrust lines that had been largely predicted. All four were into the Federal Republic of Germany. In the north, 2 Guards Tank Army pushed in past Hamburg (which had been declared by the *Senat* in despair an open city) towards the Netherlands, with one column thrusting up through Schleswig-Holstein towards Denmark. The Soviet 103 Airborne Division had already secured Bremen airfield and exploitation troops were being flown in. Further south 3 Shock Army had moved in towards Hanover, with the recognized possibility that a drive south-west towards Cologne and the Ruhr might result. It was probable, they thought in Allied Forces Central Europe (AFCENT), that this was the thrust that needed most careful watching. If it got across the lower Rhine in the Low Countries some awkward possibilities would lie ahead, particularly that of a turn southwards along the west bank of the Rhine, upstream to take the Central Army Group (CENTAG) in the rear. Further south, 8 Guards Army was pushing in towards Frankfurt. The country was less favourable to the offensive here, close, hilly and often wooded, but the depth of the NATO position in the CENTAG sector was far less than further North. The Rhine was scarcely 250 kilometres away from the frontier here, and Frankfurt little more than 100. The going, however, was far from good for armour. Well reconnoitred anti-tank weapon positions in undulating country combined with the skilful use of the tanks of armoured cavalry in fire positions which they knew well, together with the intervention of anti-tank helicopters in close co-operation with fixed-wing ground attack aircraft, slowed the armoured advance considerably.

Further south, where French command in an army group task had not yet been established, the thrust of 41 Army out of Czechoslovakia towards Nuremberg, aiming at Stuttgart, made better progress.

Such was the pattern of events, briefly stated, on day one of the Warsaw Pact offensive seen as it were, from a long way up. Lower down, at ground level, things were different. There was noise every-where, distant noise of bombs or gunfire, noise of aircraft screaming overhead, of tracks clanking and squealing as the tanks hurried by, and sometimes the enormously stupifying impact of a close and direct attack, either of crashing bombs, or multiple rockets with their re-peated and violent explosions, or those dreaded automatic mortars which fire five bombs in ten seconds, bringing down a curtain of despair. There was also weariness struggling with responsibility. Everybody was tired. Everyone had something he had to take account of. All this tended to leave otherwise quite sensible and stable men in a quivering condition of uncertainty and shock. Some ran to hide, anywhere. Others walked around in a state of dumb non-comprehension, almost as though in a coma. When the moments passed, as they almost always did, men collected themselves, called up reserves of self-control and stamina which were happily still plenti-ful if not always inexhaustible, and put things together again.

On the evening of the first day Warsaw Pact gains along the whole front had been considerable. The seizure of Bremen airfield in the north by the Soviet 103 Airborne Division at dawn had been exploited by a motor rifle division quickly flown in under heavy air cover, and a bridgehead had been consolidated across the River Weser in the sector of I Netherlands Corps. Hanover was threatened by 3 Shock Army but I German Corps, though it had been forced back by the weight of the attack some 20 kilometres from the frontier and had taken heavy punishment, was still in good order. Further south, I British Corps had yielded ground west of the Harz mountains while Kassel, at the junction of I British Corps with the Belgians, was under heavy threat, also from 3 Shock Army. Over the boundary between the Northern and Central Army Groups, III German Corps, under command of CENTAG, had been driven back by a powerful assault from 8 Guards Army through the hill country of the Thüringer Wald but yielded no more than 10 to 20 kilometres of ground, while V US Corps on its right was particularly hard pressed defending the more open terrain around Fulda against a determined effort from 1 Guards Tank Army to break through to Frankfurt. The VII US Corps on the right of the V had lost Bamberg in a Soviet penetration by 28 Army of some 30 kilometres but was firm in front of Nuremberg, while II German Corps, having lost ground to an attack by 41 Army from the Carpathian Military District, now deployed in northern Czechoslovakia, was also firm, backed by II French Corps, which had not yet been engaged.

As the pattern of the day's events grew clearer on 5 August, the Soviet High Command could view the outcome of the first day's operations with some satisfaction, even if all its hopes had not been wholly fulfilled. There had been no complete breakthrough on any of the four major thrust lines. There was no sign yet of any opening which could be exploited by the huge mass of armour in the two groups of tank armies in Belorussia and the Ukraine, which were being held there principally for this purpose. But gains had been made, particularly in the north, where Hamburg had been isolated (and, like Berlin, bypassed) and left uncertain of its fate, while the seizure of Bremen had opened, as had been intended, good possibilities of exploitation towards the Low Countries. Most of Niedersachsen was already in Soviet hands.

Morale in NATO formations, though patchy and showing signs of cracking here and there under the first furious waves of assault, with its head-splitting clamour and the thunderous menace from which there was no hiding place, had not collapsed. It seemed, indeed, by nightfall to have improved somewhat. Progress in the assault against the Americans, where easy gains had been expected, had been disappointing. The forward anti-tank guided missile defences were well sited and skilfully controlled and anti-tank helicopters acting with A-10 *Thunderbolt* tank destroyers had inflicted many armoured casualties. A weakness on the Western side, which was of advantage to the Soviets and which had been foreseen by them, was some uncertainty as to who actually owned rotary-wing aircraft, with division of opinion between ground and air commanders, as to how best to use them. Where there was a close relationship between rotary and fixed-wing anti-tank tactics, as in the action against 8 Guards Army of US formations in the Fulda area, the result had been distinctly unfavourable to attacking armour.

The movement of refugees out of the frontier areas, where the population had largely stayed in place as a result of political assurances based on forward defence, was seen as particularly favourable to the attack. Soviet air and artillery had aimed at driving refugee movement on to roads in use for rearward movement by the Western allies, and then off the main thrust lines intended for use in the Soviet advance. Orders not only to disregard civilian casualties but to maximize them to this end had been correctly carried out.

There was no doubt, however, that the first day, whatever its gains, had not shown the rate of advance expected by the Soviet High

Command. This had to improve if the plan were to be completely successful.

━━━━━━━━━

At the outbreak of hostilities the British Prime Minister had instructed that the press be kept as fully informed as possible. There would, it was hoped, be no misunderstanding of the kind that had plagued the coverage by the American media of the Vietnam tragedy. Consequently, Squadron Leader Guy Whitworth, Weapons Leader of 617 Squadron of the RAF, stationed at Marham in the United Kingdom, was not surprised to receive a sympathetic but firm invitation from his Station Commander to 'Come down and tell some defence correspondents about your Magdeburg trip'.

It was 0630 hours on 7 August. Guy Whitworth was in the Ops block at RAF Marham, just finishing his debrief to the Wing Intelligence staff. He had landed two hours previously after a three-hour trip in a *Tornado* which had taken him from the relative peace of Norfolk across Belgium and West Germany beyond the Elbe to an airfield just a few miles east of Magdeburg and through a trough of action he had yet to sort out for himself. This is his description of the flight which had taken eight GR-1 *Tornados* from Marham in an attack upon a major airfield 100 miles beyond the battle. We reprint it here as it came out in the *Christian Science Monitor* in June 1986.

❛We were briefed that this particular airfield housed a regiment of MiG-27 *Flogger* Js. These are the best of the current Soviet short-range offensive support aircraft and we have been told that they make their presence felt in the ground battle. It seems that they can operate from hard-packed earth runways, but that they have not yet begun to do so, perhaps because they can maintain a higher sortie rate by staying close to their weapon and fuel support at their main operating base. *Flogger* has a very limited night or all-weather capability and we reckoned we had a good chance of catching most of them on the deck in the early hours of the morning.

Wing Commander Bill Spier, our Squadron Commander, led the first wave of four with my navigator, Flight Lieutenant Andy Blackett, and myself as his No. 4. Each *Tornado* carried two JP-233 anti-airfield weapons, two defence suppression anti-radiation (ARM) missiles – these home on to radar emissions – and an electronic counter-measure (ECM) pod. Our object was to close the Soviet airfield down and stop *Flogger* operations for as many hours as possible.

The first leg of our flight was uneventful. After climbing out of Marham we rendezvoused with a VC-10 tanker over the North Sea. We had practised night refuelling, of course, so there was no problem there. We were passed on to the Sector Controllers in Belgium, who I think must have been in touch with one of the NATO AWACS, because the last transmission we received from the ground gave a very accurate position for the Warsaw Pact thrust lines. Andy was monitoring their accuracy through the combined map and radar displays and the TV displays. He hadn't needed a radar or laser update. Anyway, as we approached the Rhine we dropped down to 200 feet and stepped up the speed to 600 knots.

Once across the Rhine we caught a glimpse of the war. Thanks to the accurate AWACS update we were spared having to fly over Warsaw Pact armour and its accompanying SAM. We were grateful for that. Over to the left we could see a fair amount of gunfire but when Wing Commander Spier took us down a further 100 feet into the weeds the sky became very dark and very small. Our *Tornado* was now being flown by the automatic terrain following system (ATFS), following the contours of the earth as closely as its speed permitted. As we approached the northern edge of the Harz mountains the aircraft remained rock steady, wings fully swept to 67 degrees, but as we crossed the inner German border (IGB) east of Kassel it began to get a bit noisier. We heard the "bing, bing" of a surveillance radar in our radar warning receiver and then the high note of a low level SAM tracker. By this time I think we must have been spotted by one of the *Cookers*, although happily the area ground-response wasn't all that sharp, perhaps because our pre-planned route was taking us along the boundaries of 8 Guards and 3 Shock Armies.

South-east of Magdeburg we swung north. Many hours of practice over Canada had taught us that loose station-keeping at night at low level was not easy, but by no means impossible. With 20 miles to go, Andy selected the "attack" mode on the TV display and the "stabilized" mode on the combined map and radar display to bring together visually computed target and aiming markers. I monitored the sequence in my head-up display in the front cockpit, just in case I picked up an aiming error and had to take over from the auto pilot.

For a few seconds we thought we were going to achieve complete surprise, and perhaps our approach from the south-east rather than the west did give us a little extra time, but then we were well and truly lit up by several different surface-to-air defence systems. I loosed off both ARM. The automatic self-screening ECM pod was obviously working well. Andy kept his head down. I think he was grateful to have his time taken up with placing his laser range finder on the main runway of the airfield, and with the fine tuning of the aiming marker. There was a fair amount of activity below us by now as we swept over the airfield. It was then that we lost No. 2 and Eric and Ken. I think they must have been hit by the guns or low level SAM. They were just blown apart. The rest of us sprayed the base with the JP-233s. I didn't see the effect of our weapons but the sub-munitions put down by the Wing Commander spread out beautifully right across the runway. Unless our weapons failed badly, we cut it in three places and in addition scattered delayed-action mines all over the tarmac and the airfield itself. The damage will take a long time to put right. I didn't see any *Floggers* but we expected them to be in their hardened shelters anyway. They'll stay there for a quite a time now. One unexpected bonus was the presence of two *Candid* transports. Andy saw both those go up. I suppose the other side also has problems of airfield overcrowding. Our second four were thirty seconds behind us and according to their report we can assume that any additional warning the enemy had that they were coming in was more than balanced by the impact of the first wave. As the second four were clearing the area they lost one aircraft after it had dropped its weapons.

So, we headed for home, but we weren't there yet. We now had two problems to think about. First, whether there was any stray *Flogger* who fancied his look-down-shoot-down chances. After that there were our own air defence people who quite naturally get a bit tense about high-speed low-level aircraft coming out of the east. One or two of the *Tornados* still had ARM left but we had to rely on the ECM pod to get us back over the Warsaw Pact SAM. In fact, as we had hoped, their SAM (which had just rolled forward with the armour) were not as well co-ordinated as the kit we had found near the airfield. It takes time to site SAM radars and naturally they tended to concentrate on their fronts, not their rear, which was where we were coming from, still at 100 feet and still tracking quite quickly.

So we crossed the FEBA over the Teutoburger Wald at a height, speed and heading which should have seen us through. As far as I know our IFF (identification friend or foe) kit was functioning but I don't know how far it might have been spoofed earlier in the night. For whatever reason, some bastard let a SAM go. At least I assume it was a SAM. It could have been one of our own HAWK. I hope not. Andy hadn't picked up any AI (air-intercept) radar warning and we didn't see any other aircraft. It got Wing Commander Spier's *Tornado*. The aircraft simply disintegrated in a ball of flame. No one could have got out. It was ironical, because one of the last things he had said in the briefing was to take care not to relax on the home leg because that was when the greater number of losses usually occurred.

I took over the lead and we climbed to meet our tanker again. I must admit I'm glad that the mates up at the box (Ministry of Defence) decided in 1982 to go ahead with the VC-10 modification because there was no way we could have launched from Marham against Magdeburg on that routing without air-to-air refuelling. So here we are: five *Tornados* back out of eight, and one major Warsaw Pact base knocked out for several critical hours. **9**

———

The 1 Guards Tank Army, deployed at the outbreak round Dresden, came into action against CENTAG on 5 and 6 August but by now two fresh US divisions flown in from the United States to man their pre-positioned equipment had come under command and the position had to some extent improved. By 8 August all of the Federal Republic east of a line from Bremen southwards to just east of Augsburg was in Soviet hands. Both Berlin and Hamburg had been bypassed but Hanover, Minden, Kassel, Würzburg, Nuremberg and Munich had all been lost and a huge and threatening salient had developed westwards from Bremen into the Netherlands. The crossing of the lower Rhine by nightfall on that day, 8 August, had been successfully carried out and a strong Warsaw Pact bridgehead consolidated on the left bank of the Rhine as far as the River Waal.

———

6 A "Concentration Centre for Reinforcements" had been set up at Dresden. It was planned for a very high capacity and a rapid through-put, but the movement of tank armies over the Polish rail network had virtually taken up the system's whole capacity and there was a significant fall in the flow of replacements of material and of personnel reinforcements from the USSR.

Bringing 197 Motor Rifle Division back to full strength took four days instead of the stipulated two. The 94 and 207 Motor Rifle Divisions were in the area at the same time. All the T-72 tanks were taken from the motor rifle regiments of 197 Division and used to replace losses in the division's tank regiment. To the motor rifle regiments old T-55 tanks were issued instead, taken out of mothballs. The heavy motor rifle regiment was brought fully up to strength with new BMP straight from two factories in the Urals, but there were no BTR replacements available for the two light regiments of the division, which should have been equipped with BTR 70s. The remaining undamaged BTR were collected into a single battalion, with the rest of the battalions having to make do with requisitioned civilian lorries. As for men, numbers were made up with reservists and soldiers from divisions that had sustained too many losses to be re-formed.

At the Centre a collection of captured NATO tanks, armoured transports and artillery had been assembled and a training programme for officers and men was organized. The NATO equipment had usually fallen into Soviet hands as a result of mechanical failure, from damage to tracks by mines or gunfire, for example, though several prize specimens had been acquired when crews were taken by surprise in early non-persistent chemical attacks to which they had at once succumbed leaving their equipment intact as an easy prey to swiftly following Soviet motor rifle infantry. To their great delight both Nekrassov and Makarov, the latter now in 207 Motor Rifle Division, found themselves together in the programme.

There was also a small camp of Western prisoners of war at the Centre. They were available for questioning. A special sub-unit of the GRU Soviet military intelligence ensured that prisoners answered questions willingly and correctly.

The two Senior Lieutenants crawled over and under and through every piece of equipment they could find at the Centre, testing the feel of it all. They inspected the West German *Leopard* II tank and the *Marder* infantry combat vehicle. Good machines but very complicated. How could such equipment be maintained in the field if crucial repair facilities and supply bases in West Germany were lost? The US *Abrams* M-1 tank wasn't bad either, a low-lying predatory machine, but the main armament wasn't really powerful enough and it had a disproportionately gas-guzzling engine. They were both impressed by the *Chieftain* and even more by the *Challenger*, fighting machines to be reckoned with – almost impenetrable armour, super-powerful armament and a dependable engine. The *Leopard* II was good and so of course was the *Abrams*. The *Challenger* was better. A few more thousand of these in Europe and the attack would soon get bogged down.

The GRU officers were happy to give the necessary explanations. The British Army had the best tanks though too few of them, and the best trained soldiers, but it was short on automatic anti-aircraft guns. The British were practically defenceless against Soviet helicopters. The German *Bundeswehr* was both determined and disciplined with first-rate professional training. The East Germans mostly fought against the Americans.

Nekrassov asked how the Belgian and Dutch units had been performing in battle. He knew about the British.

"Not bad at all," he was told. "Their supply system is first class. Their equipment is not bad either. There are few of them, of course, but they are very good in defence. One great weakness is that soldiers query their orders. There is no death sentence for disobeying an order."

Nekrassov shook his head in disbelief and the two moved on.

They then came to the captive officers, caged like wild animals. The GRU interpreter playfully twirled a thick rubber truncheon in his hand – an instrument which served as a dictionary might, to facilitate the interpreter's job.

"Ask him," Nekrassov indicated an American major sitting in the cage, "ask him why some of their vehicles have a big red cross painted on a white background instead of the actual camouflage markings. It's stupid – just makes it easier for us to pick them out and destroy them. Why do they do it?"

Evidently other Soviet officers had asked the same question. Without referring to the prisoner the interpreter explained to Nekrassov.

"Vehicles with a red cross are ambulances," he said. "They think we should not fire on them. They say there's an international agreement to that effect."

"If there were such an agreement we'd surely have been informed."

"Of course." The interpreter shrugged his shoulders. "It would be in some manual. But I've never myself come across a reference to such an agreement anywhere. None of our books or newspapers mentions it."

"There's certainly nothing about it in the Field Service Regulations." Nekrassov shrugged his shoulders in turn.

"Then ask if it's true," said Makarov to the interpreter, "that women serve on equal terms with men in their army?"

The interpreter, again without bothering to translate the question, answered for what was obviously the hundredth time: "They do."

Nekrassov was perplexed. "That's ridiculous! Women are not men. For one thing they need proper food and rest. They won't get that in the army."

"What sort of rations do the prisoners get?" asked Makarov. He addressed the question directly to the interpreter, who simply affected not to hear.

Nekrassov had never in his whole life talked to a foreigner from the capitalist West. He wanted to ask something the interpreter would not know already, just to hear an answer from this gaunt-looking American major in the tattered uniform.

"Ask him if it's true that in America anyone can write what he likes in a newspaper, even something against the President."

"That's irrelevant," said the interpreter abruptly.

Nekrassov knew he'd gone a bit too far and allowed his friend Dimitri to hurry him off so that they could lose themselves in the crowd of Soviet officers glued in fascination to a Canadian armoured personnel carrier. One question too many and you'd end up in a cage yourself. ❥

At the further end of the Central Region in the south an Allied Army group had been set up under French command (the Southern, or SOUTHAG, balancing up the Northern and Central), with responsibility south of a line through Karlsruhe (exclusive) and Nuremberg, north of which CENTAG with four corps under command (I Be, III Ge, V and VII US) seemed, though not over-optimistic, reasonably hopeful of holding the position east of Frankfurt.

If the Soviet High Command had put in 3 Shock Army immediately behind 1 Guards Tank Army the threat to CENTAG would have been far more serious. The Soviets, however, had committed 3 Shock Army in the north, to exploit the favourable position developing there for the execution of the truly critical part of the main plan, the breakthrough to swing southwards along the Rhine on the left bank.

NORTHAG, with two British, one German and the remains of one Dutch corps under command, was now fighting grimly on a line running westwards from near Minden to Nijmegen in the Netherlands, facing north, with an ominous bulge in the south near Venlo, later to be generally known as the Krefeld salient. The I British Corps on the right had done well to stay in being, largely due here also to the successful use of anti-tank guided weapons, particularly those deployed in small stay-behind parties, operating with German *Jagd-Kommandos* in country which the British knew very well and which to the Germans was native soil. The tactics of the 'sponge', for the absorption of the flow of armour, had been paying off, but the situation could not stay the way it was much longer. In the west I German Corps was under heavy pressure along the Teutoburger Wald, the Soviet intention clearly being to drive it in very soon. Further west II British Corps with a US brigade and some Dutch troops under command was being hard pressed south of Wesel, defending the Venlo gap between the Rivers Rhine and Maas in the very tip of the salient.

———

❛The order to advance against II German Corps in SOUTHAG at 0400 hours on the morning of 7 August had been received on the previous afternoon by Major General Pankratov, commanding 51 Tank Division of 8 Guards Army on the Central Front. It found the division theoretically (though not in fact) at full strength, its personnel at an assumed total of 10,843, its armoured fighting vehicle strength at 418 T-72 tanks and 241 BMP 2s. Its artillery included 126 SP howitzers, forty-eight multiple rocket launchers (twenty-four Grad-P, twenty-four BM-27) and sixty-two heavy SP anti-aircraft equipments in combined rocket and automatic artillery units. The division was organized normally. It was a Category One formation, as was usual for those deployed in Eastern Europe, with its equipment complete and personnel at between 75 and 100 per cent, filled out to full strength in an emergency such as this. It had one motor rifle and three tank regiments, a regiment of 152 mm SP guns and one of anti-aircraft missiles, together with eight other separate battalions. These comprised a FROG 7 rocket unit, communications, reconnaissance, engineer, transport, chemical defence and repair battalions and another embodying medical services. Manpower, from many parts of the USSR, was by now some 10 per cent deficient.

The day before the advance three further battalions were added to the divisional strength, in theory under Major General Pankratov's command, in fact under the exclusive control of one Lieutenant Colonel Drobis of the KGB, the head of what was known at divisional headquarters as the Special Section. Two of these units were so-called KGB barrage battalions, manned by personnel of mixed origin with a relatively low degree of military training. There were cheerful, healthy looking young Komsomol workers alongside guards drafted from prisons and members of respectable bureaucratic families who had hitherto done little or no military service but whose engagement to the Party interest could be counted on as total.

The barrage battalions were equipped with light trucks and armed with machine-guns and portable anti-tank weapons. The function of these units was simple and their location in the forward deployment plan of the division in the attack followed logically from it. They were placed well up behind the leading elements to ensure, by the use of their weapons from the rear, that the forward impetus of their own troops was maintained and there was no hesitancy or slowing down, still less any tendency to withdraw. KGB fire power was an important element in the maintenance of momentum. This caused losses, of course, but these would be readily compensated for in the arrival of fresh follow-up formations, so that the net gain could always be reckoned worthwhile. The use of KGB barrage battalions to stimulate offensive forward movement was, moreover, an essential element accepted without question in the Red Army's system of tactical practice in the field. This was wholly oriented to the offensive. Defence played virtually no part in it at all and offensive impetus had to be maintained.

Total refusal to countenance withdrawal could, of course, at times be costly. On the first day of the offensive two tank battalions of 174 Tank Regiment, moving forward from out of woodland cover, were caught almost at once in open ground by heavy anti-armoured air attack from the United States Air Force. Temporary withdrawal into cover, which was all that made sense, was flatly forbidden by the KGB. When the attacking aircraft themselves withdrew, tank casualties on the ground were in each battalion over 80 per cent.

The progress of 51 Tank Division in the attack on 6 August had been slower than hoped for, its leading battalion hammered by United States anti-tank weapons in front, against the anvil of the KGB behind.

Of the three special KGB battalions attached to 51 Tank Division, the third was 693 Pursuit Battalion. This followed up in the advance rather further back. Its business was the liquidation of possibly hostile elements in the local population – any who were obviously reactionary bourgeois, for example, or priests, or local officials – as well as taking care of officers and men of 51 Tank Division who had shown insufficient fighting spirit.

The divisional commander stood at the operations map in the BTR 50-PU which formed his command centre. On his right stood his political deputy, a Party man; on his left, his chief of staff; behind him Lieutenant Colonel Drobis of the KGB. Colonel Zimin, commanding the divisional artillery, was just climbing down into the BTR, closing the hatch firmly behind him. It was late afternoon on 6 August.

"An important task for you, Artillery," growled the divisional commander. "We've got a valley here between two hills with a road along the valley leading towards us. We tried to break through there yesterday, but got our fingers burnt. We start to attack and the Americans bring far too effective anti-tank fire along that road from positions further back.

"If they try that again this time your BM-27 multiple rocket launcher battalion will take them out. They have to be suppressed in one go. So there's a prime task for you for tomorrow."

"Comrade General," replied the artillery commander, "permission to move the BM-27 battalion 5 kilometres back and another 5 to the south?"

"Why?" barked Lieutenant Colonel Drobis, breaking in.

"It's a question of ballistics, of the laws of physics," explained Colonel Zimin patiently. "We fire off several hundred rounds at a time. We want to cover a road which is at right-angles to the front – so the impact zone has to be spread along the road, not across it. Our present firing positions are too far forward and too far to one side to do this. So we have to fire from further back, and further to the south. We move back, fire and move forward again."

"In no circumstances," snapped the KGB Lieutenant Colonel, "none at all. You stay where you are and fire from there."

"But then the zone will lie across the road instead of along it."

"Then try to get it along the road."

"I can't do that from the present firing position, only 2 kilometres from the front line and 5 from the axis of the road."

"You want to retreat?"

"It's essential to move back at least 5 kilometres and 4 or 5 kilometres further south if the tank regiment is to break through."

"You go back to the rear, while we're in the thick of it up here? Listen Colonel, you get your zone, or whatever you call it, along the road from the front line or . . ."

"It's ballistics, Comrade. Our fire pattern depends on the laws of ballistics. We can't make those up as we go along."

"Right. No more of this. I won't allow you to retreat, and you refuse to carry out orders. Arrest him! You can discuss this further where you're going."

Two KGB sergeants pinioned Colonel Zimin's arms and dragged him out.

General Pankratov went on looking stolidly at the wall map, keeping out of this skirmish between the artillery chief and the head of the Special Section. The divisional commander could see that another disaster was due in a few hours. He knew that, for all the theory of offensive action upon which it was based, tomorrow's attack would get bogged down again just like yesterday's and for the same reason. He was sad not to be able to do anything to protect the artillery commander, who was an old friend, but he knew that it would be useless to try.

Many years ago, when the General was still a young lieutenant, he was puzzled at the irrational, even, he used to think, the idiotic way in which so much was done in the Red Army. It was not till he was studying at the Frunze Military Academy that he was able, with greater maturity and more experience, to take a closer look at the Soviet power structure. He saw it not the way it was theoretically said to be, articulated under an exemplary constitution, but the way it was in actual naked fact, a structure serving one end only, the perpetuation of the supreme power of the Party. It was also true that other elements in the composition of the USSR were more interested in the preservation of structures which embodied personal power than in their functional efficiency.

The Red Army was the only organized power grouping in the Soviet Union capable of destroying the entire socialist system without harming itself. It was scarcely surprising therefore that in every battalion, regiment and division, in every headquarters at any level, in every military establishment, the Party and the KGB kept keen and watchful eyes on all that went on. There was a Party political officer in every Soviet company, in the post of deputy commander. There were KGB secret agents in every platoon.

The KGB and the Party realized (for these were not all stupid men) that such close control kills initiative and contributes to a dullness of performance which in an army invites defeat. But what could they do about it? If they did not keep control of the army it would devour them. Here, as many realized, was a clear dilemma. An army which is allowed to think holds dangers for socialism. An army which is not allowed to think cannot be an efficient fighting force. The Party and the KGB, faced with a choice, as they saw it, between an efficient army which could threaten their own position, and an army which constituted no threat but was unlikely to give a good account of itself in battle, chose what they saw as the lesser of two evils. When war came it was even more dangerous to loosen controls on the army than in peacetime. The interference of amateurs in the persons of Party bureaucrats and the secret police in such highly professional matters as the conduct of military operations was certain to cause mistakes and even lead to disaster, but this was clearly far better than letting the army off the leash and out of Party control.

General Pankratov, a high-grade professional, was quite confident he knew how to break up an American division. Neither the KGB men nor the Party stool pigeons knew how to do this and it was not possible to show them, for they were not professional soldiers. They would mouth their Party platitudes and act according to their secret instructions. They would always, of course, have to have the last word. Tomorrow, therefore, General Pankratov would do what they wanted, without any choice, and also without either originality or initiative. He would attack the enemy head-on, for this was the only way his controllers thought a battle could take place. If he did anything else he would be killed and a new commander would take over the division. A newcomer would almost certainly act in a way that the stool pigeons from the political department and the suspicious, watchful "Comrades" from the Special Department understood. If he did not, he too would be killed and another replacement found and this would go on until a commander was found who could easily be controlled and whose every move would be easily understood by everyone.

Nothing, General Pankratov reflected, could be changed. The orders he would have to give for tomorrow's battle would be foolish ones. Soldiers, of course, would now yet again be sent to a wholly purposeless death.

Quite apart from these personal and somewhat philosophical reflections, the General was also worried over some strictly professional matters. He had found it very difficult to relate the action of motor rifle infantry in BMP to movements of the tanks with which they had to co-operate. The vehicles moved at different speeds. The BMP were highly vulnerable to even light attack from gun or missile. The riflemen were often more effective dismounted than in their vehicles, in spite of the additional armament these carried. On their feet, however, they could not keep up with the tanks and were weak in fire power. It was increasingly the case, therefore, that tanks either came to a halt because they had out-run the infantry, or moved on into anti-tank defences which there had been no infantry at hand to suppress.

Moreover, General Pankratov was again finding himself travelling round the old vicious circle. He could not call for air support unless the progress his attack had made had earned him preferential treatment over other divisions in the army. As he had already discovered, it was sometimes impossible to make the progress required to qualify for air support unless you had it in the first instance. The inflexibility of battle procedures was a good match for the tight restrictions placed upon a commander's action by the Party. The two together made an almost certain formula for disaster, which was only kept at arm's length by the enormous weight of forces the Red Army had available and the staggering degree to which the common soldier accepted casualties.

General Pankratov looked up from the tank, vehicle and ammunition states which had just been given to him – none of which made any more cheerful reading than the personnel strength and artillery states he had already seen – and in a tired and indifferent voice gave the orders for tomorrow's battle.

He would go into action in his command vehicle, wearing a peaked military cap, as always. Steel helmets were hard on the head and difficult to manoeuvre in and out of hatches. If his BTR 50-PU were hit by anything that mattered, a steel helmet would be of no help anyway. General Pankratov, like most generals anywhere, was something of a fatalist. ❥*

The performance of Warsaw Pact formations had not in some important respects proved entirely satisfactory to the Soviet High Command. Co-operation between arms had been incomplete. Artillery support had been slow in response and inflexible. Junior command had been lacking in thrust, relying too much on guidance from above. The Western allies had been quick to exploit this weakness, applying their excellent electronic capabilities to the identification of command elements which they then often managed to

* He survived the war. What has been set out here was learned in a personal interview with ex-Major General Pankratov in the summer of 1986 in his home town of Vyshniy-Volochek between Petrograd and Moscow.

take out. Coherence in units, in spite of the close attention of KGB barrage battalions, had not been high, often because of the low level of reservist weapon skill and the great difficulty in achieving co-operation between men who could not understand each other's languages. Finally, there was the greater difficulty of co-ordinating infantry and tanks in action. Only infantry, in the long run, could effectively put down anti-tank defences, however powerful the assistance of technical aids to suppressive action by artillery and fixed- and rotary-wing aircraft. The tanks were highly vulnerable to unsuppressed and well-sited ATGW, as well as to long-range fire from very capably handled Allied tanks. Without infantry the tanks of the Warsaw Pact were at a severe disadvantage. But the BMP was even more vulnerable than the tank, as well as being unable to move over the country at the same speed. It very quickly became Allied practice to try to separate infantry from tanks and this was often highly successful.

There was enormous weight in the resources still available to the Soviet High Command. There were on 14 August forty Warsaw Pact divisions in the Central Region, of which fifteen were tank divisions, and no more than half of them had been in action. Their total fire power was three or four times as great as the sum of what faced them. Time, however, was not on their side. The reasons for an expeditious consolidation of the stop-line on the River Rhine had lost none of their urgency. Failure to keep up with the timetable could have unwelcome consequences.

❢ Wing Commander Roger Pullin, Commanding Officer of 19 Squadron, could hardly believe his senses. It was 0430 hours on 15 August, he was very tired, he was down to his last five *Phantoms*, the main runway had been repaired twice, his crews – or what remained of them – were on their last legs from battle strain and sheer fatigue and now, standing on the other side of the plotting table in the hardened Squadron Ops block, between two rather self-important engine mechanics turned Squadron guards, was a real live Soviet pilot, still in his equivalent of a Mae West, "G" suit, leg restrainers, and all the rest. He was obviously a very angry pilot.

The lads explained that he had literally dropped into the middle of the Squadron dispersal area, unclipped his parachute, thrown his revolver at their feet and, muttering under his breath, marched willingly with them into the Squadron block.

Roger buzzed the Station Commander, notified the Ground Defence Wing Commander and then turned to the angry man before him. On the evening of 3 August, less than a fortnight but what seemed more than a century ago, Roger had stopped by the Officers' Mess to pick up a bottle of Scotch. There had been much to think about since then and it was still in his brief case. He now took it out and in excellent Russian asked his visitor if he would like a cup of coffee or maybe something stronger. The pilot was taken aback by the offer, as well as by the fact that it was made in his own language. The Wing Commander was a Cambridge modern language graduate, who had done a tour as Assistant Air Attaché in Moscow in the late 1970s, but his visitor could not possibly have known that. Five minutes later they were sitting in Roger's office, the door open and an armed guard a couple of yards away in the corridor.

Roger had had quick instructions from the Station Commander.

"Your man will be going off up the line as soon as they come to take him away, for specialist interrogation. What I want you to do is to get from him his own story of what happened to him and put it on a tape for me the way it might have come from one of our own boys, so that I can really get the hang of it. I gather he's a bit het up and should talk freely. You've got about ten minutes."

The visiting pilot's name was Captain Leonid Balashov, and he had just been shot down by one of his own SAM. When Roger asked him how it had all happened Balashov let out a torrent of abuse and recrimination, none of it directed against Allied air forces but against the system that had put him in the same piece of sky as was being used at the same time by a massive Allied bombing effort half an hour earlier.

What follows is taken from the account that Roger Pullin put on a tape for the Station Commander a few minutes later.

"As if it wasn't bad enough being scrambled without close ground control on a general heading towards an unknown target at 'approximately' 30–40,000 feet along with a bunch of cowboys in MiG-25s who had never shot at anything in their bloody lives and had no idea whatever about attacking as a formation, with a bunch of bloody Poles behind you and you never knew whether they would simply poke off or have a go at you before they did poke off . . . "

The *Flogger* pilot held out his mug for a refill.

"I haven't got twelve hundred hours on *Floggers* in thirteen years, and my Sniper badge, just by crawling round the Squadron Commissar. I'd guessed that this one was a biggy and I knew all about F-15s: to stand any chance at all you've got to stay low and pray your *Sirena's* working so you can pick up the *Sparrow* lock-on in time to twist away and round it. And so I ignored the brief and went in low level. It was working too; I could hear and see the mêlées going on above me and I had the main bomber stream, or some of it, on my *High Lark* radar at 15 miles when I got my tail shot off. Bloody typical: for five years now *Flogger* pilots have been told to use their 'initiative'. That was translated by the Squadron boss to mean that if a mission failed because you followed the plan, you should have done your own thing; if you did your own thing and it worked, then that proved that the boss's plan was flexible; but if the mission failed for whatever reason you should not have done your own thing. Trouble was that the SAM trogs were also being told about initiative and that really was bad news. And in any case, how could you stay a competent fighter pilot and become a mud-mover at the same time if they only let you fly for 90 hours a year. Oh yes, since 1981 they've tried to make *Flogger* G drivers do ground attack as well. Now, if instead they had spent the time and fuel working up big regimental intercept attacks, or even let the *Foxbat* clowns mix it with the *Floggers* a bit – but no one at

Army Headquarters would ever listen to the Squadron shags. They just push the bloody paper around and watch promotion lists."

The RAF police had now arrived. Balashov swiftly held out the mug just once more and broke, for the first time, more or less, into English.

"Cheers, comrade. You are good troop."

He then moved off, a little unsteadily, down the corridor. The Wing Commander reflected, as he watched him go, on the unchanging characteristics of the fighter pilot everywhere – especially at 0430 hours after being shot down by his own side!

It was clear, at least, that they had not yet solved the problem of airspace management on that side either! **9**[*]

_____

Whatever difficulties faced the Soviet High Command in the field, apart from growing concern in the Kremlin over signs of internal instabilities further back, all of which indicated a pressing need to bring the operations in the Central Region to an early and successful conclusion, there was no doubt that on the other side Allied Command Europe was in deep trouble. It is well known now that SACEUR was under urgent pressure from his army group commanders to seek the release of battlefield nuclear weapons. He was still resisting this, convinced that it would rapidly lead to the all-out nuclear exchange dreaded on both sides. He knew that the President of the United States shared this view. SACEUR recognized that he had to do three things: plug the Venlo gap, where a further heavy attack from 20 Guards Army spearheaded by the crack 6 Guards Motor Rifle Division could not be long delayed; relieve pressure there by a counter-offensive from south to north into the rearward echelons following up this attack, in the general direction of Bremen; and interdict the movement through Poland of the armour now beginning to move forward from the group of tank armies in Belorussia.

He had put together a theatre reserve, carefully husbanded and held under the command of Allied Forces Central Europe (AFCENT) with instructions not to deploy it without express instruction, of the equivalent of some seven divisions. He expected that if the trans-Atlantic air bridge held and the air and sea defences in the Western Approaches to the British Isles were sufficient to bring into port four big convoys now nearing the end of a hazardous journey, he could expect, even with the heavy losses there would have been at sea, the equivalent of two fresh US corps very soon. He had also managed to persuade the French to divert an armoured division

_____

[*] _The Hawk_ 1986, journal published by the Royal Air Force Staff College, Bracknell, England, p. 28.

intended for SOUTHAG to the north and expected it in the Maastricht area within forty-eight hours. Finally, he had great faith in the strength and capacity, as well as in the leadership, of the Allied air forces. Battered though they were they could still make a special effort and pull out something good.

The Krefeld salient near Venlo would simply have to be held by the troops already there, assisted by the French and whatever he could push up from CENTAG (a brigade or two perhaps) until his fresh troops could come in, but he would also ask for a maximum effort from his air forces in support.

The all important counter-offensive towards Bremen would be undertaken by NORTHAG, to which he ordered the allotment of four of his precious reserve divisions as from 0001 hours on 14 August, for an offensive to open at first light on the 15th.

For the interdiction of tank movement across Poland, where Polish workers were being urged by Western broadcasting media to do their utmost to sabotage the rail system, he would ask the air forces to make one supreme effort.

━━━━━━━━

❝SACEUR spoke over his discrete voice-net to Commander Allied Air Forces Central Europe (COMAAFCE) in his underground war room in the Eifel region.

"Can you cut the main rail links running west from Wroclaw and Poznan in Poland?" he asked.

COMAAFCE was startled. This would mean sending what remained of his irreplaceable F-111s and *Tornados* through the grim defences of East Germany and Poland. SACEUR's question suggested such a complete misunderstanding of what they would be up against (and what they had already done at such high cost, for that matter) that he found it hard to be civil.

"I know things are bad," he replied, "but have you gone out of your mind? If I sent thirty aircraft we would be lucky if ten got over the targets and five of them came back. And these are some of your dual-capable nuclear aircraft."

"Okay, okay," said SACEUR. "You airmen are always so touchy – I'm not telling you how to do it. I'm just saying what it is that's got to be done. Give me a call back in half an hour."

At COMAAFCE's operational headquarters the planners looked at it all ways but continued to shake their heads. They just could not see how an effective force could be brought to bear at a remotely acceptable cost in air losses. The use of calculators and operating manuals speeded up as heads drew closer together over the plotting charts.

Twenty-five minutes later COMAAFCE was back on the line to SACEUR.

"Look," he said "those Swedes are having their own war up there, but if you can get them to let us into two of their southern airfields we can do it. All we'll want is fuel for thirty aircraft between two bases. They'll arrive and leave at night and there will be no fuss. Depending on how it goes we might need to recover to the same bases early in the morning but we'll try to get them back to Britain, or at least to Norway. Of course if the Swedes could give some fighter cover on the way back from the Polish coast that would be great. But from what I hear that's against their rules."

The senior Swedish liaison officer at SHAPE listened gravely to this request and undertook to put it straightaway to Stockholm.

In half an hour the answer came back – yes, the two Wings could use the airfields, provided it was planned and executed exactly as COMAAFCE had said: namely, in and out on the same night with the highest security before and after the event. They could not agree to let the force recover to Sweden next morning unless it was in distress. Nor could there by any question of *Flygvapnet* (Swedish Air Force) fighters providing cover, for that would constitute offensive action in breach of the widely known and well recognized principles of defending Swedish neutrality.

By noon that day, 13 August, eighteen USAF FB-111s and twelve *Tornados* (six each from the RAF and the German Air Force) had been detailed for the mission from Upper Heyford, Cottesmore and Marham in England. Cottesmore was the air base to which the German Air Force *Tornados* had been withdrawn from Nörvenich in Germany. The Wing Commander who was to lead the RAF/GAF element left his crews studying their radar and infra-red target maps and took a *Hawk* jet-trainer down from Marham to see the CO of the FB-111s at Upper Heyford. These were old friends from their time together at the US Air War College at Maxwell, Alabama, and they had a lot to tie up.

The essence of the plan was that the F-111/*Tornado* force, having flown over southern Norway to Sweden, would approach Poland from the north. Flying across the Polish plain at 70 metres or so they would have an excellent chance of avoiding detection until well over the coast, when the distance to run would be only 180 kilometres to Poznan and 270 to Wroclaw, and this would be covered in twelve to eighteen minutes' flying. By refuelling and setting out from Sweden, the northern flank of the Warsaw Pact defences would be turned. This was the key to the whole operation. Evasive routing would keep them clear of the worst of the fixed defences which would anyway have minimum warning of their approach. With luck they might be taken completely by surprise. The force would be split when it crossed the Wista river north of Bydgoszcz and the two parts would then head separately to their targets. A hot reception by fighters would undoubtedly be waiting for them on their way back but they would have to rely on their speed and keeping as low as possible in the dark to get them through.

At midnight, and with a bare minimum of airfield lighting, the two Wings landed at the *Flygvapnet* air bases of Kalmar and Kallinge. All thirty aircraft were refuelled and ready in little more than an hour before taking off again on their mission at 0200 hours. The primary targets were the multi-span bridges over the Warta and Oder rivers, which carried the main railway lines to Berlin from Warsaw and Krakow. Long trains of transporter floats, each train carrying up to fifty T-72 tanks or equivalent loads, were moving slowly to the west around the cities of Poznan and Wroclaw, sometimes spaced no more than a 100 metres apart. It would be a rewarding operation indeed if that flow could be halted, but bridges had always been difficult targets in air warfare. From above, it took only a small line error to produce a complete miss and bridges were designed to take heavy loads in the vertical plane anyway. Now it was all different: they were going to be hit sideways by missiles fired from 3,000 metres' range with radar and infra-red homing weapons striking the bridge piers like giant hammers on a demolition job. Any missiles or bombs left over would be launched at whatever trains they could find in their path on the way out.

The *Tornados* led both streams as they divided over the Wista river to the north. Their first task was to bring anti-radiation defence suppression weapons to bear against the SAM systems around the cities and on the bridges and to clear the way for the heavier armament of the FB-111s.

At the first bridges they had an easy ride, but when the gunners dozing over their ZSU radar-controlled anti-aircraft guns woke up to what was happening they put up such a dense curtain of fire that four *Tornados* had gone down before the batteries were silenced. Five FB-111s went the same way and two which had been straggling a bit had fallen to SAM near Bydgoszcz to the north when the force had split. In all, four bridges went down, with spans crumpling into the rivers carrying two trains with them. This was a tremendous achievement, of critical importance to the battle on the Central Front.

Nineteen out of the original force of thirty aircraft swept round out of the target area to battle their way back along the shortest route to the Baltic west of Gdansk.

The defences were now fully alerted but it was still dark, and flying not far below the speed of sound a bare 70 metres above the flat terrain they were a very difficult target for the MiG-23 *Floggers* of the GDR and Polish Air Forces waiting for them to the north. One more *Tornado* and an FB-111 went at this stage but, although it is difficult to know even now, it was the general opinion of the crews in the easterly stream that the Polish fighters had not pressed home their attacks with much enthusiasm.

Four of the seventeen surviving aircraft with heavy battle damage made distress calls and, taking the Swedes at their word, put their aircraft down on the ground in the first light of dawn at Kallinge air base. Four Soviet Air Force *Foxbats* in hot pursuit into Swedish airspace were met by interceptors and the greater agility of the Swedish *Viggens* sent two of the *Foxbats* down before the other two turned away and headed back towards Leningrad.

The two commanders, the American and the Briton, were still in the lead of their sections as the remaining aircraft flew on low over the sea towards the west. They had agreed the day before that they would cut the south-west corner of Sweden very fast and close to the ground, before pulling up over the mountains to make their pre-planned landing at Oslo in Norway.

Next day was to see the massive B-52 onslaught on the front line near Venlo. If that was the bludgeon blow, this daring and skilful attack by night intruders had been the rapier thrust. As had looked likely, the enemy's heavy bridging equipment had been taken well forward into East Germany, where it expected to be attacked, and where, of course, it repeatedly was. This resulted in scarcity of bridging and recovery equipment further back. Many trains had now to be sent back to Warsaw and Krakow and laboriously re-routed through Czechoslovakia to the south and Bydgoszcz to the north. On the map it looked like a relatively easy exercise, but yet again the inflexibility of Warsaw Pact plans was to create difficulties. Even more resulted from widespread sabotage by Polish workers, acting on exhortation and instruction over Western radio broadcasts. In all, the rapier had added a telling thirty-six hours or so to Soviet reinforcement timings. This was to multiply and would greatly exacerbate Warsaw Pact problems after the B-52 attack on the front line next morning, 15 August. **9***

The position near Venlo on the front of II British Corps, whose four divisions were flanked on the right by a US brigade and on the left by I Netherlands Corps, was critical. By nightfall on 14 August the Soviet 20 Guards Army was not far from achieving the front commander's object, which was to force a way through the Allied forces defending the point of the Krefeld salient that Soviet forces had driven between Duisburg and Venlo, and thus open the possibility of carrying out the truly critical part of the whole Warsaw Pact operational plan. This was still, once a crossing had been forced over the lower Rhine, to swing left upstream and take CENTAG from the rear.

Already trans-Atlantic reinforcement was building up and the massive augmentation the Soviet Union had hoped to forestall was well under way. The arrival in the Central Region of a fresh US corps was imminent. Its advanced parties began to arrive in the Aachen area early on the 15th. A French armoured division was approaching Maastricht. SACEUR had released four divisions from his last theatre reserves to NORTHAG, as from 0001 hours on 14 August, for the counter-offensive north-eastwards towards Bremen to open at first light on the 15th.

This was to be a critical day in the history of the Third World War. At the point of the Krefeld salient Soviet troops had penetrated II British Corps and by nightfall on 14 August Soviet tanks were not far from Jülich. Unless the Soviet advance could be held up on 15 August the fresh US corps and the additional French division could not be brought into action in time, the NORTHAG counter-offensive towards Bremen would be stillborn, and the whole Allied position in the Federal Republic would be threatened by the Soviet thrust southward, up the left bank of the Rhine, in CENTAG's rear. This, it was clear, was the time to use the B-52s standing by at Lajes in the Azores. On the morning of 14 August SACEUR ordered COM-AAFCE to make a maximum effort at first light on the 15th, to slow down the Soviet advance and help to stabilize the position in the

---

* Air Vice-Marshal Alec Penteith RAF, *Tornados in World War III* (Chatto and Windus, London 1986), p. 265.

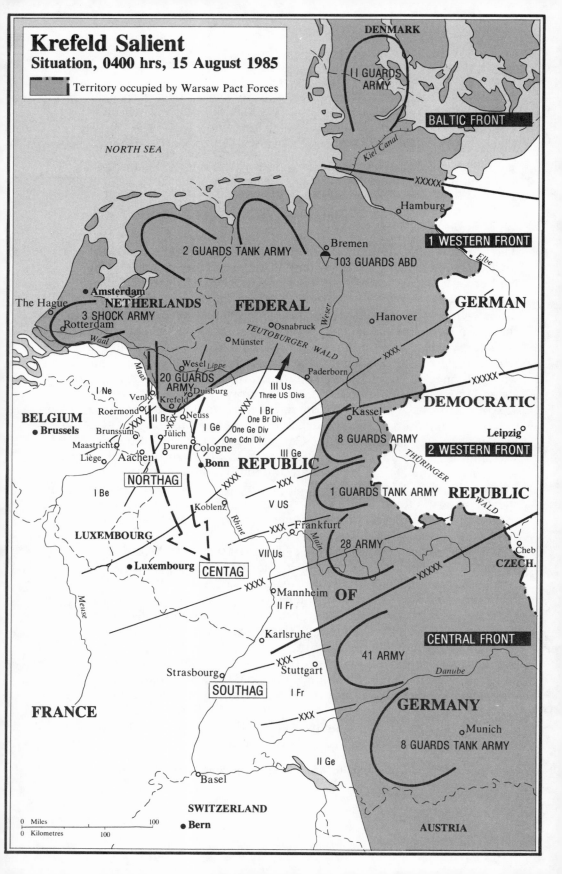

Krefeld Salient
Situation, 0400 hrs, 15 August 1985

Territory occupied by Warsaw Pact Forces

DENMARK

11 GUARDS ARMY

BALTIC FRONT

NORTH SEA

Kiel Canal

XXXXX

Hamburg

Elbe

1 WESTERN FRONT

2 GUARDS TANK ARMY

Bremen

103 GUARDS ABD

GERMAN

FEDERAL

Weser

Hanover

Amsterdam

The Hague

NETHERLANDS

3 SHOCK ARMY

Rotterdam

Waal

Osnabruck

Münster

TEUTOBURGER WALD

Paderborn

XXXX

DEMOCRATIC

XXXXX

Wesel Lippe

20 GUARDS ARMY

Duisburg

III Us
Three US Divs

Kassel

8 GUARDS ARMY

Leipzig

2 WESTERN FRONT

Maas

I Ne

Venlo

Krefeld

Roermond

II Br

Neuss

I Ge

BELGIUM

Brussels

Brunssum

Maastricht

Liège

Aachen

Jülich

Duren

Cologne

Bonn

REPUBLIC

I Br
One Br Div
One Ge Div
One Cdn Div

III Ge

XXXX

XXX

THÜRINGER WALD

REPUBLIC

1 GUARDS TANK ARMY

I Be

NORTHAG

Koblenz

Rhine

V US

XXX

Frankfurt

Main

28 ARMY

Cheb

CZECH.

LUXEMBOURG

1

VII Us

Luxembourg

CENTAG

XXXXX

XXXX

Mannheim

II Fr

OF

CENTRAL FRONT

Meuse

Karlsruhe

41 ARMY

Strasbourg

XXX

Stuttgart

Danube

SOUTHAG

I Fr

FRANCE

XXX

GERMANY

Munich

8 GUARDS TANK ARMY

II Ge

Basel

SWITZERLAND

Bern

AUSTRIA

0 Miles 100
0 Kilometres 100

Krefeld salient. The action of the B-52 bomber force, at what was a truly crucial moment of the war, deserves attention in some detail.

All were aware, ground and air commanders alike, that the practical problems raised by the decision to use the B-52s would be difficult to resolve. Defending forces would have to break contact far enough and long enough to give the B-52s a bomb line that would permit the maximum impact on Warsaw Pact armour with minimum casualties in NATO forward positions. That, COMAAFCE must have reflected pragmatically on the morning of 14 August, was now the army's problem; his was to get as many of the B-52s as possible over the Krefeld salient at 0400 hours local time the following day.

The targeting directive was received at Lajes at 1200 hours local time on the 14th. During the previous week the crews had increased the customary proportions of alert status, which ran from fifteen minutes to six hours. By 1500 hours that day the last batch of air tests was complete and thirty-nine of the B-52s were declared serviceable for the mission. It was now that the expertise built up by air crew and ground crew in several years of European exercises paid handsome dividends. One hundred MK-82 bombs were loaded into each bomb bay and, although the round trip of 4,000 miles would be well within B-52 range, a full fuel load was taken on board. By 2200 hours air crew briefings were completed. The target area was a strip of territory 10 kilometres from north to south by 2 kilometres east to west, due west of Neuss. It was believed that in that area at least three divisions of 20 Guards Army, with probably one or two of the leading regiments of the second echelon, would be concentrating for a final breakthrough. In practical terms the targets would include at least 20,000 troops, 1,000 tanks, 500 BTR and a further 1,500 soft-skinned vehicles essential to the forward momentum of the ground attack. The terrain was flat and offered little natural cover. The proximity of an *Autobahnkreuz* afforded a near-perfect identification point for either visual or radar bombing. Time on target would be 0400 hours and bombing height would be 40,000 feet.

The B-52s carried a wealth of defensive equipment but exercises during the previous five years had pointed the need for fighter escort. On this occasion that responsibility was to be shared amongst French *Mirage* F-1Cs, 2000s and USAF F-15s. The B-52s' route would take them north-eastwards across the Pyrenees and up across France and Luxembourg towards Cologne, where they would begin their bombing run.

By 0300 hours the bombing stream was cruising at 525 miles per hour at 40,000 feet over France, still on a north-north-easterly heading. Above and to either side were loose gaggles of *Mirage* F-1Cs of the Commandement Air de Forces de Défense Aériennes

(CAFDA). The AWACS screen, now pulled back over central France, detected no unusual enemy fighter movement either from the captured airfields in West Germany or across the inner German border.

From the Meuse valley area onwards, the B-52s entered theoretical intercept range of *Flogger* Gs and *Foxbats*. To reduce Allied difficulties of identification and airspace management COMAAFCE had stopped all deeper battlefield interdiction or counter-air attacks in the Central Region after 2300 hours, so that anything coming across the FEBA could be assumed to be hostile. COMAAFCE's staff had calculated that some kind of warning would reach the Warsaw Pact from agents in Lisbon and that the remaining IL-76 C *Cookers*, although now held well back over central Poland, would probably pick up the high-flying B-52 formation over central France. Seeing the formation, however, was one thing; deciding where it was headed was quite different. The known combat radius of the B-52s was so great that they could at any moment change heading and threaten troop concentrations, logistic support, command centres or any other targets anywhere between the Baltic and Bulgaria. Moreover, while COMAAFCE knew that *Flogger* and *Foxbat* units had been moved forward behind the advancing Warsaw Pact armies during the previous ten days, he suspected that the Soviets, rather like the Nazis with the *Luftwaffe* in France in 1940, had found it quite easy to deploy the aircraft themselves but much more difficult to support them quickly with enough weapons, fuel and battle-damage repair facilities to allow them to maintain a high sortie rate. It would, therefore, have been fatal for the Warsaw Pact's air defence units to be thrown into battle either too deep in NATO territory, where the French interceptors were still relatively unscathed, or before the final heading and destination of the bombers were more definitely known.

COMAAFCE also knew that the Soviets were about to have their hands forced, because as the B-52s approached Luxembourg they were joined by four F-111 EB ECM aircraft which effectively blinded all three *Cookers* and a large number of the enemy's shorter-range surveillance radars. The *Floggers* and *Foxbats* had to be scrambled towards the last known B-52 heading from bases up to 400 miles away and, as the NATO planning staffs had hoped when they had first envisaged the use of the B-52, the fighters' problems did not end there. Despite Soviet attempts to encourage pilot initiative, looser formations and reduced ground control, most air defence crews had been trained to fight in their own airspace against intruding bombers whose position and heading were precisely known. Not only were air crew conditioned to this; the aircraft were designed for little else. *Foxbat* was purely and simply a high-speed high-altitude interceptor with poor manoeuvrability, while *Flogger* G, although more flexible, was by no means an air-superiority fighter, though both would fare better at high level than at low against their NATO counterparts. A further complication was that Polish, East German and Czechoslovak pilots had expected to be defending their own homelands. Scrambling with little control from unfamiliar airfields against a vaguely defined target well away from their national airspace was not the best invitation to enthusiastic performance.

Such enthusiasm for combat as they did have would shortly be reduced still further. The formation of F-111 EB ECM aircraft was soon to be joined behind their jamming screen by forty *Mirage* 2000s and thirty of the remaining F-15s from 2 and 4 ATAF. As the bombers turned north-north-west over Cologne their crews could see outlined against the slightly lighter sky to the east the comforting silhouette of some of the most effective fighters in the world. Although the night was clouded, the city of Cologne and the river bend were crystal clear in the air-to-ground radar displays. Within a few seconds the offset aiming point, the *Autobahnkreuz* between Venlo and Duisburg, came up with equal clarity. Then, as the diary of 337 Squadron of the USAF records, 'all shades of hell broke loose both in the air and on the ground'.

It was, and is, impossible to say how many Warsaw Pact fighters were scrambled against the B-52s. The early warning *Sentries* identified eighty-five blips initially but their ability to note every target was soon lost in the very large numbers of aircraft flying in less than 100 square miles of airspace. The situation was further confused by the attempts of three Soviet Air Force *Cubs* to jam both the bomber radars and the *Sentries'* own surveillance beams. The balance of advantage, for the time being at least, remained with the NATO force. The Warsaw Pact ground controllers could do no more than direct their fighters to the approximate source of the F-111 jamming and leave them to it. But, for the first time in the war, F-15 *Eagles* were able to engage to the full extent of their equipment. There was no need to close to identify: if it was heading west, hack it. At 50 miles the *Foxbat* and *Floggers* were clearly visible on the *Eagles'* radar, and head-on at Mach 2 the enemy aircraft were well within the attack envelope of the *Eagles'* radar-guided *Sparrow* missiles.

Each *Eagle* carried four *Sparrow* and four infra-red homing *Sidewinder* air-to-air missiles. So many *Sparrows* were fired in such short time that to the bomber crews they looked like salvoes. But by no means all found their targets. A small proportion failed to detonate, one or two exploded against each other in what is called fratricide, some targets were struck by more than one missile and a few Warsaw Pact pilots were quick enough to react to their *Sirena* radar warning receivers and break the beams of the incoming missiles. It is possible, however, that more than 100 *Sparrow* missiles were fired in the first moments of contact and that some sixty attackers were hit. *Sentries* observed with interest that immediately after the opening contact, several hostile blips abruptly changed heading and set course eastwards.

Most of the fighters that had escaped the first impact, however, were not deterred and at 20 miles from the bomber stream the powerful *Fox Fire* AI (air-intercept) radar of the *Foxbats* began to burn through the F-111 jamming to disclose the B-52s. By now, however, it was 0400 hours and the first light of dawn was reaching the upper skies. Still the advantage lay with the Western allies. Now the F-15s and the *Mirages* could use their considerable advantage in agility to close, identify and kill the fast-tracking MiGs with the wide-aspect infra-red homing *Sidewinders* and *Magics*.

Then, to everybody's consternation, Soviet and Allied radar warning receivers (RWR) detected the launch of a real salvo of SAM from one of the forward Soviet battalions near Dortmund. Defection from the attackers' ranks promptly occurred as several Warsaw Pact pilots realized the implications of Soviet SAM firing into the middle of the mêlée in the air. As the salvo of SA-4 missiles was not repeated it is not known whether a trigger-happy major had been demonstrating a rare flash of initiative or whether a decision at a higher level had been hastily countermanded as a result of angry protest from the Warsaw Pact fighter commander.

In the B-52s each electronic warfare officer (EWO) sat in his compartment oblivious to the crackle of sound in his headset, intent only on the 12-inch-square cathode-ray tube in front of him which displayed the information from a suite of ECM equipment on either side. The SA-4 launch was monitored and when warning of missile 'lock on' was received the automatic self-jamming screen immediately broke the link. SA-4 homing frequencies had long been known and, to the EWO's relief, they had not been changed. None of the bombers fell to SAM attack.

Combatants elsewhere in the sky were not so fortunate. Subsequently, several pilots from both sides vehemently claimed that they had been shot down by SAM rather than by enemy fighters. Certainly they were not expecting such interference from the ground, but in fact very few of the pilots knew for certain exactly what had shot them down. The MiGs were intent on reaching the bomber stream but could not afford to ignore the *Mirages* and *Eagles*. Pre-battle tactical plans were rapidly forgotten in the confusion. RWR keys flashed continuously as aircraft illuminated each other with their AI radars. Infra-red missiles, and finally guns, were used by both sides and losses mounted, aggravated by air-to-air collisions and an unknown number of errors of identification. It was quickly obvious that while the *Floggers* were out-manoeuvred and out-gunned, if a *Foxbat* was not picked off on the first attack its ability to burst away at Mach 3 would make catching and hitting it from the rear impossible. The *Foxbat*'s speed advantage had serious implications for the B-52s.

The main air battle raged for little more than five minutes, but that was just long enough for almost all the bombers to complete their bombing runs. Below them, the units of the 20 Guards Army were completing their nightly replenishment before moving on to maintain the momentum of the advance against what must have seemed from its apparent attempt to disengage during the night a defeated II British Corps. The revving of tank and BTR engines, the rumble of fuel bowsers, engineer trucks and all the other noises of four divisions preparing to attack obscured completely the faint whine of jet engines 8 miles above. There was no warning as the first deluge of 500 lb bombs smashed down among them. In the next six minutes over 1,500 tons of high explosive thundered over an area of little more than 8 square miles. The T-72 and T-80 tanks that had survived frontal assaults from air-to-surface rockets were shattered by direct hits or had their tracks torn off by blast, while BTR and soft-skinned vehicles were destroyed in their hundreds. The impact on the Soviet ground troops was terrific. Many were killed outright or injured. Many more were stunned and paralysed. Tank and BTR crews were caught either on top of their vehicles or away from them on the ground. Most were reservists, having their first taste of battle, and many broke down under the surprise, ferocity and duration of this thunderous assault from an unseen enemy. Two forward divisional headquarters survived but 20 Guards Army in less than ten minutes of one-sided combat, had virtually ceased, for several vital hours, to exist as a fighting formation.

Inevitably, losses on the ground were not confined to 20 Guards Army. Although a bombing line 1,200 yards ahead of the defending British and Dutch troops had been defined, free-falling bombs from 40,000 feet are no respecters of bomb lines. And although the bombers' approach on a track parallel to the bomb line had reduced the risk from shortfalls, the navigator bombardiers were not all equally adept at handling their almost fully-automated bombing systems. As a result, one British battalion and some companies of Dutch infantry suffered heavy losses.

Above the ground forces, the B-52 crews had no time either to exult in their success or worry about their bombing accuracy. One EWO after another picked up search illuminations from *Foxbat* radars, quickly followed by the continuous warning of AA-9 missile lock-on. Chaff dispensers were fired and many missiles exploded harmlessly in the clouds of drifting foil or veered away sharply as their guidance giros toppled. Occasionally the tail-gunners caught a glimpse of the fighters and blazed away optimistically with their four 0.5 inch guns, much as their B-17 forbears had done forty years previously. But the *Foxbat* pilots were brave and persistent. No. 337 Squadron was the last in the wave and bore the brunt of the fighters' attack. Two aircraft were destroyed before they could release their bombs, and two more immediately afterwards. As the stream turned west towards the relative safety of North Sea airspace it suffered further losses: one B-52 was rammed from above by a *Foxbat*, while others fell to short-range AA-6 infra-red homing missiles. It was no consolation to the survivors that most of the MiGs were themselves about to be intercepted and destroyed by Dutch and Belgian F-16 *Fighting Falcons*, which were now, at dawn, able to join the fray.

Altogether, only seventeen B-52s got back to Lajes and several of those had suffered battle damage and casualties. Four more force-landed safely at bases in France or Belgium, but of the original thirty-nine, eighteen were lost, an attrition rate of over 45 per cent. Military historians will discuss that figure with interest. They will perhaps agree that no commander in history could accept such loss rates for any length of time. But as in the October War of 1973 in the Middle East, any evaluation of attrition rates must take into account the importance of the overall objectives. The alternatives to the B-52 attack had been probable failure to prevent 20 Guards Army from rolling up CENTAG from the rear, or well-nigh intolerable pressure from NATO field commanders to release nuclear weapons to relieve pressure, with all the dreadful consequences of the escalation that would almost certainly follow. In exchange for the loss of less than fifty fighter and bomber air crew and some 270 soldiers, the critical Warsaw Pact thrust had been checked, while the NORTHAG counter-offensive towards Bremen was far from being stillborn.

It had all been a very near thing. So much could have gone wrong. The actual launching of the NORTHAG counter-offensive, for example, had depended on the possession of the area around Münster, south of the River Lippe, during the day of 14 August and the following night. Without that it was hard to see how the counter-offensive could have got under way at all. Soviet pressure from the north was heavy and continuous. The Battle of the Lippe, which has been written up elsewhere,* was another very important blow in the preservation of the Federal Republic from destruction.

By 16 August the newly arrived US corps, fighting in a flank position near Aachen, was threatening any further forward move-

---

* See Sir John Hackett and others, op. cit., pp. 235–6, 238, 241, 257.

ment southwards along the Rhine. The Soviet armour never got further south than Jülich.

The Warsaw Pact timetable had now been seriously upset and regrouping was necessary, involving not a retreat but certainly some rearward movement, beginning with the withdrawal of forward divisions in the Krefeld salient now threatened with encirclement. This was not, it must be clearly understood, a decisive military defeat for the Red Army. There were still huge forces at hand which could be brought to bear before the full potential of the United States could become effective. But it was a setback, a failure to achieve the early swift success which was rightly seen to be of such critical importance. It was a demonstration that the USSR, however powerful, was neither omnipotent nor invulnerable, and this offered encouragement to any in the Soviet Union or its satellite states who hoped at some time for a lifting of the dead hand of a communist regime.

❜On 14 August a Soviet MiG-25 *Foxbat* B landed at an aerodrome near Dijon. The pilot, one Captain Belov, requested political asylum. Captain Belov reported that he had been flying an intelligence mission prior to a fresh major offensive in the central sector ordered for the next day. The attack of which Belov had given warning, but of which there were also plenty of other indicators, started at dawn on 15 August, with simultaneous thrusts at the boundaries of four NATO corps. In each case a single Soviet motor rifle division was used, followed as usual by the KGB barrage battalions and with normal artillery support. The intention was to force wide dispersal of the enemy's reserves. The 4 Guards Tank Army now formed in Poland would move in to exploit success.

The 197 Motor Rifle Division, with its two light motor rifle regiments up, was by 0630 hours beginning to force a wedge into the enemy positions at the junction of I British and I German Corps. The advance was covered by the fire of 400 guns and supported in depth by 180 attack aircraft.

The tank and heavy motor rifle regiments were still deployed along their start lines, waiting for the light infantry to find a weakness in the hostile defences.

In the early morning mist, the punishment units that had reinforced the division were preparing for battle alongside Nekrassov's battalion. Ammunition was only distributed to those units right in the firing line. They had no heavy weapons. Security at the punishment battalion rested with elderly, heavy-tracked BTR 50-PUs, from which the men in forward units were kept in the sights of automatic weapons. The punishment units were international. On Nekrassov's right, arms were being distributed to Polish workers straight from prison, covered by the weapons of an East German security company. On his left, a battalion of Soviet dissidents were downing their vodka under convoy of a Polish company.

Nekrassov was now a Captain. The previous evening, everyone who had returned from the earlier engagements had received a medal. Officers' epaulettes everywhere were brightened by a new sprinkling of stars. The regimental commander had presented Nekrassov with his new captain's epaulettes, promising him he would be a major in three days' time, if he was still alive. He himself had got to be lieutenant colonel from captain in just that time, and was now a colonel. Nekrassov was not encouraged. He stared into the distance chewing a piece of grass. It was just possible that he set more store by the support of stolid Boris, still driving his BMP, and the attentions of little Yuri, worn out and fast asleep now in the back of the BMP, than any hope of further advancement.

A curtain of black smoke hung over the wooded hills 2 kilometres away. Flights of monstrous metallic birds were again flying towards the smoke, the treetops bending in their infernal roar. Sometimes a whole squadron would fly past, sometimes they came over in pairs or fours. The noise as they screamed by made the soldiers duck, seconds after the black shadows had already flickered past over the column and were lost in the distance.

Tanks came rumbling past Nekrassov's battalion: he realized that the tank regiment was now being put in. The punishment troops rode on the tanks. They had been issued with green battledress jackets but still wore their striped prison trousers.

"Where are you lot off to in your pyjamas?" Nekrassov's men shouted at them.

But the punishment troops on the tanks did not understand a word. They were not Slavs. They were probably Romanians, put out there as enemies of the regime. Close alongside the Soviet tanks, lurching over the damaged road, BTR loaded with soldiers in Hungarian uniform were making sure that the punishment troops stayed with the tanks. Nekrassov reckoned that since the guard was Hungarian the punishment troops were almost certainly Romanian. Romanian and Soviet regimes were in full agreement on one point at least. Why feed dissenters in gaol if they can die heroes' deaths for the regime?

The tank regiment carrying the punishment troops was sent into battle on a narrow sector, followed by three barrage infantry battalions, these followed in turn by the heavy motor rifle regiment with orders to shoot in the back any from the pyjama brigade who failed to show the right spirit.

By noon there were few punishment troops remaining. The tank regiment too had suffered heavy losses. It had been amalgamated during the course of the battle into a single battalion. The heavy motor rifle regiment had got off lightly, protected as it was by the tanks and pyjama boys. Now it, too, pushed forward. Although not itself a punishment regiment, none the less a barrage battalion of the KGB followed close on its heels, just to be on the safe side. There was hardly any opposition from the enemy. Groups of attacking Soviet BMP were moving into swift thrusts at the remaining pockets of defence.

By 1000 hours it was clear that the regiment had broken through into an undefended area. The regimental commander gave the order, "No skirmishing!" The regiment was to bypass any active defence and move on westwards with all possible speed.

The army attack had been made on three thrust lines at the boundaries of four enemy corps sectors. Two divisions had been held up. One, the 197 Motor Rifle Division, had broken through. In fact, the two divisions that had been checked had been almost completely wiped out, paving the way with their casualties for a battalion or even a regiment at a time to break through here and there, charging on regardless of threats from the flanks or of shortage of ammunition, or even damage to essential equipment.

The front commander decided to concentrate on the boundary between I British and I German Corps, where the defence was crumbling before the attack of his most successful division, the 197th. This was the critical time to throw the Tank Army Group into the attack.

Polish workers and NATO air attack had ensured that only one tank army out of the three poised in Belorussia was available in time. Even so, as Nekrassov knew, a single tank army was a formidable thing. The aim of tank forces, or the Tank Army Group, was to use the narrow openings made by the divisions and armies of the first echelon to thrust westwards, smashing a steel wedge through troop positions, communication centres and administration, destroying any hope of reintegrating the defence. It had to be like a million tons of water suddenly breaking through a little crack in a concrete dam where only a few drops at a time had been seeping through before.

The roar of the endless columns of 4 Guards Tank Army was deafening. The sky had vanished. A mist hung over everything and the faint disc of the sun hardly showed through the cloud of grey dust. What could withstand this avalanche?

The 197 Motor Rifle Division had broken through but was itself disintegrating. Nekrassov's battalion, now comprising twenty-three BMP, and reinforced by a tank company with eight tanks, was on its own. All communication had been cut off. Divisional headquarters had almost ceased to function and now the regimental command appeared to have been taken out too. He could make no contact with them. Nekrassov knew that if the advanced units of the tank army were deployed on one of the neighbouring lines of advance, and not on his own, there would be for him and his command no hope at all. His regiment had split into three independent groups with no central command. There was no one behind him, only thousands of corpses and hundreds of burnt-out vehicles. If the approaching tanks attacked in his direction his battalion would be like the little fish that live round the jaws of a shark, with this tiny battalion ahead, the huge tank army behind. They would be safe.

With no orders, no information, Nekrassov suddenly sensed with certainty that the tanks had come into the attack behind him. There had been no air support for some hours past, but now the whole sky filled with the roar of rocket motors. It was clear that several air divisions had been put up to cover the attack. Now the tanks began to come swiftly into Nekrassov's view. Faster! Faster! There could be no doubt now about what his remnant of a battalion had to do.

"Advance!" yelled Nekrassov into his throat microphone. "Advance!" The troops themselves realized they were at the sharp end of a gigantic armoured wedge. Nekrassov's vehicles roared ahead, always onwards, straight ahead only. On the left of his armoured column the rear echelons of a British division were retreating on a parallel route. Nekrassov ignored them. Onwards to the west! And fast! But now the air forces and the forward elements of the tank army seemed to have swerved aside from what he had assumed was the thrust line. They were now separated from Nekrassov's column. In spite of all the orders strongly forbidding time-wasting minor engagements they had deviated from the main axis of advance. He noted what was happening with dismay. His driver Boris saw him for the first time at a loss.

Sparks flew up from the tracks as BMP clanked and roared their way forward. Without slackening speed the diminished battalion charged through a small red-brick town. The streets were full of refugees pulling small vehicles overloaded with pitiful household gear. Tearful children with frightened eyes ran screaming. Old people who remembered the last war shrank into doorways. Nekrassov's battalion broke through the panic-stricken crowds which filled the streets, tearing on westwards. The people fled in terror. Nekrassov's soldiers ignored them, the BMP running over any who stood in the way. To clear this obstacle and push on faster towards the front was all that mattered.

"Don't curse me!" shouted Nekrassov at the country people as he passed them. "I'm only a soldier. You're nothing to do with me. But the KGB pursuit battalion will come later. They'll deal with you." No one heard him except Boris at the controls of the BMP, on the intercom. No one else would have understood him anyway.

Before nightfall, however, the attack of 4 Guards Tank Army, ordered by the front commander and considered by him to be of critical importance, had come to a halt. There had been a shattering event. On a neighbouring sector, in the Netherlands, General Ryzanov commanding 3 Shock Army, in one of the most dramatic developments of the war, had declared his army the Russian Army of Liberation, sent liaison officers over to NATO and ordered fire to be opened on Soviet troops. The same thing had happened in the Second World War with 2 Shock Army, when in May 1942 their Commander, Lieutenant General Vlasov, ordered the shooting of Chekists and political commissars, and began fighting against communist troops. On that occasion the mutiny had been more or less contained, though Vlasov kept quite an important force in being, fighting against the communists, using captured equipment and supplies, up to the very end of the war, and to his own most cruel and heroic death. This time the regime was going to find the going very much harder. Ryzanov's force had to be sealed off and neutralized. This meant the withdrawal of other formations from the main effort.

Soviet battalions and regiments in some numbers, cut off deep in the rear of the enemy by the change of front of 3 Shock Army, soon ceased to be effective fighting forces. NATO commanders put this short but welcome breathing space to good use in regrouping for counter-offensive operations. The Soviet High Command's last hope of a timely resolution to the operations in the FRG (and it was a matter of growing urgency that they should soon be brought to a successful end) now lay in the other two tank armies of the Belorussian Tank Army Group, 5 and 7 Guards Tank Armies. These, however, after savage NATO air attack and civilian sabotage on the railways, were widely dispersed over Poland, with little chance of speedy concentration and deployment into action. To open opportunities for the armour moreover, the enemy's defences, now to some degree reintegrated, would once again need to be broken through. This was again a task for infantry, with strong air and artillery support, but there was now very little infantry available. It would not be possible to move sufficient fresh infantry formations across Poland quickly enough, for the same reasons that it was not possible to bring about a speedy introduction of the tank armies. Rail transportation had been heavily disrupted and the roads were breaking up.

All this was clear enough at the level of the front command, and at army group and even army level. None of it was known much lower down, in the headquarters of 197 Motor Rifle Division for example, such as remained of it, where staff officers deadened by noise and dropping with fatigue were receiving orders they could not understand and sending off others they knew could not be carried out even if they got through. In the regiments a grim confusion reigned, with half-lifeless robots going through motions lacking either hope or purpose. At battalion level little groups of people clung together, doing what they could.

As for many another this was to be Captain Nekrassov's last battle. His weakened battalion now came under heavy air attack from US *Apache* anti-tank helicopters, operating with US A-10 *Thunderbolts* and as an organized fighting unit was completely destroyed. Some of Nekrassov's men survived but he did not care. He did not even know. By this time he was dead. ❦

Chapter 12

The Scandinavian Campaign

Amongst the many documents brought out of Moscow to Sweden by a defector in the confusion of late 1985* were certain personal records, of which perhaps the most revealing is that of Colonel A. N. Romanenko, a Deputy Director of Plans in the Soviet General Staff. His notes for 15 August include the following record of a conversation between himself and the Director of Plans, General Rudolf Ignatiev:

6 At about seven o'clock this morning, General Ignatiev came into my office with a harsh look on his face.

"Those damned Americans," he said, "have landed marines in Norway. We knew a force of sorts was coming, but the navy was confident it could break it up. Well, it hasn't. We've got to get forces into south-west Norway quickly, or else the Americans will move against us in Bodö. We're doing well in the Bodö area but we've got to stay there. You have your plan for seizing the airfields around Stavanger and for getting troops into the south – we've been through it together – and I now want you to put it into operation quickly. But you'll have to look at it again, to see if it needs modifying to deal with whatever the Americans have got there."

Ignatiev said he had already put this to the Chief, who wanted the attack to go in tomorrow afternoon. The Chief reckons it would really shake the NATO governments when they see that we have to all intents and purposes completed the capture of their northern flank.

"Now we can show that it's hopeless for them to try to stop this," Ignatiev said. "We shall get real advantage from having secured air command over the North and Norwegian Seas. I know we've had heavy losses in the long-range air forces – well, now we'll make full use of our medium- and shorter-range bombers and our fighter bombers. We should have enough air defence resources to keep the enemy out. But we've got to hurry. Can we go in tomorrow?"

---

* Since published as *The Kremlin in Crisis: Soviet Documents of the Third World War*, ed. L. Wallin and Ingemar Lundquist (Gustavsson – Swedish language edition – Stockholm 1986, and Simon and Schuster, New York 1987).

All sorts of thoughts had been spinning through my mind as he was speaking – this operation was one that I had worked out myself.

"Well," I said, "we've replaced the airborne division in the Baltic Military District with 7 Guards Airborne Division from the Leningrad Military District. The new one is fresh and ready for use now. We have to find enough air transport to lift the complete division – I think we've got them but I'll get on to the VDV [Military Air Transport Organization] straight away to confirm this. There are assault landing craft still in the Danish islands and there are Ro-Ro [roll-on, roll-off] ships in Rostock and Kiel. Since we have to act very quickly, it will mean using some of the naval infantry and mechanized forces occupying Denmark."

Ignatiev was clearly impatient and looked at his watch. "Yes, I know all these sorts of things have to be arranged but they aren't a problem. I want you to get on with the operation at once. We should clear the plan by 1500 hours today, but in the meantime get some warning orders out."

"There is just one other matter," I said. "If we are to secure the airborne assault, we shall have to attack the Norwegian airfields at Trondheim – Örland and Vaernes. We can't really get at these effectively without crossing Sweden. If we are going to cross Sweden it would be better to send the air transport stream that way as well. It will be fifty times easier. Are we going to risk that?"

"Risk?" said Ignatiev. "What risk? Do you think those nervous Swedes will fight to stop us passing overhead? We've been overflying them all this last week and they've done damn little more than bite their nails. They haven't fought a war since 1814. They won't get in our way, don't worry. Get on with it, fast!" 〢 *

———————

Although the history of Swedish neutrality – based on the principle of non-alignment in peace with the aim of neutrality in war – went back a long way it was not all that well understood outside the Nordic countries. This was possibly in part because people of other countries have enough problems sorting out their own identity and history without worrying too much about others – especially when they are remote and neutral, the latter term tending to be regarded by some as synonomous with unimportant. If Sweden resented this, as it did, the country had largely itself to blame. Its impressive, passionate, and highly-armed neutrality was masked to the world by the political posturing of politicians from whatever platform they might be on at the time – 'Third Worldism', do-gooding, progressive liberalism, or whatever it happened to be. Sweden's advice to those who, in its eyes, were enslaved to power relationships and alliances was plentiful, often delivered in a high moral tone which many found irritating.

It was therefore easy to misread Sweden and fail to see the fierce

———————

* op. cit., pp. 32–3 (NY edition).

determination that buttressed its traditional neutrality beneath all the political preaching. Only military professionals, defence analysts and industrial competitors really appreciated the remarkable quality of Sweden's defence industry and armed forces, backed as they were by very high-grade planning and training and an infrastructure investment which absorbed one of the highest proportions of GNP of any country in the Western world. All of this was based on a comprehensive and well-accepted system of conscription and a sensible structure of reserves. There was much to be learnt from Sweden – not least that anyone taking it on would find it could curl up like a hedgehog and offer a very formidable resistance.

Sweden's non-alignment was not a weak-kneed opting out of European and world events but a fierce determination to preserve itself, irrespective of the folly of others. It would deter attack by its own armed strength. In a paradoxical nutshell, if Sweden had to go to war to stay neutral then it most certainly would, and it was the turn of the Swedes to be irritated that their position was so little understood, especially in the West where they had so many political and economic associations. From the Soviet Union they did not expect very much, for they realized that in a generally ignorant world the men in Moscow were bottom of the class when it came to other people's history. They were, after all, too busy cooking their own.

To the Soviet Union, Swedish neutrality was of considerable strategic importance. If Sweden threw in its hand with the West the balance in the Baltic could tilt sharply against the USSR. If war should come and the Swedes stood aside, as they always declared they would, they must understand that their country's neutrality must not be such as to stand in the way of Soviet needs in the sea and airspace of the Baltic area. Provided that was tacitly accepted there was really no reason why the Swedish people should be unduly disturbed by a major thrust into Europe. The strategic and political analysis sections in the Kremlin thought that Second World War history stood on their side in securing this balance – after all, Sweden had played both ends against the middle and come out unscathed and there was no reason to think that this sort of flexibility could not be brought into use again. Moscow assessed that continuing to play for Swedish neutrality was the best option, although contingency plans for persuasion would need to be laid should the Swedes look like failing to see where their true interests lay. With a measure of good fortune on the Soviet side, and sound practical sense from the Swedes, these contingencies need not arise. But Soviet freedom of manoeuvre in the Baltic, and its plans for Norway, were so crucial to the war plans of the USSR in the Atlantic that the posturing of a few Swedish politicians could not be allowed to stand in their way. Nevertheless, the strategic analysts cautioned, steps that might draw Soviet forces into an unnecessary campaign in Sweden should certainly be avoided.

Swedish comment and pronouncements from politicians, writers and academics had tended, sometimes with rare and much-needed fairness and impartiality, to balance the exaggerations and propaganda of the two power blocs and to illuminate the scene, somewhat naively it was often thought in the West, by adducing innocent motives for some of the Soviet Union's more questionable acts and particularly its high level of armament. The USSR found this refereeing role valuable, but after a decade of grim events in South-East and South-West Asia and in Africa the Swedes were running distinctly short of whitewash. In particular, the cosmopolitan academic society in Stockholm received a sharp shock from revelations within the vaunted Stockholm Peace Research Institute. This institute, drawing as it did on the intellects and viewpoints of clever men and women from all over the world, could not have been purer in Swedish eyes or further beyond any sort of criticism of its idealistic work. The discovery in the early 1980s that a Czechoslovak research professor in a senior post had, over a period of years, been exploiting the Institute's worldwide standing by acquiring incidental strategic and technical intelligence and remitting it to Moscow rocked the Swedish establishment to its foundations. The professor departed and the whole affair was played down but the scar that it left was deep.

The scar was shortly to be reopened very painfully by the intrusion in the autumn of 1981 of a Soviet *Whiskey*-class submarine, which stranded itself on rocks deep inside Swedish waters near the naval base of Karlskrona. The story filled the newspapers and television screens for days and nights on end. Moscow rejected the Swedish protests in intemperate fashion but gave no explanation that would stand up to examination. Sweden stubbornly refused to release the boat until it had made all the enquiries it could, in the course of which it was found – and the information was released publicly – that the submarine was carrying nuclear weapons. Swedish public opinion was incensed both by the incident and by Soviet surliness. Though the vessel was then allowed to go on its way, a seal had been set on dealings between the two countries, one that was to have its effects on subsequent events. Moscow did nothing to try to mend matters. In the next two to three years, Soviet aircraft carried out a programme of minor infringements of Swedish airspace, easily deniable but designed to remind Sweden of its geography and Soviet power.

There was nothing soft-centred or starry-eyed about the regular elements of the Swedish armed forces. Their intelligence, with the advantage of geography and good technology, was first rate and they had no illusions about the Soviet Union in any of its guises. At the same time, they were very far from blind to faults in the Western world. These highly professional men had learned to live with the contradictory tasks of leading and training their forces to the highest pitch of readiness and efficiency to serve the purposes of a perennially dove-like establishment.

It was common ground among them that in the last war Sweden had been as helpful to Britain and the USA as neutrality would decently allow. At the same time they knew, and ruefully admitted, that their neutrality had undoubtedly contributed to the woes of their sister country, Norway, under German domination. Was history to repeat itself with a single change of cast? This was an uncomfortable thought within the Nordic family.

The Swedish defence effort was considerable, the spending per capita and as a percentage of GNP being directly comparable with that of the major NATO allies in Europe. A nationwide call-up was designed to mobilize some 800,000 men and women in seventy-two hours to man defences throughout the country. The air defence was of an especially high order, remarkable for a country of such a small population, based on almost entirely home-grown products like superb *Viggen* interceptor and attack aircraft, and advanced radars and electronics, in which Swedish industry excelled. Underground shelters and hangars had been tunnelled into the mountain sides.

The navy had taken advantage of a virtually tideless sea and granite cliffs to blast out vast caverns as tunnel-docks for warships. In 1985 Sweden had a dozen modern diesel-electric submarines; four modernized destroyers, twenty-eight missile-armed fast-attack craft; anti-submarine warfare (ASW) helicopters and various mine counter-measure (MCM) vessels. As a former Swedish naval attaché in London had written: 'The Royal Swedish Navy must be prepared to operate in narrow waters on what may be called a hit-and-run basis, very often at night or in the darkness'.* The submarine force would, of course, patrol off the enemy's bases, to report and attack his forces and to intercept his invasion fleet. In peacetime, as a matter of routine, submarine surveillance would provide intelligence otherwise unobtainable; and in time of emergency this task could be critical.

Thus it was that early on 3 August 1985 the Swedish submarine *Sjöhasten*, on reconnaissance patrol just outside Soviet territorial waters, off the Gulf of Riga, sighted a large and heavily escorted convoy of Soviet amphibious vessels. Lieutenant Per Asling, the submarine's captain, was not aware of any major Soviet or Warsaw Pact naval exercise. But neither had he been told that war was

* Commander B. F. Thermaenius, 'Swedish Naval Bases', *The Naval Review*, Vol. XLVII No. 1, January 1959, p. 21.

imminent. His duty, he decided, was to remain undetected, while observing carefully the composition and course of the Soviet force. He would then make a short 'Most Immediate' sighting report, followed by an amplifying report giving full details. The first of these signals was handed to the Chief of the Swedish Defence Staff at 0957 hours that morning by his naval deputy, and together they studied the chart upon which the position and course of the Soviet force had been plotted. By noon, when the Council of State assembled in emergency meeting, with His Majesty King Carl Gustaf present, the *Sjöhasten's* amplifying report had been received. As the Commander-in-Chief of the Navy pointed out, the Soviet force, if it held on course, would pass south of Bornholm next afternoon and could have reached the Baltic exits by daybreak on 5 August. As he spoke, an air reconnaissance report was handed to him. It confirmed that of the submarine. Those Soviet amphibious craft were indeed heading for the Baltic exits. They formed the follow-up force to a division detached from 2 Guards Tank Army which, by dawn on 5 August, had reached the Kiel Canal. Before that, however, there had been much to preoccupy the Swedish Council of State, the Swedish armed forces, and indeed the Swedish people.

A key part of the Soviet plan for the campaign in Norway, which will be described shortly, rested on the amphibious assault on the port and airfield at Bodö. The airfield was an important base for Allied maritime aircraft as well as Norwegian fighters and it was vital to keep it under daily reconnaissance, immediately before and after hostilities began, to supplement the limited intelligence from agents and satellites on which they must otherwise rely. The air route via the Kola Peninsula from the Leningrad area, where the high-altitude but short-range reconnaissance aircraft were based, was over 4,000 kilometres and this would involve three refuelling stops. What was more important was that a mission on this pattern could not fail to be detected by the NATO early warning system. To preserve surprise about the amphibious assault this had to be avoided. The decision was therefore taken in Moscow to send a Mig-25 *Foxbat* B special reconnaissance aircraft at a height of 25,000 metres every day straight across Sweden from Vaasa in Finland, and such was the importance of the task that the management of the missions was exercised directly at a high level by the Soviet Air Staff itself. The reconnaissance aircraft were unarmed. The Soviets would deal with any whining by the Swedes as they had done in the past.

The first flight was made on 2 August at dawn and repeated on the 3rd. Each time, the battle flight of two *Viggen* JA-37s swept up the ramp from their mountain hangar at Västeraas air base and within twenty-five seconds were climbing with full power. But even with their high performance there was much to do and little time to do it. The *Viggens* could not, in fact, reach 25,000 metres but with the 'snap-up' capability of their missiles there was a good chance of at least threatening the *Foxbat* if they could only get into a favourable tactical relationship with it. With so short a warning time that would be difficult, but less so on the return flight when the limits of the *Foxbat*'s timing could be broadly calculated. That, at least, was how the Swedish Air Staff saw it.

When lodging his vehement protests in Moscow the Swedish Ambassador stressed that the Soviet Air Force was giving the *Viggens* little option but to engage if these violations continued. In response he was treated to an intimidating tirade about Sweden's position as a neutral country. The next day was the fateful 4 August. Sweden's armed forces, now mobilizing, had their hands full absorbing reservists. The Swedish Air Force, the *Flygvapnet*, was waiting on a Government decision to deploy some of its elements to dispersed road sites, which would of course to some extent disrupt civilian life and movement and might perhaps cause alarm. The Cabinet took the decisive step of ordering maximum air defence readiness, with the battle flights fully armed and cleared to engage any identified non-Swedish intruders without further reference to higher authority. A statement to that effect was made public to the world, but in the main the world had other things on its mind that day. In Sweden an emergency Cabinet of seven ministers was formed and far reaching powers were taken by unanimous agreement. The *Flygvapnet*, the spearhead of Sweden's defence, was as ready as it could be by noon of that day although it had to be recognized that its degree of readiness would decline for a while if full dispersal were ordered.

The emergency Cabinet decided that the *Flygvapnet* should stay as it was for the time being. There was growing relief as the day wore on, with nothing untoward happening in Swedish skies. The wishful thinking of the doves that perhaps the USSR had, after all, heeded the Swedish protests was, however, to be shattered the next morning.

This time the *Foxbat* approached low over the sea before zooming in a near vertical climb to high altitude, to evade detection by the radar system until it was too late for the fighters to react. But the *Flygvapnet* Air Defence Command was really on its mettle and, with full authority to engage, was determined somehow or other to destroy the intruder on its way back. Two pairs of *Viggens* were launched from Uppsala air base to patrol a north/south line centred on Stockholm, athwart the return track to Leningrad from where they knew the *Foxbat* had come. One pair would be at high altitude and one at medium to low, although it was unlikely that the *Foxbat* would have enough fuel to pull the low-level trick a second time. Similar blocking patrols were set up with four more *Viggen* pairs on lines centred on Sundsvall and Umeaa to the north. But the *Foxbat* pilot had his own good reasons for choosing a southerly track which headed him, with seeming carelessness, near to Stockholm at high altitude and speed.

Guided by ground control initially, the high-level fighters in the southern sector cut in their after-burners to gain the last few thousand feet to their maximum altitude on an easterly interception course which would bring them below and behind the *Foxbat*. In the underground operations centre all eyes were riveted on this highspeed drama in the stratosphere. The control staffs and senior officers could sense the nervous excitement of the pilots as they eavesdropped on the clipped dialogue with the interception controllers and watched the mesmerizing green strobes of the radar displays in the eerie half-light of the control rooms.

The *Foxbat* pilot was by now well aware of the *Viggens'* presence from his tail-warning radar. What was *not* overheard in the control room was the dialogue that he was having with someone else. In the unusual circumstances of that day it was not altogether surprising that two radar contacts moving very fast indeed from east to west along latitude 60N were not registered as quickly as they might otherwise have been. The battle flight leader was alerted from the ground but that was all that could be done. A trap had been set to teach the Swedes a lesson and they had flown right into it.

The two incoming *Foxbat* fighters, among the fastest aircraft in the world, had a height and speed advantage over the *Viggens*. Even more important, their snap-down *Acrid* missiles could engage from 45 kilometres' distance. And they were well informed about the task by their comrade in the west-bound reconnaissance aircraft. Their missiles found their mark just to seaward of the Swedish coast and sent the two JA-37s spiralling towards the sea. Captain Lars Ericsson, the pilot of No. 2 of the pair, fired his ejection seat and blasted his way through the jammed canopy of his disintegrating aircraft. As the seat separated and the main canopy deployed, he saw he was over the sea with a strong easterly wind blowing him back towards the land. There was no sign of his flight leader as he took a quick look round, but the earth was rushing up and although dazed and confused he knew he must get ready for a difficult arrival in a strong wind. He hit hard and was dragged painfully along the ground before coming to rest in a field not far from Uppsala University and his own air base.

The Soviet intention had been to shoot both aircraft into the sea so that the Swedish Government would get the message plainly without having to share it immediately with the public. But that was carrying refinement a bit too far for such blunt methods and with Ericsson under intensive care with a broken back in Uppsala hospital the cat was well and truly out of the bag. The message was all too clear: 'Be co-operative in your neutrality or take the consequences.'

In the fury and confusion of the assault in the Central Region the importance of the Bodö landing in the Soviet plan, in securing the north of Norway and denying its fiords and airfields to the Western allies, was not immediately clear to the Swedes or anyone else. The pilot of the *Foxbat* had reported, confirmed with photographic detail, the presence there of eleven RAF *Buccaneers*, four Norwegian *Orion* maritime aircraft and sixteen F-16 *Fighting Falcons*. It was correctly guessed that Joint Allied Command Western Approaches (JACWA) would decide to leave the *Buccaneers* there for future anti-shipping activity, to which the Soviet amphibious group was very likely to fall prey. With the implementation of their northern plans already under way, and such hard intelligence to hand, the conclusion was obvious – that the elimination of those forces and the denial of the airfield to the enemy was of overriding importance.

The Soviet decision to mount a sizeable attack with high-speed SU-24 *Fencers* against these valuable Allied assets was inevitable. For reasons of aircraft range (with the added bonus of surprise from a backdoor attack) it would have been operationally simpler to have mounted this across Sweden, but Moscow decided instead that it was better to let the Swedes lick their wounds for a while and take counsel of their fears. Accordingly, the attack was mounted from Murmansk with TU-16 *Blinder* and *Fencer* aircraft moved there from the Leningrad area. They were routed clear of Swedish airspace but if in difficulty could cross the tip of it, where it was in any case very lightly defended.

For the next few days the pressure was kept on Bodö, to neutralize it until the Soviet amphibious force made its landing there on 15 August. Reconnaissance flights continued to be made over Sweden, whose neutrality, now under some strain, nonetheless persisted. But the problem of what the country should do was debated intensely by Swedes everywhere, bitter, angry and frustrated by the shooting down of the *Viggens* that were doing no more than protecting national airspace. This last incident would undoubtedly have had its effect on the decision, strongly recommended by the *Flygvapnet* staff, to allow a force of thirty NATO fighters to refuel secretly at two Swedish airfields on the night of 13/14 August. These aircraft were engaged on an operation, described in Chapter 11, to attack key bridges in Poland at a critical juncture of the battle on the Central Front. If the operation was to succeed, the attacking aircraft had to approach their targets from the north, rather than fly over a heavily defended area, and for this purpose their routing over Sweden was ideal. Permission was accordingly sought via the recently installed

Swedish liaison officer at Supreme Headquarters Allied Powers Europe (SHAPE) not only to overfly but to take on fuel as well. The Swedish Cabinet – the decision was taken at that level – were divided about it but eventually agreed provided that the landing was at night and the turn-round fast. No Swedish protection would be given, nor could aircraft recover via Swedish airfields unless in distress. Some damaged aircraft did put down in the event, with Soviet aircraft pursuing them. Two of the four Soviet *Foxbats* that attempted to enter Swedish airspace were in fact shot down by *Viggens* that were watching for them. Only this part of the incident reached the press; the use of the airfields by the NATO force did not.

While the war thus developed around them, the Swedish Government debated daily the range of options over which they had some control and some over which they could see plainly they were powerless. The left-wing opposition made it clear that they would oppose any policy that took Sweden into the war; and whilst some on the extreme left let it be known privately that they would gladly give assistance to the Soviet Union short of military force, the majority were dedicated to 'maintaining neutrality in all foreseeable circumstances' – a phrase used often by their speakers in the debates in the *Riksdag* — 'which leaves the left ready to sell out to the Soviets if the going gets too rough', as a cynic on the Government side is said to have remarked quietly to a neighbour when he first heard the words.

The arguments went on. The news of the American landing in Norway had been coming in on the morning of 15 August and was clutched at with relief as the first sign of a Soviet setback there. It was then that the Soviet Ambassador asked urgently for a meeting with the Swedish Prime Minister, Bjorn Osvald, at 12.15 that day. What happened at the meeting has long since been made public. This is the Prime Minister's account of it.

The Soviet Ambassador entered and I had at once the impression of a man who had donned a mask; he was so different from the good-humoured person I had met on so many occasions.

'I have an important message from my Government,' he said, 'a message which I ask you to receive and weigh most carefully. It is this.

'At 1300 hours today, a stream of Soviet aircraft will pass over your territory. Subsequently, there will be other air movements, all of which will be notified in sufficient time to your air traffic control authorities. The Soviet Government means no harm to you in this matter. I give you a guarantee that no aerial or other attacks are to be made upon you providing that . . .' he looked up from the paper from which he was reading this message '. . . providing that you do not attempt in any way to harm or impede our aircraft. Moreover, the Government and people of the Soviet Union will not forget acts of friendly assistance granted by states which have remained aloof from its struggle for existence.'

There was a pause. It became clear to me that he evidently had nothing more to say. I was almost overwhelmed by this news. He spoke again.

'Is there any message you wish me to give my Government in reply?'

'Yes,' I said. 'It is just this. We have taken the decision to defend our territory – land, sea or air – against anyone, anyone at all, who attacks or encroaches upon us. That, of course, includes the Soviet Union. Please advise your Government not to send their aircraft across Sweden.'

'You realize this will mean war – with all the terrible consequences for your people?' he remarked.

'Yes,' I replied. I sought to keep my voice calm. 'It is of your choosing. Now, please hurry to send my reply.'

'Very well.' He left the room still, as it were, masked.

I telephoned the Minister of Defence and the Minister of External Affairs while my secretaries summoned an urgent Cabinet meeting. The decision was confirmed. The country was at war.*

This did not, of course, imply that Sweden had now become a member of NATO but it did mean a readiness to fight in association with NATO against a common enemy.

The *Flygvapnet* was naturally at alert status and the orders to defend were sent out immediately. The *Viggens* took off. Squadrons were drawn in from distant bases. After some three hours the Soviet Air Force had won a qualified victory over the defenders, inflicting heavy casualties. But almost a third of the Soviet transports and their TU-28 *Fiddler* fighter escorts had been lost or forced to turn back. The remainder had pressed on across the border into Norway.

That evening the Prime Minister spoke to the nation. The *Flygvapnet* and all the forces involved had performed superbly, he said, and a heavy price had been paid for this outrageous violation of the country's neutrality. The Cabinet had now decided that the nation must be put on a full war footing. Sweden's armed forces would defend the country against any further violations. In such grave times, he went on, he could offer no forecasts about what might happen next or where events might lead. Sweden's record in the terrible events now overtaking Europe was impeccable and he had no doubt that whatever demands or sacrifices might be involved the Swedish people would be true to themselves and the noble tradition of their country. Sweden sought peace between nations above all else. He knew he spoke for every Swede when he said they would fight on for ever to defend their country.

The people took the grave news courageously. The concept of doing all that might be needed to defend the country's neutrality was fully accepted and as the media traced the casualties of individual

---

* Bjorn Osvald, *The Crisis in Sweden, August 1985* (Swedish Government Printing Organization, Stockholm 1985, printed also in English, German and French), p. 222.

families, public opinion against the Soviet Union became embittered. Lesser incursions by Soviet aircraft continued in the next few days, in support of the campaign in Norway. The distinction between defending neutrality and being at war started to blur fairly quickly in the minds of the average Swede and a sense of Nordic kinship grew stronger. Important links were quietly established with Allied Forces Northern Europe (AFNORTH), notably for a complete exchange of early warning information. Whatever neutrality might mean, the Swedish armed forces had no intention of allowing it to prevent them from fighting in the most efficient way they could.

———

The loss of Jutland on the first day of hostilities, and the consequential loss of Schleswig-Holstein shortly after was due to the combination of an intense chemical attack on Jutland and a *coup de main* by assault forces concealed in Soviet, East German and some ostensibly neutral merchant ships on passage through the Kattegat. These had made almost unopposed landings in Aarhus, Aalborg and Frederikshavn on Jutland. Zealand had fallen after hard fighting between the reinforced Danish defence and a seaborne assault force mounted from the western Baltic ports. Unexpectedly, Bornholm, its radar and radio resources smashed by air attack, had been left to its own devices until, almost at leisure, a Polish airborne division had fallen upon it. Many of the Allied aircraft in the BALTAP (Baltic Approaches) Tactical Air Force escaped to the Federal Republic of Germany or to Norway. A daring naval operation, covered by air, was mounted by Commander, South Norway, to rescue some of the Danish and British troops from Zealand and in the final phase of the battle for the island. Though four of nine warships and transports were lost, the remainder returned intact to unload in the Oslo fiord. The aircraft and troops from BALTAP were absorbed as reinforcements to south Norway, or moved to reinforce the north.

Commander, North Norway, had been fighting an intense battle from the outset of the war when, as expected, almost all his early warning radars were destroyed and his airfields, ports and principal defence areas were raided frequently and heavily by aircraft based on the Kola Peninsula. The Soviet motor rifle division which crossed the frontier at Kirkenes on 4 August made a more rapid advance than expected through extensive use of heliborne infantry and engineers supported by swarms of ground-attack aircraft, and by heavy and medium artillery firing at maximum ranges with a frequency and weight of shell that bewildered the light forces of Norwegian infantry. As they advanced, a Soviet airborne division captured Andöya and

Evenes. A considerable amphibious force, judged to be carrying Soviet specialized naval assault infantry and a motor rifle division, was observed on passage from Murmansk. A further four Soviet divisions were seen by Allied air reconnaissance to be crossing Finland towards southern Finnmark and eastern Troms counties. Tromsö airfield was devasted. Only Bardufoss, so inaccessible among the surrounding mountains to the south of Tromsö and well defended by air defence missiles since 1984, survived as an air base.

Some looked anxiously to the western horizon for urgent relief: somewhere across the seas the carriers of SACLANT's (Supreme Allied Commander Atlantic's) Strike Fleet were active and mobile and must, surely, be moving sooner or later to attack the Kola bases and relieve north Norway. The robust Norwegian general in command of that area knew, however, that he could not immediately count on the appearance of the Strike Fleet: he had to fight a sea/air and land/air battle with the national and Allied forces he had in hand, and such others as CINCNORTH (Commander-in-Chief Allied Forces Northern Europe) could strip out from elsewhere to aid him. Fortunately, he had a wide knowledge of local circumstances, a cool head and shrewd judgment.

An early decision was made to maintain Bardufoss as a base for reconnaissance to the east and a forward operating location for air defence fighters. The British *Harriers*, dislodged from Tromsö, were kept in the north, flying from stretches of straight road and maintained from villages in the shadow of adjacent mountains. CINCNORTH's Regional Air Commander directed American F-111s from England to attack the Soviet air bases developing at Andöya, Evenes and Bodö. Otherwise, Commander, North Norway's air effort fell back necessarily upon Trondheim, i.e. Örland and Vaernes airfields. Nord-Tröndelag passed into the northern command.

Evenes airfield was recaptured on 6 August by a Norwegian brigade and their comrades in the Allied Command Europe (ACE) Mobile Force, though about one-third of the Soviet parachutists escaped to the lines their compatriots had set up to cover Andöya. This was good news for Commander, North Norway, and CINCNORTH, but each knew that bad news was on the doorstep. The first of the Soviet divisions crossing Finland was rapidly approaching the Norwegian frontier on the Finnish wedge, with another immediately behind. The northernmost invading Soviet division completed its crossing of Finnmark on 9 August, when all three began a concerted drive which was held only by committing every Norwegian soldier from Bardufoss to the north. Next day, the Soviet amphibious force turned shoreward towards Bodö and began to smash a passage through the minefields to a landing near the airfield.

The mine clearance operation was very costly to the invaders, and they suffered, too, from the guns of the Norwegian coastal forts. What triumphed was dogged persistence: the Soviet naval assault force continued to move ashore, even into the heart of Bodö, landing opposite the hotel belonging to the Swedish civil airline SAS from whose shell-broken concrete tower black smoke was rising. Air attack included chemical weapons. The guns of Northern Fleet warships fired with what seemed an unending supply of shells to cover the merchant transports moving to the quay. Warship and merchantman alike were assailed by Norwegian fast-patrol boats and there was further sinking and damage to vessels at sea. Even so, by the evening of 11 August, sufficient Soviet forces were in and around Bodö to constitute two motor rifle regiments with supplies landed to provide for at least a week's high activity. A Norwegian brigade was redeployed from Evenes and the British Marine Commando from further north joined them to buttress the Bodö sector. The main road, E6, connecting north Norway to the south, was in danger of being cut.

On the 12th, word came of the Strike Fleet's movement eastward through the Greenland-Iceland-UK gap. If the aircraft from the carriers could have intervened in the battle over north Norway on that day, the land defence might have been able to stand its ground. But the aircraft could not yet do so. As a fourth Soviet motor rifle division deployed into Troms, complemented by an air assault brigade, the defence began to feel its lack of numbers and, no less vitally, the dwindling of its supplies, particularly gun and mortar ammunition, so heavily used and with so much lost to air attack. Grimly, Commander, North Norway, ordered the withdrawal of the Allied land forces north of Bodö, while he reinforced the lines checking the Soviet force struggling vigorously to reach the E6. By the 14th, he had pulled his little army back.

En route, several attempts to delay or divert the withdrawal had been made by detachments of the Soviet special forces, wearing Norwegian uniforms, speaking accentless Norwegian. All had been negated by the vigilance and prompt reaction of the Norwegian Home Guard. South of Narvik, for example, one such attempt was dealt with in just under two minutes:

'Who are you?' asked the elderly Home Guard company commander at Mörsvik, challenging a 'Norwegian captain' who seemed to be giving contradictory orders to vehicle drivers. The 'captain' showed his identity card and told the Home Guard to mind his own business.

'Who sent you here?' The Home Guard was not going to be shaken off.

The answer he received was unsatisfactory to him. He ordered his soldiers to close in from the brief summer darkness to cover the 'captain' and his two supporters, who abused and threatened by way of response.

'We can soon settle this,' said the Home Guard. 'Where do you come from?'

'Kristiansund.'

'That's fine, the telephone is working to the south. Give me the name and address of your family or a friend there and we will telephone the local Home Guard. It will only take a few minutes.'

The 'captain' sprang into his car and drove off to the south.

'You've let him go,' said one of the Norwegians deployed on the road.

'Not really. Ole Nilsen's section is covering the road down there. There's no other route. He'll either stop or be shot.'

There was the sound of rifle fire.

'Ah, he didn't stop,' said the Home Guard commander.*

When the field army had withdrawn south, the Home Guard remained behind, drifting into the mountain uplands to continue the war in their own way.

Meantime, just after midnight on 14 August, a staff officer found Commander, North Norway, in a village close to the E6, to give him this news:

'The Marines have arrived, Sir.'

'The British commando? Surely, they have already moved south.'

'No, Sir, the Americans. They are landing now at Trondheim.'

'With their air wing?'

'With everything.'†

The United States Marines had made many dramatic entries in their distinguished history: none more timely than this. Dedicated in peace to the defence of Norway, a series of events had delayed their despatch by sea and air to their disembarkation area round Trondheim. Some units had been in process of *roulement*; some had begun deployment to the Middle East only to be halted en route, unloaded and obliged to wait for other transportation back to their bases. But now they were actually forming up on Norwegian soil, the land force together with its important air component. Here was the substance of the counter-attack force that Commander, North Norway, had been seeking to put together. He had already positioned the Canadian brigade groups and Norwegian 12 Brigade – the only two formations that had had a chance to rest and refit during the past twenty-four hours – for such a task but, of themselves, they had insufficient weight of fire power, specialized anti-armour weapons and mobility to destroy the Soviet mechanized forces. With the United States Marine brigade in their midst, they had every chance of accomplishing an important tactical riposte.

* From 'The Norwegian Home Guard in the Third World War', one of a series of articles by B. Ramstedt featured in *Aftenposten*, Oslo, May 1986.

† ibid., 'US Marines in Norway', June 1986.

At Trondheim, the port and airfields were working to capacity. The Regional Air Commander was already alarmed at the number of aircraft packing Örland and Vaernes bases – air defence fighters and fighter-bombers from the north, the local complement, now also US Marine Corps squadrons flying in. In consultation with the Commanders of South and North Norway, he arranged for some of this mass of machines to move south to the Bergen air base, Flesland, to Sola at Stavanger and Lista. The remnant of a Norwegian F-16 *Fighting Falcon* squadron was posted to Rygge, the often battered but yet surviving air station at the southern end of the Oslo fiord.

These arrangements were getting under way during the following day, 15 August, just at the time that the Deputy Director of Plans, Colonel Romanenko, having received his instructions from his chief, was sending out orders to put his plan for the landings in south-west Norway into effect with the results that we have seen.

Fairly full details of what had happened had come to CINC-NORTH as he returned to Oslo from a visit to Trondheim that afternoon. He had been in the latter city when raids were attempted by Soviet bombers on Orland and Vaernes and had seen these fail. The Soviet raiders, weakened by their encounter with the Swedish *Viggens*, had entered the Norwegian target area alerted by Swedish radar reports – reports now freely and promptly available from the Swedish authorities – to be defeated by a fighter defence reinforced by the US Marines. The raids on the south-western areas in support of the airborne assault landings had failed similarly. The air transports carrying the parachutists suffered further loss. They eventually landed about two battalions at Flesland and a weak battalion at Sola and Lista, air bases on each of which Ignatiev had expected to settle a strong brigade group. The local field forces, backed by the Home Guard, swept these intruders away by the early morning of 21 August.

On that morning, too, CINCNORTH learned from his colleague, the Chief of the Norwegian Defence Staff, that the Finns had turned upon the Soviet Forces in their country. Since early in August, the Finnish armed forces had been obliged to aid deployment of the Red army in the passage of formations, ground and air, across their large, empty land. Soviet war regulations had been enforced along these lines of communication, arbitrary demands made for resources of labour and material, war measures introduced such as the blacking out of all lights at night. The Finnish people, conditioned by the prudence of Paasakivi and Kekkonen, had complied to some extent with these requirements. But they were also the same sort of people that Mannerheim had led, a people with a clear idea of individual liberty.

When the moment came to turn upon the Soviets, it was not done by a signal from above; indeed, it followed a spontaneous act of indignation arising from the arrogant behaviour of the officers of a Soviet logistic control centre. It was not done so much on the basis of attacking a body of waning power but at a time when the Finns could no longer tolerate the position of manifest subservience to which they had been brought. Small though their numbers were, all but a handful turned to fight the Soviet forces, which had seemed to make them a dependency once more.

This was not quite the last battle for the recovery of territory occupied by the Soviet Union in the northern region. CINCNORTH had gradually been gathering together a land force for the recovery of Denmark and Schleswig-Holstein. The Commander, BALTAP, a Danish officer, driven out of Jutland on the first day of war, had been engaged since his arrival in Norway in planning the liberation of these territories. The British and Dutch Royal Marines were concentrated in south Norway on 18 August, with the Danish and British forces recovered from Zealand. Given the depletion and demoralization of the Soviet occupation forces in the Baltic Approaches, this force overall might just secure and sustain a lodgement in north Jutland under air cover from the airfields of south Norway. The prime limitation was shipping, the only amphibious shipping being the remnant recovered to Norway from the German and Danish navies in the first week of August, to which might be added a slender increment of Norwegian landing craft. It was doubted whether the numbers that these could carry in the first lift could hold territory against a counter-attack mounted prior to the return of the second and subsequent ferrying. Much hinged upon the ability of the Danish Home Guard, now operating as a clandestine and deliberately passive force, to co-ordinate uprising with an Allied landing.

Although the enemy were depleted in Jutland, CINCNORTH considered them still a force to be reckoned with. An assault landing at this stage would be very risky. He proposed instead a strong raid. The group of CINCEASTLANT's warships that had escorted the US Marine sea force into Trondheim were available to CINCNORTH for short-term contingency operations. The F-16 *Fighting Falcon* force at Rygge had been reinforced from Örland and, in the same deployment from that area, the air bases at Lista and Sola had now a notable air defence and ground strike capability. The intelligence provided by the Home Guard indicated that Frederikshavn was vulnerable to a raiding force of about two battalions and a squadron of tanks. This was now scheduled for the evening of 20 August.

Over the next two days of preparation, the operation seemed to hang in the balance. All the amphibious force was concentrating at

Kragerö and Kristiansund: could they survive there? Commander, BALTAP's answer was to put the force to sea; in the circumstances they were as safe in these waters as anywhere. They entered the Kattegat in darkness, a little late, and landed at Frederikshavn early on the morning of the 21st.

There was a brief struggle with the Soviet garrison before it surrendered. Then, suddenly, the occupation force began surrendering everywhere – to the raiders, who remained, and to the Home Guard who emerged in uniforms with weapons. COMBALTAP sent off more units to join the raiders and then seemed to disappear. A week later he met CINCNORTH in Copenhagen as the latter stepped from his aircraft to call on the Danish Government, restored to their offices and the Christianborg Palace. There was a report in a Swedish newspaper that ran roughly as follows:

'I hear you came down to liberate Zealand personally,' said CINCNORTH. 'Is it true that you travelled by train and road through Sweden with the *Gardehusar* Regiment, and then crossed the Sound on car ferries?'

'Yes, Sir,' said COMBALTAP (a Dane, as will be recalled). 'You see, it was a race against time.'

'You mean you were afraid the Soviet troops might . . .'

'No, not the Soviet troops. I was just afraid that if I didn't get a move on, Copenhagen would be liberated by those perishing Swedes!'*

He need not, of course, have worried. There had never been any sign of an intention on the part of the Swedes to move into Denmark. Whatever threats lay over Copenhagen, occupation by Swedish troops was not among them.

---

* See *Svenska Dageblad*, 1 September 1985.

Chapter 13

War at Sea

❝The cruiser *Krasnya Krim* (in Russian *Bolshoy Protivopodochny Korabi*, meaning "large anti-submarine ship") sailed from Sevastopol in June 1985, and after passing through the Bosporus and the Dardanelles, spent some days in the Eastern Mediterranean before proceeding through the Suez Canal, down the Red Sea and into the Indian Ocean. The Soviet naval force on station there came for the most part from the Pacific Fleet base at Vladivostok. But the *Krasnya Krim* had a special mission. After fuelling at Socotra in the Indian Ocean she was to call at the Indian naval base at Vishakhapatnam. From there she would visit Mauritius and then continue round Africa, calling at Angola and Guinea, before returning to the Black Sea early in August.

The *Krasnya Krim*'s mission was to test the reactions to her presence within the 200-mile Extended Economic Zones and territorial seas of a large number of the coastal states which were signatories of the UN Convention on the Law of the Sea, signed in the previous year after a series of conferences which began nearly thirty years before.

On board, besides her captain and political commissar and some thirty officers and 500 men, was Soviet academician Yuri Skridlov, who had been a member of the Soviet delegation to the United Nations Law of the Sea Conference, meeting in Washington, in Caracas, in Geneva and again in Washington. A man of honesty and high intelligence and a worldwide authority on international law, Professor Skridlov, who combined a strong personality with a deep, if concealed, detestation of Marxist-Leninist humbug, became much liked and respected by all on board the *Krasnya Krim*, including the political commissar.

Skridlov introduced a practice of taping items of world news and of regional interest, translating them into Russian and then broadcasting them on the ship's communication system each evening, with a commentary. Without being openly critical of the CPSU or of the Soviet Union, he nevertheless succeeded in presenting a fair picture of the free world and a faithful account of what was happening in it. The ship's company of the *Krasnya Krim*, cooped up for weeks on end, at sea most of the time either steaming slowly or anchored well away from land, was developing a totally new awareness. There was critical discussion of matters which had long been kept out of sight. There was an increasingly vocal expression of discontent with the system under which they lived, compared with the systems operating outside the USSR which they, of course, were either prevented from seeing or were only allowed to see under strict surveillance. The vast majority were young, unmarried conscripts. When the ship left Luanda on 23 July bound for the Black Sea, and home, spirits began to rise. After a short call at Guinea, to fuel, it moved on. It was to pass through the Straits of Gibraltar on 4 August, and the Dardanelles on the 8th.

On 25 July Professor Skridlov's News Talk suddenly took on a sharper edge. The captain had received a Top Secret signal, whose contents he felt entitled to divulge to the Professor, warning him of strained relations between NATO and the Warsaw Pact. The *Krasnya Krim* was to increase speed so as to pass the Dardanelles on 3 August. This would mean going through the Straits of Gibraltar on the night of 30 July. The Soviet Commander-in-Chief Navy also ordered the ship to prepare "unobtrusively" for war and gave her a SITREP on the naval forces of NATO that might be encountered, as well as the positions of Soviet warships and submarines. It appeared that the US Sixth Fleet might well bar the way to the Dardanelles.

The events of the next few days on board the Soviet cruiser are by no means clear. What emerges is that Soviet sailors were prepared to take dramatic steps to show their hostility to a tyrannous regime. At 2107 on 30 July the *Krasnya Krim*, after duly requesting permission from the Flag Officer, Gibraltar, entered British territorial waters and anchored in the Bay. It appeared that the fuel embarked at Guinea was severely contaminated, and it would not be possible for the cruiser to proceed on her way until the entire fuel system had been cleaned. At least, that was what the Soviet High Command was told. It was not what the cruiser's captain told the Flag Officer, Gibraltar, when he called on him next morning, in company with the political commissar – and the Professor.

They were convinced that world conflict was now unavoidable and that out of it a new Russia would emerge. The ship's company had been openly and fully consulted and gave their whole-hearted support to what was now proposed. They wished the ship and all in her to be granted asylum, fighting neither against their own former comrades nor against NATO, until the conflict was over and they could see more clearly what part to play in the shaping of a brighter future.

The request was immediately granted, in the first of what was to become a series of defections.

On 10 August a nuclear missile cruiser, sole survivor of the Fifth *Eskadra*, or Mediterranean Squadron, of the Soviet Navy also raised the British flag and sailed into harbour at Gibraltar, where she gave the shore battery a twenty-one-gun salute and dropped anchor. The ship's commander, Captain 1st Rank P. Semenov, appeared before the British Governor in his dress uniform and declared that the missile cruiser was placing itself at the disposal of the British authorities, the entire crew requesting political asylum.

"Including the political commissars and the KGB officers?" enquired the Governor.

"No," replied the Captain. "We've strung them up from the masts. Come and see for yourself." The invitation was declined, the request for asylum granted.

That same day the Soviet nuclear submarine *Robespierre* sailed into harbour at Boston, Massachusetts, under the US flag. As the submarine had no masts, there was nowhere to hang the KGB and Party representatives.

They had therefore been dropped overboard before entering harbour. The Soviet submarine was disarmed and immobilized, with the crew very comfortably interned. **'**[*]

We must now look more thoroughly at the war at sea. A convenient, if somewhat informal, point of entry into this important topic is the text of a lecture given at the National Defence College in Washington by Rear Admiral Randolph Maybury of the United States Navy in the summer of 1986. He was introduced by the Commandant.

'Good morning, gentlemen. As you know, we are continuing today with our study of the military operations which took place between 4 and 20 August 1985. Our course has been structured to provide both an "all-arms" conspectus, region by region, and amplifying accounts of the fighting at sea, on land and in the air. Since last winter, when Admiral Lacey addressed us on the naval operations in the Atlantic and the Norwegian Sea – particularly the famous *Cavalry* reinforcement convoy operation – additional data which have come to hand, and much hard work, have made it possible to present a record of the naval (which includes, of course, naval and maritime air) operations which were taking place concurrently in other areas and theatres. Admiral Maybury, here, has not long since completed this work, and we are most fortunate to have him with us to talk about it. As Deputy Chief of Staff to the Commander-in-Chief US Navy Europe (CINCUSNAVEUR) in London, from 1984 through 1985, he was well placed to see what went on. No doubt he took a hand in things also! At any rate, we're glad to see you, Admiral – and now will you kindly step up and tell us about it.'

'Thank you. It's good to be back at the National War College. When I was a student here, in 1983, the question was "What would happen, if . . .? Now, the concern is "What did happen, and why . . .?" The human race came close to destroying itself. History, as mere hindsight, may be of interest, but it is of little value unless its lessons are learned.

'I have come to believe that where we went wrong – and by "we" I mean the United States and her NATO allies – was in our failure to incorporate the Moscow dimension into our own perception of the dangers to civilization which were implicit in Soviet attitudes, beliefs and actions. We could read, for example, in the writings of Lenin:

Great questions in the life of a people are decided only by force . . . once the bayonet really stands as the first order of political business, then constitu-

---

[*] J. Heller, *Submarines at War* (Sidgwick and Jackson, London 1987), p. 184.

tional illusions and scholastic exercises in Parliament become nothing but a cover for bourgeois betrayal of the revolution. The truly revolutionary class must then advance the slogan of the dictatorship of the proletariat.*

Or the words of one of his disciples in the 1970s:

Our era is the era of the transition from Capitalism to Socialism and Communism, the era of the struggle of the two opposed world systems. The outstanding feature of its current stage is that the forces of Socialism determine the course of historical development, and Imperialism has lost its dominant position in the world arena. The USSR now represents a mighty power in economic and military respects. The scientific-technological revolution currently taking place substantially influences the development of military affairs. In these conditions the military-technological policy of the CPSU is directed towards creating and maintaining military superiority of the Socialist countries over the forces of war and aggression.†

'Reams of such stuff was made available to us, in translation. But still we tended, for practical purposes, to look at the Soviet Union's problems in the light of our own open, free-ranging understanding, according to which Murphy's Law rates equally, for truth, with the second law of thermodynamics. A Britisher who came here to talk to us one day tried to make the point this way. It seems that there had been a party at the Soviet Embassy, here in Washington, and that the vodka had flowed freely. Towards the end of the evening the Soviet Ambassador challenged the British Ambassador to a race. The British Ambassador came first. This was duly reported in *The Times* as "There was a race between the British and the Soviet Ambassadors in Washington yesterday, which the British Ambassador won." *Pravda* put it differently: "In a race between ambassadors in Washington last week, the Soviet Ambassador came in second – the British Ambassador was second from last." '

Admiral Maybury then proceeded to present his account of naval operations in four sections: the pre-war naval balance; the naval force deployments on 4 August 1985; the naval operations during the next sixteen days; and the immediate post-hostilities activity.

The following is a digest of what he said.

No doubt the debate will be recalled which continued for at least two decades before the war about the capabilities of the Soviet Navy. It was part of Western, and above all American, concern about the growth of Soviet military power in general. Were Soviet intentions to

---

* V. I. Lenin, *Collected Works*, vol. 9 p. 3, quoted in Ian Greig, *They Mean What They Say* (Foreign Affairs Research Institute, London 1981), p. 14.

† M. Gladkov and B. Ivanov, 'The Economy and Military Technological Policy', *Communist of the Armed Forces*, No. 9, May 1972, quoted in Ian Greig, op, cit., p. 57.

be deduced from their capabilities? What were their limitations? It is not easy, even now, to find valid assessments in the records. The intelligence community tended to play safe and take no risk of under-estimating the threat. Retired officers tended to 'sound off', warning the public of the grim consequences of the failure of politicians to make proper appropriations for this or that new weapon system. Various 'think-tanks' were given contracts to produce defence studies. Where the concerns putting out these contracts were profit-making, there was a suspicion that the outcomes favoured the point of view of the organization giving the contract. As one sceptic put it: 'How can you produce an objective study without knowing the objec-tive?' Obviously, too, the arms manufacturers had an interest in seeing that the Soviet threat, as perceived by the US Administration, and by Congress, matched the particular combat capability that they were in business to sell. Congress itself was not immune from this syndrome. As Admiral Miller, whose own estimate of Soviet naval capabilities stood up better than most, wrote: 'Often the version of the Soviet threat accepted by individual members is determined to some degree by the impact that version will have on the region and the constituencies they represent. If there is no defence-related industry in their particular area of interest, the charge is made that the version of the threat they consider valid is the one that requires the least financial expenditures for defense.'*

The academics who analysed military intelligence data tended to let their particular philosophies influence their deductions; journalists, over-eager to publish what would attract attention, often cared little about the balance of their version; even the active service force commander was apt to be influenced in his judgment of the threat by his own, maybe unique, experience. As to US Administra-tions, if the President came into office on a platform that promised to reduce the defence budget, it is reasonable to assume that the version of the Soviet naval threat his Administration accepted would be something less than that of a president elected on a platform propos-ing an increase in the defence budget.

Finally, how much credence could be placed, people wondered, on the books and articles on naval matters that emerged from the Soviet Union itself? Was Admiral Gorshkov's writing gospel? Was he writing for the NATO intelligence community, to inspire his own navy, to get the generals on his side, or to extract ever greater resources from the Politburo? We now know that Gorshkov believed what he wrote; that

* G. E. Miller, Vice-Admiral US Navy (retired), former Commander US Second and Sixth Fleets, 'An Evaluation of the Soviet Navy', quoted in Grayson Kirk and Nils H. Wessell (eds), *The Soviet Threat: Myths and Realities* (Praeger, New York 1978), p. 47.

it was soundly based upon Marxist-Leninist theory; that the generals neither liked nor believed it; that the Politburo both liked and believed it; and that NATO did not want to believe it. What follows is based upon Admiral Miller's own assessment of the Soviet Navy, after his period as Commander of the US Sixth Fleet, in the Mediterranean, not many years before the Third World War. As events proved, he was not far out.

As Soviet war deployments will be dealt with separately, indicating the numbers of the principal types of warship available at the start of hostilities, what follows here is confined solely to the aspect of quality. Consider, first, the Soviet surface fleet, other than aircraft carriers. The heavy cruiser, cruiser, destroyer, frigate, and smaller combatant types all included a majority of up-to-date vessels. They were impressive in appearance, quite manoeuvrable and seaworthy; and they were relatively fast and well armed, primarily with defensive weapon systems. These latter characteristics required compromises in other areas. The number of weapon reloads, for example, was rather small; living conditions for the crews tended to be restricted; space for stores, spare parts, and supplies was limited; and ship construction standards were somewhat lower than was acceptable to most Western navies. The Soviet ships, it was thought, would sink rapidly if hit. In addition, very heavy dependence upon electronics counted against the capacity of the armament to survive attack. Without adequate resistance to electronic counter-measure (ECM), the Soviet ships might find their armaments virtually useless, even if the ships themselves should remain afloat.

In anti-submarine warfare (ASW), the Soviet Navy lagged behind, even in the 1980s. The ships themselves were equipped with sonar; there were helicopters with dipping sonar and fixed-wing aircraft with sonobuoys. But the Soviets had not developed, like the US Navy, arrays of fixed sonars over large areas of the sea bottom, in order to enable hostile submarines to be detected at considerable distances offshore. Furthermore, the Soviet submarines were certainly noisier than those of the US and her allies.

The smaller combatants of the Soviet Navy were, for the most part, fast, missile-armed attack craft. Although readily countered by air attack, these craft were effective in inshore waters, under cover of shore-based fighter protection. Several of the type had proved their value in action in Arab-Israeli and Indo-Pakistani fighting. With the possible exception of the Soviet heavy cruisers of the *Kirov* class, which being nuclear powered, fast, and well armed might do much damage on independent missions before being brought to book, the surface-ship element of the Soviet naval threat did not unduly alarm the US Navy.

Submarines were a different matter. Leaving aside for the moment the strategic nuclear ballistic missile-armed, nuclear-powered submarines (SSBN), the Soviets had produced three main types of attack, or general purpose, sometimes called 'fleet', submarines. One of these types was nuclear powered and armed with torpedoes and missiles, for both anti-surface ship and ASW purposes. The other two types were armed with anti-ship cruise missiles, one being nuclear powered and the other diesel-electric driven. Within each type there were several classes, the most modern of which could run quietly and deep. In addition, the Soviet submarine fleet included a large number of diesel-electric 'patrol' submarines, torpedo armed and capable, as an alternative, of laying mines. Unlike the nuclear-powered submarines, the diesel-electric ones were bound to expose an air induction tube above the sea surface when charging the battery, and this could be detected by radar, especially airborne radar. On the other hand, these submarines were so quiet when submerged that they were extremely difficult to detect by passive means, and active sonar had therefore to be used against them. Active sonar, however, could act as a beacon for nuclear-powered submarines, which were able to proceed at high speed from a distance, closing to missile-firing range while still remaining undetected. They were able to operate in the ocean depths anywhere in the world for as long as the food and the weapons lasted, but they could not safely or effectively operate in the shallow water (200 metres or less) which covers the Continental Shelf. This factor apart, there can be no doubt that the Soviet submarine force posed a severe threat to the warships and shipping of the United States and its maritime allies in being probably able to achieve a successful attack, in the face of the best anti-submarine measures which could be taken, at least once in every three attempts, while on average only one submarine would be destroyed in every five that were detected and classified as a submarine contact.

Soviet naval aviation, on the other hand, had by 1985 hardly come of age. The first nuclear-powered, large aircraft carrier had not yet completed her trials. The four 45,000-ton *Kiev*-class aviation ships, however, with their complement of ASW helicopters and V/STOL (vertical/short take-off and landing) fighter-reconnaissance aircraft, were judged to be effective in their role. The smaller helicopter cruisers *Moskva* and *Leningrad* were thought to be no more than fair-weather ships. Soviet shore-based air power demanded much more respect, however. Admiral Gorshkov had been able to persuade the Soviet Defence Council that he must have both long-range reconnaissance to cover the Atlantic, Indian and Western Pacific Oceans, and a strong force of long-range, high-speed bombers armed with air-to-surface anti-shipping missiles. These were the *Bears* and the

Backfires. Given operational bases strategically placed, NATO and Allied shipping would be at serious risk from this air threat. If bases in North Africa were made available to the Soviet Union, even the US Sixth Fleet in the Mediterranean might be in peril.

An assessment of the Soviet amphibious forces indicated that, despite the well-advertised excellence of their naval infantry, they seemed to lack certain important elements, such as vertical airlift and integral tactical air support. For the intervention role, against light opposition, the force had to be reckoned with, but it could not compare in combat power with the US Marines. Another relatively weak aspect of the Soviet naval forces was in logistic support. There was only a small capacity for under-way replenishment of major fleet units. In peacetime, it was true, forces such as the Fifth *Eskadra*, in the eastern Mediterranean, were maintained for long periods away from their home bases, but they did this mostly at anchor, maintained by a succession of auxiliary supply ships, merchant ships, and tenders. This did not amount to a capability for sustained ocean operations. What it did mean was that if the Soviet Navy managed to achieve a surprise attack, it could inflict a good deal of damage very quickly. There was also evidence that Admiral Gorshkov had established an extremely reliable command and control system which, although highly centralized, had built-in reserves of personnel and resource. To serve the command a comprehensive operational intelligence system had long been established and was kept in constant practice.

As to the morale and efficiency of the Soviet Navy's officers and men, there were both pluses and minuses. The high command, and flag officers generally, gave the impression of knowing their business. The commanding officers of ships and submarines, also, were good, although it had been noted that many of them retained command for lengthy periods, or on relinquishment of one command were immediately given another, suggesting a shortage of really competent people. A certain reluctance to use initiative seemed also to be common. Perhaps too much was being demanded of the commanding officers. According to the Soviet armed forces regulations the commander of a unit was obliged 'to direct combat training and political education of his subordinates and to maintain perfect discipline . . . He must know the professional, political, and moral qualities of his subordinates, persistently improve their skills and act as their educator in the field of politics and law'. And, although the principle of unity of command was always stressed, in practice the Party's organization, as represented by the *Zampolit* (the commander's deputy for political affairs) was concerned not only with politico-ideological questions, but also with purely military and even technical matters.

The training load for the officers in a Soviet warship was heavy. Most of the enlisted men were conscripts and served for thirty-six months. The training was competitive, in theory. But it was not uncommon for commanding officers to exclude from various drills those officers and enlisted men whose performance might bring down the ship's score. A surprisingly large proportion of the Soviet warships' time was spent in harbour too. The standard of combat readiness and weapon-training was not invariably as high as the smartness of the ships might lead one to expect.

To sum up this section, in terms of quality the Soviet Navy was, in itself, a formidable force, but it was dependent upon the proximity of bases – both naval and air – to be capable of matching the US and Allied fleets. Indeed, the outcome of a conflict waged near the Soviet home bases would have been difficult to predict. Fortunately for the Western allies this one was waged far from Soviet home bases.

Admiral Maybury then referred to the quality of the Soviet strategic nuclear ballistic missile force. As would no doubt be recalled, the earlier types of Soviet SSBN were distinctly inferior to the *Polaris* and *Poseidon* boats of the US Navy. But by 1985 the Soviet SSBN force was mainly composed of the *Delta* class, armed with missiles having a range of over 4,000 miles. On patrol in the Barents Sea, or the Sea of Okhotsk, these submarines could range on targets over the entire United States, safe from any counter-measures. Indeed, neither the US nor the Soviet navies were capable of countering their opponent's SSBN, which retained, accordingly, their unique character as strategic retaliatory systems. Both the British and the French SSBN constituted, in spite of much smaller numbers, formidable second-strike forces. These, too, the Soviets could not counter. They could not ignore them either.

Before considering what is now known of the wartime Soviet deployments, it is as well to look at geography, and its bearing upon the operational concept on which the deployments were based. Geo-politics – ideas of 'heartland', 'rimland', 'world ocean', and so on – are interesting but probably of little practical value in formulating policies. The distribution of usable mineral resources may well determine the political map of the world in the future. But there can be no doubt of the underlying continuity of Russian foreign policy aims.

Tsar Peter the Great in 1725, shortly after his annexation of five Persian provinces and the city of Baku, and just before he died, enjoined his successors thus:

I strongly believe that the State of Russia will be able to take the whole of Europe under its sovereignty . . . you must always expand towards the Baltic and the Black Sea. You must try to approach Istanbul and India as far forward as possible. You must seek to dominate the Black Sea and be the owner of the Baltic. These actions are most important in order to achieve our future aims. You must also do your best to ensure the collapse of Persia as soon as possible and envisage opening a route through the Persian Gulf.*

In 1985 Peter the Great, the mystical-absolutist, might have conceded, had he been aware of events, that the dialectical-materialist usurpers in the Kremlin were not doing so badly. That is, until the fateful day of 4 August 1985, when the Soviet armies were launched into the Federal Republic of Germany. Tsar Peter would have been appalled at the disposition on that date of the Soviet Navy. With the most powerful of its fleets based in the remote areas of Murmansk and Kamchatka and the other two main fleets bottled up, one in the Baltic and the other in the Black Sea, how could Soviet naval power be brought effectively to bear in support of a grand design? Surely the decisive surge westward should not have been undertaken until a combination of circumstance, diplomacy and force had delivered into Soviet hands control of the exits from both the Baltic and the Black Sea?

Great emphasis had been placed upon the application of three principles in order to achieve the military aim of the Warsaw Pact, which was the destruction of the armed forces of NATO and its associates. These principles were: surprise, co-ordination of all arms, and concentration of force. Plans had been in existence, constantly updated, ever since Soviet military power had grown sufficient in relation to NATO to confer upon Soviet leaders the option of using it, if favourable circumstances should arise. It was not necessary in the Soviet Navy to risk compromising the contingency plans by any distribution below fleet commander level, and even then the directive was related to a D-day that remained undesignated until D − 5. This ensured that no change in the pattern of Soviet naval activities should give NATO early warning of possible attack. On the other hand, every Soviet warship that proceeded outside local areas had to be fully stored for war, and peacetime deployments must not take major units more than five days' steaming from war stations. Reconnaissance, surveillance and operational intelligence material had to be provided sufficient to support initial war deployments without augmentation, which might reveal unusual activity. Operational command and control of all warships, merchant ships and fishing fleets outside local areas would be assumed on D − 1 by the

* Quoted in Captain W. J. Draper (Canadian Forces), Colonel P. Monsutti (Italian Army), Group Captain B. T. Sills (RAF), Colonel M. Y. Tanyel (Turkish Army), 'In Search of a Western Military Strategy for the 1980s, a Group Study', in *Seaford House Papers 1980* (Royal College of Defence Studies London).

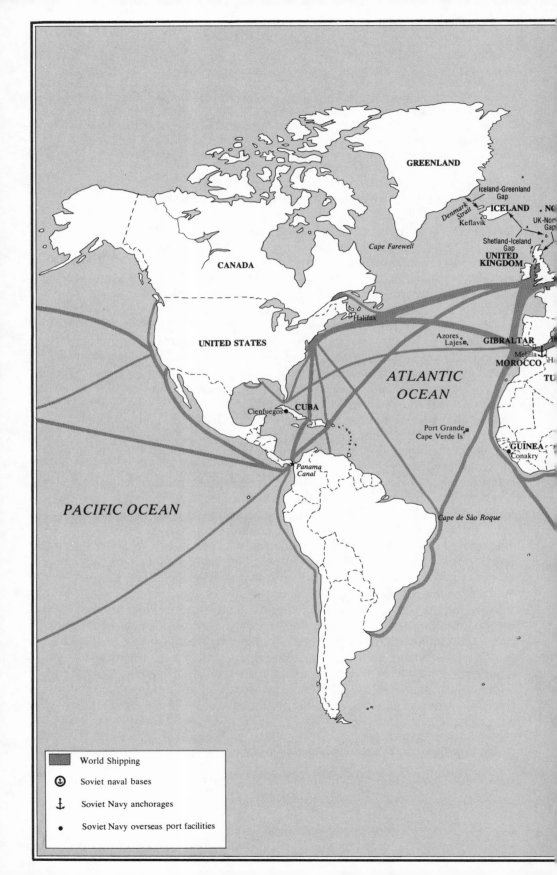

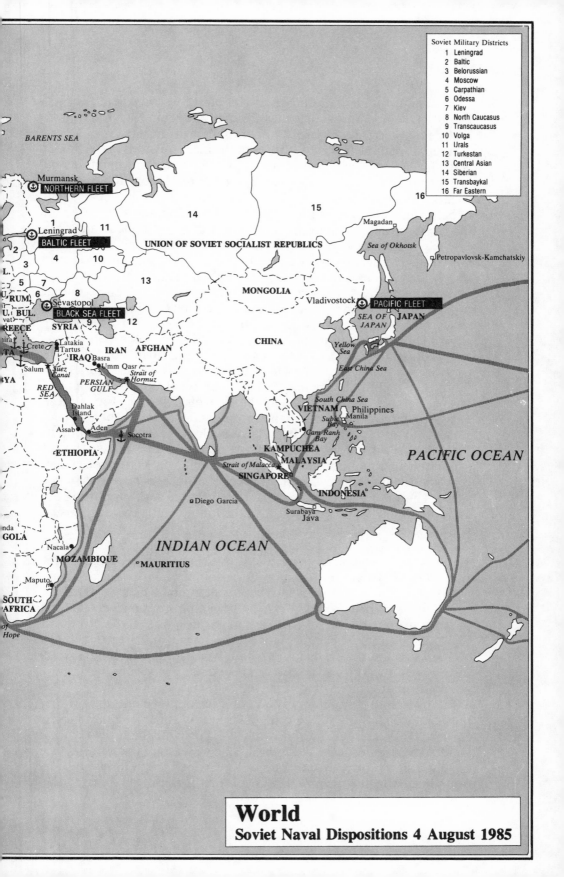

BARENTS SEA

Murmansk
NORTHERN FLEET

UNION OF SOVIET SOCIALIST REPUBLICS

Magadan

Sea of Okhotsk

□ Petropavlovsk-Kamchatskiy

1 Leningrad
BALTIC FLEET

14

15

16

11

2

3

4

10

13

MONGOLIA

Vladivostock ⊕ **PACIFIC FLEET**

5

7

6 Sevastopol
BLACK SEA FLEET

SEA OF JAPAN

JAPAN

RUM.
BUL.
REECE

8

9

12

SYRIA

CHINA

Yellow Sea

East China Sea

Crete

Latakia
Tartus
IRAN AFGHAN

ΤA

nira

L.
U.

Salum

Suez Canal

IRAQ Basra
Umm Qasr
Strait of Hormuz

South China Sea

VIETNAM

Philippines

PERSIAN GULF

Subic Bay

Manila

Cam Ranh Bay

PACIFIC OCEAN

RED SEA

Dahlak Island

Assab ⚓ Aden

⚓ Socotra

KAMPUCHEA

MALAYSIA

SINGAPORE

Strait of Malacca

ETHIOPIA

□ Diego Garcia

INDONESIA

nda
GOLA

Nacala

MOZAMBIQUE

∘MAURITIUS

INDIAN OCEAN

Surabaya
Java

Maputo

SOUTH AFRICA

of Hope

Soviet Military Districts
1 Leningrad
2 Baltic
3 Belorussian
4 Moscow
5 Carpathian
6 Odessa
7 Kiev
8 North Caucasus
9 Transcaucasus
10 Volga
11 Urals
12 Turkestan
13 Central Asian
14 Siberian
15 Transbaykal
16 Far Eastern

World
Soviet Naval Dispositions 4 August 1985

Commander-in-Chief of the Soviet Navy in Moscow, where the First Deputy Commander-in-Chief, as Chief of the Main Naval Staff, was ready to assume the control of operations worldwide.

It seems that the NATO estimate of the main missions of the Soviet Navy in the event of war was not far out. They were: to maintain at instant readiness the SSBN strategic nuclear retaliatory force, and to ensure its security from any counter-measures that might be brought to bear against it; to counter, as far as practicable, the SSBN forces of the USA, Great Britain and France; to destroy or neutralize US carrier air groups, and other major warships; to support the army, both directly by fire power and indirectly by transportation and supply, and by interdiction of enemy military shipping; to interrupt all movement by sea which directly supported the enemy combat capability; and to carry out reconnaissance, surveillance and intelligence missions as required in support of the foregoing missions.

From Soviet records it appears that the following force dispositions had been made in order to carry out the requirements of the naval contingency plan. At any moment during the last week of July 1985 there were eight SSBN, each with sixteen or twenty missiles, on patrol in the Barents Sea and five in the Sea of Okhotsk. From these locations, targets anywhere in the continental USA could be reached. In order to protect the SSBN from the unwelcome attentions of potentially hostile 'intruders', the Soviets used diesel-electric ASW patrol submarines, exploiting the acoustic advantage they enjoyed, when running on their electric motors, over the nuclear-powered opposition. There were, of course, shore-based ASW aircraft supporting the SSBN operations, and there was also the input from a comprehensive operational intelligence network.

The Soviet Union had come to the conclusion that it was not feasible to counter, completely or directly, the opposing SSBN forces of the USA, Great Britain and France. A certain amount could be done, however, to limit the damage to the Soviet Union which a retaliatory strike by SSBN could cause. The only warships earmarked for this purpose were some diesel-electric submarines – six in the Northern Fleet, and four in the Pacific Fleet – whose task would be to lay mines off the SSBN bases. Certain other counter-measures which the Soviets took were not specifically naval, and need not concern us here. They were not in any case very effective.

It is as well to recall the US/NATO force deployment upon which the Soviet Union had to base its plans – and as has been remarked earlier, the Western powers did not always provide themselves with a valid 'Moscow view'. By 1985 the US Navy was well into the service life extension programme (SLEP) for its carrier force. This would add fifteen years to the normal thirty-year life of these warships. It was designed to enable the US Navy to have at least twelve carriers in commission for the remainder of the present century. By August 1985 the USS *Saratoga* and *Forrestal* had been through the SLEP, and were 'good as new'; and the USS *Independence* had been taken in hand by the Philadelphia Navy Yard – that may have seemed tough on the Virginians, but at least Newport News was given the *Carl Vinson*, CVN-70, to build!

In a well-publicized comment, around 1981, the Chief of Naval Operations, Admiral Thomas B. Hayward, said that he was '. . . trying to meet a three-ocean requirement with a one-and-a-half-ocean navy'. It has to be accepted that, over a period of years, it takes three carriers in commission to keep one up front. Hence, in mid-1985 there were permanently on station a one-carrier battle group in the Mediterranean, a one- and occasionally two-carrier battle group in the Indian Ocean and a one- and occasionally two-carrier battle group in the Western Pacific.

None was permanently on station in the Atlantic: a Carrier Battle Group Atlantic would be formed from the forces training in home waters prior to deployment for war. Each of the carriers had an air group of about eighty-five aircraft – fighters, strike aircraft, ASW aircraft, both fixed and rotary wing, and one or two aircraft specially fitted for ECM and airborne early warning (AEW). To protect this floating airfield the US had two or three guided-missile cruisers and ten or so modern destroyers and frigates. Quite often, too, there was a nuclear 'attack' submarine in direct support.

The USSR had assumed that the US carriers could launch nuclear strikes, and for this reason had determined that they should be constantly tracked, and targeted by both torpedo and missile firing submarines; and because it was realized that the carriers might take a lot of sinking – or even neutralizing – cruisers and destroyers armed with surface-to-surface missiles (SSM) were also deployed within a day or two of striking distance and developed a pattern of closing in to firing range from time to time. In this way such a movement would not, it was hoped, alert US carrriers that war was imminent.

During this last week in July 1985, therefore, there were two missile-armed and two torpedo-armed Soviet submarines in the Mediterranean, all nuclear powered, and all from the Northern Fleet. Off Newfoundland across the line of advance of the Carrier Battle Group Atlantic were positioned three more missile-armed and four torpedo-armed nuclear-powered submarines, again from the Northern Fleet. This fleet also provided to the west of the Straits of Gibraltar two diesel-electric missile-armed boats, and two diesel-electric ballistic-missile boats were stationed within bombardment range of the NATO air bases as Keflavik, Iceland, and Lossiemouth,

Scotland. Other submarines were at sea between their patrol stations and home base in Murmansk.

The Fifth *Eskadra*, cruising or anchored in the general vicinity of the carrier battle group of the US Sixth Fleet, consisted of three guided-missile cruisers, four guided-missile destroyers, and four gun destroyers, all from the Soviet's Black Sea Fleet. Both the US and the Soviet groups were accompanied, of course, by logistic support and, in the Soviet case, maintenance ships in considerable numbers.

In the Indian Ocean, the Soviets had stationed one guided-missile and three torpedo-attack nuclear-powered submarines to cover the US carrier battle group, but their surface force in that area, consisting of one guided-missile cruiser and three guided-missile destroyers or frigates, tended to remain well out of range.

Finally, in the western Pacific, where there was a US carrier battle group based usually on Subic in the Philippines, the Soviets were able to muster another group of nuclear-powered submarines, one missile armed and the other torpedo armed while, in addition, there was a diesel-electric guided-missile boat on patrol off Yokosuka in Japan.

In addition to the submarines and surface forces tasked to destroy US carriers on station, the Soviet Naval Air Force maintained specially trained and briefed long-range bomber squadrons, armed with stand-off air-to-surface missiles, based at Murmansk, in the Leningrad Military District, and at Sevastopol and Vladivostok. These were mainly *Backfires*, in support of the Northern and Pacific Fleets, with the shorter-range *Blinders* in the Baltic and the Black Sea. The range of both types could be extended by in-flight refuelling. The US carriers and their supporting ships, whose exact positions were always known to the Soviet Union by air, submarine, surface ship and satellite reconnaissance in combination, were liable to air attack anywhere in the North Atlantic, the Mediterranean, the northern part of the Indian Ocean, and in the Pacific from the South China Sea to the west coast of the United States.

We come now to the Soviet Navy's dispositions for the support of the Red Army and its Warsaw Pact allies. From the 1970s onwards it had been evident that the Soviet amphibious capability had been increasing, and much interest had been aroused in the autumn of 1981 when exercise *Zapad* was carried out in the eastern Baltic. At the time there were some who believed that the exercise was designed specifically to bring pressure to bear on Poland, at that time suffering from something of a breakdown in political control by its own Communist Party, under pressure from the powerful Solidarity free trade union movement supported by the Catholic church. But in fact the exercise had been planned over a year previously and we now know that it was a rehearsal for the seizure of the Dardanelles. This

accounted for the unprecedented bringing together of the
helicopter-cruiser *Leningrad*, a *Sverdlov*-class cruiser, two *Krivak*-
class frigates and several units belonging to the amphibious forces of
the Black Sea Fleet and the Northern Fleet, plus the latest large
landing ship *Ivan Rogov* from the Pacific, while the carrier *Kiev*,
accompanied by two frigates, was diverted to the Baltic from her
passage back to the Northern Fleet base from the Mediterranean. In
July 1985 strong amphibious forces, well supported by anti-
submarine and anti-air defence and by shore-based air-striking
forces, were poised to fight alongside the Warsaw Pact land forces in
north Norway, north Germany, Turkey, and in the Far East, while
Soviet submarines and naval aircraft were ready to interdict NATO
support for its land forces in these theatres.

When we look at the Soviet plans for the interruption of all
movement by sea that directly supported the enemy combat capability, we must at the same time bear in mind the Soviet emphasis, in
operational concept, on the achievement of surprise and the co-
ordination of all arms. It must also be remembered that the entire
Soviet and Warsaw Pact merchant fleet, as well as the fishing fleet,
were under the operational control of the Soviet Government –
which meant, once contingency plans were put into effect, the
Soviet Main Naval Staff.

It is now clear that the Soviets had worked out very carefully how
'and where to apply pressure to the world's sea transportation system
so as to create the maximum disruption in the minimum time, priority
being given to denying to the United States and her allies the supply
of those imported materials which would have the most immediate
effect upon their combat capability.

The rapid growth of the Soviet merchant fleet in the 1970s and
early 1980s had not only earned much-needed hard currency, but had
also helped to extend Soviet political influence and provide a most
valuable auxiliary force to the Soviet Navy. Not the least of its merits
was to furnish accurate, comprehensive and up-to-date intelligence of
the world's shipping movements, the cargoes carried, and their desti-
nations. Certain Soviet merchant ships, also, could lay mines, and
many were equipped with electronic warfare devices, for both interception and jamming of radio communications. What the Soviets
planned to do, therefore, at the outset of hostilities, was to paralyse
shipping movement by executing, as nearly as possible simultaneously, a number of operations involving surface raiding forces, submarine attacks, shore-based air attacks, mining by merchant ships,
sabotage, radio jamming and disinformation. 'War zones', into which
non-aligned and neutral shipping would sail at their peril, would be
declared in the western approaches to north-west Europe; west of the

Straits of Gibraltar; in the Arabian Sea; off the Cape of Good Hope; and in the East China Sea. This concept of the 'instantaneous threat' to shipping, rather than the prosecution of a *guerre de course* – the old-style war of attrition – accorded well with the Soviet politico-military war plan for a rapid seizure of the Federal Republic of Germany, followed by a peace negotiated with the USA, on the basis of a stunning demonstration of Soviet power on land, at sea, and in the air.

The Soviet naval and naval air forces available for paralysing shipping, like those allocated for other missions already referred to, had to be in place, or nearly so, long before war contingency plans were executed. Again, therefore, they were bound to be few in number. Western operational intelligence was naturally most interested, in peacetime, in the movements of the Soviet nuclear-powered heavy cruisers of the *Kirov* class, two of which were in commission in July 1985 – one, the *Kirov* herself, with the Northern Fleet, and the other in the Pacific. Their 'electronic signatures' were well known to the US Navy – and hence to NATO – as were those of all the other main units of the Soviet fleets. It was not, however, too difficult, when the moment came, for these to be artificially altered, so as to confuse – even if only for a day or two – surveillance and reconnaissance systems. Furthermore, the *Kirovs*, being nuclear powered and extremely well armed, could operate independently and continuously, at high speed, demanding from the enemy a full-scale concentration of force in order to bring them to book.

Some *Kiev*-class v/STOL aircraft carriers, of which four were in commission in July 1985, provided the other main element of the Soviet anti-shipping surface force. Two were in the Northern Fleet, including the *Kiev* herself, and two in the Pacific Fleet. It was normal for either the *Kiev* or her sister ship the *Novorossysk* to be operating between the Mediterranean and Murmansk, with occasional cruises to the Cape Verde area, and the west coast of Africa; while the *Minsk* and her sister ship, based upon Vladivostok, operated between there and Cam Ranh Bay – that bonus to the Soviet union from its support of Vietnam – with periodical sorties into the South China Sea. These carriers were usually accompanied by a pair of the excellent *Krivak*-class frigates.

It was often assumed, on the Western side, that if war came the *Kirov* heavy cruisers would join the *Kiev* carriers, with perhaps additional frigates or destroyers, to form battle groups similar in concept to NATO battle groups. But this view was mistaken. It overlooked the Soviet determination to achieve surprise, accepting the risk of losing perhaps all of their in-place forces during the first few days, or even hours, of hostilities. Besides, why sacrifice the exceptional mobility of the nuclear-powered *Kirovs* by grouping them with the logistically-limited *Kievs* and their escorts?

As to submarines in the anti-merchant ship role, only two submarines were kept on station in peacetime with this task in mind. They were both elderly, torpedo-firing nuclear powered boats. One of them patrolled within two days' easy steaming of the Cape of Good Hope, and the other had a billet within the same distance of Cape de São Roque, the focal point off Brazil. It was their job to identify and sink particular ships, designated by Moscow, within hours of the opening of hostilities on the Central Front in Europe.

That, in essence, was the Soviet naval plan. It was a good one, and it very nearly worked.

Admiral Maybury then continued his talk on the basis of the Soviet naval objectives and dispositions already described, with brief accounts of some selected actions, all of which it must be emphasized were taking place at about the same time. He began with the heavy cruiser *Kirov*.

It was known in CINCUSNAVEUR on 1 August that this ship had sailed from the Kola inlet a day or so before and headed south-west towards the middle of the Greenland-Iceland-UK gap at moderate speed. From time to time, in the past, the *Kirov* had proceeded into the Atlantic, west of Iceland, and appeared to be acting as target for *Backfire* strikes from airfields in the Murmansk area; it was good training, also, for the Soviet maritime reconnaissance aircraft and for satellite surveillance. What was not known, on this occasion, was that the *Kirov* was accompanied by an *Oscar*-class nuclear attack submarine, keeping station beneath her, so that her noise signature could not be distinguished from that of the surface ship.

By 3 August the *Kirov* was about 350 miles south of Cape Farewell. Suddenly the US Navy *Orion* that had been trailing the cruiser detected another echo close to her. The echoes then merged, and after a short while separated. The *Orion* continued to trail what she felt sure was the cruiser, while the other echo headed south at 20 knots; both echoes were now observing radar and radio silence. It was the *Kirov*, however, that was heading south. Early on the 4th the cruiser intercepted the British container ship *Leeds United*, the exact position, course and speed of which had been transmitted to the *Kirov* by Moscow. The *Leeds United* never knew what hit her – two ss-n-19 conventionally-armed tactical missiles fired from over the horizon. During the next three days the *Kirov* destroyed, in the same way, no less than seven Allied ships, all valuable. As none of them managed to transmit an SOS, let alone a raider report, these losses went unnoticed.

Kirov's orders were to continue south towards the Cape Verde

Islands where she could replenish with missiles at the Soviet base at Porte Grande. Having already used up all her surface-to-surface missiles (SSM), her capable Captain Fokin decided instead to make all speed back to Murmansk, passing through the Denmark Strait. He knew that the US airfield at Keflavik had been put temporarily out of action by bombardment with submarine-launched ballistic missiles (SLBM) specially developed for the purpose, fitted into the old but still operational *Golf*-class boats. In the event, the *Kirov* was located by a Canadian *Orion*, which managed to keep just out of range of the cruiser's SAM. On 9 August the *Kirov* was severely damaged by *Harpoon* attack from the US submarine *Dallas*, and later sunk by torpedoes from the submarine's squadron mate, the *Groton*.

In the Mediterranean, on 2 August, the Soviet Fifth *Eskadra* came to its regular anchorage in the Gulf of Hammamet, off the coast of Tunisia; that is to say, the surface ships and their auxiliaries did. The submarines – two *Charlie* II SSGN (submarine, guided missile, nuclear powered), and two *Victor* SSN – remained in deep water, a pair consisting of one of each type patrolling to the east and to the west of Malta. On 2 August the Commander-in-Chief Allied Forces Southern Europe (CINCSOUTH) and the Commander, Sixth Fleet, agreed that it would be advisable for the carrier battle group, which was already at short notice for sea, to sail from Naples and proceed to exercise south-east of Malta. The Soviet *Eskadra* was, of course, kept under surveillance. However, the electronic deception of the Soviet force was successful, in so far as the guided-missile cruisers *Admiral Drozd*, *Sevastopol* and *Admiral Golovko* with their accompanying missile destroyers were able to weigh anchor after dark on 3 August and proceed eastwards at high speed without immediately being trailed.

The force was located at about 0300 on 4 August by one of CINCSOUTH's reconnaissance aircraft about 150 miles to the westward of the *Forrestal* and her battle group. Admiral Lorimer, commanding the Sixth Fleet, immediately ordered reconnaissance to be flown off and a strike readied. At this time both the Soviet submarines of the eastern group were in contact with *Forrestal*'s battle group and had received orders to commence hostilities at 0400. Sonar conditions, with the warmer surface water typical of the Mediterranean in summer, greatly assisted the submarines to remain undetected. A few minutes after 0400, and before the American admiral had received the order to open hostilities, his flagship was struck by two guided missiles which started fires in the hangar and among the aircraft ranged and armed for the strike. The AWACS aircraft, which had been airborne since 0300, was able to report the incoming missiles as submarine launched, and shortly afterwards detected a stream of missiles approaching from the Soviet force to the westward. This time the counter-measures had some effect. No more missiles hit the *Forrestal*, but two of her accompanying destroyers were hit. The fires in the *Forrestal* herself were being brought under control, damaged aircraft ditched and those which were intact prepared to fly off. A surface striking group was forming up, and the carrier altered round to the north-westward, into wind, to fly off the strike aircraft. This new course, as it happened, took the carrier within torpedo range of the second Soviet submarine, and at 0437 hours she was struck by two torpedoes, one of which damaged her port rudder and propellers.

In the surface-ship action that followed, the entire Soviet force was sunk, but the *Forrestal* had to seek permission to enter Maltese territorial waters, and was with difficulty brought into Marsaxlokk and anchored. That evening one of the western group of Soviet submarines was sunk by the USS *Arthur W. Radford* while attempting to get within torpedo range of the carrier.

The US battle group in the Indian Ocean was centred on the nuclear-powered carrier *Nimitz*. Sailing from Diego Garcia on 2 August, this force set course north-westwards towards the Arabian Sea. The Soviet Indian Ocean Squadron was known to be at Socotra, and it was the intention to get within air striking range of it as soon as possible. The battle group's movements were, of course, impossible to conceal from satellite reconnaissance. Using their exceptionally high speed, two torpedo-armed submarines, Soviet *Alfa*-class SSN, took up an intercepting position which would enable contact to be made with the US battle group at about 0100 on 4 August. Because the US force was steaming at 25 knots, it was unable to utilize its ASW helicopters for screening, and its fixed-wing anti-submarine aircraft, relying upon sonobuoys for submarine detection, were in the circumstances of little value. Once again, therefore, a successful submarine attack was carried out shortly after the opening of hostilities. Fortunately, however, only one torpedo hit the *Nimitz*, and although it was fairly far aft, the carrier's speed was reduced by only 4 knots; more importantly, her reactors remained safely in operation. A subsequent air strike on the Soviet squadron was not very successful. Casualties from SAM were heavy, mainly because the one electronic counter-measure (ECM) aircraft accompanying the strike lost power shortly after take-off and ditched. The carrier's fighters were able to counter, fairly effectively, an attack on the battle group by Soviet *Backfires* from South Yemen. Honours, one might say, in the Indian Ocean were fairly even during the first few days of the war, although the lack of a dock anywhere nearer than San Diego large enough to take the damaged *Nimitz* was a serious matter.

The *Kirov*-class heavy cruiser in the Pacific had followed a rather similar pattern of operation to that of the *Kirov* herself in the Atlantic. That is to say, she would from time to time sortie from Petropavlovsk and proceed south-eastwards into the Pacific for some days, apparently in order to provide a reconnaissance and strike target for the Soviet Naval Air Force. On 1 August the cruiser followed the usual course into the Pacific. Fortunately, the US submarine *La Jolla* was on surveillance patrol in the vicinity of Petropavlovsk and the Soviet cruiser had a 'tail' as she went on her way. Shortly after hostilities were opened, the Soviet ship was attacked. The stricken cruiser, hit by three torpedoes, sank within twenty minutes.

In the meantime, the carrier *Kitty Hawk* – one of two in the US Seventh Fleet at that period – which was exercising to the eastward of Yokosuka with her *Aegis*-equipped cruiser consorts and some units of the Japanese Maritime Self-Defence Force, had been ordered to intercept the Soviet heavy crusier as back-up for the *La Jolla*. But before this group had come within striking range of the Soviet warship the submarine report of its sinking was received in the *Kitty Hawk*, which then set course with her group to return to Yokosuka.

The American carrier *John F. Kennedy*, with her battle group, was in Subic Bay in the Philippines on 4 August. Admiral Carlsberg, the Commander, US Seventh Fleet, reckoned that his first duty, if the state of tension should be followed by war, was to take his force to sea and seek out and destroy the Soviet carrier *Minsk*, sister ship of the *Kiev*, which was currently using Cam Ranh Bay as an operational base. Accordingly he sailed his battle group from Subic at 1800 on 4 August after having conducted energetic ASW operations along the sortie route. What he did not know was that a Soviet submarine had that morning laid a minefield precisely where the *John F. Kennedy* would have to go when leaving Subic. The carrier duly detonated one of those mines and had to return to harbour, having first managed to fly off her aircraft. The *Minsk*'s *Forger* v/STOL fighters were no match for the strike carried out at dawn next day by the *John F. Kennedy*'s own air group, flying from the airfield in Manila. The Soviet carrier and two of her group were sunk. Two guided missile cruisers and two destroyers survived, however, and sank several merchant ships in the South China Sea before being interned in Surabaya, Java.

By this time the *Kitty Hawk* had been redeployed to Subic as flagship for Admiral Carlsberg in place of the damaged *John F. Kennedy*.

The Soviet submarines stationed off Cape de São Roque, to the west of the Straits of Gibraltar, and off the Cape of Good Hope, all sank several important merchant ships during the first few days of hostilities, and all round the world ships were kept in harbour or back from danger zones pending developments. Several vessels struck mines laid a few days previously by Soviet merchant ships. There can be no doubt that the 'instantaneous threat' had been successfully put into effect.

The final operation now to be mentioned is the launching by the Soviet armies in the south, together with Romanian and Bulgarian assistance, of a seaborne assault upon the Dardanelles. Rather than make a direct attack in the immediate vicinity of the Bosporus, the Soviet forces advanced by land from Bulgaria – strongly opposed by a combined Greek-Turkish force already deployed against just that contingency – while simultaneously launching a sea and airborne assault on the port of Zonguldak. From there it was intended to proceed westwards along the coast, supported by the Black Sea Fleet, while at the same time threatening Ankara. As is now evident from Soviet records, it was expected that this campaign would induce the Turks to come to terms following the Soviet success in West Germany: These intentions were frustrated owing to the failure to reach their objectives on the Central Front.

One general point should be made before giving an outline – and it will have to be just that – of the naval operations that followed the first two days of hostilities, which is all that we have dealt with in the war at sea so far.

It will be recalled that the Soviet aims, in seeking to occupy the whole of the Federal German Republic within ten days, was to cause the collapse of the Atlantic Alliance and to bring the United States to the negotiating table. The Soviet Main Naval Command deemed it imperative to destroy or neutralize US carriers in a surprise attack at the first possible opportunity. It was this act, more than any other, that gave the war an immediate worldwide character, and perhaps above all else ensured that, even if the Red Army reached the Rhine stop-line on time, the United States would have been very unlikely indeed to negotiate. Quite apart from the fury of the American people at what many saw as almost another Pearl Harbor and the determination of the United States to reassert naval supremacy in the Atlantic, isolationism was no longer, in the 1980s, a valid option for America. The United States was now forced to import oil and strategic raw materials from other continents – and hence had now become truly sea-dependent. Soviet naval predominance around the continents of Europe, Asia and Africa was therefore unacceptable. Yet that is what total US withdrawal from Europe would have meant.

Turning now to the sea/air campaigns that followed the initial surprise attacks, there were five separate, but more or less simultaneous, conflicts being waged within the NATO area as a whole; and of course there were worldwide attacks on shipping, with regional naval activity east of Suez and in the Pacific. The campaigns were: in the Norwegian Sea in support of the Commander-in-Chief Allied Forces Northern Europe (CINCNORTH); in the Baltic, North Sea and Channel in support of the Commander-in-Chief Allied Forces Central Europe (CINCENT); in the Western Approaches to north-west Europe and in general support of Allied Command Europe; in the Atlantic reinforcement operation; and in the Mediterranean in support of CINCSOUTH.

Taking the Norwegian Sea first, it will be recalled that the heavy cruiser *Kirov* was sunk on her way back to base in Murmansk after sinking merchant shipping in the Atlantic. Another operation of special interest in progress at the same time involved the carrier *Kiev*. She had sailed from Murmansk on 23 July, nearly a fortnight before war broke out, accompanied by the two *Krivak*-class frigates. The group arrived in Cork in the Irish Republic on the 27th for what was presented as a courtesy visit. The ships were reported to be on a training cruise to the Caribbean. The group had of course been tracked by NATO surveillance forces since leaving its home waters as a matter of routine, and it remained under observation after sailing from Cork to the south-westward on 2 August. Contact with the *Kiev* group was lost, as a result of effective Soviet electronic deception measures, on the night of the 3rd. Luckily, owing to the use of Shannon air base, the subsequent air search was successful in relocating the *Kiev* on the 5th.

Shannon extended the search radius of French anti-submarine *Atlantique Nouvelle Generation* (ANG) aircraft, and furnished an invaluable staging point for a squadron of *Tornados* of the *Marineflieger* (the Federal German Naval Air Force) which had been pulled out from Schleswig-Holstein to Lossiemouth and redeployed by Joint Allied Command Western Approaches (JACWA). Accompanied by two RAF *Tornado* interceptors, with a VC-10 for refuelling, the German *Tornados* homed on to the *Kiev* at noon on 6 August. The *Forgers* from the Soviet carriers had already shot down one of the ANG and one of the *Tornados*, while SAM from the frigates and the carrier destroyed two more. But the remainder managed good attacks and the *Kiev* was crippled. One of her frigates was badly damaged also. In the meantime, one of the British fleet submarines, the *Splendid*, had been sent to intercept. She sank both the *Kiev* herself and the damaged frigate. The second frigate, having picked up survivors, set off for Cuba but was eventually found by a US *Orion* operating from Lajes. She did not last long after that.

The main activity in the Norwegian Sea began on 5 August. The British fleet submarine *Churchill*, on ASW patrol north of the Shetland Islands, sank a Soviet diesel submarine of the newish *Tango* class (SS) which was on its way to lay mines in the Firth of Clyde. During the next three days there were several submarine encounters with hostile submarines as the first wave of Soviet boats to be sailed after hostilities began reached the Greenland-Iceland-UK gap. The exchange rate was favourable to NATO, as was to be expected given the quieter running of US boats and those of the European allies. But seven more Soviet ssn had got through to the Atlantic.

The US Strike Fleet Atlantic, consisting of two carrier battle-groups, entered the Norwegian Sea on 10 August in order to support the Norwegian forces ashore and the British and US Marines who were about to land, in their task of holding the airfields. This was of high importance. There should have been three carrier battlegroups engaged, but when the news came that the *Forrestal* had been badly damaged in the Mediterranean it was decided to detach the *Saratoga*, with her group, from the Strike Fleet Atlantic and send her to support CINCSOUTH.

The Strike Fleet's operations were also intended to give distant support to the first major reinforcement operation across the Atlantic. This consisted of a group of fast military convoys which sailed from US east coast ports on 8 August, heavily escorted. Diversionary convoys were sailed on other routes, and there was a comprehensive deception plan. Even so, the convoys were heavily attacked by Soviet submarines firing missiles from ranges of up to 250 miles. In mid-Atlantic they were also attacked by *Backfire* bombers from Murmansk, the attacking aircraft launching their missiles from a distance of up to 180 miles. The running battle that developed occupied a tremendous area of ocean. Fortunately counter-measures were not unsuccessful. The number of transports put out of action would otherwise have been much higher. Losses were nonetheless severe. Only thirty-six out of the forty-eight transports which sailed from the USA docked safely in the Channel ports, but the reinforcement they brought was just in time to play a major part in stabilizing the position on the Central Front.

We come now to the end of Admiral Maybury's presentation to the US National Defence College in Washington and offer some comments of our own.

A more detailed narrative of these operations is, of course, to be found in *The Third World War: August 1985*, published earlier this year, in the spring of 1987. It covers, also, the air/sea battle around the Baltic exits and the English Channel, where the Soviet light forces, with air cover, tried to interdict the flow of reinforcements and supplies from the UK to the continent of Europe. We have not repeated this story here.

Many mines were laid by the Soviet forces, and sea traffic nearly came to a standstill owing to the shortage of mine counter-measure (MCM) vessels. This was particularly felt in regard to the south of Ireland. It will be remembered that the *Kiev* and her group visited Cork just before the outbreak of war. During that visit, as is now known, a group of Soviet mine-laying submarines were laying delayed-action mines off Lough Swilly, Bantry Bay, Cork, Wexford, Dublin and Milford Haven. Five ships were to be sunk by these mines. It was only at Milford Haven that MCM were taken and casualties avoided.

Much of the follow-up reinforcement shipping was sent from ports in the Gulf of Mexico. Routed south of the Azores it was then brought in, where possible, to the shallower waters along the European coast. With the extra support available from Spain, as well as that from Portugal and France, this reduced the level of the submarine threat and almost eliminated the threat from the air. Outside the NATO area, where there was no established and practised sea/air operational control of shipping, or proper protection, ocean shipping remained for the most part paralysed, until some degree of confidence had been restored in NATO's competence to safeguard it. By the end of the second week after war had started NATO's worldwide operational intelligence system had provided a more realistic assessment of the submarine threat to shipping in the various theatres. Indeed, there is little doubt that the intelligence organization at NATO's disposal was of critical importance in enabling it to counter a grave threat to the ability of the Alliance to use the sea.

It may be worthwhile to dwell on this aspect for a moment. The advance of information technology had enabled the Western allies to use computers, micro-electronics and telecommunications to produce, store, obtain and send information in a variety of forms extremely rapidly and – until the enemy began to interfere – reliably. Fortunately Soviet interference was rarely effective. Every scrap of data on every Soviet submarine at sea which came within range of any Allied sensors – sonar in ships or helicopters, sonobuoys from fixed-wing aircraft, acoustic devices on the seabed, or radar contact by snort mast (when the submarine was a diesel-electric one) – could be processed almost instantaneously, analysed and compared. The NATO submarine plot would then be updated and the latest submarine report communicated to all concerned. Furthermore, the knowledge that this was being done had in many circumstances the effect upon the Soviet submariners (NATO's own submariners had a similar respect for the Soviet operational intelligence system) of imposing speed restrictions. The faster a submarine goes the more noise it makes. Even when it is not exactly located every detection of a submarine by the enemy draws the net more tightly round it. SSBN are not embarrassed by such detection possibilities because they do not have to use high speed in order to fulfil their role, and are deployed in remote areas which, at the same time, can be kept clear of 'intruders'.

It must be added, in order to account for Allied failure, where it occurred, to act promptly and with good effect upon intelligence received, that something was seen to happen which many had warned would happen. This was an inability to decentralize sufficiently to subordinate flag, or in some cases commanding, officers which resulted in what has been described as 'apoplexy at the centre and paralysis at the extremities'. In a fast-moving situation it is essential to let the man on the spot have the information he needs, and let him get on with the job as he thinks best. By far the most important function of the flag officer and his staff, especially in a shore headquarters, is to avoid the mutual interference of friendly forces – surface ship, submarine and aircraft.

In reflecting upon the outcome of the fighting at sea, it can be said that the greatest Allied shortcoming was the lack of sufficient anti-missile missiles, as well as counter-measures to the various types of guidance and homing used in the missiles of the enemy. It was quite obvious, as early as the 1950s, that the age of the guided missile in fighting at sea was upon us. This knowledge was not sufficiently exploited. The weak point in any electronic guidance system is that it can be interfered with by electronic means. Any missile with a generally usable homing system can, by definition, be decoyed and made to home on something other than the intended target. Ultimately, of course, hostile ships, submarines and aircraft must be destroyed or neutralized. In the first instance what matters most is to cope with the missiles, wherever they come from.

By the end of the second week of the Third World War, over 90 per cent of Soviet and Warsaw Pact commercial shipping, including the fishing fleets, which had been operating outside the Baltic, the Black Sea, and the Sea of Japan, had been sunk or captured, or had taken refuge in a neutral port. That was the end of Soviet sea power.

Chapter 14

War in the Air

We have already described in detail some of the air battles that raged over the Central Front, for many of these had a crucial effect on what was happening in the land battle. But air power was more important in this war than in any other major conflict; its impact deserves a wider assessment.

Air forces were everywhere involved where fighting took place. Over the oceans and their littoral states the aircraft came mainly from carriers and helicopter ships. The great proportion were mounted from the US Navy's big carriers, but the French *Foch* and *Clemenceau* and the British *Ark Royal* and *Illustrious* were also in the thick of the battles in the Mediterranean and Atlantic. The United States Navy had nearly 1,500 top-class aircraft and in addition to that global force the USAF's Pacific Air Force (PACAF), with its headquarters in Japan and wings based in adjacent friendly countries in South-East Asia, as well as a wing of Strategic Air Command's B-52 heavy bombers on the Pacific island of Guam, all played their part in the peripheral battles.

Over the Atlantic the continuous action of the US Strike Fleet carriers has rightly been well publicized; what is less well known perhaps is that on the submarine front Allied maritime patrol aircraft, operating independently or in conjunction with ships and submarines, took a very heavy toll of Soviet submarines. These aircraft, packed with electronic and sonic detection equipment and ingenious underwater weapons, exceeded even their high peacetime promise. But being large and 'soft' they were vulnerable on the ground, and on the eastern side of the Atlantic several were lost early on in the war to missile attacks on airfields from distant Soviet aircraft and submarines. Thereafter these aircraft were dispersed in ones and twos along the European Atlantic seaboard to fight a rather lonely war. With ample facilities for rest and eating on board, and a disregard for peacetime maintenance requirements, the astonishing fact is that many of these aircraft and crews spent more than three-quarters of the whole war in the air, landing only for fuel and food.

Soviet Naval Air Force action to interrupt the all-important Atlantic air bridge sent a number of large US troop transports plummeting into the sea with air-to-air missiles from modified *Backfires*, *Bears* and *Badgers*. But despite losses and damage the NATO early warning system held up well and USAF F-15 *Eagles* from Iceland and RAF *Tornados* from Scotland were a good match for them. Similarly, when the rather inadequate Soviet *Forger* v/STOL aircraft tried to intervene from their *Kiev*-class carriers, RAF *Tornados* and US carrier-borne interceptors kept them at bay until the offending mother ships were sunk. Radar and infra-red reconnaissance from high-flying aircraft and satellites in space meant that surprise at sea rested principally with aircraft and submarines.

The United Kingdom and France came under Soviet air attack from the first few hours of the war. Initially it was confined to missiles from *Backfire*, *Bear* and *Badger* aircraft directed at port installations, airfields, and radar and communications centres, as well as government and military headquarters. Although in no way decisive, these attacks sometimes hit the soft centres of important targets such as the hotel-like building housing the British air traffic control centre at West Drayton on the outskirts of London.

In the first days of the war the Soviet Naval and Long-Range Air Forces could not exert a decisive weight of attack on French and British targets from their distant bases. Their losses were high as they ventured down the Atlantic and the North Sea to get into range with their stand-off missiles. It was not until 8 August, when the Soviet Air Force (SAF) had occupied airfields in Schleswig-Holstein and were able to turn larger numbers of SU-17 *Fitter* and SU-24 *Fencer* bombers on to French and British targets, that both countries came under really heavy attack. Then US FB-111s, British and German *Tornados*, and French *Jaguars* began pounding the SAF's new-found airfields and their improvised air defences, while Soviet *Fitters* and *Fencers* suffered heavy losses in the target areas, as well as being mauled on the way by Belgian and Dutch F-16 *Fighting Falcons*. The French and British air defence systems were degraded by the gaps torn in the early warning system, the loss of fixed ground radars and airfield damage, but their modern and hardened communications survived well and the airborne early warning (AEW) aircraft proved marvellously adaptable in making good the losses in the ground radar systems. Right up to the end of the war, despite seriously depleted numbers, both French and British air forces were still offering a formidable challenge to SAF aircraft venturing into their air space.

High above the land battle in Germany, the Soviets, with a calculated disregard for losses, swamped the air with their aircraft. The outnumbered, though otherwise generally superior, Allied air forces had to respond with maximum effort. All the pre-war misgivings about what was optimistically called 'airspace management' were more than realized. Radars and communications were jammed and close control of fighters from the ground had to be abandoned. The problems of identifying friend and foe and integrating surface-to-air missiles with manned aircraft in the same airspace were so complex and difficult that they could only be met by the simplest of measures. In the absence of a foolproof weapons-locking IFF (identification friend or foe) system both sides inevitably shot down their own as well as the enemy's aircraft. Broad rules were established within hours by Allied Air Forces Central Europe (AAFCE) giving sanctuary height bands for returning aircraft and ensuring that missile fire from the ground was withheld for a few minutes every hour. Although this sometimes gave SAF aircraft an uncontested run to their targets it was the best that could be done in the intensity of the air battle.

At altitude, the US, Belgian, Dutch and Danish F-16 *Fighting Falcons*, together with the US F-15 *Eagles*, French *Mirages* and British and German *Phantoms*, hacked away at Soviet *Fishbed*, *Flogger* and *Foxbat* fighters in a relentless struggle for control of the air. It was reckoned that Allied air forces exacted a toll of 5 to 2 in their favour. This only just matched the advantage in number of aircraft that the Warsaw Pact had over them. Allied losses soon caused great anxiety to COMAAFCE and his air commanders. To add to their difficulties, fresh airfields and ground facilities had to be set up to the west as forward bases in north Germany were overrun or came under direct ground fire as well as air attack. Although it had never been part of NATO's declared policy to plan for a withdrawal, discreet re-location plans had prudently been made. So when the need arose, NATO air squadrons quickly found themselves operating from unfamiliar airfields in northern France, Belgium and the UK, where there was still some protection from relatively intact air defence systems. USAF and RAF C-130 *Hercules*, and French and German *Transall* heavy air transports, as well as helicopters, did magnificent work moving the airmen and their weapons, technical equipment and specialist vehicles back from exposed airfields. Despite chaos on many of the air bases the Allied air forces somehow kept flying and their challenge to the enemy never slackened.

Pilots and navigators in the fast jets had developed split-second reactions and when battle damage sent their aircraft out of control they fired their ejection seats by reflex. Many were lucky enough to parachute into the arms of friendly Germans who helped them back to Allied territory through gaps in the enemy lines. Some air crew returned on foot as many as four times to claim a cockpit seat and rejoin the battle. This proved a significant factor in offsetting the serious attrition of NATO's air power as each day went by.

Meanwhile, in the important counter-air operations, RAF and GAF *Tornados* and USAF FB-111s were hammering away at Warsaw Pact airfields in East Germany and Czechoslovakia, the *Tornados* flying in the ultra-low mode for which they were designed. These repeated assaults were far from being free of losses, but their specially delivered bombs and mines steadily reduced the enemy's superior numbers and disrupted the operation of his airfields, thereby redressing the balance in the high- and low-level battles over the front line. These NATO wings and squadrons were also engaged in attacking 'choke points' to disrupt and impede Warsaw Pact armoured reinforcements and supplies rolling forward into Western Europe.

After nine days of ferocious air fighting more than half of COMAAFCE's aircraft and rather less of his air crew had been lost. But the Allied air forces regained the initiative when SACEUR made his historic decision on 13 August to release his dual-capable aircraft to the battle with conventional weapons and to make use of the B-52s standing by at Lajes in the Azores. This was reinforced by COMAAFCE's parallel decision to commit his remaining reserves, made up of some Italian Air Force squadrons, disembarked French and US naval air squadrons and French and German *AlphaJet* trainers (which, like the British *Hawk*, had a useful secondary war role). These forces had been harboured safely, but with rising frustration among their crews, in southern France and Germany.

All the factors that contributed to the Western allies holding the air against superior numbers will only be known when a full study and analysis of the war is completed, but many of the reasons are clear even now. The importance attached to quality of men and machines was more than justified in battle, but it must be said that had the war continued much longer the decisive factor would have been numbers alone. The commitment of the French Air Force to the air war from the outset was undoubtedly of major strategic importance. The French Tactical Air Force (No. 1 Commandement Aérienne Tactique) with its headquarters at Metz in eastern France provided a flexible framework for the tasking and co-ordination of Allied aircraft drawn back from Germany on to French airfields. Without that prompt commitment and ready adaptability, together with the uncovenanted involvement of several hundred French Air Force *Mirages* and *Jaguars* and their skilled crews, the margin of success in the air might well have rested with the other side.

Chapter 15

Conflict in Space

❝When active hostilities began on 4 August 1985, the space orbiter *Enterprise* 101, with a four-man crew under Colonel "Slim" Wentworth of the USAF, had already been in orbit on a multiple mission for over forty hours. Photographic and electronic reconnaissance was its initial purpose and, as the orbiter made its regular passes over the Soviet Union ten times a day, an impressive quantity of valuable material had been returned. The spaceship was also, however, furnished with programmes of tapes for broadcasts to the USSR and satellite countries in the event of war, inviting disaffection and revolt. This was perfectly well known, through their own intelligence sources, in the USSR and plans had been made to eliminate *Enterprise* 101 if the current state of alert were to be followed by hostilities.

Early on 4 August a *Soyuz* 49 mission set out to intercept. Its fourth orbit brought it to within 150 metres of Wentworth's craft, just as he had himself gone on visual look-out. A laser beam sweep from the Soviet craft blinded him at once. Further sweeps and attack with minelets did such damage to the craft as to put controlled re-entry into the atmosphere and return to earth out of the question. Only a recovery mission by a space shuttle orbiter could effect the rescue of Colonel Wentworth and his companions, and the damage that had been done to *Enterprise* 101, particularly to its controls and electric power generators, would result in the failure of life support systems before long. This was, therefore, a matter of urgency.

The Colonel's wife Janet, a tall good-looking brunette, was with Nicholas aged ten and Pamela aged six in the light and generous living room of the Wentworth home in Monterey, California, listening to the dramatic news coming from the commentator on breakfast-time TV. The family usually had breakfast in the kitchen but they were in the living room now because the bigger TV screen was there. They had heard that the country was at war now but what was uppermost in the minds of all three was that a beloved husband and an adored father was already out there in space.

"He'll get back all right," said Janet, clearing the breakfast things, "just like the other times."

She spoke with more confidence than she felt.

The telephone rang.

"Slim's in trouble," said a voice that Janet knew well. A close friend of them all was ringing her from Space Control.

"You'll get it on the news any time now but I thought I'd warn you. He's hurt, in the eyes, otherwise he's OK. The ship is in poor shape but we'll get him back."

Almost at once there was some news on the TV screen. Even as Janet put down the phone, the commentator was saying: "One of our spacecraft has been damaged in an attack from a Soviet space interceptor. A rescue mission for its crew is being mounted and should soon be under way."

"Marvellous!" said Janet to the children. "They'll bring him back all right. You'll see!"

There was someone at the door. An officer, who identified himself as coming on orders from Space Control, was with two Air Force men bringing in a TV set of a type Janet had not seen before. It was clearly not a model for domestic use. It looked like service equipment. The officer set it up, plugged in the power and made some adjustments.

"You can talk to Colonel Wentworth now," he said, "when he comes up. He has been told to call you."

What did all this mean? Janet found herself in the grip of a terrible fear.

She walked around the strange TV set, not touching it, and called the family friend in Space Control.

"There's a shuttle going up to bring him out, isn't there?" she asked. "They said there was."

"I hope that's true," was the hesitant reply. "There aren't many shots left right now. Everything depends on how the Joint Chiefs propose to use them."

An hour later he called again. She had not yet been able to bring herself to touch the set.

"Janet, bad news. There's only one rocket left that can get up there before the life support systems run out. The Joint Chiefs have ordered that shot to be used to replace a critical reconnaissance satellite taken out by Soviet interception."

"You mean – they're going to let Slim die, out there, when they could save him?"

"They have only one space shot left," was the reply, "until *Enterprise* 103 can be pushed out again. That will take at least three days. With the damage done in the Soviet attack the systems in Slim's ship won't last that long. The only shot they have ready to go at Vandenberg is already set to take up the reconnaissance satellite they have to have there and I am afraid there is no way of changing that. The TV set they have brought you will bring in Slim. You can see him and talk to him. Turn it on – but you are going to have to be brave."

"But . . . but . . . the newsman said a rescue mission was being urgently prepared and would soon be on its way. He said that."

"I am sorry, Janet, truly sorry. That's only PR to allay public anxiety. You have to be told the truth."

Janet was silent for a moment.

"What about the others in the crew out there?" she almost whispered. "What about them and their families too?"

"That's being taken care of," was the reply. "But time is running on. You can switch on the set now and pick up Slim."

She did so. There on the screen was Slim, her beloved Slim, one of the only three people in her whole world who really mattered. He was in the cabin of the spacecraft surrounded by all the gadgetry but blundering about in his spacesuit even more than usual and uncertain in his movements. His eyes looked strange.

"Slim!" she said.

"Hello, love," he said. "My eyes aren't so good and I can't see you but my God it's good to hear you. How are things?"

"Good," she lied. "Nicholas and Pamela are here. Say hello to daddy, children."

"Hello, daddy," came up in chorus.

"That's great," was the reply.

Janet watched a weightless, sightless spaceman fumbling about in the cabin. The voice was the same. That was Slim's voice.

"Janet," it said, "I love you."

"Oh, Slim . . ."

"It can't last long now, perhaps an hour or so, perhaps only minutes. I love you, Janet, I love you dearly and I am switching off." The image vanished.

Janet, in her much loved and lived in home, sat down upon a sofa, dry-eyed and too stricken even for grief.

Suddenly a wail came from deep within her as from a dying animal.

"I hate you all!" she shouted and then in a flood of tears snatched the children to her and held them close.

When the war ended, a space mission recovered the orbiting bodies of the Captain and crew of *Enterprise* 101 and brought them back to earth for burial with military honours in Arlington National Cemetery. The occasion was made an important one. The President sent an aide. Janet Wentworth stayed away. **9** *

In the three decades before the war, with vast investment and marvellous inventiveness from the superpowers, space technology and its applications raced ahead. Apart from well-publicized programmes for peaceful purposes, there was a strong military thrust behind this effort. All space activity had some military significance but at least 65 per cent of the launches before the war were for military reasons only. By January 1985 the Soviet Union had made 2,119 launches compared with 1,387 by the United States. The latter generally used bigger launching rockets with heavier payloads and their satellites had longer lives and wider capabilities.

Among the military tasks performed by unmanned satellites were reconnaissance, by photographic, electronic, radar and infra-red means; the provision of communications, early-warning, navigational and meteorological stations; and finally there were the interceptor/destroyer (I/D) counter-satellites. Manned vehicles like the orbiter *Enterprise* 101 were reserved for combinations of tasks which

---

* Mary McGihon, *Women in War* (Dutton, New York 1986), p. 348.

were interdependent or where the opportunity might be fleeting or variable. China, France and Britain also had modest space programmes and put up satellites for research and communications. France and China used their own launchers while the British, who were considerable designers and manufacturers of satellites, depended on US launchers, as of course did NATO, which had a three-satellite communications system.

Before the war ordinary people around the world had little idea of what was going on far above them. This was principally because much of it was shrouded in secrecy, but it was also because their attention was only drawn to space sporadically when people were shot up into it and the TV cameras followed their progress. As things turned out, heroic exploits in space did not figure much in the war. Human beings were needed in space for certain tasks and especially so in the early days of the research programme. When it came to military applications they were usually more of an encumbrance than an advantage. There were notable exceptions when multiple tasks needed direct human judgment and control. Colonel Wentworth's tragic flight in *Enterprise* 101 was a dramatic example. But in the main space was best left to the robots.

To appreciate what happened in space during the war a little understanding of the governing science is helpful. Man-made earth satellites have to conform, as do natural planets, to laws discovered in the seventeenth century by the German philosopher/scientist Johann Kepler. What is probably most significant in the context of this book is that the plane of an earth satellite (or planet) will always pass through the centre of the earth. Under the inexorable discipline of this and the other laws, the movement of satellites is inherently stable and predictable. They can only be manoeuvred by the thrust of 'on-board' propulsive forces, usually in the form of liquid or solid fuel rocket motors. These manoeuvring engines and their fuel have of course to be carried up from the earth in competition with all other payloads. As the fuel is quickly exhausted, manoeuvrability is limited. It has in any case to be paid for at the price of other payloads.

The amount of electric power available to activate the satellite's systems is another limiting factor. Solar cells can convert the sun's rays into electricity quite readily but there are early limits to the power that can be generated and stored in this way. That is why satellite radars, which played such an important role in the war, were at some disadvantage. Radar hungers greedily for electric power. It was for this reason that the Soviet Union made use of small nuclear reactors as power generators in its radar reconnaissance satellites. It may be recalled that it was a Soviet satellite, undoubtedly engaged in ocean surveillance, that caused worldwide concern in 1978 when it went wrong and scattered radioactivity over northern Canada as it burnt up on falling back into the atmosphere.

Even without such mishaps a satellite's useful life does not last for ever. It is largely determined by the height of its orbit and the endurance of its power supply. The exhaustion of its power supply sets an obvious limit to its functional life as distinct from the life of the vehicle. The lives of satellites range from days and weeks to (theoretically) thousands of years, depending on their orbits. Generally speaking, the lower the orbit the shorter the life and vice versa. The height of the orbit is determined by the characteristics of the satellite's launch and is set to suit the tasks it has to perform. Photographic satellites are usually the lowest and are set as low as 120 kilometres from the earth. At the other end of the scale, the United States nuclear explosion detection VELA (velocity and angle of attack) satellites were pushed out as far as 110,000 kilometres into space in the war.

Although space enables man-made objects to move at fast speeds over great distances in near perpetual motion, everything that moves in space is a captive of Kepler's laws. Once a satellite is in undisturbed orbit it will turn up precisely on time in its next predicted position above the earth. Manoeuvring can change the height or the plane of the orbit but at the end of the manoeuvre the satellite – unless it is brought back into the atmosphere – settles once again into a predictable orbit. So although the exact purposes of some of the earth satellites were not always known in the years before the war, space was very 'open' and all the satellites, old booster rockets and other debris orbiting the world, were monitored, numbered and registered in computers at scientific agencies like the Royal Aircraft Establishment at Farnborough, England. Indeed, under a widely accepted United Nations convention (with the USSR among its signatories), countries were obliged to notify the launch and leading parameters of every satellite. Within broad limits this was done.

Satellites can be seen by the naked eye at night when they reflect the sun's light, but more scientifically they are tracked by telescopes, radar, and electronic means. Space activity is so open to observation and deduction that the news that Plesetsk, in the north of the USSR, was the Soviet Union's major launch complex first came to the knowledge of the world from Kettering Boys' School in England. A group at the school under the leadership of an enthusiastic science master kept a continuous watch on space and periodically released details of earth satellites that had newly arrived in orbit.

Among many advantages that flowed from pre-war space programmes was the acceptance by the superpowers (because of its scientific inevitability) of the concept of 'open space'. This removed one of the difficulties in the strategic arms limitation and reduction negotiations (SALT and START), in that numbers of launchers and missile sites could be so easily verified from space reconnaissance. Verification by 'national technical means' was the euphemism adopted in protracted negotiations over satellite surveillance. Both sides knew exactly what it meant. Such reconnaissance had its limits: it could not count reserve missiles kept concealed, nor could it penetrate the secrets of the multiple re-entry vehicles within the nosecones of the missiles themselves.

Man's activities in space in peacetime, therefore, tended to be stable, both scientifically and politically. Indeed there was considerable co-operation. Sometimes this was even political, as when the USSR advised the United States that South Africa looked to be preparing for a nuclear test in the Kalahari Desert. This intelligence was extracted from Soviet *Cosmos* satellites manoeuvred over the Kalahari in July and August 1977.

Although the methods chosen by the USA and USSR to get into space differed widely in technical ways, the comfortable feeling generally enjoyed by the uninitiated in the West was that the USA must surely be in the lead. This was not obviously so, and in different respects each was ahead of the other. The US put an enormous effort into the *Apollo* 'man on the moon' programme. The USSR, with less fuss, put their *Salyut* space station into orbit, and by changing crews rotated some forty astronauts through it on different research tasks. Both those 'men in space' programmes were very remarkable but they were very different achievements.

Telemetry enables information gained by optical and electronic sensors in space to be transmitted instantly to earth. In the war these systems were jammed, partially or completely, by both sides, using earth and space jamming stations. Space photography, which involved complicated systems of ejecting the film and sending it back to earth for processing and interpretation, was fine in peacetime but took too long in war. On the other hand, the transmission earthwards of its product in this way could not be jammed. The satellite communications system, which had been well established before the war, was invaluable in keeping political and military centres in touch and in the control of a war moving at an unprecedented pace. But here too the effectiveness of the system was degraded by jamming and other interference.

Satellites were destroyed or damaged by limited rather than widespread counter-satellite action; the numbers of I/D satellites was limited on both sides and they were reserved for high-value targets. In the main, these were the electronic intelligence (ELINT) satellites which gained key information about the enemy's electronic systems and above all his operating frequencies. Some of the satellites knocked out were replaced by new ground launches, but when this was done great care was needed to ensure that the direction of launch, and the location of the site, involved no risk that the launch of the rocket would be confused with an inter-continental ballistic missile (ICBM) attack. This very sensitive and vital discrimination was well within the state of the art and the facilities available for rapid computer analysis; it was also part of the tacit understanding between the superpowers that such a process of replacement would need to go on in war. As space was well stocked with satellites of all types in the months before the war, replacement launchings were not numerous. In consequence, the much slower launching rate of the US system, with its big satellites and big rockets, did not turn out to have the great disadvantage that some of its pre-war critics had forecast.

Destruction or jamming of the ELINT satellites hurt the West much more than it did the USSR. This was because NATO placed such great reliance on electronic counter-measures (ECM) and ECCM (in which they proved to have a substantial but not overwhelming lead) to offset the numerical inferiorities and unfavourable starting deployments they would have at the beginning of a war. Because of this, the ELINT effort in space, the heavy initial Allied air losses, the congestion in the intelligence system, and what we have recounted in chapter 6 as the story of the Gdansk incident were all tied together. It is also why the events in that particular tale, with its interesting human overtones, were so important at the beginning of the war.

With the strategic and military opportunities that spaceflight offered, it was inevitable that the superpowers would turn their attention to counter-satellite systems. They did so as early as the mid-1960s. The Soviet Union demonstrated its ability to make a rendezvous between satellites during their *Soyuz/Cosmos* programme in 1967 and the US did the same somewhat earlier in the *Gemini* series. By the second half of the 1970s it looked as if the USSR was firmly committed to a system whereby the interceptor would approach its target in a similar orbit from below to launch minelets at it or to close with the target and then blow itself up. The war showed those deductions to be correct and both methods were used effectively. Satellites are in essence 'soft' targets and very little in the way of impact or explosion is needed to put them out of commission. The principal US system depended on a quite low relative speed collision between the interceptor and the target. These interceptors were launched into space from beneath the wings of F-15 *Eagle* fighters flying at very high altitude in the atmosphere. Both sides used infra-red homing for the terminal stages of the interception.

Direct ground-launched anti-satellite missiles were also considered but discarded, even though the United States did have some initial success in early trials in the Pacific. As with the anti-ballistic missile (ABM) system permitted under the SALT I Treaty, the problems of target tracking and split-second missile-aiming from the ground proved too complex and costly as a practical proposition. Another possibility was to offset inaccuracy by the use of nuclear warheads in space but this risked some very unattractive consequences in escalatory effects. Anyway, the 1967 Outer Space Treaty banned nuclear weapons from being orbited in space and, although the treaty might not have held in war, it put an effective brake on trials and development in peacetime.

Much science fiction has proved strikingly prophetic, but space-age tales in the pre-war years in which men promenaded weightlessly in space with death-ray guns found no echoes in the real space war. Colonel Wentworth and his crew in *Enterprise* 101 were put out of action by a Soviet I/D and he was blinded by a laser beam. But it is now known that this was an experimental chemical laser system of limited range and application. The damage done to *Enterprise* 101's engine nozzles, power supplies and flight controls was almost certainly caused by small minelets exploded near the orbiter by the Soviet interceptor.

Fiction and fantasy are one thing and scientific intelligence is another and their relationship is a curiously close one. There was another matter brought to public notice from time to time that caused understandable anxiety and doubt. This was, quite simply, the 'charged-particle beam'. The theory of charging, or 'exciting' atomic particles to concentrate great energy in a narrow beam had been well understood by physicists for a number of years. A charged-particle beam would make short work of any earth satellite – but what was more important, it could almost certainly detonate and destroy incoming ballistic missiles if the tracking and aiming problems could be solved. But like fusion energy – so long heralded as our liberator from the bondage of fossil fuels – while the equations were understood the engineering was not.

It was a Soviet scientist – Gersh Budker – who set the ball rolling in 1956 by demonstrating that once the gases in a magnetic field had attained a certain velocity they could become self-accelerating. With broad parity in strategic and space systems between the superpowers in the 1980s there was much to be said for sitting firmly on the lid of this Pandora's box. It was thought none the less that the USSR was perversely assigning large scientific resources to trying to prise it open, though there was some dispute within the US intelligence community over the extent of the Soviet programme, the timescale within which an operational system could be expected to appear, and what the United States should be doing to develop such a system.

We now know that charged-particle beams were not employed in the war, but international scientists have recently inspected the great Soviet research complex near the Sino-Soviet border that was dedicated solely to this area of physics. We do not know their full findings but it is clear that Soviet scientists were still some way from being able to reduce the cyclotrons used in this research to a size where they could be used in a ground-based system, let alone one in space.

A less well advertised skeleton in the space cupboard was what the scientists called 'electro-magnetic pulse' (EMP). In its simplest terms this was the effect caused by gamma rays hitting the atmosphere suddenly after a nuclear explosion in space. The scientists calculated that the associated electro-magnetic surge would destroy or disable electrical and electronic systems across a wide area of the earth's surface. Furthermore the 'footprint' could be controlled and directed to contain the area of impact. All of this could happen without any of the normal blast and radiation effects on earth of a nuclear explosion in the atmosphere. If this was true (and some unexpected side effects in Hawaii after an American nuclear test in the Pacific in 1962 suggested that it might be) the whole system of command and control of a modern war machine could be paralysed.

Because of the 1963 Partial Test Ban Treaty, the observance of which was well monitored from ultra-high satellites, the EMP theory could not be tested even on the smallest scale. That and other restraints, such as the risk of confusion with nuclear strike, kept this genie firmly in its bottle. All that could be said to the claim of a science correspondent in the London *Times* on 4 December 1981 that two nuclear explosions in space would immobilize NATO was that if the theory was correct then another two could immobilize the Warsaw Pact as well. There was certainly no general defence against this possible danger when the war started in 1985; but at least some protective measures had been adopted by the industrialized countries in the widespread modernization of their communications in the early 1980s. In broad terms this amounted to the hardening of input circuits in key electronic equipment and the increasing use of fibre optics in the main systems for the distribution of power and information. It is quite possible that the communications for waging war could have been seriously damaged by EMP; but it would not have stopped the war and for reasons of calculated strategic advantage neither side was moved to put the theoretical opportunities of EMP to the practical test.

VITAL PERIPHERIES

Chapter 16

The Elephant Trap: Central America

In the last three years before the world war, Central America was an elephant trap and a ticking time bomb. The United States very nearly fell into the one and detonated the other.

At the lowest stage of America's fortunes in early 1984 a Vietnam-style war seemed in process of exploding right across the threshold of America's southern backdoor. It looked like being a war that the United States would lose and that communist Cuba and Sandinista Nicaragua would win, although Cuba's and Nicaragua's own economic experiments were proving an unmitigated disaster for all their peoples. It was a war that started in El Salvador, but then spread also to the four other non-communist countries of Central America – militarist Guatemala and Honduras, troubled Panama, even democratic Costa Rica.

The crisis was made suddenly worse because it seemed that America's ally, Christian Democrat Venezuela, was going to become embroiled in war with Cuba-leaning Guyana; and there were absurd dangers that all of the important countries of the Caribbean (Trinidad-Tobago, anti-colonialist Grenada, Jamaica) might find themselves to some degree on Guyana's side.

The crisis was averted in the most unexpected manner; partly because the United States engaged in eyeball-to-eyeball confrontation with Cuba, but also because Venezuela (at first to America's horror) went Social-Democratic in December of 1983. Thereafter a Venezuelan-Mexican alliance became an important stabilizing force in the region, and in the nick of time brought peace and compromise to it. If it had not, if at this juncture the Caribbean had become a Soviet lake and Central America a Soviet base area, the Western Alliance would almost certainly have gone down in the Third World War.

For all elephants that need to tread delicately in this post-war world, possibly as dangerous and unstable now in 1987 as at any

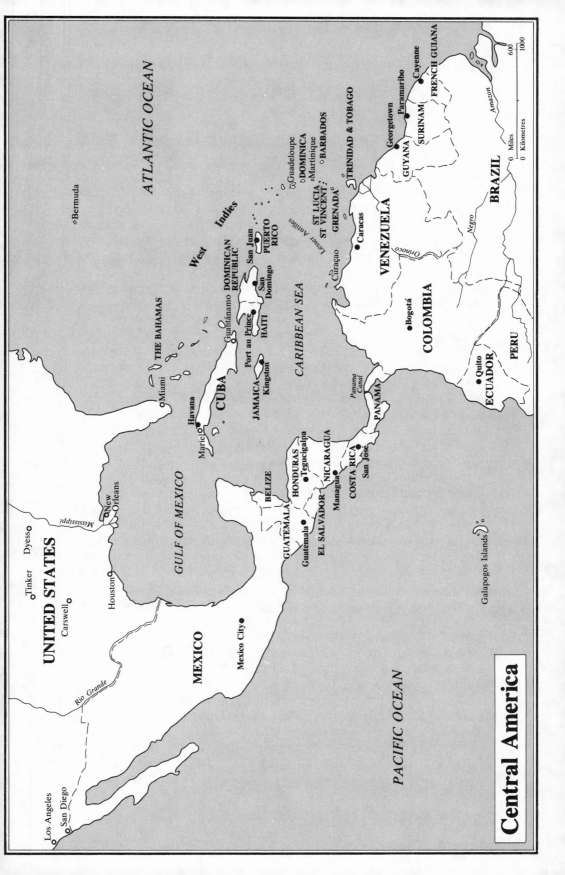

Central America

time in living memory, the story carries disturbing lessons. It also
carries a message of hope.

———

As the decade of the 1980s opened, the forces of change in Central
America were not all revolutionary or Cuban-supported. There were
also moderates and reformists trying both to stop the revolutionary
tide and to implement reform in countries that had for generations
been oppressed by too few rich families and too many soldiers, and
where there were some of the lowest per capita incomes in the world.

To the left of centre among these moderate reformists was the
Socialist International, closely related to the social democratic parties
in Venezuela, Costa Rica and Mexico, and influential with groups in
El Salvador. It had at one time also been influential with the rulers of
Nicaragua, but Sandinista Nicaragua was slipping under communist
control. To the right of centre was the Organizacion Democrata
Cristiana de America (ODCA), presided over by a Venezuelan
(Aristides Calvani) and influential with President Duarte of El Sal-
vador and with several political parties in the Caribbean.

The Cubans and Soviets decided to try to cause trouble for ODCA
(ie, El Salvador and Venezuela) first.

Already in 1980 Cuba's leaders had held a secret meeting with
Central American Marxist leaders up country in Nicaragua, to discuss
their intended polarization of the region. They could by then cele-
brate a considerable triumph.

This triumph had been the military victory of the Sandinista
movement in Nicaragua, and the overthrow of the Somoza dynasty.

The United States was completely isolated in its last lukewarm
attempt to preserve 'Somocism without Somoza'. The importance of
this event was threefold and to the United States Administration
deeply unsettling. It showed that a guerrilla movement in Central
America could fight successfully against a US trained, politically
demoralized army like Somoza's National Guard. It brought to
power a mainland government in a Central American country that
had a strong pro-Cuban faction in its midst. The Sandinistas in
Nicaragua, until they turned almost entirely communist, clearly
enjoyed wide popular support.

At the 1980 meeting in Nicaragua of rising Marxists the voice was
that of Fidel Castro, but the hand belonged to the Soviet Union's
President Brezhnev, who was already propping up Cuba's ineffective
economy to the tune of forty million dollars a week. The Soviets had
become attracted during 1980 by the possibility of drawing the
United States into a deep trap just outside its southern backdoor,

where it could flounder ineffectually while critical events beyond its control unrolled elsewhere.

Soviet strategists believed that both Central America and the Caribbean were now ripe for revolution. They saw that Cuba could be used as the springboard of a powerful politico-strategic movement of support for subversive forces throughout the area. This diversion would tie down US forces and compromise American prestige, allowing the Soviet Union to strike more decisive blows and develop its own initiatives in other areas of the world. It would be difficult for the US to cast the issue of Central American conflict in purely East-West terms and so involve its allies. The Soviets were confident that American public opinion would hysterically oppose a major commitment of troops for a counter-insurgency war in an area to which American TV commentators could commute almost daily. The outlook as seen from the Kremlin was good.

Despite the appalling mess into which his economy had sunk, Fidel Castro started the 1980s in buoyant mood. The emigration of more than 125,000 Cubans out of his island, after the port of Mariel was opened in the spring of 1980 to all who wanted to leave, had strangely given him a political respite. It had enabled him to get rid of some thousands of hard-core criminals and a good many mental patients. Almost all of the Marielitos had settled in Florida, bumping up the murder rate in Miami and the trade in drugs through the state to become the worst in America. Politically, by exporting at the same time the best of his opposition, Castro was again able to unite around him the different factions of the Cuban political elite: the military, the radical-revolutionaries and the remaining and wetter of the moderates, the latter led by the Minister of Economics Carlos Rafael Rodriguez.

Castro now saw an opportunity to stage a comeback to the Latin American mainland, break away from the regional isolation in which Cuba had found itself for many years, and open an outlet for the energies of the powerful Cuban armed forces after their African adventures. He told his fellow Marxists in Nicaragua that in the United States he would now be mobilizing his racial assets. There were going to be black and Hispanic riots if the new conservative Administration in Washington cut its welfare spending, as it almost certainly would. In Central America the main target was civil war in El Salvador, at least in part as a reaction against the return to power of the Christian Democrats in Venezuela.

Until December of 1979 Venezuela was ruled by the Social Democrats, who were careful to avoid confrontation with Cuba. After the election in that month it was ruled by the Christian Democrats who had campaigned for a policy of open confrontation against Cuba and for closer ties with the US. It appears from information available in Havana, where leaks were as common as in Washington at about the same time, that in 1981 Castro sent a memorandum to Brezhnev in Moscow, of which the gist is as follows: 'The Government in Venezuela is the key US ally in this region. Without Venezuela the US could be isolated in Central America and we could probably bring forward revolutions in El Salvador, Guatemala, Honduras – while the radicalization of the Sandinista Government would go much faster. The Venezuelan Government has adopted a very anti-Cuban line. It recognizes the spread of communist influence in Central America and the Caribbean as a serious security risk. It is capable of mobilizing the help of other Latin American countries, notably Brazil, in order to face that threat. Luckily we have two advantages. First, there is strong domestic opposition in Venezuela to this Government's policies. Secondly, this Government has made a fool of itself by being the decisive influence in bringing a Christian Democrat stooge to the presidency of El Salvador. The Americans think that this man will (a) be an adequate figure in holding his military junta in check (actually he is too weak); (b) look like a charismatic moderate, although in fact he is unconvincing on American television, especially when he tries to speak English; (c) be accepted by Mexico (which he won't). It is against El Salvador that the revolutionary forces of communism now need to strike.'

This assessment was not entirely different from that being made on the other side of the hill. A document laid before the new President of the US at this time (and finding its way, as was not unusual then, almost at once into the hands of newsmen) ran as follows: 'Faced with a dilemma between revolution and repression in Central America, the United States must try to find a middle course. While helping the military governments in El Salvador, Guatemala and Honduras the US must also: (a) pressure those governments into implementing reforms aimed at undermining support for the revolutionaries; (b) urge them to reduce the levels of 'official terrorism'; (c) protect the present El Salvador Government from an extreme right-wing coup; (d) oppose resolutely, and if necessary by military means, the direct despatch of Cuban troops to the guerrilla movement in El Salvador; (e) try to wean the area's Social Democrats away from supporting the communists. The first approach must be to Social Democratic Mexico.'

The approach to Mexico did not work. A special US adviser in Mexico City has since made public that he filed back the following report: 'We are caught on the horns of a dreadful dilemma. The Mexican analysis of the Central American and Caribbean situation differs fundamentally from that of the US. The Mexicans think subversion in this region is the result of socio-economic backwardness and political oppression. They believe that the military governments of El Salvador, Guatemala and Honduras cannot survive much longer. They say that stability in the area will be best served if these dictatorial regimes are quickly replaced with centre-left popular governments, willing to implement agrarian reform, to institute democratic freedoms, and to dismantle secret armies under right-wing control.

'The Mexicans do not differ from us about what the ideal solution to the crisis would be, but they disagree on the methods to accomplish it. Mexico will not support the Government in El Salvador. The Mexican ruling party has close connections with the Socialist International. It believes that social change is inevitable and that opposition to the military regimes offers the best hope for long-term stability.'

It is possible that the US Ambassador exaggerated Mexico's real beliefs. When talking to a distinguished but unofficial American, the Mexican President asked, 'Why on earth did the US allow those communist Sandinistas to take over Nicaragua?'

'But,' said the surprised professor, 'Your Excellency made speeches in favour of the Sandinistas.'

'Oh,' said the President, 'those were politics.'

All this helped set the springs of the elephant trap.

The first stage of the crisis was the intensification of the revolutionary war in El Salvador. What had begun as a series of skirmishes by a small, badly-trained and poorly-equipped army against a few guerrilla bands developed into a serious war, covering large sections of the countryside. The Salvadoran Army received help from the US, the guerrillas from Cuba.

The President of El Salvador was a good man as troubled men go, and as troubled men go he went. In the elections in early 1982 only those bitterly opposed to the guerrillas dared to stand or vote, and they voted by a small majority for a coalition government to the right of the Christian Democrats. If there had been an election among Protestants in Northern Ireland at that time, a majority would also have voted that anything attempting to be centrist was 'too soft'. Some moderates tried to join and restrain the new coalition for a while, but – under attack from their own colleagues as too gentle, and from American newspapermen as 'accessories of the fascist murder gangs' – they later withdrew. The resigning centre-right politicians bitterly blamed the 'so-called moderate opposition' for the failure of the 'democratic experiment', and accused them and leftist American newspapermen of wickedly contributing to the continuance of civil war.

For a number of right-wing officers, the moderates' departure was welcome news. Hard-line soldiers and demagogues took over power and vowed to prosecute the war against communist subversion until the guerrillas were completely exterminated. There were brutal murders of people even vaguely attracted to the opposition movement. Many moderate-minded people then foolishly joined the communists, and the civil war gained in intensity and destructiveness.

That had desperate consequences for the peasant masses of this tiny but heavily populated country. Unfortunately for the US, there could be no pretence now that democracy was being defended in El Salvador. An outright and firm decision in favour of or against the all-military government was necessary.

The US Administration chose to favour it. With the help of American advisers and the provision of significant quantities of weapons and equipment it started a major counter-insurgency effort of the sort that could not work. El Salvador's military, reinforced in their 'win or die' stand by this show of support, raised the level of violence in a war that by now had become something very like a popular insurgency. From both the Government and the guerrillas ever more widespread brutality was used against the civilian populace.

In America, the liberal opposition exploded. The Cubans had laid their plans in 1981 for Hispanic and black demonstrations against the welfare cuts they correctly expected from the US Administration, but they had shown their usual inefficiency in not getting the demonstrations (which had already been paid for) mounted on the target date. This inefficiency now proved for the Cubans a great advantage. Just as had happened in 1968, subsidized demonstrations spread with increasing violence across America. Decent young people and others looking for political mileage also, quite understandably, joined in protests against the 'new Vietnam'.

By late 1983 El Salvador's war was spreading across Central America. It looked at one stage likely to involve all of Central America's five other republics.

Even before the right-wing coup in El Salvador the Sandinista Government in Nicaragua was going further down the sad Cuban road. Under pressure from a deteriorating economic situation, Nicaragua started putting local and even multi-national businessmen in prison, because they were 'slandering' instead of aiding the national economy. The US responded by cutting off economic aid, and Venezuela followed suit. This led the pro-Cubans in the Sandinista leadership to ask for Cuban and Soviet economic and other assistance. Cuba loudly and angrily denounced the 'US-inspired interventionist measures against Nicaragua', and claimed that a 'mercenary army' paid for with US and Venezuelan money was being trained in Costa Rica 'to make war on the Nicaraguan revolution'.

More Cuban military advisers and weapons were rushed into Nicaragua. Mexico was not helpful at this moment. It said that America's action in cutting off economic aid was pushing Nicaragua into the hands of the Soviet Union.

Some rather more sinister folk began to fear (or hope) the same thing. In Guatemala, a well-organized and equipped guerrilla army made the military apprehensive that a full-scale revolutionary war might develop very soon. The trouble spread to Costa Rica, a country possessing no armed forces but only police, long admired for its domestic tranquillity and its pacifist international stand. Reductions in the standards of living in Costa Rica's hitherto well-off and civilized society, and the fall in the prices of coffee and other exports, set the stage for the appearance of something unheard of in that country – tiny, but highly efficient, terrorist groups. The same happened in Panama, where the death in 1981 of the spectacular General Torrijos had left a power vacuum that contributed to the resurgence of left-wing revolutionary activities. Rioting near the Panama Canal caused grave disquiet among senior officers of the US Navy.

Foolishly, Guatemala now intervened in El Salvador, and Honduras in Nicaragua. In the late summer of 1983 the Guatemalan military government, faced with a major guerrilla insurgency of its own, sent forces through the frontier to help Salvadoran Army units engaged in fierce battles with the guerrillas in the northern part of the country.

Honduras allowed attacks to be launched on Nicaraguan border areas by former Somocista National Guardsmen. Consequent clashes between border guards developed into sharp, bloody encounters throughout the months of September and October 1983. No war was declared. Hondurans accused the Sandinistas of promoting revolution in their country. The Nicaraguan Government denounced a Honduran 'invasion' and mobilized popular militias 'for the defence of the fatherland'. The Organization of American States (OAS) called a meeting in October which passed a weak resolution 'condemning all aggressions'. The war in Central America was suddenly looking like a trans-national one of left against right. National boundaries might be about to lose their significance.

At this moment it began to look as if there would be a Venezuela-Guyana war as well.

The Venezuelan general elections were due at the beginning of December 1983. During the Christian Democrat period in El Salvador, Venezuela had acted as a hard-line ally of the US. Its own people did not like this. Public opinion polls even at this stage showed that only 10 per cent of Venezuelans thought that their country should get involved in El Salvador and help the junta. Nearly 60 per cent thought that Venezuela should continue to give aid for the reconstruction of Nicaragua.

The struggle which began with Cuba-leaning Guyana at this time was welcomed by some extreme right-wing nationalist groups in Venezuela, plus some of the Venezuelan military, but it was really initiated by Cuba-leaning politicians in Guyana itself. A quarrel between these countries is always easy to ignite, because Venezuelans think that two-thirds of the land area of Guyana should actually belong to Venezuela. Some Guyanan politicians wanted to integrate their country more closely with Cuba because this would advance their own careers. They could feel fairly certain that the movement of armed bands across the disputed areas, spilling occasionally over the frontier, would trigger a reaction from Venezuelan generals. The trigger was pulled, and the reaction came. The spectre had now been raised of a war on the South American mainland.

Guyana asked for Cuban military help, and new teams of Cuban 'advisers' quickly turned up. All the other Caribbean countries tried to persuade Venezuela and Guyana to come to terms peacefully, and their general mood was against Venezuela. A left-wing inspired campaign against 'Venezuelan imperialism' spread throughout Trinidad, Tobago, Curaçao, anti-colonialist Grenada, Dominica and even Jamaica. It was embarrassing to the US that its key ally in containing subversion in Central America and the Caribbean should start to lose sympathy in both regions as a result of a ninety-year-old territorial dispute with a black-dominated, English-speaking Caribbean country. Cuba did not miss the opportunity to show its anti-colonialism. It prepared to station military units on the mainland 'at the request of a friendly government, threatened by foreign aggression'.

In November of 1983 America's fortunes in Central America therefore seemed at their lowest ebb. The US Administration, committed to a policy of containment of subversion, but not opposed in principle to moderate change, had almost given up hopes that any middle-of-the-road alternative was feasible in countries torn apart by extremists from left and right. Mexico persisted in its anti-US stand, willing to take risks with the centre-left and more extreme left-wing movements. The Venezuelan Government had lost most of its capacity for action as the election approached, and it was unpopular internationally because of its border disputes with Colombia as well as Guyana. The Soviet Union was delighted to see the United States caught in the elephant trap and wallowing ineffectively, while the Soviet Union's Cuban ally was recovering political prestige and gaining opportunities to intervene militarily at the request of 'friendly governments', as it had done in Africa.

As only one example, Cuban technicians now accelerated work on the new airport in Grenada, begun in 1980, which was clearly going to be able to service sophisticated combat aircraft. The United States had to decide whether it was going to take military action to stop 'new Cubas' from arising right across Central America and the Caribbean.

The US Administration adopted, as the only possible way out of the trap, Teddy Roosevelt's old policy in the area: 'speak softly, but carry a big stick'. The big stick hit the headlines. The United States gave warning to Cuba that the despatch of any more Cuban troops to countries outside its borders would be regarded as a *casus belli*. Units of the United States' Atlantic Fleet took up stations around the island. If any attacks were launched on these ships, Washington announced, selected targets in Cuba would be attacked from the air in return. The soft speaking at this time was the US President's statement that in view of the 'crisis towards which the Soviet Union is now clearly moving, there can be no sense in any Caribbean or Central American country so far from its borders remaining under its vassalage. We will hold out a genuine hand of friendship, and aid, to governments which wish to break away from that vassalage. We hold no animosity against leaders now in power.'

The policy worked. The ships were not attacked, and no more Cuban troops were despatched to the mainland or through the Caribbean. The CIA triumphantly attributed this to the big stick. As was reported in the *New York Times*, the CIA view was that 'The moderates within the Cuban elite are worried at the appalling economic conditions in Cuba and at the mess developing in the Soviet Union. They might have moved to oust the Cuban leadership if it had sent missiles against the American ships.' Cuba's excuse for running away looked more subtle. 'We can afford to be patient,' a communiqué from its premier said. 'The revolutions against the repressive regimes of Central America are already irreversible. If America tries to prop them up, it will fail. If America were to move to encourage less fascist regimes in the junta-run countries, then it might be worthwhile exploring new relationships with it. But let us stir no more pots until the Christian Democrats have lost the Venezuelan elections in early December.'

They duly did so. The Social Democrats (Accion Democratica) won the Venezuelan election with a substantial majority. The US Administration, horrified at first, later found good reason to be pleased.

The new Venezuelan President-elect, who was to assume office next April according to Venezuelan constitutional procedures, held several early meetings with US and Mexican leaders. He made it clear

that Venezuela would no longer follow the US line of interpreting
conflicts in Central America in purely East-West terms. He wanted to
try to bring moderate elements into the governments of El Salvador
and Guatemala. Venezuela, explained the President-elect to US
representatives, accepted the US policy of a 'big stick and soft words'
towards Cuba. As regards the stick Venezuela would never condone
military intervention from foreign powers in Central America or the
Caribbean. As regards the soft words, Venezuela like Mexico
regarded Cuba as a Latin American country which, it was thought,
could be gradually weaned away from the Soviet embrace by a policy
of cautious rapprochement. This had been Mexico's policy for twenty
years; it was Venezuela's policy from 1973 until 1978, and now from
1984 onwards it would again be the official attitude of the Venezuelan Government.

The new alliance between Venezuela and Mexico proved patient,
systematic and rather efficient. The isolation of the military regimes
in El Salvador and Guatemala, supported now only by a tiny minority, made it surprisingly easy for Venezuela and Mexico to create a
democratic alliance against them.

Mexico and Venezuela persuaded leading Salvadoran Social
Democrats to separate themselves from the most radical elements in
the Marxist revolutionary 'Farabundo Marti National Liberation
Front' and to accept a 'common front' for a provisional government
with other democratic organizations such as El Salvador's Christian
Democrats. The US was asked to propose the establishment of an
international conference with the participation of all democratic
Salvadoran political organizations, supervised by Mexico and Venezuela. The main role of the US would be to persuade the extreme
right-wing members in El Salvador's military government to accept a
transition towards democracy. To these Salvadoran members of the
junta, the only offers would be that there would be no prosecution for
'crimes of war' and that there would be an honourable end to their
careers, still as quite rich men.

The initial response to these proposals by the right-wing military
and the Marxist guerrillas in El Salvador was the same: total rejection. The Marxists condemned 'those who are trying to steal the
triumph of the Salvadoran people'.

This inclined the US Administration to accept the Mexican-
Venezuelan plan. Washington made three conditions: (a) no Cuban
participation at any stage of the proceedings; (b) the exclusion of
Marxists and pro-Cubans from key positions in the new Salvadoran
Government; (c) general elections to be held six months after the
installation of the Provisional Government.

In the US there were some who regarded the change of policy as a sell-out of loyal allies, as with Thieu in Vietnam. For others, it was a wise decision, leading to an enlightened solution such as that in Rhodesia-Zimbabwe. Optimism spread because the Nicaraguan Government, under the pressure of a great economic crisis and disheartened by the lack of new Cuban support, was swinging back to the centre. The new Venezuelan President made an early state visit to Nicaragua in the month of May, only three weeks after his inauguration. He was welcomed by an enthusiastic populace, who had not forgotten the Venezuelan contribution to the overthrow of Somoza in 1979 and the hopes then surging for a better and more democratic future. The message was not lost on the left-wing Sandinista leaders who had been losing support among the masses. They wanted to avoid regional isolation.

Cuba's premier made a last-ditch effort to avert the tide of Mexican-Venezuelan-sponsored political reforms. He travelled to Nicaragua at the same time as delegates started gathering in Mexico City to draw up a plan for democracy in El Salvador. But his effort to create a 'rejection front' proved unsuccessful, even in Nicaragua. The US discreetly let it be known to the more moderate of the Sandinistas that it would consider re-establishing diplomatic relations and the flow of aid if the Sandinistas freed political prisoners, sanctioned civil liberties and let opposition newspapers be printed again.

By the beginning of 1985, therefore, Cuba had to reconsider its position, and started to do so fairly fast.

———

When the Third World War started in the summer of 1985, El Salvador had just become insecurely democratic. Guatemala and Honduras were still (but now less securely) military dictatorships. The President of Mexico had, sadly, been assassinated in January but everybody assumed that Mexico and Venezuela would soon arrange a 'political solution' in these two countries too. In Nicaragua the moderates now had a more powerful voice in the civilian leadership (which was drawing aid from the US and Venezuela, and had also applied to the International Monetary Fund), but the military and security forces in Nicaragua were still very left wing, because they had been systematically penetrated by Cuba. The IMF's investigators considered Nicaragua still too much run by soldiers who thought they were socialists, which in their view was economically not a good combination.

Cuba was rethinking its posture rather desperately when the Soviet tanks rolled into Western Europe. The orders from Moscow were explicit: 'Proceed against the United States into full-scale war.' The

Cubans sensibly half-ratted, and the Americans foolishly over-
reacted to what little the Cubans did.

After a desperate high-level meeting in Havana through most of 4
August 1985, the Cubans sent a long coded telex back to Moscow.
The first thirty pages consisted of obsequious expressions of support
for the fundamental revolutionary justice of the Soviet cause. The
decoder in Moscow working on the complicated Atropos decoding
system could not conceal his impatience. Eventually he got to the
sentences the Kremlin was waiting for, and they did not say what the
Kremlin wanted. The vital parts of the Cuban message to Moscow on
5 August ran: 'The risks before socialist Cuba are enormous, considering the possibility of US nuclear retaliation. Our options are in fact
very few. Cuba does not have the military capacity to mount an
invasion of a major Latin American country. To attack the US by air
is too risky. Sea actions are out of the question; the Cuban navy has a
capacity only for a limited degree of coastal vigilance and self-
defence. American naval predominance in this region is total.
Attacks against specific objectives in the Caribbean (for instance,
Puerto Rico) have been most seriously considered. It is the unanimous view here that they would be ineffective, indeed actually harm-
ful for the Soviet cause at this stage of the conflict.

'We have nevertheless determined on the most courageous action
in support of our socialist cause. This action will take three forms.
First, we will accelerate our aircraft lifts of ammunition, supplies and
some soldiers to selected spots on the mainland of Central America
already under socialist or guerrilla control. Secondly, we will alert air
squadrons and missiles on our airfields, and be ready to attack
American shipping and US convoys bound for Europe. We are sure
that you recognize, however, that this assault must be launched at the
appropriate moment, when we can strike most violently and effectively. If we strike prematurely, before the really vital targets are at
sea, we may be destroyed by American nuclear missiles; and our
great usefulness to the common cause – as the independent socialist
country nearest to the heartland of capitalism – could be wiped out in
five minutes. Thirdly, as our most immediate contribution, all Cuba
has been mobilized for war. Our armed forces are concentrating
against the Americans' Guantánamo naval base. An assault will be
launched upon this at the moment when our attack on American
shipping begins.'

This Atropos coded message was read, after decoding, by two very
different generals, one in Moscow and one in Miami.

Army General I. P. Seriy of the Second Main Directorate (military
intelligence) of the Army General Staff (the GRU) accurately
minuted for the Soviet High Command: 'Cuba is clearly deserting us

as disgracefully as Mussolini deserted Hitler in 1939. The Cubans will join the war only when they think we have won it. After Soviet victory we should treat their renegade leader far less kindly than the sentimental Hitler would have treated Mussolini if he had won in 1945.'

The United States had broken the Atropos code even before Japan's all-conquering Fujitsu computer company signed a joint-venture agreement with America's biggest computer company in 1984. Before General Seriy had received his decoded message, Lieutenant General Henry J. Irving, Chief of Staff of the Rapid Deployment Force (known to his friends as 'Humdinger Hank'), had got his. Minuted General Irving: 'It is clear from decoded messages that Cuban communist forces, while pretending to lie low, will attack US convoys with missiles and aircraft as soon as they put to sea, and that attacks (possibly with biological weapons, probably with nuclear and chemical) will start against Guantánamo at that delayed moment. It is essential that America's non-nuclear war plan be launched against Cuba from this moment, well before the Cubans strike.'

The US plan was activated. From military airports in Florida, and from the decks of Atlantic Fleet carriers, attacks were made against military and industrial targets in Cuba, with devastating effect. The weight of the attack wholly overwhelmed the Cuban air defences and caused very many casualties. A total naval blockade was imposed, cutting Cuba off from the rest of the world. US forces (particularly Cuban émigrés and Filipino mercenaries) massed to invade the island.

The United States had not anticipated the reaction of the rest of Latin America. The Secretary-General of the OAS sent an urgent message to the US President on 10 August: 'Although all my members are in principle on America's side in its global confrontation with the Soviet Union, I must tell you that there is general opposition and revulsion among them against the possibility of the US killing more civilians in Cuba. The Cubans have not yet launched any warlike actions against you, but you are bombing them. I beseech you to send me an instant assurance that in no circumstances will American nuclear weapons be used against Cuba, and that civilian casualties there will be kept to a minimum.'

'Humdinger Hank' regarded this message as appalling impudence. Fortunately, the speed of events in Europe cooled his actions before invasion of Cuba could actually take place. On the day when it became evident that the Soviet Union was breaking up, Cuba's Economics Minister minuted to the premier: 'Our great Soviet ally has lost this war, so let us be as sensible as General Franco was when Hitler was defeated in 1945. We have an advantage that Franco did

not have in a totally de-Nazified Europe in 1945. Many of our fellow
Latin American countries are allies of the US, but they are not blind
servants of US national interests. They will see the Soviet defeat
as a mixed blessing. They will fear that the US, free from the limitations previously imposed by Soviet power, may try to gain rigid
control over its Latin American area of influence. Previous fears of
"subversion from the Soviet Union and Cuba" in Latin America may
now be replaced by fear of US neo-colonialism.

'In these next few critical days we should therefore tell our volunteer troops still fighting at the side of guerrillas on the Central
American mainland to surrender to Latin American governments,
asking perhaps for Mexican and Venezuelan protection. But we
should not accept any US ultimatum for unconditional surrender by
Cuba itself, and we should say that any US invasion of Cuba will be
met by our armed forces fighting to the last man.'

This was agreed. Some of the remaining Cuban troops on the
mainland were anyway isolated and running out of supplies. Most of
them surrendered, coming in together with guerrilla troops through
November 1985. Only small pockets of about platoon size still kept
fighting, but no peace treaty had yet been signed between Cuba and
the US.

The Secretary-General of the OAS sent another urgent telex to the
US President in late November: 'Let me be very frank. The Government and people of Cuba still expect an invasion from the victorious
US. Nearly all my members think such an invasion would be a great
mistake. Bluntly, I must give you a warning that will distress you. If
you continue with an aggressive stance towards Cuba, then the Mexican (and possibly the Venezuelan) Presidents will fly to Havana to
sign with Cuba a treaty of assistance for the provision of food and oil.
In helping Cuba, countries such as Mexico and Venezuela will be
protecting their own freedom of action.

'It is believed among my members that the US is now confronted by
both a great danger and a great opportunity. The danger is that the
US, free from the limitations previously imposed by Soviet power,
may try to encroach upon the independent policies of other American
countries. The opportunity is that of creating a united Latin American front, including a tamed Cuba, willing to play a more assertive
role in world affairs.'

Hardliners in the US, as General Irving's memoirs* show, were far

---

* Much use has been made in the preceding few pages of material to be found in
Lieutenant General Henry J. Irving's memoirs, entitled *Line of Duty* (Grosset
and Dunlop, New York 1986), see particularly pp. 263, 264–5, 271, 279. We have
not been able wholly to endorse General Irving's approach but are grateful for the
source material his book so freely makes available.

from pleased by this message. The President and his close advisers wisely accepted the advice it contained.

A decisive influence was that of Brazil, now one of the principal promoters of Latin American unity. This country – together with Argentina, Mexico and Venezuela – soon began to play a significant role in providing the food and oil urgently required on the other side of the Atlantic, which gave Latin America leverage with a US Government facing a situation of unprecedented international change and turmoil. The US agreed to suspend the blockade against Cuba on the condition that all the few remaining Cuban troops in Central America surrendered, and that Cuba stopped all military and political activities in support of subversion in Latin America. This was quickly accepted. As this book is being written, Cuba is already moving towards far-reaching reforms in its internal policies.

The crucial new factor is Latin America's unity and its will to preserve its freedom of action in the international arena. The US has survived a war against the Soviet empire, but this has not solved the structural problems of Latin America, still less has it done anything to reduce social and political unrest.

At the inter-state level, a new situation is being created, in which Latin American governments are acting on the basis of common policies towards the US. Cuba is being incorporated into this new grouping, on the understanding that its foreign and internal policies will profoundly change. The domination of the communist party in Cuba is about to disappear in fact as well as in name. The end of the Third World War, however, did not bring an end to crisis in Latin America, and the situation there may yet turn into another period of what will be called anti-colonialist confrontation with the advanced, triumphant Western powers. We believe this will not happen, for there is evidence of a truly profound change in attitudes in the US towards Latin America.

We have dealt at some length with the struggles with which the US freed itself from the trap into which the Soviets wished it to fall because of the importance of what has been a profoundly educational and sobering process, whose consequences will be felt far outside the Americas. In its perceptions, orientation, judgment and method the foreign policy of the United States is unlikely, after the experiences in Central America and the Caribbean in the first half of the 1980s, ever to be the same again. This looks like being particularly relevant to US relations with other countries in the Americas. It will probably become more and more apparent in US policies in other regions too, in ASEAN for instance, and in South-West Asia, and in the Third World generally. The world is likely, whatever else may happen, to become on that account alone in some degree a safer place.

Chapter 17

The Middle East

In the Middle East, not unfittingly for a region where violence and conflict had so long been the order of the day, it was first the threat of general war and then that war itself which at length brought about peace. Indeed, had it not been for strong, effective action by the United Nations in the summer of 1984, the Third World War might well have started a year earlier, and started moreover in the Middle East itself. As we look back from this year 1987, only two years after the brief but cataclysmic clash between the superpowers, we may recall that during the early 1980s events in Arabia, in South-West Asia and in Africa too, moved along lines which brought closer the very circumstances and confrontations that the Western nations had been seeking to diminish or avoid. Among such events might be included the fighting in Afghanistan, Iran's agony, the Gulf war, Libya's expansionism, Israeli strikes against Iraq and Lebanon together with colonization of the West Bank and annexation of Golan, South Africa's action in Namibia and Angola, and a worrying disparity of view between the United States and Western Europe. At the same time, other events made for further stability and international understanding, such as UN and EEC initiatives on Palestine and Namibia, the relatively harmonious developments in Zimbabwe, US and Soviet attempts to discuss arms control, the general urge to relieve Third World poverty and the workings of the Gulf Council for Co-operation.

These developments, whether disruptive or otherwise, had in common not only the areas in which they took place. They also illustrated a cardinal point of both Soviet and US policy, that whereas their struggle for influence and gain in the Middle East and Africa could be and was waged by proxy, they did not wish themselves as the two principals to become directly and personally engaged in confrontation and conflict. This policy was easier to realize in southern Africa than it was in the Middle East, for although these two areas shared many features in common, there was one very important difference.

Both areas contained a nation at bay, people fiercely dedicated to

250

their own survival, striking out against those neighbours who threatened their destruction, withstanding the pressure of United Nations Security Council resolutions which called upon them to surrender territory in order to move towards peaceful solutions. Both areas were and are of great strategic moment, both were fertile markets for arms dealers, both provoked Soviet troublemaking and Western ambivalence. In neither was the Soviet Union or the United States content to allow the other to gain an upper hand. Indeed it seemed as if the two superpowers looked then on the Middle East and southern Africa as arenas, not for co-operation, but for competition. This last similarity underlined the crucial difference. Whereas in southern Africa the prospects of a direct Soviet-American confrontation seemed small, in the Middle East they had been growing more likely and more dangerous month by month. There were clear reasons for this – the greater strategic prizes of the Middle East, its close vicinity to vital areas of military power already deployed or readily deployable by the two rivals and, perhaps most marked of all, the immense complexity of the Middle East problem.

In southern Africa the situation could be measured in simple terms, in terms, as it might be put, of black and white. The early 1980s in the Middle East told a very different story. There we saw not just the aspirations of developing countries against a background of superpower rivalry attempting to influence policies and events. We saw an Islamic world divided against itself in spite of the strongest possible motive for unity – a shared hostility to Zionism. Some events threw a strong light on this central issue, particularly Israel's policy of procrastinating over Sinai, colonizing the West Bank, annexing the Golan and surrounding Jerusalem with high concrete buildings. Other events obscured it: Iran and Iraq at war; Syria and Libya supporting Iran, not for sympathy with the ayatollahs, but out of enmity towards other Arab nations; Jordan dangerously linked to Iraq and beginning to lean, like Syria, towards the USSR; Egypt trying to reconcile the irreconcilable by aiming to be on good terms with Israel, the USA *and* the moderate Arab states; Saudi Arabia, Oman and the smaller Gulf states seeking to pursue policies of moderation in an environment largely given over to extremism; the PLO divided in its leadership and in no mood for compromise; the two Yemens keeping an eye, with Soviet interest in the background, on the main chance. Yet many of these other events arose from the apparent inability of any power, super or not, to get to grips with the central Middle Eastern issue itself, the deadlock over Palestine. Meanwhile the USA seemed to stick firmly to three aims – a Camp David peace, the exclusion of the Soviet Union and an uninterrupted flow of oil. The Soviet Union seemed equally prepared to interfere with these aims.

Southern Europe, Middle East, and Northern Africa

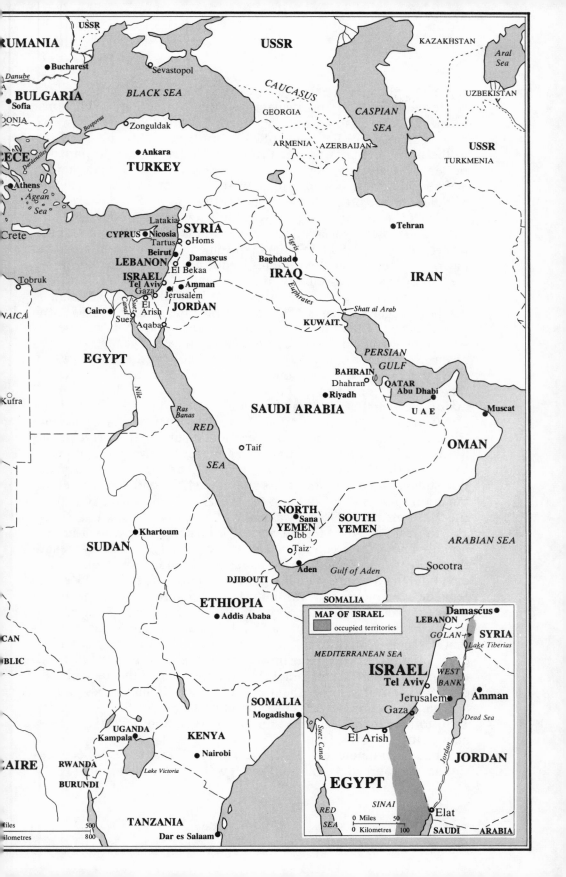

In short, the very dangers of a world war between the superpowers, because either might miscalculate the other's intentions and actions in the Middle East, were heightened. Indeed the new phase of peacemaking which began in 1982 did bring the USSR and the USA to the brink of war. At times their very rivalry seemed to impede, rather than advance, their policies. Some of the United States' activities that were designed to keep Soviet influence away from the Middle East had precisely the opposite effect. The US-Israel strategic agreement, unstable though it was, drew even the moderate Arab states into closer association with the Soviet Union, so that in the end it was the fact of US and Soviet involvement in Arabian affairs that narrowed their respective interests into a common one, the promotion of peace and stability in the region.

It was in 1982 that real progress towards breaking the Palestinian deadlock began to be made. Up to this time the status quo had been maintained, not because it was generally desirable, but because of what seemed to be immovable obstacles to any change. If these obstacles could be weakened or removed, however, a way forward from stalemate might be found. The conditions that had produced this deadlock were many, but they could perhaps be distilled into four major ones. First, no matter what other strategic interests the United States might have had in Middle Eastern, particularly Arab, countries, its continued military and economic support for Israel – as illustrated by intermittent strategic agreement between them – had been such that Israel's military superiority over the Arab confrontation states had been more or less guaranteed. Second, Israel's determination to annex the whole of the West Bank and Gaza, as well as East Jerusalem and Golan, was always likely to be totally unacceptable to Arabs and the Moslem world. Third, persistent Arab disunity, notably among those countries that neighboured Israel, simply meant that there was no local threat to Israel, nor would there be until they did unite. In this connection Egypt's obsession with getting back all of Sinai delayed moves towards unity and (at that time) made negotiations for Palestinian autonomy something of a fraud. Fourth, the PLO's unwillingness to play what was commonly called its 'last card' – that is, recognition of Israel's right to exist – ruled out the possibility of negotiation between Palestinian leaders whether from the PLO or its National Council, and Israel. These were some of the main obstacles. Weaken or remove them and different circumstances would prevail. It was precisely this process which began in 1982 and led in 1986 to the emergence of the autonomous state of Palestine and a new status for Jerusalem.

It had been nineteen years earlier, in 1967, that the UN Security Council had agreed Resolution 242. It will be remembered that from the principle of 'the inadmissibility of acquisition of territory by war' the Resolution had called for 'withdrawal of Israeli armed forces from territories occupied in the recent conflict . . . to secure and recognized boundaries' and had stressed the necessity to guarantee 'the territorial inviolability and political independence of every State in the area'. There were, of course, other matters concerning refugees, demilitarized zones, and freedom of navigation through international waterways, but the Resolution's architect, Lord Caradon, summarized the two crucial requirements: Israel must be secure and the Palestinians must be free. In the early 1980s certain variations on the theme gathered momentum, in particular Crown Prince Fahd's eight-point plan. This was put forward in 1981 but was rejected at the Fez summit in the same year. It envisaged:

(1) Israeli withdrawal from all Arab territories occupied in 1967.
(2) Establishment of an independent Palestinian state with East Jerusalem as its capital.
(3) UN control of the West Bank and Gaza in the transitional period, which would last only a few months.
(4) Recognition of the right of Palestinians to repatriation, with compensation for those who did not wish to return.
(5) Removal of all Israeli settlements established in Arab territory since 1967.
(6) Guarantee of any agreement by the UN or some of its members.
(7) Guarantee for all religions to worship freely in the Holy Land.
(8) Guarantee of the right of all states in the region to live in peace.

While there were those who dissented from the idea of East Jerusalem as the capital of Palestine, hoping that a different solution for Jerusalem would emerge, and while the practicability of compensation for non-repatriated Palestinians was questioned, Prince Fahd's proposals received such substantial and varied support, including that of the authors of the EEC Venice Declaration and of Crown Prince Hassan of Jordan, that they acquired a kind of mantle of authority which led to their general acceptance as a blueprint for peace in the Middle East. This general acceptance had been made easier by concurrent progress on a plan for Lebanon's future, which was designed to allow Lebanon itself to take over responsibility for its security and to re-establish its political identity. First, the Christian Phalangists by abandoning their association with Israel would be enabled to reinforce the idea of Lebanese nationalist autonomy. At the same time, Palestinian military forces would evacuate the whole of South

Lebanon, as would Israeli forces too. Their place would be taken by the UN Force in Lebanon (UNIFIL). Beirut itself, formerly garrisoned by both Palestinian and Syrian forces, would also be looked after by the newly constituted Lebanese Army. All this would enable the Syrian Army to evacuate Lebanon completely except for the El Bekaa valley bordering Syria itself.

These processes of military readjustment were intended to assist political realignments so that a central and national Lebanese government, incorporating all parties except Palestinians, could be established. Saudi Arabia's commitment to and sponsoring of this idea continued to advance its general political position in the Arab world, while it was hoped that Syria's dependence on the Soviet Union and its former hostility to the Fahd eight-point plan would be further reduced. If there appeared to be little of value in these various comings and goings for the Palestinians themselves, they could at least console themselves with the thought that the inter-relationship between the Saudi and Lebanese plan could lead to more general support for their own national aspirations.

All this sounded admirable in theory. But it was still theory, and there still had to be found some means of getting once again under way those international initiatives without which there could be no breaking of the deadlock. The key to finding these means lay in Egypt.

In 1981 and 1982, as had been expected, the newly appointed Egyptian President continued with the Camp David peace process in order to regain the whole of Sinai, yet he tried to reconcile this process, which required the co-operation of the United States and Israel, with a move back into the moderate Arab camp. At the same time, Israel itself had been tempted to slow down the hand-over of Sinai in order to gain time to judge further influences and policies. Such temptations, however, were removed by intense pressure from both the United States and Western Europe. Indeed the United States, which had already given some indication of future intentions by further military assistance to Saudi Arabia following the AWACS deal in 1981, made it clear that the balance of military aid could switch away from Israel to Arabia if the Sinai were not handed back on time. There was not yet any progress from Camp David to a proper re-assessment of how both the PLO and Israel could be persuaded to acknowledge each other's rights in order to pave the way for negotiations on the lines of Prince Fahd's plan. Once all the Sinai had been handed back to Egypt, however, and a peacekeeping force, which included Third World, American and European troops, had been established, a new set of circumstances emerged.

In 1982, with the Sinai back in Egyptian hands and the so-called normalization of Egyptian-Israeli relations still proceeding, the Saudi Arabian Sheikh Faisal Abdullah, who had long been working for a rapprochement between Egypt and his own country, succeeded in arranging a meeting between the Crown Prince and the President of Egypt. It took place in Geneva and was to set in train a series of events which, unlike all previous initiatives, began to break the Palestinian deadlock. In essence the policy they agreed upon was that Arab unity would as far as possible be restored. Disruptive movements, such as Moslem fundamentalism or adventurism in the Sahara, would be controlled by friendly, or if this failed, unfriendly persuasion. Given a degree of Arab unity, irresistible pressure should be brought to bear in two quarters: first on Israel, through the United States, to make the Israelis sit down and negotiate the future of an autonomous Palestine; secondly on the PLO, to oblige it to acknowledge Israel's right to exist and thus also sit down at the negotiating table. The weapon to be used against the United States and thus its Western allies would, of course, be oil. In simple terms, the bargaining would be: no Palestine, no oil. This position had to be taken seriously and a settlement based on it did in the end come about. But the voices of those not present at the Geneva meeting still had to be heard. The principal voices, both demanding and entitled to be heard, were those of the United States, Israel, Libya, Jordan, Syria and the Soviet Union.

During the remaining months of 1982 and the early ones of the following year these voices made themselves heard in various bilateral and multilateral meetings, and in doing so helped to shape the final outcome. We must shortly consider the way in which the United States was persuaded to sponsor a formula for peace, broadly acceptable to the bulk of the Arab nations and to which Israel could be obliged to submit. We must also examine how the Soviet Union took a hand in the game which all but brought the superpowers to a direct clash in the very area they were seeking to pacify. But first, we must clear out of the way two other obstacles which were impeding solution to the central problem. The first was Libya, the second Iran.

Libya's leader, whose preposterous behaviour had caused flutterings in so many dovecotes, overreached himself at last in the same year – 1983 – as negotiations for a Palestinian settlement were gaining ground. He actually committed his country, with the promised aid of Pakistan (whose paymaster he had capriciously been, stopped being, and was again) to the establishment of a nuclear armoury. At the same time, his further interference in the Sudan and Niger, covered more fully in the next chapter, so enraged the moderate Arab nations, headed by Saudi Arabia and Egypt, that, choosing a time when Libyan forces were also heavily engaged in suppressing another uprising in Chad, Egypt was authorized to deal with the Libyan leader once and for all.

Egypt's armed forces struck, and struck hard. Libya's air force was destroyed on its airfields. The relatively small number of serviceable tanks in the Libyan Army were knocked out by the anti-tank helicopters which Egypt had bought from Britain, while hundreds of non-running tanks were impounded in depots. What remained of Libya's infantry, such as were not deployed in Saharan adventures, felt disinclined to argue the toss with the armoured and air forces that Egypt was able to put into the field. It was clear from the way in which the Egyptians conducted their campaign against Libya that they had modelled themselves on Wavell and O'Connor rather than on Alexander and Montgomery. Speed, surprise and audacity characterized the whole operation.

On D-day, the Egyptian Air Force destroyed all Libyan aircraft at Benghazi, while parachute and heliborne forces seized the Al Kufra oasis and its Soviet-made missile sites. Meanwhile, as armoured and mechanized divisions with strong air support drove for Benghazi, Tobruk was taken by commando groups. Within a week the Egyptians had consolidated these gains and destroyed or captured the main Libyan forces deployed in eastern Cyrenaica. In this consolidation they were assisted by the Senussi who had long chafed against rule from Tripoli. While mechanized troops continued to advance westwards on the coast road, mopping up half-hearted garrisons, Tripoli air base was put out of action by Egyptian bombers, and further seaborne and airborne operations captured El Agheila, Sirte and Homs. The main oil-producing areas between Gialo and Dahra were occupied by follow-up echelons, and communication centres like Al Fuqaha and Daraj were controlled by groups of parachute and light reconnaissance forces. Spearheads of the main armoured thrust drove into Tripoli after a final skirmish with garrison troops.

The whole affair had something in common with what Rommel had once described as a lightning tour of the enemy's country. In this way Libya was subdued and all but annexed by Egypt. But the fight had been against the Libyan leader – who found refuge in Ethiopia – not against the Libyan people, whose new government was formed by a triumvirate, all of whom were recalled from exile, comprising the former commander of Tobruk garrison, Libya's Prime Minister in the pre-military regime, and the man who was the eminence grise of Libya's last king, the Senussi Idris.

Protests by the Soviet Union at this action by Egypt had no more effect than protests from the West when the Soviet Union invaded Afghanistan. With the United States Sixth Fleet patrolling the central and eastern Mediterranean, the Soviet Mediterranean Squadron, the

Fifth *Eskadra*, had been ordered to remain at anchorage and avoid confrontation. The Soviet High Command was much more concerned with free passage of the Dardanelles than with Libyan port facilities or the fate of the Libyan leader. The latter's removal and his replacement by a regime sympathetic to moderate Arab policies were widely seen as almost wholly beneficial. Interference in Chad, Niger and Sudan stopped. The financing of international terrorism dwindled. Temptation to make a stir in the world simply for its own sake was put aside. Arab unity was further enhanced. Moslem fundamentalism suffered a setback. Encouragement for the less benevolent policies of South Yemen, Ethiopia and Syria ceased. What is more – and this in Western eyes was not wholly beneficial – the Arab oil weapon became more powerful with Libyan oil now under Egyptian control. Nor were the benefits confined to that part of the Middle East alone.

The fall of the Libyan military regime made it easier for Iran to escape from the pitiless rule of the mullahs in a way which also frustrated Soviet hopes of securing control of the country. The Soviet Union had long been infiltrating Iran with arms and agents for the revolutionary guards, at the same time attempting to subvert the army. They had been assisted by Libya which had subsidized a fanatical group of left-wing Iranian Army officers. To moderates who sought to overthrow the ayatollahs, a coalition between this group of fanatics with the pro-Soviet Tudeh communists and the revolutionary guards seemed a highly unattractive alternative to the mullahs themselves. Now, however, the influence in Iran of moderate, anti-revolutionary officers of the army and air force grew and infiltration into Iranian Azerbaijan was curtailed. The revolutionary guards' endeavours to replace the army as the country's main military force came to nothing. There was in addition a man for the moment at hand.

General Ahmed Bahram, former army commander, exiled by the ayatollahs, had established his headquarters and his army of counter-revolutionaries in Turkey in 1982. He held two strong cards in his hand. The first was his agreement with the Arab nations and particularly with the new military leadership in Baghdad that he would recognize Iraq's shared need of the Shatt al Arab and harmonize their respective policies over Kurdistan. The second and even more important card was that he enjoyed a secret understanding both with the generals commanding the principal garrisons of Iran and with the leaders of the Mujaheddin Khalq, the Iranian People's Militia.

General Bahram's takeover of Iran was relatively bloodless, and the blood which was spilled could easily be spared as it was largely that of the revolutionary guards. The Tudeh communists proved to be insufficiently armed or concentrated to stand up to the alliance of regular and irregular forces, whose coup was staged with such precision and pressure.

The establishment of a more moderate and pro-Western regime in Iran, together with an end to the Gulf war, strengthened still further the axis between Saudi Arabia and Egypt, and gave still more coherence to general Arab unity. The Gulf war had done much to separate Arab countries and distract them from the very issue – Palestine – for which unity and concerted action were indispensable. Instability and violence in Iran itself, bearing in mind that Soviet troops were on Iran's eastern frontier, had always conjured up fears of direct Soviet military intervention there too. Now, with a military ruler determined to re-establish economic, social and political order, these fears were to some extent dissipated. It was not a return to the sort of Western alliance there had been with the Shah, but it offered at least some additional defence against Soviet expansionism. All in all, therefore, the Western nations had reason to be satisfied with developments in Libya, Iraq and Iran. The fly in the ointment, however, particularly in United States' eyes, remained the immensely strong position from which the Arab nations could now wield the oil weapon.

As was to be expected, it was wielded not bluntly or brutally, but with forbearance and subtlety. The Saudis had long understood that next to knowing when to seize an opportunity, the most important thing was to know when to forgo an advantage. Opportunity had to be nourished before it could be seized. Advantage, which would follow, had to be savoured before it could be forgone.

The Arab summit at Taif in mid-1983 appeared at first to underline some continuing disagreement rather than to signal a unified stand which would enable Arab leaders to persuade the United States to bring further pressure upon Israel. There appeared to be little change in the position of the rejectionist front. Despite Libya's forced acceptance of Egypt's way of thinking, Syria, South Yemen and Algeria were still opposed to any arrangement with Israel. There appeared to be no general acceptance of Egypt's return to the Arab camp, although at Saudi Arabia's insistence Egypt was represented at the conference. Iraq and Jordan seemed still to be at odds with Syria. The PLO although accepted as a voice to speak for the Palestinians, persisted in omnipresent intrigue and still presented the face of timorous foe and suspicious friend. It was even thought that they had had secret meetings with the Israelis in Vienna. Nonetheless the representative Palestine National Council – the so-called parliament of the PLO – began to take a more positive and constructive part in PLO leadership.

Such appearances, if inauspicious, were deceptive. The Saudis, who as hosts had more control of the agenda and procedures than anyone else, displayed to advantage their singleness of purpose and toughness in diplomacy. The eight-point plan of Crown Prince Fahd, in spite of not having been endorsed at the 1981 Fez summit, remained firmly the vehicle for discussion and agreement. This plan had, of course, the respectability and authority of being not merely an Arab plan, but a Saudi Arabian one. Saudi Arabia had long enjoyed a special position as the custodian of the Holy Places of Islam. Now, with Egypt once more by its side, and with the fruits of consistently moderate statesmanship and inexhaustible economic strength to draw upon, Saudi Arabia's claims to the political, as well as the religious, leadership of the Arab nations were hard to challenge. Moreover, their determination to bring about United States partici-pation in putting intense pressure on Israel remained unchanged. In this they were supported (which was indispensable for their pur-poses) by the bulk of other Arab nations, including the oil producers. In effect, and despite the continued uncertainties of Syria, Algeria and South Yemen, the *jihad*, or holy war, which Prince Fahd had called for three years earlier as the only means of asserting Islamic rights in Jerusalem and breaking the Palestinian deadlock, was now a reality. Furthermore, Syria's reluctance to conform was to some extent offset by the PLO's further detachment from Syria and by its willingness to play the 'last card' as a preliminary to actual negotia-tions over the outstanding issues.

During the Taif summit the US President's special envoy to the Middle East sat in Cairo, being briefed by all those emissaries from Taif and elsewhere whom he chose to see. Outwardly he remained serene and his despatches to the President were couched in the language of a diplomat whose options remained open. But in fact these options were rapidly dwindling to only two: silence or placate the Jewish lobby in New York, Washington and the rest of the USA, or let the Western world go short of Middle Eastern oil.

At the same time, Western European governments had been active. The former British President of the Council of Ministers of the EEC had put his and Western Europe's weight behind a drive for two objectives, whose achievement they felt would greatly enhance the possibility of new international peace initiatives. One was that the implicit acceptance of Israel's right to exist contained in the eighth point of Prince Fahd's plan – guarantee of the right of all states in the region to live in peace – should somehow be made explicit. The other was that the PLO's part in the peacemaking machinery should be acknowledged by all concerned, including Israel itself, on the under-standing that explicit mention of Israel's right to exist in security and peace was in turn endorsed by the PLO. At the time of the Taif summit in mid-1983 these objectives seemed to be within reach.

Much still depended, however, on the United States' willingness and ability to change Israel's position and policies. In 1983 the governments of the major European members of NATO made a proposal which could not fail to be attractive to the United States, and at the same time would relieve some of their own anxieties. It was, in brief, that the European members of NATO would now at last reduce their real vulnerability by more efficient co-operation between them in defence efforts and less reliance on US forces in Europe. It was to be hoped that this would enable the United States to pursue more vigorously a Middle East policy leading on from Camp David to a full settlement, an essential feature of which would be to oblige the Israelis to accept the need to involve the Palestinians and the Arab nations on the basis of Prince Fahd's plan, perhaps with modifications. This European proposal added much weight to the pressure on the United States from the more or less unified Arabs, particularly since it was accompanied by the setting up of machinery, in the shape of the Western Policy Staff, to consider common action by NATO member states outside the NATO area where common interest arose. This the United States found particularly gratifying. Faced with the prospect of either antagonizing the Jewish lobby or denying the Western world adequate supplies of oil – and comforted by the reflection that he would not again be standing for office – the President chose the former. He would try to hold the Jewish lobby at bay.

Once more the President despatched his special envoy to Tel Aviv. This time his mission was made public by carefully orchestrated leaks to the media. In plain terms the United States' message to Israel's leaders was this: either Israel must now agree to move on from Camp David and begin to negotiate a settlement of Palestine and Jerusalem, or US military and economic aid would be run down.

The reaction of the Israeli Government was as capricious as it was self-destructive. In a desperate but fruitless demonstration of their immediate strength, but ultimate impotence, they announced their intention of annexing South Lebanon and instantly mounted air attacks on airfields near Damascus, on Syrian troop concentrations in the El Bekaa valley, and pushed aside UN troops in South Lebanon. Syria responded in kind with artillery, missile and air attacks on the Golan Heights. While the reaction of the United States Government might have been predicted, what took the world by surprise was that for once the United States and the Soviet Union were at one – Israel must be made to toe the line. In an unprecedentedly cordial and fruitful meeting between the US Secretary of State and the Soviet Foreign

Minister, which took place in London late in 1983, it was agreed that unless Israel instantly accepted the conditions for peace negotiations based on the Fahd plan, economic sanctions against it, including total blockade of its ports of entry, would be initiated at once. The Israeli Government thereupon resigned and was replaced by one from the main opposition party with the declared policy of negotiating peace with the Arab nations in order to solve the problems of Palestine and Jerusalem.

One by one the obstacles to negotiation had been going down. A significant degree of Arab unity had been restored; the PLO together with Arab leaders had expressed their willingness to acknowledge Israel's right to exist; pressure had been brought upon the United States both by the Arab nations and Western Europe to take that uneasy leap from Camp David to the determination of Palestinian autonomy; and now Israel, responding to a choice of action put before it by the United States and the Soviet Union, had a new government willing to reciprocate by formally declaring abandonment of the previous Israeli policy of colonization and annexation. The way for negotiation at an international peace conference was at last open. What was now wanted was an agreed formula and machinery to enable negotiations actually to begin. During December 1983 work towards these ends proceeded. At length, after intensive international diplomacy in the Security Council of the United Nations, agreement was achieved and a new Security Council Resolution emerged.

The main difference between this new Resolution and 242 was, of course, that Palestinian self-determination was now a cardinal feature of it. In bringing the original Resolution up to date and providing for its implementation, therefore, the new one did much to acknowledge, while not absolutely conforming to, Prince Fahd's eight-point plan. The new Resolution dealt with five main issues:

(1) Cessation of all violence and all Israeli settlements in occupied territory.

(2) Creation of a boundary commission to hear both sides and make recommendations for a permanent 'secure and recognized' frontier.

(3) A period of international trusteeship over East Jerusalem, the West Bank and Gaza (and also the Golan Heights) during which period the Palestinians could exercise self-determination, elect their own leaders, and decide both on their own constitution and on their relations with neighbours.

(4) Provision of international guarantees (together with demilitarized zones, and restriction on the deployment of

certain weapons systems, particularly SSM and SAM) to preserve the right of every state in the area to live in peace 'free
from threats and acts of force'.

(5) A final peace conference to take place in Geneva under the
joint chairmanship of the United States and the Soviet
Union as before (with the Palestinians represented by their
chosen leaders) to prepare and sign the peace treaties.

The unanimity of support for Resolution 242 in 1967 had been
thought remarkable. Unanimity on this new Resolution was no less
so. In particular the readiness of the Soviet Union to comply with
what was so clearly identifiable as a United States' interest was
remarked upon. Reflection, however, reminded observers that sixteen years had elapsed between the two Resolutions without there
being much implementation of the first – if in this respect Camp
David might be left aside. In any case, it was not at this time the Soviet
Union's intention implacably to antagonize the moderate Arab states
under the leadership of Saudi Arabia when the USSR believed that
its own proxy Arab states, like Syria and South Yemen, could, when
actual negotiations to implement the new Resolution got under way,
safeguard Soviet interests under the guise of their being Arab ones.
So it turned out to be.

Before we examine how actual negotiation turned into a more
dangerous confrontation between the superpowers, it is necessary to
say a word or two further about Jerusalem. It had always been clear
that there could be no peace in the Middle East without peace in
Jerusalem. Yet real peace in Jerusalem was unobtainable through
divided domination; it had to be brought about through united freedom. Jerusalem itself had to become a kind of gateway to peace.
Concurrently, therefore, with the diplomatic activity in the Security
Council during late 1983, European initiatives in the General
Assembly, with Great Britain taking a particular lead, had led to the
adoption of a Resolution dealing with Jerusalem, the implementation
of which was intended to be in parallel with that of the broader
Resolution of the Security Council. Its essential outlines, after the
preamble dealing with the Holy City's future role as a symbol of
peace and freedom, recognized and respected by all mankind, were
these:

(1) There would be an Israeli Jerusalem and an Arab Jerusalem
each exercising full sovereignty within its own territory but
with no barriers and no impediment to freedom of movement between them.

(2) The Secretary-General would appoint an impartial boundary commission to hear representations from those concerned and make recommendations to the Security Council

as to the boundary between the Israeli Jerusalem and the Arab Jerusalem.

(3) The Holy City would be completely demilitarized.

(4) The Secretary-General would appoint a high commissioner (and deputy) to be stationed in Jerusalem, to represent the United Nations and to work with all concerned to secure and ensure the purposes of the Resolution, and to report appropriately for the information of the General Assembly and the Security Council.

Thus not only had the need for concerted international action to bring permanent peace to Jerusalem and the Middle East been reaffirmed, but both a formula and machinery for its implementation had been established. We need not at present concern ourselves with the detailed working of this machinery during the last months of 1983 and the early part of 1984. It is the end which mattered, rather than the means. But what must now command our attention is what happened in Syria in the summer of 1984, which nearly brought the whole peacemaking procedure to a close and the two superpowers to the brink of war in the Middle East itself one year before actual war on the Central Front of Europe.

It became plain at this time that as well as peacemakers, there were peacebreakers at large. It seemed at first as if a whole series of peacewrecking events was being directed by implacable extremists. Yet so capricious and multitudinous appeared to be the motives and targets, that paradoxically these events might have been the work of a single internationally organized network, such as Black International, or even a combination of Black and Red International. The connection was never firmly established. It was suggested by Western sources that a kind of multinational strike force had been structured round the Palestinian Rejection Front, which had, of course, been armed by the Soviet Union, and was now – so argued these sources – being directed from Moscow. It was hardly surprising that the Soviet Union and its associates took a different stance, and put all the blame squarely on to the CIA. All such views were coloured of course by the political attitudes of those who expressed them. Initially, however, it was not so much the direction behind the terrible events which ensued that mattered. It was the effect of the events themselves.

The bomb explosions in Cairo airport were bad enough, killing or maiming as they did more than 350 people. Then came the assassination of the President's special envoy in Tel Aviv, which caused some cynics to observe that this was the best blow for peace the PLO had so far struck. The murder of sixteen members of the United States contingent in the UN peacekeeping force in Sinai was similarly attributed to the Palestinian Rejection Front – certainly the bullets found

in them had been fired from Soviet-made weapons. All this soured
the United States view of the Soviet commitment to peace. Nor was
the Soviet Union less sceptical about the USA's real intentions when
the former's representatives at the peace conference were kidnap-
ped, tortured and executed. There may have been evidence to show
that it was the doing of the Italian-Nazi-Maoist group, but this did not
prevent the Soviet Union attributing the whole affair to the CIA.
These accusations and misunderstandings hardly made for smooth
progress at Geneva.

The worst events of all took place in Syria, and the Syrian
authorities were not slow to condemn hard-line Israeli groups, who,
they claimed, were operating in Syria with the Mossad's support. In
Damascus the President's office was blown up during a high-level
meeting. Again the levity of some political commentary let it be made
known that the meeting continued at an even higher level, but the fact
was that the President, his brother, other ministers and some senior
military officers had been killed. Simultaneously, sabotage at a dozen
military bases, together with the destruction of fuel depots, power
centres and telecommunications so disturbed the Syrian Government
that it declared martial law. If this was a last mad attack on Syria by
Israeli clandestine forces, it was certainly effective.

Then two more acts of violence shocked the world. In the Syrian
naval base at Tartus two minesweepers and a visiting Soviet frigate
were destroyed by limpet mines, killing and wounding many Syrian
and Soviet sailors, while at Riyadh an AWACS aircraft which was about
to be handed over by the US Air Force to the Royal Saudi Air Force
disintegrated in flight. All on board perished.

Fear, increased by uncertainty, gripped the peacemakers. The
Soviet Union accused the United States of sabotaging peace efforts in
order to maintain a position of strategic dominance in the Middle
East through its ally Israel. The United States in reply taxed the
Soviet Union with the intention to establish a military base in Syria,
from which to spread its influence east and south.

For this last accusation there appeared to be some grounds. Syria,
either motivated by panic or manipulated by those determined never
to compromise with Israel, had once more appealed to the Soviet
Union for instant and substantial demonstration of friendship and
fulfilment of their security pact. The appeal was not made in vain.

The Soviet Mediterranean Fifth *Eskadra* moved to Syria's naval
base at Latakia, and reinforcements from the Black Sea Fleet were
moving through the Dardanelles as frequently as the Turkish
Government would permit, under the Montreux Convention. The
surface ships of the Soviet Indian Ocean Squadron, consisting of a
missile cruiser and two frigates, with three auxiliaries, returned to

Aden. Meanwhile a stream of *Antonov* transports bringing arms, equipment and troops to Damascus overflew Turkish airspace, having given minimum warning through normal diplomatic channels. Turkey protested in strong terms and received a discourteous and threatening reply from the Soviet Union. Notwithstanding these threats, Turkey moved air and ground units nearer to the Syrian frontier, as did Iraq and Jordan, while the Turkish Navy concentrated some of its submarine, mine-laying and patrol craft astride the Dardanelles. Egypt moved more combat aircraft and armoured formations into the Sinai. The United States reaction demonstrated its determination to go on reassuring its friends while cautioning the Soviet Union. Units of the US Air Force and Rapid Deployment Force were despatched to Egypt and Somalia. Even Jordan accepted some US advisers and AWACS aircraft. The US Sixth Fleet took up a waiting position south-east of Cyprus. Two US destroyers exercising in the Red Sea with the Egyptian Navy, off Ras Banas, departed to rejoin their carrier group further south.

So serious did the situation appear to be that NATO commanders called for certain alert measures to be taken in Europe, while Warsaw Pact forces prolonged and reinforced manoeuvres which were under way in Bulgaria. In Britain some reserves were recalled and the House of Commons debated the question of embodying the Territorial Army. France and Italy undertook joint naval exercises in the western Mediterranean.

Worse was to come. There were several sharp sea and air engagements in the eastern Mediterranean between US and Syrian forces and between Soviet and Israeli, all naturally disavowed or hushed up at the time. By good fortune there were no TV cameramen present at any. Both US and Soviet forces were under strict orders to avoid direct engagement with the main antagonist, but it could only be a matter of time before, whether by accident or design, they fired upon each other. It really appeared as if the superpowers were on the brink of war. And all for what? For Syrian intransigence. The hot line between Washington and Moscow became very hot indeed. What was said lent great strength to the UN Secretary-General's call for an immediate international conference under his chairmanship in Geneva to resolve differences and resume Middle East peace negotiations. All parties concerned agreed to it.

So it was that in the latter months of 1984 negotiations as to the future of Jerusalem and the establishment of an autonomous Palestinian state, together with international guarantees designed to preserve the right of all states in the area to live in peace 'free from threats and acts of force', resumed, and might be said to have been crowned with success, for by the spring of 1985 a peace conference had been convened to take place in Geneva later that year under the joint chairmanship of the United States and the Soviet Union to make preparations for the signature of peace treaties by all the parties involved.

By this time much progress had been made. Violence had ceased. Israeli settlements had been withdrawn from occupied Arab and Palestinian territory. The boundary commission had made its recommendations, which had been endorsed by all sides. The future of Jerusalem on the lines of the UN Security Council Resolution was assured. The Palestinians had agreed on their future constitution and the Palestinian National Council together with members of the PLO made up the majority party of the newly-elected Palestinian Parliament. The principal guarantors of these new agreements were to be the Soviet Union and the United States with peacekeeping forces to be established along previously disputed frontiers, these forces to come mainly from Third World nations and exclude both US and Soviet troops. All that remained was final signature of the treaties and their implementation.

It was not to be, or at least not in this way. Events in the Middle East were overtaken by the outbreak of the Third World War.

The superpowers came very close to war in the Middle East and it is of interest to note the potential for waging war there that the various countries of the region, and those from outside it who had interests there, possessed.

If numbers alone could have determined the military balance, it would have been firmly tipped in favour of the Arab nations. Egypt, Syria, Iraq, Saudi Arabia and the Gulf States – to say nothing of the Sudan, Algeria and Morocco – mustered between them the best part of a million men under arms, excluding reserves, while Israel's total armed forces were some 170,000, although mobilization, which would be rapid, more than doubled this figure. There were, of course, peacekeeping forces from the United Nations in positions close to previously disputed frontiers – in the West Bank, Gaza, Sinai, the Golan Heights and Jerusalem – but these forces were small and lightly equipped. As for the United States and the Soviet Union, their presence at the centre of things near the new State of Palestine and in the countries neighbouring Israel was confined largely to advisers and training teams. It was true that the Soviet Union still had nearly 100,000 troops in Afghanistan, but they were being kept very busy, while the naval and air units which both superpowers deployed periodically in friendly Arab ports and air bases were, after withdrawal from former confrontation, of modest proportions.

But the game was not one of numbers alone. As tension in Europe became greater and the forces of the Warsaw Pact and those of

NATO began their processes of mobilization, redeployment and reinforcement, so comparable processes were to be seen in the Middle East. It then became clear that the Arab states, led by Saudi Arabia and Egypt, far from abandoning the peaceful settlement on which they had embarked, were not intent on using their military strength against Israel, but were determined to harbour it in order to keep open the path to peace. At the same time Israel had to be kept quiet. The United States would have to help. The Arab nations, in forgoing what might have seemed to be a temporary advantage, were thus able to combine magnanimity with policy, the fruits of which were to be seen in the successful conclusion of the Middle East peace conferences soon after hostilities between the superpowers had ceased.

So it was that Egypt, whose new relationship with Libya had allowed a greatly reduced force to patrol that frontier, did not increase its forces in the Sinai from the two armoured and two mechanized divisions already there, but did reinforce the garrisons in the southeast near Ras Banas, while leaving a strong reserve near Cairo and Suez. The Egyptian Air Defence Command with its 200 interceptors and missile brigades still guarded central strategic bases and the approaches from north-east and south-east. The air force's 300 combat aircraft were deployed roughly in proportion to the army, and the navy remained with its customary distribution of submarines, destroyers and patrol craft between the eastern Mediterranean and the Red Sea.

Saudi Arabia's main concern was with North and South Yemen. Two Saudi brigades with supporting arms and aircraft remained in the north-west, the remaining four brigades with strong air support, and patrol units from the Frontier Force, were in the south-west. Saudi naval corvettes and patrol boats were on station in both the Red Sea and the Gulf.

Iraq's army of some twelve divisions was broadly divided between a force on the new frontier with Iran, a grouping facing Syria, and a central reserve, with the Iraqi Air Force's 350 combat aircraft supporting the army deployment and the navy's missile and patrol vessels at readiness in the waterways and the Gulf.

Iran, like Iraq, had largely made good the losses already sustained in the war between them. The bulk of the Iranian Army's ten divisions, half of which were armoured, were divided between the north-east sector facing Afghanistan and the western front, with strong reserves held centrally and in the main oil-producing areas of the south-west. The Iranian Navy patrolled the Gulf, and the 200 or so combat aircraft supported both army and naval deployment.

Syria's forces – none of which were by this time deployed in

Lebanon (where UN peacekeeping forces backed up the small army) – were located with two armoured divisions each in the northern and eastern commands, while the two mechanized divisions remained near Damascus. Syria's strong air force and air defence command, which included 450 Migs, was deployed to challenge attack from any quarter.

Jordan's four divisions, all armoured or mechanized, were concentrated in the northern and eastern sectors, supported by nearly 100 F-5s, with a small naval force at Aqaba. Oman's relatively small, but efficient force of some 15,000 were deployed both to resist any further incursions from South Yemen and to guard the sea approaches. The two Yemens had armed forces of roughly similar size, the South primarily equipped with Soviet arms, the North with a mixture from the USSR and the West. Each had armoured and infantry brigades, MiG fighters and patrol craft. Both could threaten Saudi Arabia. Aden was virtually a Soviet naval base.

Thus were the various forces disposed when peacemaking in the Middle East was brought to a temporary halt. It was plain that when the two principal guarantors of the 1985 peace agreement were themselves at war – war moreover brought about by events far removed from the Middle East scene – the principal strategic aims of the Arab countries, with the exception of Syria and the inevitable dissension of South Yemen, were twofold. The first was to preserve the integrity and security of their own countries; the second, to preserve the political and military conditions that would enable them to resume implementation of the peace settlement as soon as possible. It seemed therefore to Saudi Arabia and Egypt, together with their supporters – Jordan, Iraq, Oman, the other Gulf states, Libya and Sudan – that their policy must be to isolate Israel and keep it in check; to prevent any interference by North or South Yemen; to support Iran both in maintaining its internal security and against Soviet incursions from Azerbaijan and Soviet-inspired activity in Baluchistan; and with the assistance of the United States and NATO to maintain or re-establish control of the eastern Mediterranean, the Red Sea and the Gulf.

It is not intended to give detailed accounts of how these objects were achieved. Indeed in the event there was, with two major exceptions, very little war prosecuted in the Middle East or South-West Asia during the few weeks of the Third World War. What fighting there was took place largely in Europe, and at sea and in the air. Enough to say here that the prospect of hostile action by Iraq, Syria, Jordan and Egypt, together with explicit United States warnings, kept Israel in check. Syria disallowed any Soviet proposals to fly in reinforcements, and was more conscious than ever of the proximity of

Turkey, which together with the rest of NATO was by this time at war with the Soviet Union and had closed the Bosporus with mines, submarines, land-based weapons and other means. The first aim of joint Arab policy was achieved without bloodshed.

The second aim did involve some bloodshed. North Yemen, under intense pressure from most Arab nations, agreed to accept a joint Egyptian-Saudi Arabian force to assist North Yemeni troops in suppressing once and for all the Soviet-armed guerrillas infiltrating from South Yemen. Sanaa, Taiz and Ibb were all successfully cleared, and effective anti-incursion forces were established along the frontier between North and South Yemen.

Support for Iran – the third policy requirement – did not take the form of troops or arms, but rather guarantees of co-operation in frontier control, shipping protection in the Gulf and economic aid. Iran was thus able to enhance its internal prosperity and external security without fear of threat from any of its western neighbours. The greatest threat to Iran would be from the north. The need to remove this threat was one of the reasons that brought war to the Middle East. The other was control of the sea.

Those who had previously been sceptical about the effectiveness or even the employability of the United States Rapid Deployment Force, with possible contingents from Great Britain, France and Italy, were agreeably surprised by both the rapidity of its deployment and its strength. The United States battle group in the Indian Ocean, despite torpedo damage to the carrier *Nimitz*, succeeded in neutralizing the Soviet squadron. The United States air reinforcement of Egypt and Saudi Arabia, together with the best part of an airborne division that landed near Cairo, gave them the capability of countering any Soviet intervention overland. The joint naval force of British and French frigates, plus a US Marine amphibious force and embarked air wing, secured the Gulf. The Arab four-point strategic policy, desirable in concept, had now been accomplished.

Removal of the threat to Iran from the north was the work, not of the Western allies or of the Arab nations, or even of the Iranians themselves. It was the work of the Afghan guerrilla movement. The substantial re-arming programme that had been in progress since 1982 reached its height in 1985. By this time there were plenty of essential weapons and ammunition, including SAM-7 launchers (which were extremely effective against helicopter gunships), machine-guns, mortars, assault rifles and anti-tank guided missiles. Even more important was the degree of central command and control exercised by the guerrillas' formidable and respected leader whose main area of operations was in the provinces of Nangarhar and Paktiar. His great chance came when the Soviet Union began to withdraw some of its

armoured and helicopter formations from Afghanistan after the outbreak of hostilities on the Central Front in Europe. Allowing the first
contingents of these powerful armoured and mechanized forces to
retire unmolested, he chose his moment, declared *jihad* and supervised a concerted attack on every Soviet unit left in Afghanistan.

In 1842 the British Army had suffered a 'signal catastrophe' when
it retreated from Kabul. There had been but one survivor, Surgeon
Brydon, who succeeded in reaching Jalalabad. Rudyard Kipling had
had some unpleasant things to say about what happened to British
soldiers if they were wounded and left on Afghanistan's plains – 'an'
the women come out to cut up what remains' – but neither of these
points applied to the Soviet catastrophe. There were no wounded for
the women to cut up. There were no survivors. The Soviet Union,
during the remaining short period when it existed under that name,
made no attempt to re-enter Afghanistan or to interfere in Iran.

One of the most satisfactory features of the peace conference in
Geneva, which continued on and off for the whole of 1986, was the
expedition with which the former Middle East peace treaties were
reconsidered and signed. The United States was at once able to
enforce Israel's compliance and help to guarantee its right to exist.
The guarantors were now the United Nations themselves with the
United States and the Arab nations foremost among them. The
essential conditions for peace had been realized. Jerusalem had
become a symbol of unified freedom, the Palestinians were autonomous and had their own chosen constitution and Israel was secure.
Harmony between most of the Arab nations had been achieved.

It has been argued that just as peace in Arabia was dependent upon
a settlement in Palestine, so peace in Africa was dependent upon a
settlement in Namibia. If peace in the Middle East promises to be
lasting, it is perhaps because it sprang from confrontation which led to
negotiation. If peace in Africa, particularly southern Africa – to
which we must now turn our attention – appears to be less durable, it
is perhaps because it is the result of negotiation which can only lead to
further confrontation.

Chapter 18

Southern Africa

In the Middle East the central issue of Palestine had been tackled and resolved. In Africa the central problem of what to do about South Africa had not really been tackled at all, still less resolved. This was not the only contrast between the two areas. In the Middle East the goal of a peaceful settlement for Palestine and Jerusalem had commanded the support of nearly all neighbouring nations and had more or less unified the Arab countries themselves. No such accord was to be found in southern Africa. There the problem was not how to create an autonomous state from peoples and territory that had been overrun and occupied as a result of war. The problem was how to persuade a sovereign independent state of great economic and military strength to change its political system to the immediate disadvantage of those whose system it was and who enjoyed the fruits of its power and privilege.

A generally declared commitment on the part of the black front-line nations that majority rule must replace apartheid was all very well in principle. But it seemed to endorse Bismarck's celebrated observation that when you say that you agree to a thing in principle, you mean that you have not the slightest intention of carrying it out in practice. In practice there appeared to be no effective means by which these front-line states or the Organization for African Unity (OAU) or any other body could induce South Africa to change its system and its policy. Moreover, the priorities pursued by the black nations were, understandably enough, to provide themselves with some degree of economic prosperity and political security. Yet in the early 1980s there had been one or two encouraging signs. One was in Namibia, another in South Africa itself.

We can perhaps look back four years with satisfaction at the emergence of an independent Namibia in 1983, when the great difficulty of reconciling the contradictory positions of South Africa on the one hand and the South-West Africa People's Organization (SWAPO) on the other had at length been overcome by the tireless efforts of five Western powers – Britain, the United States,

Canada, France, and West Germany – known as the Western group. It will be remembered that UN Security Council Resolution 435 had in plain terms proposed a ceasefire that would be controlled by a United Nations force, followed by elections, also to be UN supervised, and then a proclamation of independence. South Africa's particular objection to this plan lay in what appeared to be general acceptance by most other African states and the UN as a whole that SWAPO was the sole representative of the Namibian people. In those circumstances the impartiality of the UN observers and supervisors could hardly, so South Africa claimed, be guaranteed. And if SWAPO was by such lack of impartiality to win a sweeping majority in the elections, what was to prevent it establishing a one-party socialist – in South African eyes, communist – state and so put southern Africa on the road to international communism? SWAPO itself favoured Resolution 435 proposals simply because of the freedom of intimidation that it might allow it and the consequent freedom for constitutional adjustments which a substantial victory would then give it. To bridge the gap between these two positions and to secure the confidence of the Namibian internal political parties, as well as of SWAPO, South Africa and the other African nations, the Western group presented their alternative plan in the latter part of 1981.

No proposal could have been equally liked by all parties concerned, but the new plan commanded sufficient support among those who were in a position to influence the waverers that it formed the basis for implementing Resolution 435. In essence this new plan was that the ceasefire would be followed by elections to a constituent assembly; this assembly would then be required to pass by a two-thirds majority a constitution; an election under the constitution would in turn open the way for independence itself. The system of government under the proposed constitution was to have three branches: an elected executive branch responsible to the legislature; a legislature elected by universal suffrage; and an independent judicial branch. The electoral system, being based on membership from both the constituencies and the parties, would ensure proper representation in the legislature to the various political groups among the Namibian people throughout the country. The constitution was also to contain a declaration of fundamental rights to guarantee personal, political and racial freedom.

Throughout the first part of 1982 international diplomacy at the United Nations and intensive negotiations in Africa itself gradually removed the obstacles to agreement to implement a revised UN plan which was finally reached at the 1982 Geneva conference. The wise statesmanship of Zimbabwe's Prime Minister did much to facilitate the finding of a solution to the vexed question of the ceasefire – who

NIGERIA

CAMEROON
• Yaoundé

CENTRAL AFRICAN
REPUBLIC

Bangui •

SUDAN

ETHIOPIA

SOMALIA

Fernando
Poó

EQUATORIAL
GUINEA
• Libreville

GABON

CONGO

Brazzaville •
• Kinshasa
ZAIRE-
CENTRAL
KINSHASA

• Luanda

Congo

EQUATEUR

HAUT-ZAIRE

ZAIRE

BANDUNDU

KASAI-
OCCIDENTAL

KASAI-
ORIENTAL

SHABA

UGANDA

Kampala •

RWANDA
KIVU
BURUNDI

Lake Victoria

• Mogadishu

KENYA

• Nairobi

TANZANIA

Dar es Salaam •

Zanzibar

ANGOLA

ZAMBIA

Lusaka •

MALAWI

Lilongwe •

Salisbury •

ZIMBABWE

Zambezi

MOZAMBIQUE

Mozambique Channel

MADAGASCAR

NAMIBIA

Windhoek •

BOTSWANA

Limpopo

Gaborone •

TRANSVAAL

Pretoria •

Johannesburg ◦

SWAZILAND

ORANGE
FREE S/
LESOTHO

CAPE

PROVINCE

SOUTH AFRICA

Maputo

Maputo

ZULULAND

Orange

NATAL

TRANSKEI

Durban

INDIAN OCEAN

Cape Town ◦

Cape of Good Hope

SOUTH ATLANTIC OCEAN

**Central and
Southern Africa**

0   Miles   600
0   Kilometres   800

would supervise it and where would South African and SWAPO
forces withdraw to? His proposals enjoyed the authority of experience and the attraction of simplicity. Broadly, an international force,
which would police both ceasefire and elections, would be drawn
from black and white Commonwealth countries (including Zimbabwe itself, Nigeria, Canada and New Zealand), Scandinavia, the
Philippines, Venezuela, Eire, Finland and Switzerland. They would
be commanded by an Indian general whose reputation for persua-
siveness, impartiality and common sense had been greatly enhanced
by his handling of previous peacekeeping operations. The camps to
which the opposing forces would withdraw, broadly in the north for
SWAPO and south for South African, were chosen with a view to
combining ease of monitoring and administration with inability to
intimidate or influence local opinion. Two sensitive and difficult
problems – first the actual methods of conducting and supervising
elections, second, the future integration of SWAPO troops with the
existing South-West Africa Police and Territory Force – were to be
handled roughly in the same way as had been so smoothly and
successfully done in Zimbabwe.

This was but one demonstration of how practical difficulties facing
those striving for a peaceful way forward were tackled. There were
many others. First and foremost was the future constitution itself, and
here the principal hurdle to be cleared was how to reconcile the
differing views of SWAPO and the Namibia National Party (which
had the largest support from the 100,000 Afrikaner population –
out of Namibia's total of roughly one million) backed by Pretoria.
Constitutional guarantees could mean different things to different
groups, and only safeguards of minority rights in which those concerned could believe were likely to satisfy the Namibia National Party
and the Democratic Turnhalle Alliance. None the less a constitutional conference to draft the basis of an independent Namibian
government convened at Geneva late in 1982, and the fact that it did
so had been brought about by a number of other agreements and
disagreements involving the United States, South Africa and the
black African nations, particularly Angola.

In a climate where moderation had begun to assume support which
it had formerly lacked, two immoderate lines of policy had fortunately lost credibility and been put aside. One was the attempt by the
African group in the United Nations to secure agreement for imposing economic sanctions on South Africa because of this country's
refusal to comply with the original plan under Resolution 435. The
move was blocked by the vetos of France, the United States and the
United Kingdom. More important was the realization by the African
group that only some accommodation with South Africa could in the

end lead to an independent Namibia – short of continuing the fight with infinitely greater resources, rather more success than had hitherto been achieved, and non-interference by the United States should this elusive success be sought by increasing Soviet or Soviet-proxy support.

With the idea of sanctions out of the way, progress could be made elsewhere. Notable here was the second abandonment of immoderation. At one time the United States had had the curious idea that a settlement in Namibia could be linked to a withdrawal of Cuban forces from Angola. Indeed one State Department paper had contained the extraordinary suggestion that African leaders would be unable to resist the Namibian-Angola linkage once they were made to realize that they could only get a Namibia settlement through the United States and that the US was in earnest about getting such a settlement. In this bizarre notion there was one element of realism. The African states did understand the importance of the US role in securing a settlement in Namibia, but it had little to do with Angola. It concerned essentially America's relationship with South Africa.

The persuasion which the US was enabled to apply to South Africa at the continued meetings between the former's Secretary of State and the latter's Prime Minister during the early months of 1982 did much to open the 'new chapter' of relations which the two countries were henceforth to establish and cement. The most immediate benefit from these meetings was that South Africa agreed to support the Western group's plan for an independent Namibia and undertook to ensure that Namibia's internal political parties would do so as well.

In parallel with this advance, the black African nations, led by Nigeria, Zimbabwe and Angola, were able to induce the leader of SWAPO that this Western plan – despite its constitutional guarantees for minorities – was the best, indeed at that time the only, basis for seeing to it that Namibia's future would be determined by himself and his organization. After all, they pointed out, if SWAPO was justified in its claim to be the sole representatives of the Namibian people, what had it to fear from requirements for multi-party democracy with elections at prescribed intervals, or from a bill of rights to protect minorities? Conditions relating to the non-expropriation of private property or guaranteed representation for whites in parliament need not be a deterrent. They had not deterred Zimbabwe. Better surely to go for the legitimate, albeit slow, path to ultimate black domination, as in Zimbabwe, than the more rapid, more dramatic, but still disputed triumphs of the Popular Movement for the Liberation of Angola (MPLA).

In Angola the position was still an unhappy one. Ill discipline, corruption, rivalry and inefficiency seemed to be the pattern there.

Shortcomings in the transport system alone seemed to make impossible the proper distribution of food. The war against South African forces had robbed the civil transport system of half its vehicles. UNITA (the National Union for the Total Independence of Angola) guerrillas further disrupted railways in the centre and south of the country. Ambushes by the Angolan National Liberation Front (FNLA) forces interfered with life in the north. If Angola were to climb out of its pit of incompetence and strife, it would hardly be by encouraging SWAPO to continue the fight against South Africa and pledging its support to that fight. Happily, the leader of SWAPO found these arguments convincing.

The Geneva conference on Namibian independence did bear fruit. A ceasefire was declared, supervised and honoured. Elections took place early the following year – with not unexpected results. It was true that SWAPO commanded a majority in the constituent assembly, but it was a slender majority. The strength of the other parties, in particular the Democratic Turnhalle Alliance and the Namibia National Party, were such that the two-thirds majority necessary to pass the new constitution ensured inclusion in it of the guarantees about which South Africa, the Afrikaners of Namibia and the Western group had shown such concern. And so to the world's mild astonishment and relief, 1983 saw the success story of Zimbabwe repeated in Namibia. As we shall see later, this success story was not to go on for very long. None the less, in 1983 there were other grounds for encouragement.

Progress in South Africa itself may have been less striking, but was significant in that there was progress at all. Apart from Pretoria's long declared intention of introducing a programme of gradual reform, a further reason for making some political concessions was growing confidence in South Africa's military strength through measures taken to counteract the insecurity which many South African whites had previously felt. These feelings were understandable. There were after all some 300 Soviet tanks in Mozambique together with the most sophisticated air defence weapons. Soviet, East German and Cuban advisers assisted with both manning equipment and training, and although Mozambique's armed forces were no more than 30,000 strong, they were becoming efficient both in their own right and in supporting guerrillas of the African National Congress (ANC).

Zimbabwe, which had signed a secret defence pact with Mozambique, had finally, after early setbacks, successfully integrated its regular and guerrilla forces and now commanded a well-equipped and well-trained Defence Force of 50,000 men greatly experienced in the very sort of fighting that would be appropriate to any confrontation with South Africa. Botswana's army was very small, a mere few thousand, but they too had taken delivery of Soviet tanks and other vehicles, weapons and ammunition. Angola had regular armed forces of roughly the same size as Mozambique – some 30,000 – and were supported by 20,000 Cuban, 3,000 East German and several hundred Soviet advisers. Between them they operated aircraft and heavy equipment, provided advice and training to the Angolan armed forces, and could if necessary be used in actual operations. Angola's Organization of Popular Defence backed this up with a paramilitary force of about half a million men.

Thus the conventional military strength on which the black front-line states could call was by no means insignificant. In the past, South Africa had attempted to safeguard both its internal and external security by punitive cross-border raids – notably from Namibia into Angola, to say nothing of raids on Maputo. While it was clear that South Africa's armed forces, with their superior numbers, equipment and training, could always produce local successes in cross-border raids, there was no question of their contemplating military operations to occupy a neighbouring country. Indeed these raids themselves were often conducted by non-South African black troops, led by white officers. The South African-led raids in Angola, for example, made use of former FNLA black Angolans who were opposed to the MPLA. They also supported UNITA forces to disrupt SWAPO guerrillas. Similarly, South Africa made use of members of the Mozambique National Resistance (MNR) for the raids on ANC guerrilla houses near Maputo. In Angola the raids disrupted the economy and served to demonstrate the penalties to be paid for harbouring anti-South African dissidents. In Mozambique they interfered with ANC guerrillas and made it plain to those who supported them that they could not do so with impunity. There had also been raids into Zambia and Zimbabwe before negotiations about Namibia's future began to be taken seriously. Even relatively harmless support given to refugees from South Africa in Botswana and Lesotho, neither of which countries had associated themselves with ANC military activities, did not go unpunished.

The South African Defence Force was substantial, mustering about half a million men, of which some 200,000 were actually under arms, and the remainder readily mobilizable. Apart from the regular forces and national servicemen, who made up between them about 100,000, there was a Citizen Force of 50,000 and local militia commandos of similar size. In addition, the South African police amounted to 40,000, with half that number again in reserve. It was essential that the loyalty of those under arms was beyond question, for the real threat to South Africa's security came from within.

The Marxist ANC was not the only black opposition group but it was certainly the most important. Much of its support came from Moscow. It had gained general international standing by both its discipline and its realism. Its military wing, *Umklonto we Sizwe*, could call on perhaps 10,000 trained guerrilla fighters, and although there were no ANC bases in South Africa itself, it did have within the country far-reaching political support from the black population and had established an underground network. Its guerrilla operations mainly involved industrial sabotage which was directed at targets such as the oil refineries and electrical power stations and grids in Cape Province, Natal and the Orange Free State. There were, however, those in the movement who favoured widening the range of targets to heighten feelings of insecurity among the whites and give pause to Western sources of either investment or participation in South Africa's economy.

Other opposition organizations – from which many defected to join the more powerful and effective ANC – included the South African Youth Revolutionary Council, which had a strong base in Botswana; the Black Consciousness Movement of Azania; and the Azania People's Organization, which had been particularly successful in controlling some of the new black trade unions and disrupting work at a number of international industrial concerns. The ANC were quick to applaud such activities. It regarded trade union action as a crucial force in the struggle for liberation, not least because it was able to engage in this struggle within the law.

Also within the law was the Inkhata, the largest black organization in South Africa, based in Zululand and headed by Chief Kwazulu. Kwazulu, a direct descendant of the great Zulu warrior King Cetewayo, had always been a controversial figure. Indeed to be denounced by Pretoria and the ANC yet remain on constructive speaking terms with both put him firmly in the centre of South African politics. However dangerous this ground might be, it did offer some hope of compromise in adjusting South Africa's constitution so that it corresponded more closely to the racial balance within the country.

Just as moderation and compromise had for the moment won the day in Namibia in the face of opposing extremes, so a comparable course was charted for non-violent change in South Africa itself. Kwazulu's proposals for power-sharing were in essence that the white-administered state of Natal and the neighbouring black homeland of the Zulus should be merged. Although the ANC had not hesitated in 1977 to condemn Kwazulu's acceptance of limited self-government, they found his new proposals more difficult to reject. Indeed they recognized that while urban black support for the ANC was still far greater than for Inkhata, an increasing number of ANC militants were joining Inkhata because, in their own words, 'It was the legitimate offspring of the ANC'. Implementing Kwazulu's proposals for Natal, with their emphasis on *black* power-sharing, might well be a preferable course of action to a war of liberation. No matter how wide the support for military action might be within the ANC itself and among young blacks elsewhere, fighting a full-scale war against the whites at that time could only result in a very large number of black deaths, further repression and continued white supremacy and apartheid for another generation.

However reasonable Kwazulu's proposals might be and however much the ANC might be prepared to wait and see, no progress towards reform was possible except by the ruling National Party itself. But in the elections of the early 1980s, the National Party had not received a mandate for reform. Indeed, the far more extreme Herstigte National Party had gained support although it had won no seats in parliament. Yet within the country there was a growing body of liberal support for a programme of gradual reform. It was because of this, together with South African undertakings to open a 'new chapter' of relations with the United States (which would bring great economic benefits to South Africa), that the Prime Minister determined to embark on a programme of reform in 1983. There were other reasons for not leaving it any later. He wished to exploit what goodwill might be forthcoming from the valuable progress that had been made over Namibia. He was also conscious that by the end of the century the white South African population could not possibly provide all the skilled workers that would be needed. Above all, the Prime Minister wished to avoid conflict.

He reconciled himself to the creation of a black middle class by training and education to fill higher posts in industry and government, to decentralized regional development to enhance the prosperity of the homelands, and to granting more political representation to non-whites in order to start a process of co-operation and consultation that would at length lead to responsible power-sharing. In this mood, he was at least prepared to consider what Chief Kwazulu had to propose. It was unfortunate that the Prime Minister's programme of *Verligtheid*, which could have led to genuine liberalism, was interrupted by the outbreak of war. The restraint so admirably exercised by the Arab states towards Israel was not displayed by the black front-line states in their actions against the Republic of South Africa. When war broke out the armies of Mozambique, Zimbabwe and Botswana, together with a largely SWAPO and Angolan force launched from Namibia, simultaneously invaded South Africa.*

---

* See Sir John Hackett and others, op. cit., pp. 266–76.

Their unwillingness to forgo an advantage put back a solution to the injustices of apartheid many years, and the solution when it came was accompanied by violence.

Violence was no stranger to the African scene, as we shall see if we examine what was happening elsewhere during the early 1980s. Much of this violence had occurred because Libya had attempted to set up a Saharan hegemony to incorporate Chad, Niger and the Sudan, and even to link up with Ethiopia, so that Egypt could be encircled and isolated. Fortunately for Libya, and indeed for that part of Africa as a whole, things did not develop exactly as the Libyan leadership had planned. In the first years of the 1980s, however, if revolutionary zeal, large oil revenues, weak, irresolute or distracted neighbours and unlimited arms supplies from the Soviet Union could be said to be the right ingredients for indulging insatiable ambition, Libya was clearly on to a good thing. Chad had an army of three infantry battalions and a few guns and mortars; Niger had an even smaller army, but was still rich in uranium; Sudan, it was true, had respectably sized armed forces, but many of them were deployed in the troublesome southern areas of the country and to the east near the border with Ethiopia, both to maintain security there and to keep an eye on Eritrean guerrillas. In any event, Sudan's 250 tanks and forty combat aircraft looked puny enough compared with Libya's estimated strength of 3,000 tanks and over 400 MiGs and *Mirages*. Moreover the air mobility lent to Libya's twenty-five battalions of infantry, Pan-African Legion and Moslem Youth by the transport squadrons of *Hercules* aircraft and over 100 troop-lifting helicopters would make easy the concentration of superior forces against Sudan.

Libya had soon recovered from the temporary setback in Chad at the beginning of 1982 when the OAU peacekeeping force had replaced its own troops there. The Libyan regime persuaded those who controlled the principal Arab tribes in Chad to form an uneasy alliance with the leader of the main rebel forces in the eastern provinces near the Sudanese frontier. Thus with two of the three private armies on its side, Libya was still able to deploy some of its own troops at Abéché and continue to harass the Sudanese, all with a view to subverting the rule of Sudan's President. This subversion was directed not only from Chad but also from Ethiopia. To the west of Chad, Libya's sponsorship of the Tuaregs had resulted in continued fighting between its so-called Islam legions and Niger's small army.

All these manoeuvrings, designed to isolate Egypt and create Libyan hegemony over the Sahara, were brought to an end in 1983 as a result of action against Libya by Egypt itself which removed the Libyan military regime once and for all. The effect of its fall was generally beneficial. Libyan troops, who had not relished the experience or the prospect of being hideously and agonizingly mutilated by the savage tribesmen of Niger and Chad, were allowed to return home to the far more agreeable duties of garrisoning their own country. The Sudan-Chad border quarrels were patched up and the border itself policed by OAU patrols. Niger settled down under its military ruler, looking to Algeria and France for further assistance both with its security and its economy – indeed Libya's interference there had facilitated some degree of rapprochement between these two countries. Sudan was able to concentrate more on its internal difficulties in the south, while keeping an eye on the activities of Ethiopia and further cementing good relations with Egypt. Somalia's position was strengthened, while the Egyptian-Libyan axis, as we have seen in the last chapter, helped to give great impetus to growing Arab unity and a peaceful settlement in Palestine.

The great game between the superpowers of reassuring both their friends and themselves that they could be relied upon in times of danger or tension was still much in evidence in Africa during 1983. The continuing exercises by the US Rapid Deployment Force were of some comfort to Somalia and Sudan and were answered by comparable Soviet manoeuvres in South Yemen and Ethiopia. Much more serious was the Soviet build-up of arms and advisers in Mozambique, Botswana and Angola; indeed support for the latter was so extensive that some of it was clearly destined for Namibia. By 1984 there were some 10,000 Cubans in Mozambique together with increased numbers of Soviet and East German advisers. Botswana had contented itself with accepting technical and tactical experts from these two countries to help with the training of its own gradually expanding army, but it had also established in the north-east a number of training camps for ANC guerrillas who were being equipped with Soviet-supplied small arms, rocket launchers and mortars, together with hand-held SAM. In Angola the number of Cubans and East Germans had roughly doubled. Apart from their traditional tasks of manning sophisticated equipment and training the Angolan armed forces, they were now also involved in welding a large number of former SWAPO guerrillas, who had taken refuge in Angola after the Namibian independence negotiations got under way, into an all-arms force of roughly brigade size for future use in Namibia. These ominous advances in the front-line states' conventional and guerrilla capability – coming as they did at a time when the National Party in South Africa was running into more difficulties with its reform programme and ANC industrial sabotage was on the increase – did not augur well for southern Africa.

Zimbabwe, on the other hand – and this was consistent with its positive initiatives over Namibia – remained ambivalent in its attitude towards the Soviet Union. There were perhaps two reasons for this. One was the closer economic ties which Zimbabwe continued to seek with the West; the other was its association with China. China was willing to back any movement that would advance the struggle against apartheid, yet at the same time it wished to check Soviet influence in southern Africa generally. Quite apart from its special relationship with Zimbabwe, China was also on friendly terms with Mozambique and Angola, offering them limited aid and exploiting the inevitable frustrations and restrictions caused by the Soviet and East German presence in the two countries. In Zambia and Tanzania, too, China was able to build on earlier friendly co-operation, while in Namibia it gave strong support to Western initiatives to bring about a settlement. Despite all China's friendliness, however, Soviet influence in southern Africa's black states remained paramount.

The same could not be said of west Africa. In 1981 Equatorial Guinea had rebuffed the Soviet Union's attempts to reinforce its footholds there and had, moreover, invited the country's former colonizers, Spain, to return and help with the re-organization of the army, the economy and constitution. The USSR had suffered comparable setbacks in two former Portuguese colonies, Guinea-Bissau and the Cape Verde Islands. France, meanwhile, felt able to swallow some of its socialist-inspired disapproval for the more despotic behaviour of dictatorships in French-speaking west Africa and pledged continued military and economic assistance to the Ivory Coast and the Central African Republic. Perhaps the most encouraging developments of all had been those in the western Sahara. The withdrawal of Libyan aid to the *Polisario*, continued Saudi Arabian economic props for Morocco, and the OAU's refusal to recognize the Saharan Arab Democratic Republic, all made for compromise, and a solution was at last agreed during 1983 between Morocco, Mauritania, Algeria, and the *Polisario* itself. The idea of a separate and independent Saharan state was abandoned, or at any rate postponed. Instead, federation with Mauritania of much of the disputed territory won the day.

Nigeria and Zaire were two other countries in Africa where Western anxiety for moderation and cohesion did much to reconcile them to the necessary price that had to be paid – substantial foreign loans to these countries. Nigeria's problem was one of reduced oil exports and thus revenues. This made the import of sufficient food, which constituted more than half of all imports, very difficult. A reduction in imports had in the past inflated prices disastrously. It was essential for the civilian government's success in the 1983 elections that there should be neither food shortages nor crises over prices. Its broad programme for alleviating these difficulties was a conventional one –

cuts in government spending, delay in satisfying creditors abroad, general austerity in federal and state allowances, abandonment of new projects. These measures alone were not sufficient, but combined with sensible progress towards a sound oil policy and proper loan guarantees they did much to make possible the necessary borrowing on the international market.

Zaire's political instability arose not only from the need for international monetary credit – indeed this need had been temporarily taken care of by the enormous IMF grant of $1 billion spread over three years. It had arisen from dissatisfaction with the former President's tyrannical methods and his inability to cure the unrest in Shaba and, worse, in Kivu where the Parti Revolutionnaire Populaire pursued its guerrilla campaign against central authority. The new President, however, was able to reassure both the President of France and Belgium's Prime Minister to the extent that they felt able to co-operate more fully both militarily and economically.

Thus, as the United States and the Soviet Union moved towards war during the latter part of 1984 and the early months of 1985, the greatest danger of this war's being waged by proxy in Africa was not in the Arab countries of the north-east, nor in the Sahara, nor west Africa, not even in the relatively stable centre and east. It was in the Horn of Africa and in the south. In the event, as we saw in chapter 17, the Horn of Africa was partly neutralized by the astonishing speed and force with which the United States and its allies strengthened their position in Egypt, the Red Sea and the Gulf. South Yemen was contained by naval action, and by powerful deterrence from North Yemen and Oman. In a similar way Ethiopia was contained by United States military reinforcement of Somalia and Sudan. The fighting in southern Africa, however, was prolonged and savage. It has been described in some detail in a previous book* and it is not intended to reiterate here either an account of the military operations or of the gradual withdrawal of black African forces and ANC guerrillas from South Africa. Nor need we concern ourselves with the immense United Nations activities which dealt with the problems of relief, reconstruction and repatriation, although it should be noted that the Cubans, the East Germans and what remained of the Soviet advisers were repatriated, in many cases after lengthy hospitality from South African 'camps' which made the treatment they were subjected to by their own countrymen, when they did return, less disagreeable than it might otherwise have been. What does command our attention now is the effect that war in southern Africa had on the central problem itself – the future of the Republic of South Africa.

---

* ibid., pp. 266–76.

One result of the brief but cataclysmic war between the Warsaw Pact and NATO was that it prolonged, with results whose severity and disruption have yet fully to be seen, the unjust and oppressive regime based on white supremacy in South Africa. It seemed that during the early days of recovery from this last world war, South Africa's leaders – faced with all the pressures for and against reform, some internal, some external – chose to risk the mounting black discontent and violence for the sake of white control. When war came, the activities of the front-line states' armies, together with ANC guerrillas, did little to endear the Afrikaners to their northern neighbours, except in so far that the South African Defence Force's eventual successes in holding on and beating back all invaders strengthened conviction in their own supremacy. Indeed the poor showing of the ANC guerrillas when it came to actual battle reinforced the views of hard-line Afrikaan leaders that they would be able to perpetuate their own political dominance. White control was something they understood and thought they knew how to deal with. The consequences of a programme of reform and reconstruction were not understood and were as a result feared and shunned. There had been ample grounds for misgiving even before the war began. In Namibia constitutional government had been overthrown in 1985 and SWAPO dictatorship established. In Zimbabwe gradual decline from democratic practices had been more or less completed in the same year; Botswana's greatly enhanced support for both foreign and ANC revolutionary militants had simply ensured the misery of its own people; and Mozambique had seemed helpless in trying to escape from the contradictory grips of communist mercenaries and national resistance movements.

There may have been one or two unexpected dividends in South Africa for those who advocated a policy of gradual reform and power-sharing. One was the revulsion felt by black and white South Africans alike at the indiscriminate bloodlust shown by some of the ANC guerrillas during the transitory and haphazard instances when unarmed civilians were at their mercy. Another was the stand taken by black homeland units, like the Transkeian Defence Force, the Bophuthatswana National Guard and, most notably, by the Inkhata Army, which so furiously and successfully resisted the Cuban and Mozambique attempts to invade the Zulu homelands. Yet examples like this of loyalty to the Republic did little or nothing to reconcile those who had previously questioned the principle of liberal reform to a new initiative for a *verligte* policy. On the contrary, there was an even greater swing to the *verkrampte* line advocating the exploitation of South Africa's economic hold in terms of food, transport, technology and goods, over its neighbouring black countries, so creating a kind of buffer between white supremacy and the ANC, and abandoning the reformist schemes that had raised so much hope in the early 1980s.

The policy of black homelands would continue. The so-called independent nation states would continue to be totally dependent on Pretoria financially, economically, administratively. The multi-racial President's Council which had formerly been used as machinery for introducing constitutional reforms, was dismantled. There would be no question of a single, racially-mixed parliament. Ethnic 'self-determination' would be maintained. There was to be no limited franchise system for regional councils and no question of any coloureds or Indians – let alone blacks – in a central legislative body. There was to be a clear division of power between the various racial groups. In short, apartheid was there to stay. *Also sprach* the Herstigte National Party.

Thus South Africa set itself on the path of blood, violence and revolution. Argument as to the future of that country has inevitably been taken up once more by all those who disagreed: the black front-line states as they begin to recover some degree of political, economic and military cohesion; the ANC in exile, together with all the other black revolutionary movements; the trade unions within South Africa itself; almost all the rest of black Africa with their support in arms, agents and money; the Third World in general. And unless, by the sort of diplomatic activity in the United Nations and elsewhere that made possible a peaceful Middle East solution, a way can be found to put such intolerable pressure on Pretoria that wiser counsels prevail, South Africa will find that the injustices of apartheid are corrected on a far bloodier battlefield than ever it saw during the short-lived Third World War.

Chapter 19

The Far East

The collapse of colonialism in South-East Asia, where three empires, British, French and Dutch, had sprawled untidily over the map, left the area without regional coherence in a clear need for it. The fall of Saigon in 1975, at the end of the second Indochinese war, marked the end of the brief period of American dominance and, apparently, of external intervention. The United States, scarred by the internal divisions caused by the costly and ultimately unsuccessful war in Vietnam, turned with huge relief away from the commitment of American troops on land in South-East Asia towards a purely maritime strategy for the region, based on the islands and island states of the Pacific.

There was a price to pay for this: it was no longer possible to exercise influence over events on land in the area. Governments were toppled or put in place by small, hard, wiry men crossing land frontiers, not by the actions of ships at sea or by unscrewing the nose cones of missiles. This had to be accepted. Domestic politics would stand nothing more. This was not to say that the United States was leaving Asia. Far from it; the US had every intention of remaining a power in the Pacific basin, the fastest growing economic area in the world. America's centre of gravity, however, would henceforward be in North-East Asia, built around the security link with Japan and, as it turned out later, a growing understanding with China. The naval and air bases in the Philippines would still be needed for US maritime strategy. Washington hastened to renew the leases for them. Manila was initially hesitant, not merely to drive a hard bargain but because the waning of American strength and influence was creating a climate of caution. But Vietnamese actions in Indochina soon put an end to regional hopes for stability and the other ASEAN (Association of South-East Asian Nations) states pressed the Philippines to sign, to enable the United States to keep a strong military presence in the area. South-East Asia was looking to Washington once more; the countries needed powerful friends again. In January 1979 the new agreements for American use of the Philippine bases were concluded.

It was the men in Hanoi that brought all this about. The North Vietnamese had emerged in heroic guise from the longest and bloodiest war of independence that South-East Asia had seen, unifying a country which now had military power far greater than its neighbours, allied to a fanatical determination to go on using it if need be, regardless of the opposition. In the aftermath of the war the ASEAN hope was that the Vietnamese energies would be channelled into uniting the hitherto divided nation and into rebuilding the war-torn economy. The fear was that communist or nationalist fervour would prevail instead, with Hanoi pursuing the aim of controlling the whole of Indochina, the long-held ambition of Ho Chi Minh. And then what? Further into South-East Asia?

The ASEAN leaders put out friendly feelers, making clear their desire for stability and their willingness to encourage and help with economic consolidation. Japan offered economic aid to Hanoi. This was perhaps the best way of drawing Vietnam towards peace and the West and away from the Soviet Union, now Hanoi's principal patron. The United States was unhappy at the idea of rewarding the intransigent in this way, at least so soon, but itself none the less conducted discreet negotiations with Hanoi to pave the way towards normal relations when the wounds had healed a little. Vietnam seemed willing to contemplate this, but all stopped when in November 1978 it concluded a treaty with the Soviet Union and shortly afterwards invaded Kampuchea (Cambodia), overthrowing the admittedly hateful and genocidal regime of Pol Pot and installing its own puppet, Heng Samrin.

Conflict in South-East Asia had thus broken out again, heavily supported, indeed only made possible, by the military assistance given to Vietnam by the Soviet Union. China, traditionally sensitive to Vietnamese ambitions, soon reacted in support of Pol Pot and in February 1979 briefly invaded Vietnam. While this attack certainly exposed China's military inadequacies, not least to Peking, it none the less imposed great costs on Hanoi, drawing a large part of Vietnamese military strength northwards to the frontier regions, where it was tied thereafter by the threat of renewed hostilities.

Thailand, faced with the insurgent activities of the ousted Pol Pot supporters spilling over the common border with Kampuchea, turned to the United States for aid and was promptly given military supplies. The ASEAN nations banded together against the Vietnamese and Soviet expansionism and turned to the world outside for support and in particular for help with the flood of refugees that had begun to pour out of Indochina. Most of all they looked to Washington, as the power in the area best able to counter the military strength of the Soviet Union. Thus the United States became once more politically involved

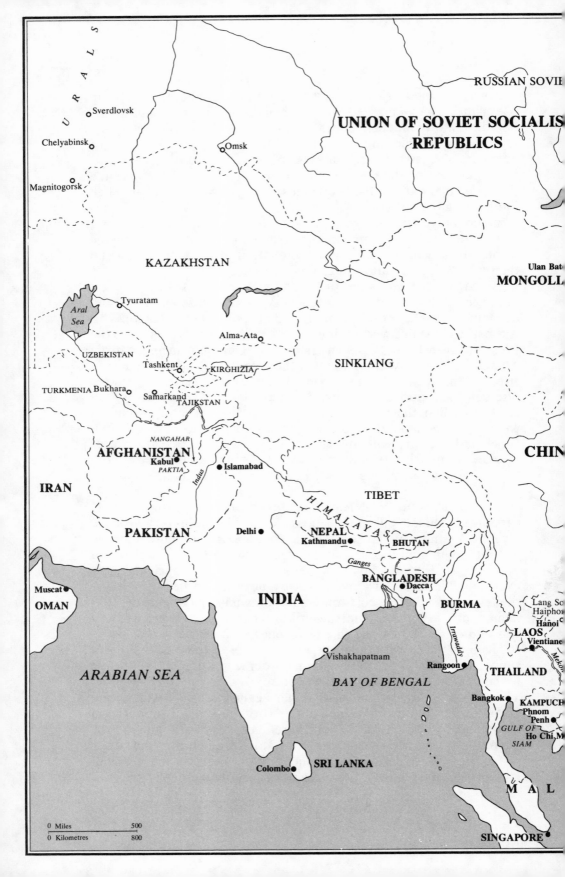

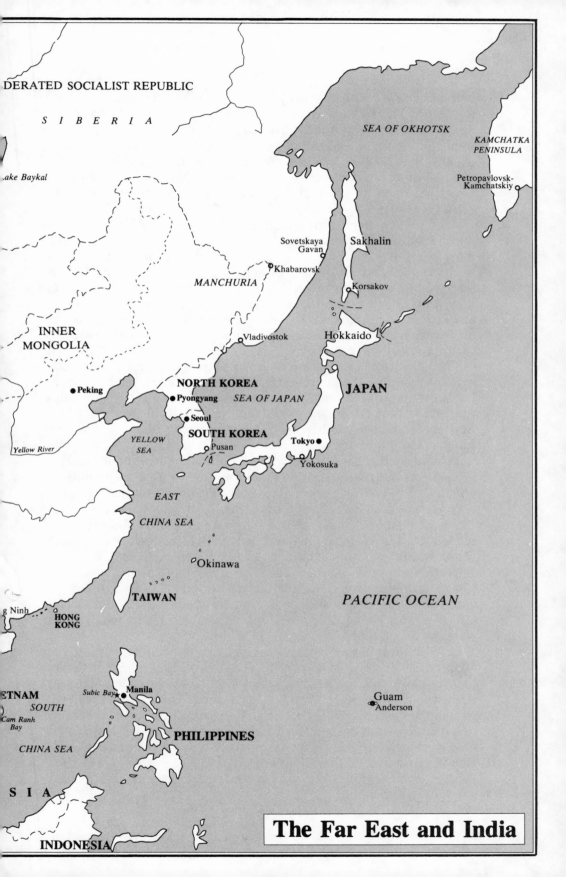

DERATED SOCIALIST REPUBLIC

S I B E R I A

Lake Baykal

SEA OF OKHOTSK

*KAMCHATKA
PENINSULA*

Petropavlovsk-
Kamchatskiy ○

Sovetskaya
Gavan ○

Khabarovsk ○

MANCHURIA

Sakhalin

Korsakov ○

**INNER
MONGOLIA**

Vladivostok ○

Hokkaido

● Peking

NORTH KOREA

● Pyongyang *SEA OF JAPAN*

JAPAN

● Seoul

SOUTH KOREA

*YELLOW
SEA*

Tokyo ●

○ Pusan

Yokosuka ○

Yellow River

*EAST

CHINA SEA*

Okinawa ○

PACIFIC OCEAN

TAIWAN

g Ninh

**HONG
KONG**

ETNAM

SOUTH

Subic Bay ★ ● **Manila**

Guam
Anderson

*Cam Ranh
Bay*

CHINA SEA

PHILIPPINES

S I A

INDONESIA

The Far East and India

in the region, only a few short years after leaving Vietnam. This time it was not for the containment of China, the original focus of US South-East Asian commitments. Rapprochement with Peking had removed the need for that. Now it was Soviet military activity and expansion that had to be checked. Soviet policies in South-East Asia were all of a piece with its activities elsewhere in the Third World – assertive, opportunist, anti-Western, anti-Chinese; in short, pro-Soviet and with a traditionally Russian flavour to boot.

ASEAN, the association which brought together Malaysia, Singapore, Thailand, Indonesia and the Philippines, had for long been the most promising grouping yet seen in the region, though its purposes were primarily political and economic. Each of the members had its own security problems or preoccupations, some of them severe, but they were of a separate nature. Collectively they did not recognize any external threat to their security and since there was no consensus on security, nor apparently any particular urgency, there was no security structure in ASEAN.

The area ASEAN covered had some strategic significance, however, not only for the energy sources and raw materials it contained, but for its importance as a waterway. Among the hundred or so ships that were passing through the Malacca Strait daily in the early 1980s were those that carried the bulk of Japan's imports of oil and iron ore. For the United States and for the Soviet Union the waterway was important as the passage between the Pacific and Indian Oceans. Access to trade with the region and the preservation of stability to enable this to continue seemed to offer a common interest to all the powers, and the Soviet Union in particular was at pains in the later 1970s to woo the ASEAN states – after initially being ill-disposed to recognize the organization – and to seek closer links. For a time Moscow touted a proposal for an Asian Collective Security Pact, but since this was transparently aimed at opposing China it found no takers in an area conscious that it had to find some way of getting along with that huge and unpredictable country. Yet the Soviet Union was also determined to support Vietnam and the two policies were not compatible.

ASEAN drew away from the Soviet Union, sharply so after the Vietnamese invasion of Kampuchea, and some of its members began to forge closer links with China. The Soviet Union became isolated in Asia, its only allies being Vietnam and a North Korea that was careful to maintain links with China as well. Soviet forces did, however, reap the benefit of the support for Hanoi, in the form of air and naval bases in Vietnam. The Soviet navy began to make use of Cam Ranh Bay in particular, admirably placed halfway between the Far East Fleet and the Soviet naval force in the Indian Ocean, and affording surveillance over the activities of the US Seventh Fleet in the south Pacific.

It was almost inevitable that ASEAN would, under the new circumstances that were unfolding, pay more attention to security concerns. By 1980 the military expenditures of the member states had risen to $5.47 billion, 45 per cent more than the year before and a near doubling compared with 1975. Thailand, dangerously close to Vietnamese military activity in Kampuchea, was already devoting 20 per cent of its budget to military purposes. All were buying modern weapons, with Singapore, Malaysia and Thailand acquiring new tanks, indicating a readiness to resist any incursions by Vietnam. An interesting feature was the growing adoption of American weapons. All the countries operated one model or another of the F-5 *Tiger* fighter and the A-4 *Skyhawk* fighter-bomber. The US M-16 assault rifle was the standardized personal arm. American military advisers were in many countries, and ASEAN officers trained in hundreds in the United States. American military aid to ASEAN members went up by 250 per cent to some $7.5 million in the five years up to 1980 and was to more than double in the four years after that.

There were military links with other countries too. Indonesia, as an island chain, concentrated largely on sea and air forces, buying in 1980 three missile corvettes from the Netherlands, four missile ships from South Korea and two submarines from West Germany, together with fighter aircraft from Britain as well as from the United States. Malaysia bought frigates from Germany and mine counter-measures vessels from Italy. Military facilities were expanded too, notably in Malaysia. A new air base was built in Kelantan state, facing the Gulf of Siam, which became operative in 1983. A new naval port was also built in Perak state on the Strait of Malacca, which opened in 1984.

So ASEAN military strength grew with the heightened awareness of the need for it, and with this the transformation towards a military grouping slowly developed. Staff talks, with shared exercises and intelligence, paved the way militarily. Thailand, most threatened, and Singapore, most conservative and realistic, led the way politically, with Malaysia coming along more slowly. Indonesia had a special reluctance to draw nearer to China, remembering past Chinese involvement in the activities of the Indonesian Communist Party – which were, it must be said, brutally put down. But no country was quite sure about Chinese aims; after all, Peking would not renounce support for communist elements in South-East Asia despite its wish to be on good terms with governments. As an overtly communist state aspiring to the leadership of the Third World, perhaps such a renunciation was simply not thinkable to the ideologically pure in Peking, even if their more pragmatic colleagues saw that other things were much more important for the time being.

By early 1985, ASEAN, after feeling its way for some time, had become a reluctant but none the less real military alliance. The struggle in Indochina had in the meantime been continuing, with various insurgent factions managing to survive, even to prosper, on the strength of arms and other help reaching them from China via Thailand. Vietnam had something like 250,000 men tied down by Kampuchean guerrillas and more men were occupied trying to maintain control of Laos, where again China was giving active help. There were constant clashes with Chinese troops along the common border, which suited Peking very well since it locked up large numbers of the best Vietnamese troops and prevented them from being used against the Kampucheans and Laotians.

In short, Vietnam was bogged down. The economic strain was huge and Moscow, angry at Hanoi's total unwillingness not only to listen to advice but even to accept that it might be needed, began to keep it on short supplies as a means of applying leverage. Military material was carefully rationed on one excuse or another; spare parts for the almost entirely Soviet-made equipment were limited and slow in arriving. The Soviet Union had become disenchanted with the lack of success of the South-East Asian venture and was alarmed at the way ASEAN had now banded itself together in open opposition. It is possible, just possible, that Soviet pressure might eventually have forced some compromise or change of course on Hanoi, on the hard-faced leadership there which had known no other life but that of armed struggle to attain its own ends. But war now broke out in Europe. Soviet supplies almost instantly dried up; Soviet forces left; the ships in Cam Ranh Bay scurried off. The whole political scene changed dramatically.

When war came to Europe, the nations in Asia were immediately fearful that it would come there too, for surely the conflict would spread around the world. American and Soviet warships both put to sea at once. Merchant vessels made for the nearest safe port. Defences everywhere went on the alert. Diplomats worked feverishly. Nobody knew quite what to expect. They simply feared the worst, as people will.

The Soviet Union faced the most difficult problems. Though Europe was the primary theatre, the vital one in which the war against the Western Alliance would be won or lost, the Soviet Union had to remain fully on guard in Asia too. There it was confronted by China, an implacable enemy whose military strength had steadily been improving. Chinese weapon systems and formations were no match for those of the Soviet forces but their numbers were huge. The Soviet

Union, accustomed to using men in mass, found it profoundly disturbing to face vastly superior masses. The thinly populated Soviet Far Eastern territories were vulnerable to long-term Chinese expansionism and Moscow was not a little aware of the political and cultural appeal that China might exert, if things went badly for the Soviet Union, on the peoples of the Soviet Asian republics.

Soviet foreign policy in Asia had long been dominated by the need to contain China. Since 1969 strong forces had been built up along the 4,000-mile border, amounting to almost a quarter of the Red Army, around fifty divisions in all. They were there simply to defend the border, to prevent China from altering it by force (it was disputed in many places) and to see that if fighting did break out the Soviet Union would get the better of it. There was no intention of using them to mount an invasion of China: that would be to fight the way Peking wanted it. The Chinese would welcome the chance to draw an attacker deep into their often brutally inhospitable country and then wear him down with an inexhaustible supply of hardy defenders. That was not Moscow's idea at all.

There was the United States to worry about as well. The US Seventh Fleet had recovered considerably from a low point after the Vietnam war and had now built up its strength once more. It had the advantage of being able to operate from forward bases in the western Pacific, giving it a flexibility that the Soviet Pacific Fleet with its own limited bases and virtually no allies did not have. The new US *Trident* II submarines were now able to operate from waters near the US west coast, forcing Soviet attack submarines to deploy over considerable distances to try to counter them. The United States also had allies, notably Japan, whose forces were now quite strong.

It was very much the fault of the Soviet Union that Japan had in the late 1970s and early 1980s begun to change its security policy. As Soviet military strength in the Far East increased it was impossible in Japan to ignore its presence. Soviet garrisons were built up in the Northern Islands which Japan claimed as her own; Soviet aircraft infringed Japanese airspace; Soviet naval activity was prominent. Overt Soviet support for Vietnam and markedly insensitive Soviet diplomacy towards Tokyo in the wake of the Sino-Japanese Peace Treaty of August 1978, an obvious sign of displeasure, created in Japan a distinct awareness that the world around it was no longer benign. Public consent for an increase in defence spending, so grudgingly given in the past, slowly emerged. A programme of modernization was started, notably in the maritime and air self-defence forces, which quickly picked up speed, aided by the ability of Japanese industry to deliver the goods. A sense of nationalism, of being under threat, began to take over. As always in Japan, when a consensus had been formed, change was swift. The maritime self-defence force acquired an anti-ship capacity and took over sea control of the Sea of Japan and out into the open sea lanes, freeing the US Navy for offensive tasks. The air self-defence force, re-equipped with F-15 *Eagle* interceptors and with new air-to-surface and air-to-air missiles, and with AWACS and new radars as well, was able to take over the defence of Japanese airspace and give support to naval vessels. Again, US aircraft were freed for offensive tasks.

By late 1984, when acute East-West tensions were inexorably leading to world war, the strategic setting in Asia was not at all in the Soviet favour, despite her own force expansion. While the Soviet leaders could feel with some reason that events in the Middle East and Africa were moving their way and could feel confident about the outcome of a war in Europe, about Asia they had real doubts. Soviet strategy was therefore plain: try to keep the region quiet. China and Japan must be persuaded that it was in their interest to keep out of any war between the Soviet Union and the United States. If that did not prove to be possible, China would have to be contained until the war in Europe was won. It could then be dealt with, and harshly. But at all costs there must be no war on two fronts.

Moscow was, on the other hand, more than happy to have the United States involved in such a difficulty. At some quite early point in 1985 – just when is not quite clear – a Soviet emissary went to North Korea to press the leadership there to be ready to take, at the least, some military action against the South, at best to launch a full-scale war at the right moment. The idea was an ingenious one. It would draw US forces to Korea, men who might otherwise go to the Gulf or Europe. The US Navy would have to get their equipment there, which would hamper its operations in the Indian Ocean. A large number of US aircraft would be tied down in Korea and Japan. As a bonus it would present China with a dilemma: should it give help to North Korea, a communist state and an old ally, but at the cost of opposing the United States and thus indirectly aiding the Soviet Union; or refuse help, in which case North Korea would become a Soviet client? Japan, too, would have to decide whether to allow the United States unfettered use of bases in Japan. If it did and China helped North Korea, that would set Japan and China at odds with each other, which would be good for the Soviet Union. If Japan refused to allow use of the bases this would cripple US support of South Korea and split the United States and Japan. All in all, the Soviet Union had much to gain if trouble could be started in the Korean peninsula.

Peking, however, had highly-placed friends in Pyongyang, where reasons of ideology and personal ambition promoted factions that gave their support, open or hidden, either to the Soviet Union or China and not always consistently at that. The Chinese leaders got wind of the initiative and had no intention of allowing events to develop as Moscow planned. A very senior member of the Politburo and, just as important, the Deputy Chairman (a general) of the Chinese Communist Party (CCP) Central Committee's Military Affairs Committee (the supreme military command) went with him. Quietly but very firmly the North Koreans were told that if they started a war at this particular juncture there would be no Chinese 'volunteers' this time; they would be on their own.* Both knew there would be no Soviet assistance beyond a few weapons; Soviet troops would be too busy looking after their own security on the Chinese border and elsewhere.

This blunt warning, impressed not only on the politicians in Pyongyang but also on the North Korean generals, many of them known personally to the Chinese general from the Military Affairs Committee through their service together in the Korean War of 1950–3, seems to have gone home. At all events, North Korea did very little when the time came, mounting just a few minor raids. The North was clearly not going to risk the enmity of a growing China, just as China was not going to risk having Pyongyang fall into unfriendly hands; North Korean territory was too close to Manchuria for that. Perhaps also the North thought the time was not appropriate anyway; after all, the emissaries had been careful during the talks not to rule out action later on, when circumstances might be more suitable. Better wait and see how the Soviets got on first.

The raids, principally with light naval units, did cause the Americans and the Japanese some alarm since it was not quite clear at the time whether they presaged something bigger. The South Koreans, of course, mobilized completely and appealed to Washington, describing the threat in their usual rather dramatic terms. Washington was not so sure about things, but did send two fighter squadrons, to comfort Tokyo. Preparations were made to move some ground forces to the peninsula but the Soviet Union collapsed before they arrived and the men were in the event sent instead to Vladivostok to supervise the surrender of some of the Soviet forces in the Far East.

Just as the Soviet Union wanted to avoid full-scale war in Asia, so did the United States; they both had their hands full elsewhere. China did not want it either, and was not ready for it unless the Soviet Union emerged from the war very much weaker, in which case China might well be tempted into taking advantage, in the Marxist jargon, of the

---

* See the article by defecting North Korean Ambassador, Kim Kwon-sang, in the *Dong a Ilbo* of 31 October 1985 (Seoul, South Korea).

new correlation of forces. Japan did not want war at all, despite its
new foreign policy direction. To its relief it saw the danger approach
and then happily recede, though its new strength left it able to throw
useful weight into the Western side of the scale had it been needed.
Japan also took the opportunity later of profiting from the Soviet fall.

Asia, then, saw much tension but no global East-West war. What
fighting there was largely took place out in the Pacific and something
of this has already been described in Chapter 13. The Soviet Pacific
Fleet had put to sea, under the guise of one of its regular exercises,
before fighting in Europe erupted. It was shadowed by American and
Japanese warships and aircraft, and the submarines of both sides
stalked each other. Soviet aircraft maintained their usual surveillance
over south China and Soviet ships were active in and around Vietnamese waters. But that was before the war in Europe started. When
it did start they all left. Vietnam would have to look after itself for a
while. There were naval actions between Soviet and US naval units
but not many. Perhaps the war went too fast for that; both navies had
intense preoccupations in other theatres. Japanese ships were
involved in one minor action, when a Japanese escort group north of
the Tsushima Islands was fired on by an unidentified fast-patrol boat,
later known to have been part of a small North Korean force returning from a lightning raid on Pusan in South Korea. The missile – a *Styx*
– was intercepted and the Japanese destroyer, commanded by one
Captain Noda, a lively and aggressive officer, fired back with one of
the new Japanese-built missiles. Like many another piece of Japanese
equipment, it worked splendidly. The radar showed a hit and the
target disappeared. This was the first shot fired in action by the
maritime self-defence force and, as it turned out, the only one of the
war.

In the Korean peninsula nothing much happened, despite the
heavy concentration of troops there. The North Korean decision to
pay more attention to Peking than to Moscow proved a canny one,
and its minor forays produced little more than defensive actions by
South Korean forces, who were discouraged by the United States
from any wish they might have had to upgrade the fighting. While
Seoul and Washington had both heard of the warning given by China
to the North (through confidential information gleaned at the time by
the US Ambassador in Peking) they were aware that the Chinese
attitude might well be different if major war were launched by the
South.

So the clash between East and West did not spread to Asia as the
countries of the region had feared. But that did not mean that nothing
happened there. Far from it: a lot of what might be called tidying up
went on. The breakdown of authority in the Soviet Union provided a

heaven-sent (so to speak) opportunity for putting right a few wrongs and settling old scores.

The first of these was in Indochina. The drawn-out struggle there had been going badly for Hanoi, as has already been described. Soviet supplies had been thinning out and when the war in Europe started they stopped altogether. The Soviet advisers, who had already concentrated in Haiphong for their annual indoctrination and conference found themselves conveniently placed to leave for a safer place on 3 August. It is thought that they did this on the *Ivan Rogov*, the large amphibious ship usually stationed there. The *Ivan Rogov* was sunk a few days later, along with one of its escorts, by a US attack submarine. The submarine's elated skipper, Commander David Redfern, had long been waiting for such an opportunity and had worked hard for it, helped, it must be said, by a patient patrol aircraft working with him, which unfortunately did not survive the action.

In Peking the Politburo and the Military Affairs Committee had been in almost continuous session since early August. Daily they had argued, often heatedly, over the merits of a variety of actions that might extract some profit from the war between the superpowers. They had discussed what could be done to encourage the Kazakh unrest in the Soviet Union, of which they were getting news, not least from the Kazakhs on their own side of the border. They decided eventually to order large-scale military exercises on the border, but that was not until Kazakhstan had seceded from the Soviet Union after the destruction of Minsk by nuclear attack on 20 August. Manoeuvres were ordered at the same time, on the border with Uzbekistan, in both cases to dissuade the Soviet Union from launching punitive action. Exercises on a smaller scale were also set in train in Manchuria, but with caution. The Chinese were conscious of their military weakness, in Manchuria above all. They decided on a course of prudence, to wait and see what events brought. In relation to Mongolia, however, they thought it worthwhile to send some very tough messages, making it distinctly clear that the time had come, in their view, for the Mongolian leaders to invite the Soviet divisions there to go home. If they did not, it was gently hinted, life might later prove very uncomfortable indeed for those leaders when the Sinic peoples inevitably drew together again.

Vietnam seemed to offer a more immediate chance of doing something that would be to Chinese advantage. Mei Feng, the aged but experienced Chairman of the Military Affairs Committee, had no doubts. China had learned from the abortive invasion in 1979. The People's Liberation Army (PLA) was in much better shape now, but the Vietnamese were not. Mei Feng's view was that Chinese forces should go in, and this time as far as Hanoi. Once they were in control there, the Soviet Union would be unable to dislodge them, even if it won the war. The rainy season should not deter them; it would hinder the enemy aircraft and armour but the Chinese soldiers could manage all right, they would take to it like Peking ducks to water.

Mei Feng's counsel prevailed. A Chinese attack on Vietnam, long prepared and needing only the signal, was launched on 19 August, with the PLA itching to show the results of the change of leadership, training and tactics that had gone right through the Chinese Main Force divisions since 1979. The invasion, for that is what it was, followed something like the pattern of February 1979, for the PLA was still tied to some extent to its old thought processes and beliefs, except that forces went in through Laos as well. The aim of this was to split the defenders and force them to divide their resources among a number of fronts, any one of which could develop into something bigger. And, of course, messages had gone out to the Laotian insurgents, with whom Chinese 'advisers' had been working, and to the various factions fighting the Vietnamese in Kampuchea. It was not a model of co-ordination but under the conditions of insurgent fighting in the jungles this was hardly to be expected. The transistor radios carried by guerrilla groups crackled out the message that China had attacked and within a day or two all the various fronts, if such a term can be applied to actions varying from ambushes to divisional attacks, burst into life.

This time the PLA made rapid progress at the outset. It seems that something like twelve divisions were used in the opening assault, which was launched against the fortified Vietnamese positions and defences along the length of the border and through the jungles of Laos as well. Then the attack bogged down for a time as the regular Vietnamese formations moved in to support the largely local defences that the PLA had broken through at considerable cost. By this time Birmingham and Minsk had been destroyed followed by the swift crumbling of the Soviet empire. Some sort of description of these events would have gone out on Chinese radio, though it may not have meant very much to the wet and weary peasants who formed the bulk of those fighting on both sides in Vietnam. The news spread like wildfire through Hanoi, though, as it did through the cities of ASEAN. The men in the Vietnamese front line – and the women too, since they shared in the fighting that had occupied most of their disturbed lives – may not have taken much notice of the news, but the Vietnamese leaders certainly did. The pro-Peking faction which had always existed under the surface began to show itself, as personal survival came to depend again on backing the right horse. Now there was clearly only one horse to back, for the time being at least. And the sooner the bet was placed the better.

The Vietnamese Politburo had no doubt been in session all this time but it has recently become clear that the hard-liners who had held power for some years, since the conclusion of the treaty with the Soviet Union in 1978, had slowly been losing it. Ample accounts have come out via Peking of the activities of the pro-Chinese elements in the Vietnamese leadership, subdued for some years but never absent. Now, it seems, their influence began to be exerted, first among the few southerners still in responsible positions, then among the military. The battle was going badly and, of course, all hope of Soviet support was lost. There was a coup, aided, it is thought, by a 'heart attack' or two – a terminal illness when caused by a bullet in the right place. Within days negotiations with China were taking place through intermediaries, almost all of whom were pro-Peking Vietnamese returned from exile.

As is now known, the fighting stopped when the PLA was on the point of breaking through at Lang Son and Quang Ninh, ready for a drive with fresh divisions astride Routes 1 and 18 towards Hanoi and Haiphong. A new government was installed – or installed itself, as is the way in such circumstances – and a formal ceasefire was concluded shortly afterwards. This was not all plain sailing; China not only wished to see the Vietnamese divisions totally disarmed but also to see them hand over their equipment to the PLA at once. Peking made it clear, too, that Vietnamese forces were to withdraw from Kampuchea and Laos. The new administration in Hanoi was more than happy to agree to most of this but wanted it done in an orderly fashion, handing over to responsible elements. The hand-over of weapons posed a problem but this was solved by allowing Vietnamese forces to retain certain of them, to enable the new leaders to secure their position against disgruntled pro-Moscow dissidents. Heavy equipment was centralized under Chinese guard and later moved to China by the PLA, though some weapons in the south of the country undoubtedly fell into the eager hands of groups in Kampuchea. A provisional government was set up in Kampuchea, from factions broadly acceptable both to China and to the ASEAN states, and at ASEAN instigation a conference was called (which did not meet for some months because of disagreement over who the potential leaders of a new regime would be) to nominate a new government that would have international backing.

So ended what was, from the Chinese point of view, a satisfactory interlude. Militarily a little messy, it was politically uncomplicated, neatly achieving the aim of removing Soviet influence from Vietnam. It produced a government there that was, on the face of it, likely to be in harmony with Peking, at least for the time being. Since there had been friction between Vietnam and China for 1,000 years, erupting into conflict from time to time, it was perhaps too much to expect harmony in a few short weeks – or to expect it to last. The ASEAN states were relieved at the changes, since the new men in Hanoi promised to turn to peaceful activities. And as we write in 1987, so it has turned out. There has been stability, even in Kampuchea, helped, fortunately, by some good harvests and generous aid from around the world. Perhaps this will endure and the example of the prosperity of the states in the Pacific basin spread to the whole of South-East Asia. One can but hope so. The signs are fairly good.

When Peking decided to use force in Vietnam, the war in Europe had not reached its climax and the Soviet regime had not fallen. The moment this happened, the Chinese leaders had plenty on their minds besides disciplining Hanoi.

Their simplest problem turned out to be that of Mongolia. Messages had been sent to the leaders in Ulan Bator and others now followed, telling them that they should regard themselves from that point on as being under Chinese protection. Soviet forces should therefore surrender. They had in fact already gone, though under whose orders is still not quite clear. The divisions apparently went in good order, taking all of their arms and equipment with them. This, of course, was not quite what Peking had in mind but they were in no position then to influence the situation. The Mongolian Government sent fraternal messages to China pledging its allegiance, though not at once, for these matters take a little time.

It is not yet clear whether there were leadership reshuffles on any scale in Ulan Bator, though some of the men formerly in charge have not been seen since. At any rate, to strengthen the durability of Mongolia's allegiance, China sent an intimation to its leaders that Mongolian defences would be bolstered, against whatever ills there might be around, by a PLA garrision. More precisely, it was requested that the barracks vacated by the three Soviet divisions should be occupied by three PLA Main Force divisions. 'Would the Mongolian Government be so kind as to make them ready.' This was, of course, done at once, since it would have been impolitic to do otherwise. Some time later, the Mongolian leaders went to Peking and were fêted. To nobody's particular surprise they agreed that Mongolia's destiny lay with China, that it was, indeed had always been, a part of China. So was the Autonomous Region of Mongolia formed. Another bit of 'tidying up' had been successfully completed.

But this is to run ahead a little. The dramatic events of late August 1985 did not always lead to such readily acceptable solutions. When the Government in Moscow was toppled, Washington was diplomatically very active around the world. The American ambassadors in the various Asian capitals were kept fully informed all along, of course, and normally provided the local governments with the fastest, sometimes the only, news of what was happening. The US Ambassador in Peking had kept his eye on what was going on in Vietnam, with which he broadly agreed but about which he could have done nothing if he had not, and he had intimated to the Chairman that Washington would quite understand if China had certain ambitions for Mongolia. This was by way of a sweetener, because he also made it clear that the surrender of the Soviet forces in the Far East, which he confidently expected any day, would be handled by the United States. It was, after all, the United States that had been at war. China had no standing in the matter, so to speak, 'but its interests would naturally be carefully safeguarded in whatever arrangements were made'.

Similarly, the US Ambassador in Tokyo carefully let loose the offhand remark that he imagined Japan would have views about the Northern Islands, but if so he would rather not know about them, at least not officially. He conveyed the message that the US troops that had been on their way to Korea would, in all probability, now be diverted to the Vladivostok area, to accept the surrender of Soviet forces there. The timing of this was, however, a little uncertain and he formally asked, under the terms of the Japan-US Security Treaty, for agreement to their staging in Japan if need be.

The hint about the islands fell on receptive ears. The Northern Territories – four islands close to the east coast of Hokkaido, the northernmost of Japan's four main islands – were claimed by Japan as its territory but had been occupied by the Soviet Union after the Second World War. Soviet garrisons were installed there then and substantially built up in the early 1980s. Japan badly wanted them back, but the Soviet Union was totally unyielding; Moscow was not and never had been in the business of returning territories it had acquired. The issue united all Japanese; even the mildest section of the press was fiercely nationalistic about the islands.

The Cabinet in Tokyo had naturally been watching matters closely. Whatever arguments there might be about the Soviet title to the islands (and there were unresolved legal arguments, though not in Japan), Tokyo had no doubt at all that if the Soviet forces vacated them then they would revert to Japan one way or another. Accordingly, Japanese reconnaissance aircraft had been watching the islands closely, and on 22 August, or thereabouts, reported that amphibious landing vessels were leaving them. There were still some guns there and some aircraft, but it seemed as if the Soviet garrison might be moving out.

As we now know, that is indeed what was happening. The unfortunate Soviet commander of the Far Eastern Military District, under whom the garrison came, had been without any coherent orders from

Moscow for days. Most of his forces had not been involved in the war so far, the fighting having been essentially confined to the Pacific Fleet and various maritime and other aircraft in support. Marshal P. Y. Pavlovsky was understandably a worried man, not merely because of his unhappy situation but also because he felt that the new men in Moscow would be no friends of his. He clearly could not continue a war by himself – setting aside any question of whether his men, in all the circumstances, would be willing to fight. But he did not care at all for the idea of having, perhaps, to surrender to Chinese forces. Nor would his men. Far better to hand over to the Americans, or even to the Japanese, though that thought did not give him much pleasure either.

It was then that he decided that there were at least some problems that could be solved. He would bring in his outlying garrisons and get them under his own hand. So he gave orders to the divisions in Mongolia to move back into Soviet territory, and for the troops to come back from the Northern Islands. He did not want to have to hand them back to the Japanese forces who would almost certainly arrive before too long.

The return of the Northern Territories did not take long. Before August was out the Japanese self-defence forces were in. It was an emotional occasion. Quite a flotilla went there, with the Japanese Prime Minister on board the flagship (his words hit the headlines: 'Prime Minister Sato Eisaku secured the return of Okinawa; I am deeply honoured that it has fallen to me to secure the return of our Northern Territories'). Garrisons were installed. The Japanese press went wild.* There were some murmurings in the corridors of the United Nations about premature, some said 'illegal', acts, but Tokyo was content to deal with that little difficulty some other time. Ambassador Kunihiro in New York would have no problem with that.

But to return to Marshal Pavlovsky, sitting in Headquarters, Far Eastern Military District, at Khabarovsk with a group of officers around him, including the Deputy Commander of the Soviet Pacific Fleet. By now, into the early days of September, some things were beginning to fall into place, others were falling about his ears.

The Marshal had, several days ago, received very clear instructions from the Americans that he was to arrange the surrender of his forces to emissaries who would arrive very soon. In the meantime he was held responsible for their good conduct and so on. The Commander of the Pacific Fleet had also received orders to recall all his ships to Vladivostok, Sovetskaya Gavan, Magadan and Korsakov. These

---

* For a splendid account of all the excitement, see the article by T. Sakanaka in *Asahi Shimbun*, 30 August 1985.

orders had come from the Americans too. Moscow had been told about them and had simply wired back 'Comply'. That was clear enough, no problem there. But was Moscow in charge? And what of? Pavlovsky had also received news that was altogether more unsettling and heady: in Omsk, Colonel General Chervinsky, whose guts he detested but who was, he had grudgingly to admit, a man not without a certain panache, had set himself up as a sort of independent military leader and taken over his area. As far as he could gather this was tolerated by the Americans – fools they must be – perhaps so that he could keep law and order. If he knew Chervinsky he would keep lots of other things as well. All the same, it was an interesting idea.

Pavlovsky had been musing over it for days and had made up his mind; he now had to carry others with him. He would copy Chervinsky. It might not last for long, but it could achieve what he was intent on doing, which was to ensure that the Soviet Far East came under whatever administration the US had in mind, and not under the Chinese. He was quite sure he would have no problems with his staff on that particular point. Much more difficult would be to persuade the Americans to let him keep his weapons. He was chilled at the thought of his forces being disarmed and left facing China and its millions. There was no future in that.

The Marshal was in fact surprisingly successful. Washington had also been wrestling with the problem of how to keep China from demanding all the Soviet equipment. Of course, not all of it was still there; many men had simply left their units, with their own weapons, and gone home. Aircraft had flown off too, to airfields further away from the Chinese. All Soviet soldiers, certainly those of Russian origin, wanted to get away from the Chinese. Two warships had been scuttled and more might be yet; it was hard to put guards on everything. The Americans decided that Pavlovsky could be left with most of his forces for the time being and should operate a sort of military government in the Far Eastern coastal region – a Chervinsky under licence, so to speak. All the heavy equipment and the important naval vessels were under strong American guard, mounted by troops diverted from South Korea. Some of the latest submarines were towed off by the US Navy.

That raised the question – a vital one – of the nuclear warheads with both the ground and air forces in the Far East. The naval ones were less of a problem – it was clear where they were – but the warheads with the ground and air forces were less easily located and accessible. Acutely worrying at the beginning, of course, was the fear of unauthorized nuclear action. Peking sent very urgent signals to Washington and was, it was plain, more than anxious to get hold of warheads itself. In fact this whole question of what was to happen to the Soviet weapons caused great friction with China. The United States was left in no doubt by any of its allies in Asia that they did not want China to get more than a very small proportion of them, and no nuclear weapons. The Chinese readiness to invade Vietnam for the second time had been disturbing. Some weapons the Americans wanted themselves, naturally.

Peking was rebuffed by Washington; China had not been at war, but some conventional weapons would certainly be handed over. In the meantime China had nothing to fear, Soviet forces would be separated from their heavy weapons before their formations were disbanded altogether. Nuclear weapons would be guarded by special US units and later on handed over to the United Nations, to the UN Fissile Materials Recovery Organization (UNIFISMATRECO). Marshal Pavlovsky and the Pacific Fleet staff did in fact work admirably to trace warheads and see that they were handed over.

Soviet soldiers and sailors in the Far East were thus left initially under their own command, to be demilitarized eventually. Pavlovsky, an efficient and tough man, remained in charge even when a civilian administration was slowly formed. He looked balefully at the Chinese and they at him, but his business was essentially with the Allied Demilitarization Commission, made up mostly of Americans. On these China had no more than liaison groups. But the American head of the commission had many a difficult time with the Chinese; their aims and his were not exactly coincident and the strains were evident.

The map of Asia was, as a result of all these events, 'tidied up' a little. Some problems were solved, some were probably merely moved on to the back burner. What would happen in the region in the decades ahead was hard to predict, since it depended in large measure on the policies of a China steadily growing in power and confidence and no longer checked by its Soviet adversary.

THE END AND A
BEGINNING

Chapter 20

The Destruction of Minsk

As it became more and more evident that the Warsaw Pact programme of operations on the Central Front had fallen critically short of achieving its main objective in time and more and more cracks were opening up in the Eastern bloc, it was abundantly clear that a completely new situation was developing.

Debate at the highest level raged in both East and West as to what to do next. There was pressure in the US, with some German support, to allow the momentum of warlike preparation in the West, and above all in the US, to follow its logical path, to mobilize the national aspiration long dormant in the Soviet Union's subject peoples and move Allied forces in to push the Soviets back where they came from and restore freedom in Eastern Europe. Agreement among the Allies on a matter so complex and of such far-reaching importance was unlikely to be reached easily. In the first place it would be a mistake to suppose, as was very quickly pointed out, that the forces of the Warsaw Pact had been defeated. In spite of the desertion, almost *en masse*, of General Ryzanov's 3 Shock Army in the Netherlands, Warsaw Pact forces continued to be far more powerful than those facing them on the battlefields in Europe. Moreover, the Soviet Union's nuclear capability was still intact. But time was running out. There was something approaching open revolt in Poland and in the forward area a Polish regiment, following the example set in 3 Shock Army, had surrendered en bloc to the Americans. Defections from Warsaw Pact armies were increasing daily, in spite of the KGB. The total now ran into many thousands. It was not only in countries of the Warsaw Pact that there were signs of growing discontent. In the Baltic states of the Soviet Union itself, as well as in Belorussia and the Ukraine, there was mounting disaffection.

None the less it was certainly not a foregone conclusion that subject nations would everywhere be easily aroused to revolt. The habits of servitude and resignation were deeply ingrained. The Communist Party had been actively engaged for so long and with such assiduity in the detection and ruthless liquidation of any source of opposition that leadership would be difficult to establish and response to it might be sluggish – unless truly dramatic events provided a powerful stimulus. Just such a stimulus, as events proved, was not far off.

In the Soviet Union the Defence Council had been since early July in complete control, though the full Politburo was summoned from time to time to broaden the scope of discussion, to allocate responsibilities and review the performance of individuals. The Politburo was now summoned for 8 am on 19 August to meet in the VKP, the Volga Command Post built into the granite near Kuybyshev, 600 kilometres south-east of Moscow, in Stalin's time and greatly enlarged and improved since then. The most urgent requirement was to discuss the possibility of nuclear action.

The five members of the Defence Council had met the previous night but had been quite unable to agree. The pattern of disagreement formulated in a meeting of the Politburo on 6 December 1984, when the Operational Plan for 1985 had been discussed, had persisted essentially unchanged ever since. Aristanov, Chairman of the KGB, and Marshal Nastin, Minister of Defence, both members of the Defence Council, had always supported the view that operations against the West should be nuclear from the start. The Supreme Party Ideologist Malinsky, who was also a member of the Defence Council, had strongly opposed this, ably supported by two members of the Politburo, who were not, as it happened, also members of the Defence Council. These were Berzinsh, Leader of the Organization of the Party and State Control, and the Ukrainian Nalivaiko, responsible for relations with socialist countries. The milder view had prevailed in December and was later accepted as official policy. There would be no nuclear opening to an offensive against the West and nuclear weapons would not be used as long as victory could be seen to be certain without them. It was agreed, however, that if there were a setback in the operation, and the plan did not look like being completely successful in a non-nuclear mode, the matter would be urgently re-opened. The moment to re-open it had now come.

At the Defence Council meeting, which went on to 3 am without agreement, Malinsky, who still opposed the use of nuclear weapons on the grounds that at this stage it would be premature and on balance do far more harm than good, had been in a minority, with two members strongly against him, Aristanov and Nastin both arguing for a full-scale nuclear offensive at once, using all weapons, while the other two members remained undecided. It was Malinsky who succeeded in causing the full Politburo to be called. This was duly summoned for 8 am. In between meetings the General Secretary, advanced in years, clearly unwell and seen by some to be visibly failing (though they could hardly say so) summoned both sides separately. One was for using all, the other for using none. He himself, it appears, was in favour of one powerful strike on a prominent Western satellite nation, a European member of the Alliance with influence in Europe. The target would not be the capital: that would be needed in the future and its destruction might in any case be counter-productive for the purpose in mind. This was to issue a dramatic warning to the world, while at the same time inviting the US to immediate discussion of a ceasefire.

Neither Aristanov nor Malinsky, though they could hardly discuss it, thought much of this. They were both, in the last resort, men who would back all or nothing and reject half measures.

At the meeting of the Politburo the General Secretary steered discussion towards the conclusion he had chosen. The Chief of the General Staff was invited to advise on a country and a target. After a short adjournment to consult advisers he came back to propose attack on Birmingham in England. On the strong representations of Aristanov and Malinsky, for once in agreement, the matter, before the issue of any executive order, was taken back by the General Secretary for further consideration by the Defence Council, which was ordered to meet in an hour's time. When the Supreme Party Ideologist and Chairman of the KGB turned up for the meeting they found the door closed and two of the General Secretary's personal security guard, automatic pistols in hand, barring the way. It was apparent that they were not wanted. Inside, the General Secretary had no difficulty in arriving at a joint decision to carry out a single warning strike and the President of the Soviet Union was then informed of what was expected of him.

A very precisely detailed plan was made to allow him to warn the President of the United States over the hot line immediately the strike had been launched that one, and only one, missile was on its way and to indicate its target. He was to emphasize that this was in the nature of a warning to the Alliance, a warning which, it would be noted, though severe, was being given without doing any harm to the United States. It was not the initiation of an inter-continental exchange, in which, he was to remind the other President, the Soviet Union disposed of a very powerful second-strike capability. President Vorotnikov would hope and most earnestly urged that the US would now agree to very early discussions. Otherwise there could be further selective strikes.

The hot line conversation, amid frantic speculation on the Allied side, was arranged for 1020 hours Greenwich Mean Time (1320 local time) the next day, 20 August. President Vorotnikov duly delivered his message.

At 1030 hours GMT exactly, the one megaton warhead launched

by the USSR detonated at 3,500 metres above Winson Green, in Birmingham, with results which we have recorded elsewhere.*

At 1035 hours GMT the British Prime Minister and the President of the United States agreed on instant reprisal. The French President gave his concurrence and the Allies were all informed, even as instructions were on their way to two nuclear submarines, one each of the United States and Royal Navies. As a result of these the ancient and beautiful city of Minsk was totally destroyed, in a devastating attack even more dreadful in its power and its appalling results than that on Birmingham, and the events were set in train which were to tear the imperial structure of the Soviet Union apart and leave the world in general bewilderment, with parts of it in total chaos.

The hideous and gigantic doom which descended upon the unsuspecting city of Minsk in the early afternoon of 20 August stunned the world. Following hard upon the disaster which had overtaken the city of Birmingham in England less than an hour before, it did much to alter the outlook of people in our time with, beyond any doubt at all, a powerful impact on history in time to come. Is it possible, people ask, and will go on asking, that human beings can allow themselves to be driven into situations in which they find no alternative to this?

The four missiles, each of between 200 and 300 kilotons, which detonated over the centre of the city of Minsk at 1350 local time (1050 GMT) on 20 August at 3,000 metres, set up a towering fiery beacon which would be seen nearly as far off as Moscow, 600 kilometres away. The missiles did not, as distant observers noted, all detonate at once. One exploded, then almost immediately two more, and after a second or two the fourth. Ground zeros were all within a circle, as subsequent investigation has established, of a radius of roughly 1,000 metres.

The fireball of the first soared up in dreadful majesty alone from its point of detonation at 3 kilometres to a height of nearly 12, a beacon of light more searing than the sun. The next two, very near to each other in time and space, closely pursued the first, the fireballs of all three merging into one gigantic, blinding pillar. The fourth and last followed a few moments later and did not rise so high, reaching up some 10 kilometres into the base of an immense and growing mass of cloud. What seemed about to form huge mushrooms was now writhing in promethean patterns, turning, twisting and whirling,

---

* See Sir John Hackett and others, op. cit., chapter 25, 'The Destruction of Birmingham', pp. 287 ff.

beginning within one minute of the first explosion to form a single colossal cloud rising to a height of some 25 kilometres across a span of 30 or 40 and now spreading in one single blanket across the sky. The blinding light from the central pillar lasted a full twenty seconds even in the clarity of an August afternoon sky.

The unbelievably fierce effect of the downward heatwave was felt first. At a range of over 15 kilometres from the epicentre people clad in ordinary summer clothing in the open received burns which demanded immediate medical attention if they were not to prove fatal. Such attention was almost never forthcoming. The epicentre of the attack, above which the missiles had been set to detonate, was the grandiose building of the Central Committee of the Communist Party of Belorussia, built in the late 1930s in the style then current to emphasize the power, extent and modernity of socialism. In front of it stood a full-size statue of Lenin. Within a few seconds of the first detonation this immense structure was no more than a great pile of rubble. Somewhere in there the statue of Lenin, the principal architect of all this huge disorder, lay pounded into dust. Up to some 5 kilometres from the former Communist Party headquarters, everything combustible was immediately set on fire. Fires were also springing up further out from the centre but the heat pulse was followed in a few seconds by blast waves of terrific power which extinguished many of the fires raging in the centre itself. The huge pressures developed by blast crushed everything immediately below, so that within 5 kilometres of the centre everything above ground level, of whatever construction, was brought crashing to the earth. The effect of the blast wave declined as it travelled outwards and some buildings of stouter construction still remained standing, if badly damaged, further out, though structures more lightly built, if not immediately destroyed by blast, were often torn apart by the hurricane winds that followed it. As far out as 12 kilometres from the city centre railway trucks were hurled from the permanent way, oil tanks were split asunder and their contents spread, while overhead wiring everywhere came down.

The noise of these explosions, in a continuous roar, lasted for more than thirty seconds at Dzerzhinsk, for example, some 30 kilometres away to the south-west and an important centre of local administration with a key railway station, as it also did at Borisov, about the same distance away from Minsk on the direct railway line to Moscow in the north-east. Damage at this range was relatively slight, though very many windows were broken, but the terrifying burning fiery furnace, with its stupefying noise, stunned all who saw it, even those who saved their sight by turning away.

The attack came quite without warning and though there were

shelters available for at least a part of the population, very few people were in them. Of the one and a quarter million inhabitants of the city of Minsk, some 50,000 were killed almost instantly. Some, so badly burnt in the first thermal pulse as to have no hope of survival, were mercifully killed in the blast wave which almost immediately followed, while many were buried alive in the piles of masonry from buildings thrown down by the shock.

Something that could be seen from near Moscow, some 600 kilometres' distant, was even more clearly manifest in important places nearer to Minsk itself. It was visible in Riga, capital of Latvia to the north-west, in Kiev in the south-east and in Warsaw some 450 kilometres to the south-west. The pillar of fire was seen and the rumble of the detonations clearly heard at Vilnius, the capital of Lithuania, only 170 kilometres away, while in the important Lithuanian city of Kaunas, 100 kilometres further off, the disturbance in the sky was also clearly visible and the rumble of the bursts was plainly heard. The inhabitants of Bobruisk, also in Belorussia and only 150 kilometres away from Minsk, were shocked and terrified. Much was seen and heard in Smolensk, Vitebsk, Gomel and Brest, on the Belorussian/Polish border. In all these important places, each with its own political interests, there was confusion and uncertainty and everyone was gripped by a fear approaching panic as to what might happen next.

In the suburbs of Minsk, where there were still wooden buildings, something approaching a firestorm was developing, generated in the tremendous currents of air caused by the impact of the blast wave. It was scarcely possible that any living thing could survive in the inner part of the city and if any did it could not be for long. On the outskirts burnt and blinded people, many bleeding badly from the effects of flying glass and other debris carried through the air by winds approaching hurricane force, all in a severe state of shock, were stumbling about in a forlorn search for parents or children and for medical assistance of which there was no hope at all. Others whose injuries prevented movement or who were pinned in wreckage from which there was no possibility of their rescue lay where they were in a state of stunned despair.

Soviet provision for civil defence had been held up in the early 1980s as something to admire and imitate. It is true that there were in the neighbourhood of Minsk concentrations of civil defence expertise and equipment at places like Borisov, Bobruisk and Baranovichi. All available resources were mobilized and moved in towards the disaster area. The authorities, however, were less concerned with the alleviation of personal distress than with the control of the movement of refugees, pathetic crowds of people who came pouring out from the outskirts of Minsk and its neighbouring regions along the roads towards Orsha and Bobruisk, people still alive, unlike those in the city, but suffering greatly from burns, injuries from falling masonry and a thousand other sources of distress. Almost all came on foot. By the outbreak of war the private ownership of motor vehicles in Minsk was at the level normal in Soviet cities, that is, at about that found among black South Africans. The few that there were had, of course, at once been requisitioned. Here and there in this heart-rending horde there would be a military or official motor vehicle, or one seized by force. For the most part the crowd just stumbled hurriedly on, carrying bits of household gear or food or bedding, wheeling perambulators, or handcarts upon which old or injured people sometimes lay. They only wanted, for the most part, in their state of stunned stupor, to get away.

The problem of controlling their movement, daunting though it might be, was in the Soviet fashion fairly easily solved, at least in the first instance. The USSR had raised more than 1,000 KGB battalions in the process of mobilization. It was not difficult to put a barrage round Minsk at a distance of some 12 kilometres from the centre and shoot anyone not belonging to the Party structure or the military who wished to come further.

At a distance of some 30 kilometres (in front of Borisov for example) a further ring of KGB troops was established. It was their business not to shoot down anyone attempting to get through but simply to send them back, with the exception of any individuals who could prove an official connection.

The headquarters of the Central Committee of the Communist Party of Belorussia had moved out from Minsk on the outbreak of war and was established, together with the headquarters of the Belorussian Military District, in Orsha. These two centres of power, the military and the civil acting jointly, with the military commander technically in charge but the Party First Secretary as his deputy the real source of authority, now faced a truly frightening task of relief and reorganization. It was quite beyond the resources of the republic of Belorussia. It was formidable even for the USSR and could hardly be contemplated without despair.

Only much later would the question arise why such an appalling disaster should ever have been invited and who was to blame. There will probably never be an answer. What is sure is that it should never have happened and must never be allowed to happen again.

Chapter 21

Soviet Disintegration

Minsk was chosen as the target for the Western nuclear attack because of its general comparability with Birmingham as the Soviet target. To destroy Moscow or Leningrad would have been a fast jump up the ladder of escalation. An important provincial city was required, far enough from the capital so that no direct physical effects would be felt there, but near enough for immediate political repercussions on the seat of government. Minsk answered this bill. It was not just a specimen city of the Soviet Union, but the capital of the Belorussian Republic, one of the principal constituent units of the USSR, and singled out for special prominence by being allotted a fictionally independent seat at the United Nations. The stability and coherence of the area was weakened by the frontier changes after the Second World War, when Poland was pushed bodily westwards, absorbing parts of Germany, but losing territory, and population, to Belorussia and the Ukraine. As a result there were important Catholic minorities in both these republics. The destruction of Minsk would clearly add to the internal strains in the whole area.

The Ukraine, lying immediately to the south of Belorussia, is far larger and more important. It occupies an area greater than that of France and has a population of about the same size. Before the war it produced more steel than the Federal Republic of Germany, with major armament works at Kharkov and Kiev. Kiev was the capital of the First Russia, before the Tartar invasion and before the emergence of Moscow. But the Ukraine had never been an independent state. It was a battlefield between Poles and Russians, Turks and even Swedes, before it was was finally absorbed by Russia in 1654. However, the memories of former greatness and the idea of Ukrainian independence had never wholly died. They had, indeed, been revived by Stalinist persecution and by the repression of a fragmentary independence movement in 1966.

After Minsk the Ukrainians could well fear that Kiev or Kharkov would be next on the Allied targeting list. There was another more long-standing anxiety: insurrection was now widespread in Poland

315

and receiving active and increasing support from the Western allies.
As we have seen, this was already weakening the Soviet military
effort in Germany. The destruction of Minsk would make it even
more difficult for the Soviet Union to control the situation in Poland.
If Poland were to escape from Soviet hegemony, one of its first
ambitions would probably be to recover the Polish territory lost to
Belorussia and the Ukraine. The Ukraine would be wise not to lose
much time in claiming its own independence and looking after its own
interests rather than those of its Soviet overlords.

To the north of Belorussia, the brief independence of the three
Baltic states, Latvia, Lithuania, Estonia, had also been extinguished
by the USSR in the Second World War, but they had never been
wholly assimilated and were now likely to be early candidates for
freedom. Minsk therefore proved politically more significant in death
than it had ever been in life. Its destruction triggered the dissolution
of the whole western border area of the Soviet Union, not only by
showing the vulnerability of Soviet power but by releasing, through
the psychological shockwaves of four nuclear missiles, the nationalistic passions which had lain dormant for so long.

This particular denouement had not been in mind when the young
Vasyl Duglenko, a promising graduate from the Kiev police
academy, was infiltrated by Ukrainian nationalists into the KGB,
thanks to a favourable recommendation from no less than Khrushchev himself. It was this action, nevertheless, and Duglenko's
subsequent appointment to the security section in the Kremlin, which
made sure that the Soviet system could be overthrown from within,
and that it would be followed by the establishment of separate nations
on the ruins of the Soviet empire.

The mechanics of conspiracy are hard to unravel. To misquote the
old epigram, if treason prospers it is not treason but a constitutional
change of regime: and the secret plotting is swept under the carpet in
the hope that it may not serve as a model for the next attempt at
change. But three main elements were required for the success of the
momentous coup which toppled the CPSU: the Ukrainian network in
the KGB which had access to the inner sanctum of the Command Post
being used at the time, to which Politburo and Defence Council had
transferred their functions from the Kremlin; the disaffection of some
of the Politburo members who had struggled under the leadership of
Chief Party Ideologist Malinsky against the nuclear decision and now
saw their attitude vindicated in the appalling devastation of the
capital of Belorussia, with stupendous human suffering, and the
gigantic surge of feeling which could lead to disintegration in the
western regions; and influential officers of the Soviet High Command
anxious to preserve a core of military strength as the foundation and

guarantee of a successor Soviet state. For these were conscious that any further nuclear attack on the Soviet Union would destroy the chances of survival of organized authority and they knew that this could now only be provided by the armed forces.

All these groups had watched with growing apprehension the checks to Soviet forces on western fronts, the reverses of Soviet policy in the peripheral adventures, the signs of approaching break-up in Central Asia, and above all the incapacity of the leadership to understand and to adjust to what was happening. This was particularly noticeable in the formerly all-powerful General Secretary of the Central Committee of the Communist Party, whose physical and mental deterioration was so marked that total breakdown could not be far off. The need of each group for allies in the right places overcame their seasoned caution, and contacts had begun to be made. Duglenko found a fellow Ukrainian in the highest ranks of the General Staff in Colonel General Vladimir Borisovich Ivanitskiy, Chief of the First Main (Strategic) Directorate. The latter knew the divisions in the Politburo intimately and had no difficulty in identifying the right members to approach at the crucial moment. The decision to bomb Birmingham gave them all the evidence they needed that the Party Secretary had lost his head (and some would even go so far as to say his reason) and should be removed at a very early opportunity. From the effect of the nuclear attack on Minsk they drew the assurance that Soviet forces west of the capital would be in no position to support or to restore the existing regime once it was overthrown. The example set by the defection of a great part of 3 Shock Army, under General Ryzanov, now freely co-operating with the British, German and Dutch in the Northern Army Group, supported and maintained by them in armed hostility to forces loyal to the regime, was being already followed in other parts of the Soviet forces as well. For the overthrow of the regime it now only remained for the method to emerge and the moment to be chosen. The Minsk disaster had become the fulcrum upon which the lever of popular disaffection already labouring to displace the Soviet regime could now operate. The method was there, the moment was there, but time was short. A meeting of the Politburo had been summoned to meet early on the following morning, 22 August.

The start of the October revolution of 1917 had been signalled by a cannon shot from the *Aurora*. On this occasion, in 1985, it was evident that a more prosaic pistol shot would have to suffice, but if it could be aimed precisely at the General Secretary himself it would do all that was required. Duglenko assumed responsibility for this part of the operation, counting on his access, for security purposes, to the most closely guarded parts of the Command Post currently in use.

Some vital problems still remained. Who was going to take power in succession to the Secretary, and how were the conspirators to make sure that they, and no one else in the hierarchic succession, secured the physical levers of supreme power, that is to say, control over the nuclear command system? Unless they had this control there would be a serious danger that some frustrated hard-line party or military group that had managed to secure it could decide that holocaust was preferable to surrender and start the ICBM attack on the West which would bring about the near-annihilation of the world. The conspirators had viewed with irony but also with apprehension the conflict of claims to authority by the top members of the US Government when the President of the United States was shot and nearly killed in 1981. The American version of 'hunt the black box', the search for the package containing the relatively simple apparatus without which, whatever other authority he possessed, even the President could not authorize nuclear release, had been farcical. A Soviet version in present circumstances could end in universal tragedy. The actual guardian of the box itself at the time, an army signals officer, would therefore have to be made to transfer his allegiance rapidly from the General Secretary to the conspirators' choice of successor, and not merely rely on the devolution of authority down the normal line of orthodox command. This was a practical detail to which Duglenko gave very close attention.

Just before the meeting, ordered for 5 am on that fateful morning of 22 August, it was learnt that the General Secretary had been taken seriously ill and would not be able to attend. In this crisis, both of the country and the Communist Party, with the leadership faltering, it was imperative to defer what looked like developing into a personal power struggle over the succession in the Politburo – or more probably, between the five members of the Defence Council – until decisions of the most pressing urgency had been taken, first of all on what was arising out of the nuclear attack on Minsk. In the absence of the General Secretary the chairmanship of the meeting had to be in the hands of someone of the highest prestige who, at the same time, would not be taken too seriously as a contender for personal power. The not unprecedented, though unusual, step was taken by common consent of bringing in the titular head of state President Vorotnikov to take the chair.

All ten members of the Politburo (excluding, of course, the General Secretary) were expected to attend the meeting. Duglenko's first task was to see that his own chief, Aristanov, Chairman of the KGB, did not. He had moreover not only to be prevented from attending this meeting but any other that might be held subsequently. With the help of his Ukrainian driver, Duglenko did not find the fatal accident which was required for the purpose impossibly difficult to arrange and, of course, it was Duglenko himself who could expect to be called in to explain the absence of the chief he should have accompanied to the meeting.

As soon as the Politburo assembled, under the chairmanship of President Vorotnikov, KGB Chairman Aristanov's empty chair was at first assumed to be the result of pressing state security business in Belorussia, but also raised fears that the KGB were plotting independent action. Only one of the members knew that the actual plotters were already within the gates. This, of course, was Taras Kyrillovich Nalivaiko, the member of the Politburo responsible for relations with socialist countries and a fellow Ukrainian. Some others were to have ample leisure in future to reflect on the poignancy of the always unanswered question: *Quis custodiet ipsos custodes*, or in Soviet terms, if you give too much power to the state security force, what is to prevent it from taking the rest?

Power was soon to come flaming from the barrel of a gun, when Duglenko was invited to represent the KGB Chairman and present his report and, instead, drew a revolver and shot the unfortunate Vorotnikov, President of the Soviet Union, through the heart. As Duglenko saw it, whoever was in the chair which would otherwise have been occupied by the General Secretary was the only proper target, if he were to achieve his aim of establishing control over the gathering. The room now quickly filled up with Ukrainian security personnel, and as Malinsky, Supreme Party Ideologist, began to speak asserting his own claim to the leadership, two of these removed Vorotnikov's body. Duglenko promptly occupied his chair. The man with the black box (who, as it had been contrived, was also a Ukrainian and a party to the conspiracy) ostentatiously moved in behind him, confirming the newly established leadership with this obvious demonstration that it was well on the road to nuclear command. Duglenko then announced his assumption of supreme authority. A few of the members of the Politburo who protested were quickly removed and the others, including Malinsky, forced smiles and came out with a round of ritual applause.

As for the General Secretary, it was known before the morning was out that he had been struck down by a heart attack and was dead. This caused no surprise and curiously little sadness. It also had almost no effect on the course of events, for the General Secretary had already for some time been seen by his colleagues as a burnt-out case and largely disregarded. The man who once bestrode the narrow world – or a great part of it anyway – like a Colossus as the successor in a line from Lenin, through Stalin and Khrushchev, in the exercise of absolute power over huge domains, had simply failed and faded out like a candle in the wind. He had done much to increase the worldwide power and influence of the Soviet Union, and the absolute dominion within it of the Communist Party. It was here, in the attempt to protect and perpetuate the position of the Party, that he had himself sharpened the contradictions which in the end would bring it down.

Duglenko was faced with an almost impossible task. It is to his credit that he put first things first and dealt with some of them, erecting at the same time a few breakwaters against the engulfing chaos. What were the priorities? First of all came the situation in Belorussia and all that arose from it. The relief of the appalling human suffering which resulted from the Western response to the nuclear destruction of Birmingham threw a huge and immediate burden on the Soviet Union. This and its associated security problems could certainly be carried, given a little time. There was, however, already widespread fear, almost amounting to panic in some western areas – in the Ukraine for example, and the Baltic republics, apart from Warsaw Pact states – about what would happen next. Supposing this disaster were not the last but only the first of many? What comfort would the citizens of Kharkov find in the confident assurance that if they and their own city were destroyed the incineration of Detroit would follow? Could any governmental structure, however absolute, however well provided with the apparatus of repression by brute force, contain the consequences if questions such as these were asked? If the structure were one forced upon unwilling men and women whose aspirations to national independence, though deeply hidden, were still strong, might not these now explode and so destroy the hard case in which they had been hitherto enclosed?

Relief of the position in Belorussia, the stilling of panic fears in central Europe and an end to the fighting were all aspects of one problem. There had to be a nuclear stand-down and a ceasefire ending the war in such a way as to avoid a general *sauve-qui-peut* of the Soviet armies. Then there was the nationality problem, that is, as Duglenko saw it, the independence of the Ukraine and its defence against Poland. And finally there was food. The food shortages, leading to riots (which we look at in the next chapter) were a phenomenon of the great cities but, since government also perforce resided in great cities, the food had to be brought in if government was to continue. Returning armies, too, needed food if they were not to turn into a rabble of looters.

Here were critical elements of a proposal for armistice which had rapidly to be put to the Americans. First of all Duglenko would propose a ceasefire worldwide with the stand-down of all nuclear forces at 0001 hours local time 23 August. This had to be followed by a massive relief operation in Belorussia, for which advanced planning parties were invited to arrive within thirty-six hours. Soviet ships were already being recalled to base and Soviet armed forces would leave occupied territory by stages to be agreed under arrangements made by Supreme Headquarters Allied Powers Europe. Grain would be shipped from the West and distributed under Red Cross auspices to relieve distress in Soviet cities outside the Minsk disaster area and provide minimum rations for Soviet forces provided they followed agreed withdrawal plans. The territory of all countries in Europe would be respected, pending a peace treaty, but the Ukraine and Belorussia, and such other of the Soviet republics as wished, would immediately assume responsibility for their own territories and would be free to decide whether they wished to join with others in any larger group, though the Warsaw Pact would be immediately abolished and could not be re-created.

Having established his authority at the head of the Soviet system, which he was about to liquidate, and having ordered an immediate standstill of Soviet forces, Duglenko was able to speak on the hot line to the US President less than thirty-six hours after the destruction of Minsk to report what had happened and to propose the terms of ceasefire and armistice. The West could perhaps be pardoned for a period of stupefaction and confusion at the extent of their success – or more correctly, perhaps, the failure of their opponent. In other circumstances they might have been able to appreciate rather more accurately the hollowness of the new Soviet regime. There were also hawkish Westerners who wanted to demand unconditional surrender and have it proclaimed before the world media in the Kremlin. They were outvoted in favour of terms based on those put forward by Duglenko, for two reasons.

The first area of an Allied advance would be the GDR. Western occupation of this territory would pose inescapably the question of German unity, which was still a bugbear to Western Europe, even to many Germans in the Federal Republic. The argument of disorder was also powerful. Had not the Bolshevik success in 1917 been made possible by the return to Russia of defeated and mutinous troops, who became the agents of revolution? Was it not also the Kerensky Government's brave decision to continue the war against Germany which contributed greatly to its downfall? Now, in 1985, there was a rare chance to reverse the previous disastrous course of history: to make peace with the provisional government and, instead of sending a communist revolutionary in a sealed train, as the Germans had done with Lenin in 1917, to send trucks of grain.

The massive relief operation in the Minsk area was put in hand by the United States at once, with immediate Allied help, and then handed over to the United Nations. The ceasefire was agreed within the proposed time limit. The armistice had to take a little longer, and delegates from both commands met at the NATO headquarters in Brussels. Western representation was fairly straightforward. On the Eastern side, however, there had not been time for all the communist regimes to be replaced by something else. Representation was therefore confined to the Soviet High Command, Poland (where the leaders of Solidarity had lost no time in emerging from prisons and internment camps and assuming the power which had so narrowly escaped them in 1981) and the newly established independent governments of the Ukraine, Belorussia and the three Baltic states. A Kazakh from Alma-Ata arrived halfway through the proceedings to announce the independence of the Central Asian republics.

The armistice was of course only the beginning of a very long process of reordering the political geography of large parts of Europe and Asia. It is still going on. A major threat to mankind's future had been eliminated, but this did not mean that mankind would at once become as angels. Indeed, the relaxation of fear and of dictatorship gave freedom not only to breathe again, but to resume many of the ancient and modern quarrels which had been temporarily suppressed by the greater danger. Their resumption took place, none the less, under the tragic but in its own way salutary recollection of the terrible events which took place in Birmingham and, far worse, in Minsk. Before looking at the re-ordering of the map, however, we might catch our own breath and very briefly examine some of the reasons which conditioned the resolution of the main drama and take a look, at close quarters, at its effect on ordinary Soviet citizens.

Chapter 22

The Experience of Defeat

❝ "They'll be shooting us all soon," sighed Nikolay Kryukov. Other prisoners turned to him, but he just went on musing aloud, talking to no one in particular. He was a huge rough man from Murom, an ancient city 200 kilometres east of Moscow.

"When things are so unstable it's dangerous for the Party to keep us alive, even in prison. Sasha here has tried to organize a free trade union. Peter has taken part in a strike. I am known to have read books on the banned list, Adam Goldman has joined in demonstrations, Jan Bruminsh raised the national flag in Riga, Dima Nalivaiko did the same in Kiev. They must see us as detonators in a powder store, so they've isolated us, surrounded us with guard towers and machine-guns, barbed wire and dogs.

"During the Second World War opponents of the regime held in Soviet camps were systematically shot. That's in the official histories.

"Why should we wait until one by one they start shooting *us*? We must act now. *Now*. I haven't talked about this earlier because we've got provocateurs here. Our only chance lies in immediate action, all together, with little or no preparation. When this rest break ends, we'll all go back to work and then move instantly. What I'm going to say now is for the provocateurs. I don't know who you are, but you're here for sure. We've got seven minutes left until the end of the break. That's when we get under way. Anyone attempting to approach the guards before the break ends will be considered a provocateur, and I'll kill him with this shovel." Kryukov raised a shovel, which was like a toy in his great paws.

"I now want all the tractor drivers over here. Not all at once: we don't want to attract any attention."

Over by the central gate to the building site the supervisor banged on a piece of rail suspended from a post. The sound echoed across the site, signalling the end of the break. Slowly the prisoners got up and wandered off back to their work. A heavy tractor coughed into life, the circular saw started up, cement-mixers were turning. Everything seemed to be as usual. One of the tractors lumbered slowly off. Then, suddenly, it turned on the spot and the driver in a prison pea-jacket jumped down, while the tractor slowly crawled on towards one of the guard towers. A second and then a third tractor followed suit, each ploughing its stolid way towards a separate tower. The guards, taken by surprise, soon reacted and began to pour machine-gun bullets into the first tractor. It just carried on its way, until, meeting with the resistance of the guard tower, slowly and methodically pushed it aside. With a cry the man on guard came down, his machine-gun with him. The tractor carried on past the crumpled tower towards the rows of barbed wire. The second tractor was not so lucky. It missed the guard tower and, deflected by a rock at the first line of barbed wire, failed to break through. The third tractor brought down its guard tower and moved effortlessly through the barbed wire beyond. The way to freedom was open.

Hundreds of shouting prisoners tore through the breaks in the wire under a hail of wild machine-gun fire. Dogs tried to head them off but cascades of toxic foam from fire extinguishers, snatched up at the towers, held them back. A machine-gun from one of the towers was seized by the crowd. The scene was a terrifying one: 700 raging men armed with hammers and spades, with fire-extinguishers and, now, a machine-gun. And they still had one tractor in reserve. They turned it towards the guards' barracks. The guards ran shouting and screaming out of the doors or jumped out of the windows, straight into machine-gun fire. A second attack was under way. The grey-black crowd roared towards the central gates. One of them had picked up an automatic lying on the ground and still yet another machine-gun fell into the prisoners' hands. Fire broke out in the more distant guard towers. But the guards there had long since deserted their posts and fled into the forest.

The throng of prisoners pulled down the gates and were free.

"Wait!" shouted Nikolay Kryukov, a machine-gun in his hands. "Listen to me. In this situation prisoners usually go off into the forest in small groups, on the basis that you can't catch a lot of hares in one go. But we're no hares, and times have changed now anyway. The communists haven't the forces to hunt us through the forest. I'm forming a National Liberation Detachment. Anyone who wants to join – come with me. If not – then go off separately or in small groups."

Kryukov got 193 men for his detachment.

Immediately after the uprising the Lithuanian prisoners formed their own group of twenty-seven. They thanked Kryukov, took their leave of the other political prisoners and set off back towards Lithuania. It was a long way off but what else could they do? A group of Armenians followed suit with even further to go, as well as a score or so of Baptists making for Kursk. There were a couple of hundred common criminals in with the political prisoners; some asked to join Kryukov, but he declined to take them. Some of the politicals had to be left behind too – if they were seriously wounded or suffering from leg injuries which made walking difficult. A small camp was organized for them on an island in the swamp, where they were left with an automatic rifle and sixty rounds of ammunition, together with such stores and medicaments as had been seized. Kryukov's detachment then set off into the forest.

Kryukov himself realized that they should not go far. He would be hunted in the woods and marshes, so it would be better to hang out near a camp, where no one would think of looking for him. The detachment made a great loop through the forest, coming back to where their tricky journey had started. The following night they attacked a neighbouring camp for political prisoners. The guards' attention was directed inside the camp, not towards the perimeter – an ancient and natural instinct of prison guards. Hence the attack could go in quickly and quietly, without much shooting and with few losses to the attackers. Six hundred political prisoners and 400 criminals were then set free from the camp. There were also rich pickings – 100 automatics, several cases of ammunition, many grenades. Kryukov now had

297 politicals in his detachment. The prisoners hanged the entire prison guard from the gateposts and guard towers and the detachment then took cover in the forest. This time Kryukov held a council of war and decided to head straight for the industrial area in the Urals – to Chelyabinsk and Magnitogorsk . . . **'** *

The question is still being asked, how was it possible for Duglenko's conspiracy to succeed; how could a system established for so long, buttressed by the largest security apparatus in the world and governed by an all-powerful Communist Party, be overthrown in a few minutes' gun battle in the inner sanctum of the Politburo in the Command Post?

The general answer is that the system, in spite of all appearances, was already permeated by decay, like a wooden structure devoured by termites, when only the outer shell remains and can be knocked over by a minor accident. Considered in outline, the situation brought into being by the war held powerful elements of change. The check to the Soviet advance in Europe, the defection of units of the armed forces to the enemy, the fear of total nuclear devastation following one horrifying disaster, and the initial signs of break-up in the east – all these might have been weathered if the system had been generally sound. As it was, they brought into the open the disillusion and hatred that so many in the USSR had long been harbouring in their hearts. Reactions to failure, to fear and to hunger were for the first time stronger than the customary caution of the citizen towards the secret policemen and the informer. The 'masses' on whom the regime was supposed to be based now at last realized the strength that numbers could give.

Three primary weaknesses were exposed. First of all, the system was grossly inefficient in producing material goods because of the distortions inherent in central planning in a state of the size of the Soviet Union, and because ideology still dominated economic theory. Secondly, agriculture was a disgrace and cause of shame. How could a vast area like the Soviet Union, with some of the most fertile soil in the world, not produce enough to feed its own people? Agricultural failures had been concealed because there was enough gold and gas produced in Siberia to find hard currency for American wheat and maize, but now, with the always inefficient distribution system upset by the demands of war, the lack of food in urban centres became a pressing matter of public order.

---

* Alyosha Petrovich Narishkin, *A Phoenix Out of Ashes* (Bantam, New York 1986), pp. 55–6.

Last but by no means least was the contrast between the way in which 'we' and 'they' lived. The Bolshevik revolution had triumphed in the name of a classless proletarian society determined to root out aristocratic privilege. It succeeded in this task, but only to substitute another privileged group for the old aristocracy. It was tragic that the Soviet Union, which was founded in the name of egalitarianism and love and brotherliness, should become the land of privilege and hate and police-state cruelty.

Societies turn unstable when distribution of incomes is too uneven. Revolutions like those of 1789 and 1917 and 1985 have usually broken out when the top decile of privilegentsia is more than, say, fifteen times richer than the mass of population. In stable countries like the United States, Japan, China and all West Europe, the after-tax incomes of the richest decile in the inter-war (1945–85) years were rarely more than seven to eight times the incomes of those even on welfare relief. In the Soviet Union, because of the system of buying goods through special shops, the top 2 to 3 per cent of the privilegentsia had after-tax living standards more than fifteen times those of the ordinary toiler. They have paid a terrible price for it.

Such was the situation, in general outline, in which the Soviet imperial system disintegrated. So much effort has been applied over the years, however, to the falsification of the historical and philosophical background to this gigantic and cruel swindle, that a little further reflection on what lay behind it, and how it developed, may not be out of place. The simple fact was that the Soviet Empire was destroyed by its own inner contradictions, under an inexorable historical dialectic whose existence Marxists had long suspected but apparently never fully understood. The basic contradiction lay in the fundamental incompatibility of freedom and socialism. Marxism, offering such rich early promise to a humanity suffering under its own human limitations, had long shown itself to be romantic, unscientific and obsolete.

It was inevitable that Marx would be followed by a Lenin, whose observations on the tactics necessary in the Bolshevik revolution are revealing: 'We must be ready to employ trickery, deceit, lawbreaking, withholding and concealing truth . . . We can and must write in a language which sows among the masses hate, revulsion, scorn and the like towards those who disagree with us.'

Lenin in his turn, if a communist system were to survive, could not fail to be followed by a Stalin, in a dictatorship marked by merciless repression and wholesale butchery. How many people, to help stabilize the regime, were killed under Stalin? Twenty million? Fifty million? A hundred million? Bukovsky puts it at rather more than fifty.

In the last eighty years of Tsarist rule, up to 1917, some seventeen people, in what were thought to be fairly turbulent times, had been executed every year. The Bolshevik secret police, the Cheka, in a report on their work in 1918 and 1919, recorded that in those two years more than one thousand people *a month* had been executed by them without trial.

But it was not moral squalor that undid Marxist–Leninism in the end. The system was not undermined by its essential fraudulence, though that was plain enough. What killed Marxist–Leninism, and destroyed Soviet Russia, was simply that the doctrine had never been, and probably never could be, realized. It did not work.

The birth of the regime, in the October Revolution of 1917, is shrouded in the myth that this was the result of a vast popular movement which swept into power the rulers of its choice. The truth is very different.

The government from which the Bolsheviks unlawfully seized power in 1917, though it was weak and unpopular, had at least come into existence constitutionally and is now recognized to have been fairly representative of the people. The promises of the minority group who by force and fraud were able to overthrow it were certainly attractive. Besides equality, liberty and fraternity, they guaranteed power to the workers, land to the peasants and peace to the people. Every one of these promises was broken. Under Bolshevism, workers were never given anything but a nominal share in government. Real power in representative bodies, the Soviets, was soon taken over by the Party, to which any show of opposition was brutally crushed. Land was, in the early stages, distributed to peasants but very soon taken away into state ownership. Most people who found their living on the land were forced into collective farms. Huge numbers of the most capable and hard-working were physically eliminated. Solzhenitsyn's researches showed him that fifteen million peasants were transported to extermination in the two years 1929 and 1930 alone. As for peace, quite apart from the more famous rebellions such as those in Murom, Yaroslavl, Rybinsk and Arzamas, and Antonov's, with its centre in Tambov, which were all put down with the utmost savagery, the Communist Party had embarked upon a civil war against its own population which was to continue for half a century, a war in which the dead far outnumbered those of any other war in the whole history of mankind. In place of equality, liberty and fraternity, the hallmarks of an increasingly corrupt society were coercion, fear and distrust. Words themselves seemed to have acquired new meanings in a socialist context. Equality meant no more, as we have seen, than privileges for top Party bureaucrats, with their special shops, foreign travel, high salaries and luxurious homes. There were equal rights for all others, as Bukovsky has put it, to share a common misery, to accommodate themselves to a society they knew was totally corrupt, to stand for ever in queues or else to perish in a Gulag. The total alienation this produced between Party and people brought about in time a general disillusion with socialist aspirations.

By the 1970s hope had long given way to cynicism. A continuous process of petrification seemed to have overcome the bureaucratic machine, producing economic policies and political practice as dogmatic as they were inflexible. The general atmosphere had become one of stagnation. Workers, denied any real incentive, took little interest in their work. Virtues and abilities went unrecognized and certainly, unless they were applied to meeting the state's requirements, earned no promotion. Advancement depended upon conformity. Ideology penetrated the structure of the machine at every level but those who operated it had long since shed any adherence to truly socialist principles. The Party never comprised more than 10 per cent of the population of the Soviet Union and probably not one Party member in ten in 1970 still believed in communism. The process of candidacy for membership to the Party, in which the candidate had to satisfy one Party committee after another of his devotion to the CPSU, and give proof of it, became an elaborate exercise in falsehood.

The cumulative effect of all this on the Soviet economy was by the mid-1970s disastrous. Central planning imposed restrictions on local initiative in situations ill understood at the controlling centre. Local needs, in materials, equipment, spare parts, even roads, were either not known or disregarded. People in the localities made their own arrangements for some fictitious show of meeting planned targets.

The targets, constantly derided by the populace, always rose and were almost never met. Workers anxious to meet them, where any did, faced only the hostility of workmates. Low salaries and shortages stimulated theft. Factories and shops, if unwillingly, fed the black market, under which 30 per cent of the whole of the country's economy by 1983 was operating.

Peasants cultivated their own plots for subsistence, selling any surplus on the black market for the cash they needed. In 1981 it was calculated that these plots – 3 per cent of the totality of arable land – were producing half of all the agricultural output. State investment in the early 1980s to enable peasants to earn more money only resulted in their producing from the land what they themselves needed for their own purposes. Parts of the Soviet Union were in fact, in the early 1980s, approaching starvation. Only a loosening of control could correct this tendency but that would lead, as it had in Hungary, in the direction of a free market economy, which was a trend the system could not tolerate.

By 1985 the growth rate of GNP in the USSR was negative, with a positive growth rate in the population, by far the greater part of the increase being in non-Russian peoples. Pauperization was now a great and growing menace. Inflation, already high and always rising, could no longer be concealed by official manipulation. Within the Soviet Union more and more people were turning to religion, often in forms the state found sufficiently hostile to proscribe. The weaknesses built into the system from the start were beginning to destroy it.

The events of the August war in 1985 worked in two ways to bring matters to a head. The political leadership had long been discredited by developments in Poland. It was the first time a governing European Communist Party had been shown to be unable to cope with dissidence and ideological opposition. Moscow was faced with the choice between direct intervention by Red Army troops and the takeover of Polish security by the Soviet KGB, or recourse to Polish military government. The latter, chosen through old men's inertia rather than conscious decision, put off for a time the international outcry which Soviet military action would have caused, and partially evaded Soviet responsibility for Poland's debt. But it signalled the abdication of the Communist Party of Poland from the control of political life.

The enormity of this breach of ideology and tradition was not everywhere fully recognized in the West, which was accustomed to military takeovers in Latin America and the Middle East, and tended to regard them as a recurrent and unsurprising reaction by the forces of order faced with administrative or parliamentary chaos. But to doctrinal communists the implications were of a different order. The Party, the fountain-head of doctrine and decision, the network which made a certain rough and ready sense in a hopelessly over-centralized bureaucracy, had shown itself powerless, divided and incapable of decision. Solidarity may have been temporarily overcome in Poland, but in its downfall the movement won a famous victory by demonstrating that the Communist Party in a communist state was no longer the all-powerful guardian of the state's authority.

The shock waves of this ideological explosion flowed back into the Soviet Union, exposing even the CPSU to doubt, and seeming to enhance the potential of the Soviet military leadership, which it appeared might one day have to play a similar role to that of Poland. So it was doubly traumatic to those inside the hierarchies when the check to the Soviet advance in Europe demonstrated that the military leadership had feet of clay. They were seen to have made faulty assessments, to have failed to adapt to changing tactical circumstances, and to have based their plans on an operational doctrine geared exclusively to rapid and complete success. When this success was not entirely forthcoming, the military machine was stalled, and the only alternative was nothing more brilliant than a futile nuclear demonstration which could not hope to restore the lost momentum of the Soviet armed forces.

These reflections went far to explain the demoralization of the nerve centre of the Soviet apparatus which made it ripe for Duglenko's takeover. The popular disenchantment had simpler causes, the same as those of many earlier revolutions: empty bellies on one side of the privilege line and full ones on the other. The demands of the war on civil transport had exceeded plans and expectations. The peasants were hoarding stocks of food, as if aware of impending catastrophe, rather than taking it for sale to the towns. The great ones of the regime still found enough in their special shops, but for the man and woman in the street too little food was at last too much for their patience, and the acute shortages in many towns gave rise to riots and disorder which overwhelmed the security militia.

The food riots, which began in Moscow, soon spread to most major towns and cities. For a firsthand view of them in their earliest stages we turn to a local source. The following piece appeared in *Russkaya Misl* in Paris in November 1985, filed by a special correspondent in Moscow.

————————

❝A figure, matronly but none the less imperious, appeared in the shop doorway. There were gold rings on her thick fingers.

"The shop will not be opening today," she announced. "We have nothing in stock – no bread, no sausage – nothing. So just go away."

A groan of disappointment rose out of the long queue which already stretched the length of several blocks from the shop door.

"But we've been waiting all night!"

"What will our children eat?"

After a few moments individual shouts began to merge into a continuous murmur of indignation. Nevertheless, the crowd's rage was short-lived. The queue broke up and people began to wander away. They were used to this.

"I've lived in this place for seventy years," mumbled an untidy and toothless old man. "It's nothing but queues. A whole lifetime in queues."

Suddenly a small boy's shrill voice rang out above the crowd, directed, it seemed, to the matronly figure.

"You're lying about the bread, fatty. Your car's just around the corner. I saw you carry three bags out to it in the night."

There was a roar from the crowd. A hundred or so rushed around the corner to the car. Others ran back to the shop into the queue. They all wanted to believe that the shop would now open and everyone would be able to buy a loaf of bread. Those who had been at the back of the queue hurried to get to the front. Others who had been at the very doors of the shop insisted on having their old places back, whilst those from behind insisted that this was a new queue. There was pushing and scuffling as the crowd pressed forward. There was a sound of breaking glass. The shop window gave way. A dozen or so people found themselves flung into the shop. Some got to their feet and tried to get back on to the pavement, afraid of being accused of looting. But a score of hungry people had already burst through the broken window. The electric alarm bell went off, calling in vain for assistance. The crowd got noisier, for the shelves were empty. More pushed their way in. The door to the storeroom was broken down and its meagre contents were rapidly dispersed.

Those who had made for the fat woman's car realized that very soon nothing would be left inside the shop for them and decided to make the most of what was in the car. They broke the windows and hauled out bags with whole smoked sausages and bars of chocolate and even tins of caviar in them.

Shop windows were being smashed all along the street as crowds gathered. Militiamen appeared at the crossroads. They were greeted with a hail of stones and wisely withdrew. A crowd of several thousand was now on the rampage. These were hungry people with families to feed. The long grey streets echoed to their shouting.

None of the shops had anything much in stock except the liquor store, where there was vodka, beer, wine and champagne. Crates of bottles were carefully lifted out on to the street, without a bottle broken. The bottles passed from hand to hand along the street, everyone taking a swig in turn. But there was no food. No shop in the street had been left unplundered, and still there was no food.

"Intourist!" shouted someone.

"Intourist!" The cry spread.

A menacing crowd surged across the bridge towards a great box-like hotel reserved for foreign visitors. This place had long been hated. To proclaim the successes of the communist regime "paradise zones" had been built for foreigners in many parts of the main towns, with splendid hotels, restaurants, shops, hospitals, sports stadia. The Party and the KGB carried out an intensive campaign to win "friends for communism" in these zones. Ordinary citizens were strictly barred from access to them. Amongst the people, especially old folk who could still remember the Tsarist regime, this was a source of great indignation. Why should they not have the right, in their own country, to go into the best restaurants, hotels and shops?

When war had first broken out, the hotels for foreigners in Moscow and the other towns had all been cordoned off by KGB detachments. All the foreigners in them were arrested and many were now being shot in the hotel cellars, with little or no enquiry as to whether they were friends or enemies. After all, there was nothing now to feed them on, and no one to guard them. Lorries had been heard the night before near the Metropole Hotel. They were carrying away the corpses of foreign citizens.

Hungry crowds of Muscovites assumed that the lorries were only making the usual nocturnal deliveries. The mob now came streaming from all parts of the city in search of food.

In the inner courtyard of the Metropole Hotel, prisoners from the Lefortovo prison, guarded by a small squad of mounted militiamen, had just finished loading corpses of foreign guests of the capital of communism into the lorries. At the head of the convoy a militia lieutenant on a horse gave the order to open the gates and started to walk his horse on through them. In front of him, advancing round the corner on to the square, came a solid wall of people armed with sticks, stones and chains. Along the way some had torn up iron railings and the long rods with their pointed ends bristled above the crowd like the pikes of a mediaeval army.

"Close the gates!" shouted the lieutenant. A couple of militiamen jumped to do so. But the crowd had already caught sight of the long grey vans in the courtyard, and a menacing roar filled the square.

"They've got bread there."

"And meat!"

"Smoked fish!"

"Comrades!" shouted the officer, "there's nothing in the lorries. There's no food there!"

"Then why have you shut the gates?" they shouted back at him. "Give us the bread!"

Half a dozen mounted militiamen came hurrying to the officer's side. Three more quickly set up a machine-gun by the gates.

Just at that moment, a square-built red-haired lad poked the rump of the lieutenant's mount with a long spike. The horse reared up on its hind legs, throwing its rider. There was a howl of triumph, and a hail of stones deluged the militiamen. The crowd pressed forward, pulling off the antique gates and filling the inner courtyard. They broke into the lorries and tore off the tarpaulins.

"Bread!"

Bewilderment, disappointment, despair, hatred and horror filled the courtyard. Instead of bread they had found dead bodies. The thousands of people filling the square outside did not know what had happened in the courtyard but seemed to guess instinctively that something dreadful had been discovered.

To get a better view a few climbed up on to the statue of Karl Marx.

"Break the old bastard up," came a call from the crowd. People nearby burst out laughing. Some who had managed to get hold of a metal post began bashing at the granite pedestal.

"That's no good. We'll have to pull him down."

A thick wire cable was produced from somewhere and its end passed up to the people sitting on Marx's head. They wound the cable round his granite neck and threw down the end. It was eagerly seized and the huge grey granite block came tumbling down to the triumphant roar of the crowd.

"Lenin too!"

"And Dzerzhinski!"

The growing crowd had filled the square and now surged on to Red Square. The higher the dam, the louder the roar when it collapses. The more apparently tranquil the million tons of water held in by the dam, the more terrifying and destructive its force when it finally breaks out into freedom.

On the square, by the Historical Museum, the single barrel of a 57 mm anti-aircraft gun thrust upwards to the sky. A few batteries of these guns covered the city centre. The roaring crowd appearing round the corner caught the gun crew completely unawares.

People swarmed over the anti-aircraft gun from all directions. They offered the soldiers opened bottles of wine. Then, suddenly, from the Kremlin walls a machine-gun cracked its leaden whip. People fell injured and dying.

"Brothers, soldiers – defend us!"

The sergeant commanding the gun crew drew his pistol and aimed it into the crowd. Instantly, one of his own soldiers bayoneted him in the back. The crowd ducked under the walls for shelter from the machine-gun fire. The Kremlin guards' fire was answered by a hand-held machine-gun from somewhere in the crowded square. But the Kremlin machine-gun behind the ancient and mighty walls was invulnerable. Then the anti-aircraft gun swung smoothly round. The loader threw a clip of ten shells into the breach, the weapon swallowed and discharged them, and disgorged the empty cartridge cases on to the stone pavement. Ten explosions so close to each other as to be almost simultaneous broke through the ancient wall, into the embrasure in the Spassky Tower through which the machine-gun was firing. The square was shrouded in brick dust and filled with the smell of burning explosive.

"Hurrah-ah-ah!"

"And again!"

"Aim at the stars, the stars!"

"At the gates!"

"At Lenin!"

But the gun crew knew better. The loader threw in another clip and this time the gun swung slowly from left to right, firing off single unhurried shots at the Kremlin walls, breaking the merlons which concealed the automatic weapons of security guards. The high building immediately behind the Kremlin wall was now in its turn being torn apart by exploding shells. Masonry and glass came crashing to the ground. A roar of approval from the crowd accompanied every shot. The gunners would gladly have fired at the doors of the Lenin Mausoleum but there were people there already trying to break their way in with improvised battering rams. Instead, the barrel of the anti-aircraft gun swung smoothly upwards and with a tongue of flame in one single shot shattered to smithereens the red star topping the Spassky Tower.

The Mausoleum guards had fled but the black marble doors of the Mausoleum itself stood fast.

"We'll have to break it open, all the same," someone shouted in the crowd, "and have him out."

"No use! Lenin rotted years ago, it's just a wax effigy there now!"

"We'll get in and see!"

"It's not Lenin that's rotted," someone had to make a speech, "it's Leninism. It rotted when Lenin broke up the Constituent Assembly . . ."

But there was nothing to be done: the Mausoleum had been well built in its time. The crowd cleared out of it on to Red Square where they strung up without ceremony several men who had been identified as members of the Central Committee, indiscriminately mixed with ordinary Kremlin security guards. *Aux lanternes!*

It was the members of the Politburo that were now being sought by this rampaging crowd, but they were nowhere to be found. They had escaped by an underground passage into the Metro where an armoured train was waiting to whisk them away.

Not the Kremlin itself but the buildings housing the Communist Party bureaucracy within the Kremlin were ablaze. The Kremlin churches were unharmed. People flocked into them, praying on their knees for the Lord God to forgive the sins of His long-suffering people.

For sixty-eight years Moscow had not heard church bells. Now, high above Moscow, Ivan the Dread, the great bell of all Russia, awoke from his slumber. His mellow chime rang out over the ancient city, where the communists in little more than half a century had destroyed so many more people than even the Tartars in 300 years. Hear what the ancient bell has to say – "forgive our enemies . . . " – What? Nobody is doing any forgiving here. *Aux lanternes!*

Along the avenues of Moscow, members of the Party, many protesting to the end in vain that they were not really communists, hung like bunches of grapes from the lamp posts. So many of them! It was done quickly – some by the neck to die, some by the legs already dead. Rope ran out. Electric light cable did very well instead. At the Lyubyanka a battle raged. It was a vast building, with 1,000 people inside, all armed with pistols. On the square in front of the memorial to the founder of the Cheka, Dzerzhinsky, lay the mutilated corpses of members of what was now the KGB. The building itself had so far remained inviolate. The secret police knew what awaited them and were putting up a spirited defence. Anti-aircraft guns towed along from various parts of the city rained shells into the windows but those within refused to give themselves up.

Then, above the block of the Lyubyanka, a column of smoke rose up to the sky. The heads of the KGB, like the members of the Politburo, had abandoned the building and made their way to safe hiding in the Metro through a secret underground passage. The fate of ordinary officers left to beat back the pressure of the crowd was no concern of theirs. Before leaving they had set fire to the building from within, to destroy the archives. The fire spread with amazing rapidity. There were plenty of documents to feed it. One thousand Chekists now found themselves caught in a rat-trap. Flames raged in the corridors, but the windows on the lower stories were secured by substantial grilles. It was only possible to jump from the second floor, from the burning windows straight down on to the asphalt below. Legs were broken in the fall but this was of minor consequence. The crowd trampled on those who fell, stoned them, beat in their skulls.

"Put out the fire!" came the cry. "Put it out! There are millions of names there of people we want. Save the archives!"

Too late. The floors and roof were well alight. Staircases and ceilings fell in. Well, perhaps the safes would survive. We'll sort it out afterwards and square up accounts somehow.

From the Lyubyanka to the Old Square a huge crowd was now milling. There was something even more interesting going on there. This was the location of the Central Committee of the Communist Party, in several blocks, solidly built and united into one large building complex with hundreds of kilometres of corridors. There were even more people here than at the Lyubyanka, though those buildings were older perhaps, more solidly built, and well armed.

The thousands of inmates of the Central Committee building saw they had no option. They gave themselves up without a fight. A security guard was hurriedly formed from amongst the crowd to preserve what could be saved from the archives. Then, in several places on the square, the officials and security police were lined up and executed in turn after a brief pretence at trial. There were not enough guns, not enough rope, nor even in the event enough electric cable. The executions were carried out when all else failed with firemen's axes, or the officials were simply bludgeoned to death or thrown down from the windows or rooftops. White and shaking men who had only the day before been holding their own country and almost half the world by the throat came creeping out. They were all lined up and made to await their punishment.

There was laughter in the gloating crowd. "Now its your turn to queue. You lot have never had to wait in a queue. You can do it now!"

Meanwhile at the Lyubyanka a heavy tractor had fixed a hawser round Iron Felix, the statue of Dzerzhinsky. He soon came crashing down on to the corpses of those who were the successors of his Cheka, startling a flock of ravens, who flew up croaking into a sky darkened by the smoke from burning buildings.

There was swift and cruel vengeance everywhere, bitter retribution and a bloodstained payment of account. But there was still no food. **9**

Chapter 23

A New World

One of the main preoccupations of the United States authorities in the very rapid planning which they had undertaken about the future of the Soviet forces and the Soviet empire had been to assume control and possession of the nuclear weapons remaining in Soviet hands. The regrouping of Soviet divisions which occurred at Omsk and Khabarovsk was authorized by the Allied authorities only on the condition that all nuclear weapons in the possession of these forces were handed over to American teams sent in for the purpose. Other small American task forces operated dispersed over Soviet Asia searching for and taking possession of, by force if necessary, the weapons still held by units which had scattered throughout the vast expanse of Siberia. The Americans and Chinese met by prior arrangement at the Soviet missile testing ground, which was not, in fact, at Bykonor in Kazakhstan, as was always publicly put out by Soviet disinformation services, but not very far away at Tyuratam. The decision was taken to set up a group of experts to make a common study of the relevant Soviet technology. They also agreed that nuclear material on the site should be removed for disposal rather than incorporated in the nuclear forces of either party. This agreement symbolized American acceptance of the fact that they could not hope for the de-nuclearization of China. They were certainly in no position to enforce it. Since they did not believe that the present Chinese regime would make use of nuclear weapons in a manner contrary to the interests of the United States or of world peace, they were content to make a virtue of necessity.

The situation was, however, quite different with regard to other possessors or possible possessors of nuclear weapons. The Non-Proliferation Treaty of 1968 had failed in its object of restricting the possession of nuclear weapons to the five powers possessing them in the 1960s (the USA, Soviet Union, UK, France and China) and there was reasonable evidence to support the view that others had them or had the capability of making them at short notice. The most certain candidates for inclusion in this group were Iraq, Pakistan, India, South Africa, Israel. Libya might have attempted to purchase one with its oil money but could now be happily struck off the list. The others, however, still represented the danger of a possible use of these weapons in the local quarrels which were only too likely to continue after the general war came to an end.

There seemed to be a small window of opportunity in the excitement and euphoria of the Soviet collapse in which America and the West could compel rather than persuade others to accept the total extension of non-proliferation. Here again it was possible to direct the enthusiasm of the nuclear disarmers in the West into more fruitful channels now that the absurd claim could be dropped that unilateral disarmament in the West would 'encourage' the USSR to follow suit. It could be much more plausibly represented that the renunciation of nuclear weapons by Britain and France would provide much improved moral justification for imposing such renunciation on other possessors, actual or potential, of these weapons. Even so, this was too difficult for everyone to swallow all at once and the Americans had to be content with a solemn and binding promise that the nuclear weapons of Britain and France would be phased out over a period of ten years (thus just avoiding the necessity for Britain to complete the distressingly expensive purchase of the Trident system) on condition that other countries concerned renounced all intention to produce nuclear weapons and allowed the facilities that existed for this purpose to be destroyed under international supervision. Proposals to this effect were put to possible nuclear powers with the clear intimation that if they refused to agree, the facilities in their territories would be destroyed, probably by air attack, but with any other military action thought to be necessary. This they would clearly be in no position to resist.

Apart from the one overriding necessity of making the world comparatively safe from nuclear warfare for another generation, the Western allies generally resisted the temptation to play God except where this seemed unavoidable. In Europe, despite the ruined areas, there has been real hope that we are witnessing the construction of some sort of European community from the Atlantic to the Urals. In this region there has been a note of innovation, excitement, enthusiasm and intellectual daring – an attractive throwback to the European spirit of the late 1950s which had seemed to be sleeping since. This is not to say that the road to an allied extended Europe is likely to be smooth.

The worries being felt by the five Atlantic powers of Europe's far west – Britain, France, Spain, Portugal and Ireland – were well summarized in the views of a prominent member of the new coalition

government in Britain, in a brilliant speech at Harvard soon after the
end of the war.

In what is now generally known as the Harvard 'Address', this
thoughtful, perhaps heretical, British politician told an American
audience that for some time before the war many Europeans had seen
a degree of stability – precarious but precious – in a world in rough
balance between two superpowers, the Soviet Union and the United
States. Now one of the two superpowers had gone, but it was unlikely
that the whole globe would wish to live for ever under a single *pax
Americana*. The burden of world domination today was certainly too
heavy for any one country to bear, and there would be constant
revolts if any country tried to take it on.

It would therefore be greatly to America's advantage, and good for
everybody's peace of mind, that there should soon be either two or
three friendly superpowers again. As the unorthodox British politician put it, 'The President of the United States should be hell-bent
on the dissolution of the unintended American empire.' If there were
two superpowers, most people would guess they would be the United
States and the Japan-China co-prosperity sphere, facing each other
(one trusts in amity) across the Pacific Ocean.

There were much greater attractions in this possibility than there
had been in the pre-war system where the two superpowers of the
United States and the Soviet Union faced each other in some enmity
with Western Europe in between. But if the centre of the world were
to move to the aptly named Pacific, with one of the two superpowers
on each side of it, said the British politician, 'this would have some
disadvantages, both for us in Europe and for you on this east coast of
these United States.'

The main disadvantage of 'this east coast' of the United States was
that it was already enormously attractive to live in California, if only
because of the weather (the speaker looked out on the driving snow
of Massachusetts in January). If the Pacific were now to become the
ocean across which passed most of advanced world trade, the pull to
California would become much greater. 'There is a danger that this
east coast may become a depressed area in North America.'

That had serious implications for Europe, on 'the other side of our
Atlantic millpond'. For the first time in its history, there was a danger
that Europe, in the new Pacific century, could become isolated from
the centre of the world. It was therefore greatly to the advantage of all
eastern Americans, and of all people in the United States who valued
the European heritage, that Europe should become the third new
superpower.

Europe would not quickly become a coherent superpower. At best
it would be a confederation that was 'untidy and not at all well

organized but very well meaning'. At worst there were two dangers in this Europe from the Atlantic to the Urals which might be called the danger at the peripheries and the danger at the centre.

The trouble at the peripheries was that the Urals were at present the border between Western civilization and an eastern part of the old Soviet Union where new and uncertain structures had to be created out of a chaotic void. 'It is not a comfortable posture for any new European superpower to have one foot on these Urals and one on an Atlantic Ocean that may be about to become a waterway through a depressed area.'

The danger at the centre of the new Europe was one that diplomatic people were less willing to talk about, but it should be brought out into the open. 'With all respect to the great German people, who have behaved better, since 1945, than any European people except the Poles have done for centuries, there are worries on my continent about the emergence of a reunited and thus possibly re-Prussianized Germany.

'It is important for us in the EEC to see that the sort of Europe we rebuild should not be one liable to tribal wars. The rest of Europe, both East and West, will be frightened if the two Germanies unite. They would then form too dominant a European power. It is important that each Germany should be a member of the EEC, and be united within the EEC to the same degree that France and West Germany are, but no more than that. The same applies to all the former communist states, including the European states of the former Soviet Union. This is how we must build our new Europe from the Atlantic to the Urals.'

In fact, German reunification was not the only alternative option. The Germans had to choose whether they would, as two separate countries, West and East Germany, be members of the enlarged European Community on the same basis as the other participants, or whether they would see a more interesting future as the protagonists of a revived *Mittel-Europa* based on German industry, technology and finance, and extending through Hungary, Austria, Czechoslovakia into the Ukraine and the Balkans, perhaps even so far as to participate in Turkey's potential resources of manpower, raw materials and food in the south.

The arguments for *Mittel-Europa* were compelling from a historical point of view. What had never been quite achieved with the Berlin-Baghdad railway project before the First World War, or the push to the Caucasus in 1942, was the challenge to the German nation – now two-headed, like its former imperial eagle. This solution would avoid much complication and committee work. German leadership would be uncontested, unlike the give and take (which so often seemed to be 'Germans give and others take') in the con-

voluted negotiations of the Community. On the other side there was
the attraction of the wider world, the creation of an element in a
world system equivalent at least in economic power to the United
States and China-Japan. As with most politicians and diplomats, the
Germans naturally hoped to have the best of both these systems, and
hoped also that they need not be mutually exclusive alternatives. So,
at the time of our writing, the much enlarged European Community is
in process of formation. Within it the two German states are making
good their claim to be the leaders in a joint, and not yet exclusive,
Drang nach Osten.

The option of reunifying the two Germanies was rejected largely
from considerations of West German politics. The Christian Democrats were the largest party in 1985 and, though not members of the
governing coalition, had a blocking vote in the *Bundesrat*. It was at
first supposed that they would be the party most in favour of reunifying West and East Germany. This supposition proved wrong.

As East Germany moved towards its first democratic elections in
late 1986, the public opinion polls suggested that the so-called Freedom Party would probably win. This had connections with the
Catholic church as well as some Protestant evangelists. The Christian
Democrats in Bonn originally assumed that it would be an ally of
theirs. A visit to the Freedom Party by a prominent West German
academic provided the following rather unexpected report to the
Christian Democrat party machine.

'The population of East Germany is accustomed to living standards under one-half of those in the Bundesrepublik. If the two
Germanies unite, we will be importing seventeen million proletarians
into our system.

'Although all East Germans hate communism, the Freedom Party is
by our standards socialist. Its idea of economic democracy is that workers' councils have the main say in how to run factories. The folk heroes
there are the old Solidarity trade unionists in Poland. Even the Catholic
church glorifies them.

'The only two features of East German life which are more
advanced than in the Bundesrepublik are the provision of public
sports facilities and free health care. If East Germany joins with
West Germany we will almost certainly have to proceed to socialist
medicine and a wider-ranging pattern of government expenditure. In
this, most East Germans will vote with the political left in the
Bundesrepublik.

'It should also be realized that, even after forty years in a different
system, some East Germans are anxious to get back to the old
Prussian virtues of frugality, a sort of puritanism and a feeling of
superiority towards neighbours on either side. They feel they are

more advanced than the Slavs to their east, and morally superior in some ways to us decadent Rhinelanders to their west. This could introduce philosophies into our Bavarian and Rhineland way of life which most of us were rather relieved to jettison in 1945.'

It was fairly clear that the Christian Democrat Party in West Germany was not going to be overkeen on reunification.

Irrespective of the larger structure that might encompass central and eastern Europe, in the form of an enlarged Community, or, less probably, a German oriented *Mittel-Europa*, there were clearly going to be local tensions to be resolved and local scores to be settled. Like other empires, the Soviet empire had largely suppressed old quarrels and rivalries in the territory which it dominated. With its removal, the Czechs and Slovaks, for example, were more conscious of their differences than of the need for Czechoslovak unity; Hungary and Romania were inclined to flex their muscles about Transylvania, largely inhabited by a Hungarian minority; Poland prepared to renew dormant territorial disputes with the Ukraine and Lithuania. This was reminiscent of the break-up of the British Indian empire into two, then three, warring countries, or the civil war in Nigeria, or the confusion in Indochina following French and then American withdrawal. Events in Czechoslovakia were the first to precipitate a change in the old order.

The collapse of the Soviet regime left the Czechoslovaks unable to rely, as the Poles could, upon a self-confident leadership to pick up the reins of government, though the country was still far from the total confusion prevailing at the same time in the GDR. Their leaders believed – rightly or wrongly time alone will show – that a split into two more homogeneous parts would help to solve the many problems that freedom brought with it. So Czechia and Slovakia set themselves up as two separate states. In the eighteen months which have elapsed they have not been able to do much more than hold constituent assemblies and draft terms for new elections in each. Industrial production, down to near zero in the autumn of 1985, has picked up somewhat, but the disastrous central European harvest of that same year has left the Czechs and Slovaks no less dependent on food supplies from the Americas and Australasia than the people of other former European clients of Soviet Russia.

The year 1986 was one of unprecedented flourishing for the Hungarian economy. This country, whilst still under Soviet hegemony, had managed to move away from socialism, to reduce the intervention of its bureaucrats in the economy, and to renounce state subsidies in industry and in agriculture. The Hungarian economy developed swiftly, following the laws of competition rather than state planning and regulations. As soon as the war ended, Hungary made rapid progress in improving the wellbeing of its population. The Government introduced the lowest taxes in Europe and abolished all state intervention in economic problems. This caused an economic boom and an unprecedented influx of capital. The temptation to exploit success was too great and in the summer Hungarian forces attempted a rapid movement into Romania, with the classic objective of protecting the Hungarian minority in Transylvania who had been transferred to Romanian sovereignty in 1919. Only partial success was achieved, in spite of Romania's simultaneous trouble on another front.

In the remains of the dismembered Soviet Union itself, the approaching winter of 1985 looked like being a savage one. In many parts order had completely broken down. Marauding bands dominated huge tracts of country searching for food. Ethnic groups, driven by necessity, were banding together for their own survival. Soldiers returning to their homes, often with weapons and sometimes in organized units and formations, if they did not turn to banditry were forming local defence forces. Centres of order slowly began to emerge.

For the Western allies the occupation and administration of all that huge hinterland was quite out of the question. It was essential, however, to establish secure areas both as refuges and as nuclei of civil government. These were set up initially in Petrograd (no time was lost in shedding the hated patronym of the source of so much evil), Moscow, Archangel, Odessa, Smolensk, and in the vicinity of Gorki and Kuybyshev on the Volga. Each secure area was the responsibility of one Allied division, operating with an organization strong in infantry and specialist troops (particularly in engineers, communications, logistics and transportation) but not in heavy weapons. A Control Headquarters at the level of an army group was established in Petrograd, which swiftly became the capital of the North Russian Republic, soon also incorporating Novgorod and adopting in its entirety Novgorod's ancient code of laws. The Control HQ, set up in the first instance by NATO in late September 1985, passed under the control of the United Nations, where it still rests.

The most pressing problem was the provision and distribution of food, which was immediately taken in hand under the United Nations in an operation of unprecedented magnitude. The full co-operation of all nations was most urgently sought, and in nearly all cases very generously given. Due to the short duration of the war and the relatively restricted areas of high damage, most of the economies of the world were still functioning almost normally. Surpluses which had been an embarrassment to the EEC were now of the highest value. The worst aspects of famine were avoided in the former territory of the Soviet Union, but not by a wide margin and shortages in the more important foodstuffs still continue even now to cause concern.

It is not the business of this book to explore every detail of the slow and often painful evolution of the successor states to the Soviet Union. But as pieces in a vast and complex jigsaw puzzle the fate of Moscow and the early evolution of the Ukraine, Belorussia and the Moslem Central Asians may be mentioned.

Moscow raised special problems. It was a natural rallying point for the criminal, the violent, the rejected – the undesirable in any form. A quadripartite system was established, not greatly dissimilar, except in one important respect, to that set up in Berlin in 1945 with United States, Soviet Russian, British and French participation. The difference between Berlin in 1945 and Moscow forty years later was in the origin of the security forces involved. Instead of contingents from the four powers, as in Berlin, troops of the former Red Army were used, drawn from 3 Shock Army, which, under General Ryzanov, had earlier defected to the West.

By comparison the Ukraine was almost a success story. This newly independent republic now ranked with Great Britain, France and West Germany in terms of area, size of population and economic development. The Ukrainian National Assembly lost no time in proclaiming a constitution for the new state, in which it was declared that the economic freedom of the people was the basic principle of political freedom. A man cannot be politically free if his livelihood depends on the state, the trade union or a monopoly association. At its first congress the National Assembly passed laws forbidding state intervention in the private lives of the country's citizens and in the economy. In addition, laws were passed against the emergence of monopolies and trade unions with more than 10,000 members. The first benefit of free enterprise was felt in agriculture, and the Ukraine set out on the way to resume its position as one of the world's chief suppliers of agricultural produce.

All was not sweetness and light however. The western provinces, whose population was Roman Catholic, were demanding autonomy. Groups of Crimean Tartars, deported from the Crimea at the end of the Second World War by Stalin's security forces, had begun to return to their homeland. They too declared that they did not want to remain part of the Ukraine. A new knot of contradictions was beginning. Moreover, Poland claimed its rights to the part of Ukrainian territory at the centre of which lies the town of Lvov, and a border conflict threatened to break out.

The neighbouring republic of Moldavia had been incorporated into Romania, but here again a border clash arose between the Ukraine and Romania. Both countries considered the Dniester delta and the town of Odessa as their own territory. On the night of 13 July 1986 two tank divisions and three motor rifle divisions of the newly-formed Ukrainian People's Army made a surprise attack on Moldavia and seized the town of Kishinev. The Ukrainian Government demanded that Romania renounce all claims to Odessa and to the Dniester lowlands in exchange for which the Ukraine would remove its forces from Moldavia.

The fate of Belorussia turned out more tragically. Its capital, Minsk, had perished in the nuclear catastrophe, and with it many of those who might have taken a lead in bringing the state to successful independence. There was not a single political party, group or movement capable of taking power into its own hands. The western Catholic part of Belorussia indicated its wish to rejoin Poland. The eastern part remained independent, but there was a strong tendency among the refugees returning from the army and other parts of the Soviet Union to feel that they should become part of Russia in order to preserve their orthodox religion and national traditions, no matter what the political regime in Russia might be. Otherwise the whole country might be seized by Poland and converted to Catholicism. The trouble was that Russia did not exist. In the place where Russia had been there was confusion and widespread fighting, often approaching a state of civil war.

As one further example of the myriad difficulties arising from the disintegration of the Soviet Union, Cossacks presented, and continue to present, a problem. They form a distinct nation of Slavonic origin, dispersed in several widely separated localities. There are groups, for example, on the Don and the Kuban, in the Caucasus, in Astrakhan and Siberia, forming eleven separate tribal districts. It is by no means yet clear how these groups, which cannot be physically co-located, can be associated with successor states in their vicinity, whether in one form of association or several different forms. An Allied mission is at present established with each one.

Before moving on to the rather separate fate of Central Asia it may be appropriate to reflect that whatever problems the collapse of the Soviet regime may have solved, many others have rushed in to fill the resultant empty spaces. There are inevitably those who argue now (as some even argued before) that to struggle along in a world divided by the rivalries of two superpowers doing whatever was possible to smooth the rough edges at the interface made more sense than to try to resolve the situation by the destruction of one of them. Had the USSR offered any convincing gesture of willingness to accept peaceful co-existence the Soviet Union might still be a great power today. It did not because it could not. Acceptance of the legitimacy of capitalist democracy was a contradiction wholly intolerable to the Marxist-

Leninist ideology. The rugged strength developed by the structure in its sixty-eight years of life made sure that when it was destroyed by its own weaknesses it would go down, as it did, in a bloodbath of terrifying magnitude.

The problems left behind are still with us, some brought into being by the disappearance of Soviet imperialism, others existing before, but now made greater still. We have at least been spared the worst on two major counts.

The first, of transcendental importance, is our almost miraculous escape from total nuclear war. Some say it was never very likely anyway, since it would have led to something approaching so close to annihilation for either side that both were determined to avoid it. Others do not agree and argue that given the unpredictability of human behaviour under stress it could very easily have happened.

The second was that the US had, at last, learned the lesson it ignored, with disastrous consequences, in the Second World War – that war must never be waged except to a clear political end. The American approach had been that a war was to be fought by the military, to whom the politicians deferred until the war was won. Politics then once more took over and the President could turn from being primarily Commander-in-Chief to the resumption of his other and more important functions as head of government and head of state.

The overriding and very nearly the sole consideration in war, under this approach, was the defeat of the enemy in the field at minimum cost in American life. Nothing else mattered nearly so much. Eisenhower was therefore halted on the Elbe in 1945 to let the Soviet steamroller drive on into Berlin. Patton was within a day's march of Prague when he too was halted, again to let the Soviets do the job. Meanwhile Alexander in Italy, in spite of Churchill's strong opposition, had been deprived, in order to mount a futile Allied operation on the French Riviera, of the troops which would have got him safely, before the Russians, to Vienna. Berlin, Prague, Vienna – all gifts to Stalin from the United States, gifts which paved the way to Soviet imperial dominance of Eastern Europe, and helped to make a Third World War inevitable.

Whether or not US policies can be described as fully effective in the disordered world left by the collapse of Soviet imperialism in 1985, at least the lesson had now been learnt that postwar policies deserve most serious consideration not only before hostilities end but even before they begin. This is only one of many important lessons learned by policy makers in the United States over the years. Another, too recent to be fully evaluated, was the result of events in the Caribbean and Central America, events in which the United States could have lost the war in Europe before it began, and which have been described in chapter 16.

East of the Urals the collapse of central authority left about half the land mass of Asia in a state of high confusion. The centres of influence consisted of the important towns along the Trans-Siberian railway and the ancient cities of Central Asia and the remains of Soviet commands with such forces as had continued at their disposal. After urgent action had been taken to obtain control of the nuclear weapons left in the hands of the Soviet forces, two factors dominated the problem of what was to become of this enormous area and the many millions of its inhabitants.

First was the question of China's intentions with regard to what were traditionally described as frontier rectifications: how much territory would China attempt to get back, claiming that it had been surrendered by unequal treaties in the past? Secondly, there were the autonomist movements based on the ethnic character of the majority of the inhabitants in southern Central Asia. But it was still unclear whether they would wish and would be able to take advantage of the sudden collapse of Soviet control to establish independent states based on their national affiliations and on the Moslem religion.

Events had moved so fast in the latter part of the campaign in Europe that there had not been much time for concerted planning by the Western allies about the future of Russia in Asia. In the Second World War there had, after all, been at least two years of joint negotiation and planning between the United States, the Soviet Union and the United Kingdom about the future arrangements for Europe, including the division of Germany into zones of occupation. It could be said that the results were not brilliant from the Western point of view. Nevertheless, there had been time to codify the often conflicting interests of the participants and arrive at a system which was well known to them all at the end of hostilities and so avoid an armed struggle for territory and influence between victorious Allies. This was not the case in the Far East in 1985, when there had only been the most rapid and sketchy conversations between the United States and China, on a highly secret and hypothetical basis, in the months immediately preceding the outbreak of the Third World War.

As a result of the enormous difference between the political and administrative systems of the United States and China the discussions had to begin at a very basic level and a lot of misunderstandings had to be cleared out of the way before it was possible to get down to bedrock and talk about realities on the ground. This meant that the agreement had to be limited to a very few basic considerations and the edges had to be left fuzzy. Moreover, there were precedents that, on the Western side at least, should be avoided. Yalta was etched in the minds of those who had personal recollection of the disasters which it had inflicted on central Europe and this acted as a grave warning against the precipitate carving up of other people's lands and other people's loyalties. On this occasion the conditions were more favourable, which led to a greater possibility of agreement that might meet the requirements of both sides. Neither China nor America was aiming at world domination and neither was seriously worried about being attacked by the other – two important factors which were lacking in the negotiations with the Soviet Union at Yalta and at other wartime conferences.

The disintegration of the Soviet Union had removed the greatest threat against China. The size of China was already enormous. It was doubtful whether a single government could indefinitely control a billion people. There was no obvious advantage in gaining some millions more by extending the frontiers to the north and west. Moreover, the demographic situation was more or less under control in China so that there was no insatiable land hunger. If a certain deference could be paid to history, respect for which had survived the cultural revolution, and some lands which had historically belonged to China could be reunited with it, there might well be a basis for a fairly reasonable settlement which included a renunciation of further major expansion. On the other hand, the smaller states of East and South-East Asia were going to be in some fear of Chinese intentions and would need American reassurance or guarantee.

As far as military material was concerned, there was a possibility of reasonable compromise. The Americans (and their European allies) were anxious above all to make sure that Soviet nuclear weapons did not fall into the wrong hands. They wanted examples of the latest Soviet technology, particularly the *Typhoon* and *Delta* submarines and their missiles, but for the most part they were indifferent to the acquisition by China of such conventional weapons as could be salvaged from the Soviet forces, though it must be said that some of the Asian states had distinct misgivings.

There could also be ready agreement between China and the West that no attempt would be permitted to restore or create a central authority over the whole of Soviet Asia. There was little risk of this occurring in the circumstances at the end of the 1985 war but a mutual guarantee that any future attempt to restore a central authority would be resisted by both sides helped considerably to smooth the negotiations.

The future of the ethnic minorities in Central Asia had many complications. The most important in the context of the American-Chinese negotiation was that there were people of the same ethnic origin and culture living on both sides of the Soviet-Chinese frontier and the establishment of independent states out of the remains of Soviet Central Asia might seem to the Chinese an undesirable magnet for some of the Moslem peoples of Sinkiang. The Chinese might have been prepared to make use of this circumstance to subvert the Soviet Central Asians before and during the period of the war, but it was a different matter if there were to be independent states of thirty to forty million Turkic-speaking Moslems on the former Soviet side of the border who would obviously be in some sort of relations with their co-religionists on the Chinese side. An attempt to ensure that such states should be under ultimate Chinese suzerainty of the kind once enjoyed by Tibet was rejected by the Americans in the name of self-determination and in the interests of Western relations with the rest of the Moslem world. Equally, it had to be conceded on the Western side that it would be wrong to attempt to create or to permit the creation of a single state embracing all the non-Soviet peoples of Central Asia. Since this was not in any case the wish of the Soviet Central Asians themselves, it was easy to make the concession. Their national identity, in so far as they had been able to maintain under Soviet domination their separate languages and cultures, was as Uzbeks, Kirghiz, Turkomans, Tajiks and so on, not as a conglomerate of Central Asian Moslems.

The most suitable structure seemed likely to be a federation of these various nationalities with a fairly weak central government and a high degree of local autonomy, which was also sensible in view of the long distances between the centres of population and the disastrous state in which communications had been left by the war and subsequent tumults. It was possible, therefore, to reach agreement with the Chinese that both they and the Western allies would favour, or at least do nothing to oppose, the creation of a loose federation of this kind and that neither would seek to establish a dominant position with regard to it.

These Central Asian republics were inhabited by the remains of the Turkic and Iranian peoples after the great westward migrations from this area which had overrun first Iran and then Asia Minor. They had themselves had a glorious past but had more recently sunk from sight after conquest by Tsarist Russia and incorporation after 1919 in the Union of Soviet Socialist Republics. Only recently, in the 1970s, had their historical cities and monuments become the target of Western tourists, dazzled by the romantic names of Bokhara, Tashkent and Samarkand, and by the still brilliant remains of tombs and mosques and palaces.

Their populations now amounted to some forty to fifty million people, the vast majority still speaking Turkic or Iranian languages as their mother tongues, in spite of strenuous efforts by Moscow to promote Russianization, and still maintaining allegiance to the Moslem religion, in spite of the closure of mosques and much hostile propaganda by the Soviet bureaucracy.

There had not for many years been any evidence of nationalist agitation in this area. Material living standards had greatly improved since the period of native rule and there was just enough latitude in the use of the native languages and the promotion of native culture to satisfy the rather mild aspirations of the ethnic leaders. It was the events of 1979–80 in neighbouring Moslem territories which began to draw the attention of the inhabitants to the outside world, and made them more aware of the existence of fellow Moslems. They could not fail to note the contrast between the comparatively tolerant behaviour of the Soviet masters whom they saw in their midst and the behaviour of the same Soviets in Afghanistan, where a people of similar stock to themselves were visibly oppressed by the imposition of a communist regime and then violently attacked when they tried to express their opposition to it.

The first Soviet occupation troops in Afghanistan had been largely drawn from the nearby Central Asian territories but the strain upon them had been too great when they were ordered to shoot at fellow Central Asians and fellow Moslems. These units were accordingly quite soon withdrawn, to be replaced by others with a higher proportion of non-Central Asian and non-Moslem conscripts. But the continuing lack of success of the Soviets in their attempts to 'pacify' Afghanistan and the continuing casualties which were reported as occurring in their forces (exaggerated no doubt as a result of the suppression of genuine news) led to a significant build-up of nationalist feeling in the Central Asian republics. People were already beginning to remind themselves that the constitution of the Soviet Union provided for the voluntary secession of any of the constituent republics, even though in practice the discussion of this possibility had led to a sticky end for those who had been rash enough to try it on. It should therefore have been no surprise to the Soviet authorities that the check to their advance in Europe, the defection of units fighting there whose men came largely from the Central Asian area, and the marked unwillingness of the Soviet forces in Afghanistan to carry out their warlike operations once the news from Europe turned sour, should precipitate an outbreak of nationalism. This happened first in Uzbekistan, where the populace took to the streets and proclaimed independence, and soon after that in other Central Asian republics of the Soviet Union as well.

Looking now further south it is clear that India will be in no better state after 1985 than before to enter into any far-reaching economic or defensive international system. With population increase still out of control and with sprawling bureaucratic confusion as the nearest approach to government, the struggle to maintain a place in the modern world is going to seem increasingly forlorn. The loss of the Soviet counterpoise to China will upset the Indian external balancing act, and the break-up of a neighbouring empire may stimulate fissiparous tendencies in the Indian federation. If China, or a Sino-Japanese co-prosperity system succeeds, there will be many Indian politicians pressing to follow this example. But the more likely chance must be that India will long remain an inward-looking depressed area, whose future, like that of much of Africa, will depend on the successful restoration of the north-south dialogue, never yet very fruitful and now grievously interrupted by the 1985 war, and the even more pressing agenda of post-war settlement in northern Asia.

All this has left the vast expanse of Siberia to an unplanned future, which is hardly surprising, since the interests of the rest of the world in it were never more than marginal. Its water resources might have to be exploited sooner or later to improve food production in Central Asia, though not on the grandiose lines of the Soviet plans to reverse the flow of great rivers. Siberia's mineral resources and the oil offer a powerful attraction to Japanese economic exploitation, but this might well take place without the necessity of political control.

The Trans-Siberian railway and the string of railway towns along it are a monument to Russia's historical conviction of a manifest destiny to march ever eastwards, as well as southwards, until it reached the sea. When the USSR turned its eyes towards the West, however, the settlements along this fragile line of communication were obliged to seek local solutions for their political future. The Soviets had from time to time tried to bring Siberia within the sphere of their own political and economic system. Khrushchev had proclaimed the importance of the new lands in Kazakhstan for revolutionizing the agriculture of the Soviet Union as a whole and had managed to persuade some millions of ethnic Russians to settle in this inhospitable desert, but the plan had never worked. There had also been a deliberate attempt to offset the growing demographic preponderance of the Central Asians by moving Russian settlers into the towns of Central Asia but this had not succeeded in making much change in the proportions between native Russians in the area and its Moslem inhabitants.

Apart from these spasmodic and unsuccessful efforts to Russianize Asia, there could be no doubt that the general impression uppermost in the minds of most of the inhabitants of European Russia about their dominions in Asia was of their being used both in Tsarist times and again under communism as a penal settlement. After the war geography took its revenge and the traces of Soviet occupation began to disappear, except in the few centres in which former Soviet troops established settlements rather like the earlier Macedonian and Roman settler colonies of retired soldiers.

In the longer term the fate of Asia, and not only of the former Soviet territories, is going to be shaped largely by the answers to questions about China. Can any system, can any set of men, successfully govern a country of a billion people? Assuming that, for a time, they can, will such a country be land-hungry, or power-hungry, or will it seek to control a vast defensive glacis like its predecessor as a world power in the Eurasian landmass? It is still too early to attempt an assessment. In the short period since the war, China's external effort has been fully devoted to absorbing Mongolia and managing Vietnam. After the liquidation of the Soviet maritime command at Vladivostok it was inevitable that the United States with the connivance of its allies (including Japan and South Korea) should set up and maintain, however reluctantly, a Russian-manned centre of government and command until more permanent arrangements could be arrived at.

Japan was for the time being busy settling into the Northern Islands it had now repossessed. It betrayed no overt interest in Sakhalin, but was no doubt concerned about possible Chinese ambitions in an area so recently a part of the Soviet empire. There will be hope that this, if it is made, will be China's 'last territorial demand' and that a period of stability will be seen to be required if China is to have any hope of remaining among the leaders of the twenty-first century.

The answers to the questions about China will turn also on relationships with Japan and India. Japan will seek to give economic leadership but to avoid the political entanglement of its previous intervention in the mainland. Even so, the melding together of two such disparate economic systems will demand a fuller measure of tact and subtlety than has in the past always characterized Japanese policy. On the Chinese side much will depend upon whether the present pervasive state control of every facet of life can co-exist with the freedom of enterprise which all experience – including the recent negative experience of the Soviet Union – has shown to be necessary for economic development, even for economic survival. The United States will not be able to stay out of this vastly complicated process, as it might have hoped. If China is to remain a nuclear power, Japan is likely to feel the need for a continuing US guarantee of ultimate nuclear support against any nuclear threat from China. The non-proliferation argument seems likely to win the day, with the consequence of a US-Japan security arrangement continuing for an indefinite future. If such a guarantee were not maintained Japan would have to give thought to its own protection.

But this is only one element in another long story of which we can now scarcely glimpse even the chapter headings.

Postscript I

It was not long after midnight in the Lefortovo prison in Moscow, in late August 1985. Two prisoners, tried, convicted and condemned to death, facing execution at dawn, had been brought together for their last night on earth in a cell which had, of course, for occasions such as this, been fitted with appropriate equipment for the recording of their conversation. One was Constantin Andrievich Malinsky, upon whom the mantle of Supreme Party Ideologist had fallen, as a successor to Suslov.

The other one was Alexei Alexandrovich Nastin, lately Marshal of the Soviet Union and Defence Minister of the USSR.

The record of their conversation proved to be of no great value to those who listened to it later. They had never been friends (who, at a high level in the CPSU, ever had any friends?) and had little to say to each other. Their differences in the past had been quite well known and each regarded it as something of an affront when, after perfunctory visits from their families (and offers, accepted by Nastin and refused with contempt by Malinsky, of last rites from the Church), they had been put into this cell to spend their last few hours together.

"I recall," said the ex-Minister of Defence, after a long silence, "that in that meeting where we discussed the use of nuclear weapons, near the end of last year, you were very much against it. Your argument was, I seem to recall, that there was no point in extending socialist rule over a world half destroyed, and that it was better to keep the world going more or less as it was, and move in by degrees. So when war came we did not use our nuclear armoury either from the start, as I advised, or even with its full weight when we were checked in central Europe. And this is where *that* has got us!"

"I also recall," said Malinsky, the some-time Supreme Ideologist, "I also recall, Comrade . . ."

"Do we use that form of address any longer?" said the other.

"It's a habit," was the reply, with a shrug. "It does not matter a great deal how we address each other now, anyway. What I recall is that our difference of view was on a question of all or nothing. I thought we should use none. You thought we should use the lot. I do not think either of us was in favour of anything in between. We both recognized, I imagine, that once nuclear weapons were introduced there would be no possibility – as some misguided folk in the West seemed to suppose – of controlling their use at some arbitrary level."

"Using all we had was in the Russian traditional mode of making war. Using none was not. Never mind that now. What happened in the event was that the really incredible decision was in fact taken to do neither one thing nor the other. We would not use the lot nor would we refrain from using any. We would instead attack an important city (though not the capital: we should want that) of a major satellite in one high-yield strike and then ask for negotiations with the United States. It was almost unbelievable. I always thought the old man had gone over the top . . ."

"Did you ever say so?" asked the former Supreme Ideologist.

"No, of course not. Neither did you, and for the same reasons. Even in his dotage he held all the strings."

"Never embark on a journey, they used to say where I grew up, unless you mean to arrive. To go half way, or even less, and allow yourself to stop there, is asking for trouble."

"That is precisely what got us here," said Marshal Nastin, the former Minister of Defence.

Through the little window high up in the wall, behind its heavy iron grille, a paler shade of night heralded the approach of dawn.

"Can't be long now," said Malinsky.

Even as he spoke boots sounded in the corridor outside and a key rattled in the lock.

There had been good times, in the past, difficult times, but good times. That was all over now.

The cell door opened.

"Come," said a voice. "It is time."*

---

* The taped record of this conversation found its way into the hands of an enterprising Italian journalist. The version given above was published in *La Stampa* on 25 June 1986.

Postscript II

Dimitri Vassilievitch Makarov had to find Nekrassov's father as soon as he could but he had first to make some enquiries. Soviet prisoners of war, after their surrender, were only lightly guarded, the policy of the Western allies being early controlled dispersal. For many of their guests in the concentration areas there was no great incentive to leave. Food was freely available here but very scarce outside. Considerable freedom of movement was allowed during the inevitably long delays before the very large numbers of ex-members of Warsaw Pact forces involved could be got to wherever in this huge area they wished to go, making the utmost use of what had lately been their own military transport.

Officers and men had been collected and concentrated at the places where they laid down their arms, so that the personnel of divisions remained more or less together, at least for the time being. Nevertheless, it was more by luck than good management that Makarov found the man he was after. This was Boris Ivanienko, the driver of Andrei Nekrassov's BMP who, Makarov had learned, was still alive. Dimitri Vassilievitch heard from him of many others in the battalion who were not. Andrei's old Sergeant Major from No. 3 Company, for example, Astap Beda, with whom Andrei had maintained touch till near the end, was dead. Little Yuri had disappeared. Boris Ivanienko, however, before he found transport back to his Ukrainian home in Poltava, had much to tell Makarov in his own quiet way. He had got very close to his officer. Little could be said on either side but this was a relationship in which, on his side at any rate, there had been understanding and sympathy. He felt that there had been the same on the other, too. He spoke of how a compassionate and sensitive young man, good professional though he was, seemed increasingly to suffer under the strain of the madness that had engulfed them all, so that the BMP driver sometimes feared for his reason. What Makarov heard moved him greatly.

Boris still had with him the soldier's kitbag with the drawstring at the mouth, carried by officers as well as men to hold the few little articles of spare clothing and personal possessions each carried, the whole material sum of a private life on the battlefield, which he had taken from Nekrassov's body when the cannon-shell from the American gun-ship helicopter had struck him down. He handed it over, with its meagre but highly personal contents, to Makarov.

The journey down to Rostov was not easy, nor was it easy to find the elder Nekrassov's dwelling when he got there. The habit of not answering questions from strangers, still deeply engrained everywhere, would take a long time to die away. He found where his friend's father lived in the end – not in a dacha in its own grounds, which would have been appropriate to an officer retiring as a general, but in a small apartment on the eleventh floor of one of the square, grey tower blocks, grim and cheerless, of which all Soviet cities were now mostly composed. Cats were foraging in piles of rubbish round the ground floor. Children with dirty faces were quarrelling in the stairways. From a window on the eleventh floor it was at least possible to get a distant glimpse of the River Don.

The older man stood waiting for him at the entrance, as he had done every day since word had reached him that Makarov was coming.

He knew at once who it was. It could be no other.

He went forward to embrace the younger man and turned, with an arm about his shoulder.

"Come in, my other son," he said, "and tell me."

Envoi

'We will bury you!' was the irritated retort of Khrushchev to an ill-considered interpolation. He was misunderstood by many, who thought he was threatening the early destruction of the capitalist West in war.

What he was doing was no more than to echo, in his own way, the prophetic words of Lenin.

'As long as capitalism and socialism exist we cannot live in peace: in the end one or the other will triumph – a funeral dirge will be sung over the Soviet Republic or over world capitalism.'

It has been sung.

Author's Notes and Acknowledgements

The team that put together the earlier book, *The Third World War: August 1985*, has gathered again, some four years later, to take a further look at the events we imagined then and to amplify and explore them a little further. In these years, though much of what we then had to say has since become even more closely relevant to the world about us, as recent events in Poland, for example, suggest, the scene here and there has changed. The Shah has gone. Egypt is no longer dependent on the Soviet Union. The story we now offer takes account of these events. Our purpose, however, has remained the same. It is to tell a cautionary tale (with such adjustment as the passage of time suggests) in an attempt to persuade the public that if, in a dangerous and unstable world, we wish to avoid a nuclear war we must be prepared for a conventional one.

We have assembled the original group, with one or two important additions. Air Chief Marshal Sir John Barraclough brought us unsurpassed experience of air matters and cool judgement; Sir Bernard Burrows, former Ambassador to Turkey and then to NATO, had much of high value to contribute in the political sphere; Vice-Admiral Sir Ian McGeoch's long and distinguished naval career, much of it in submarines, which also included NATO command, as well as post-graduate university work on Soviet armed forces and his editorship for some years of *The Naval Review*, has been of great value; Norman Macrae, Deputy Editor of *The Economist*, enlivens and illuminates everything he does, and here has run true to form; Major-General John Strawson, a highly literate soldier, lately retired, with several books to his own credit, now working with Westland Aircraft, has given us some thoughtful and penetrating work on the peripheries; and finally, of the old team, Brigadier Ken Hunt, one of the best known of military analysts, not only makes a notable contribution to the content of this book, particularly on the Far East, but has also applied his renowned editorial skills in helping to put it together.

The most important new element in this latest book is some investigation of what it all looked like from the Soviet side. Here I acknowledge a deep debt to a new colleague in Viktor Suvorov, from whose experience and advice I have profited greatly. His own first book, *The Liberators* (he commanded a motor rifle company in the 'liberation' of Czechoslovakia in 1968), already published, demands attention. He has another book coming out soon.

I am also deeply indebted to Vladimir Bukovsky, a man who in the non-communist world rightly commands enormous respect. The advice he has given me has been most valuable. His own book *To Build a Castle: My Life as a Dissenter*, is of profound importance.

I have also to thank one of the wisest and kindest of men in Lord Caradon, a very old friend, who gave good counsel and helped us particularly over the Middle East.

I owe more gratitude than I can say to the patience of my wife in putting up with the domestic commotion caused by the creation of this book. I am also deeply indebted to Mrs Carole Beesley, without whose cheerful and efficient help it could hardly have been finished, and to my daughter Elizabeth, whose assistance was crucial. To Jane Heller, finally, of Sidgwick and Jackson, more thanks are owed than any of us in the team could adequately express.

Having said all that I have to add that, although a good many hands have shared in the preparation of this book, the responsiblity for anything that may be found wrong with it rests with me.

J. W. HACKETT

Coberley Mill, Gloucestershire
February 1982

Index